Citizens, Civil Society and Heritage-Making in Asia

The **ISEAS – Yusof Ishak Institute** (formerly Institute of Southeast Asian Studies) is an autonomous organization established in 1968. It is a regional centre dedicated to the study of socio-political, security, and economic trends and developments in Southeast Asia and its wider geostrategic and economic environment. The Institute's research programmes are grouped under Regional Economic Studies (RES), Regional Strategic and Political Studies (RSPS), and Regional Social and Cultural Studies (RSCS). The Institute is also home to the ASEAN Studies Centre (ASC), the Nalanda-Sriwijaya Centre (NSC), and the Singapore APEC Centre.

ISEAS Publishing, an established academic press, has issued more than two thousand books and journals. It is the largest scholarly publisher of research about Southeast Asia from within the region. ISEAS Publishing works with many other academic and trade publishers and distributors to disseminate important research and analyses from and about Southeast Asia to the rest of the world.

Institute of Sociology, Academia Sinica is devoted (1) to implement indigenous research and to build up the identity of Taiwanese sociology; (2) to strengthen research on neighboring societies, aiming to foster regional and cross-national comparative studies; (3) to deepen and further to systematize the findings of important fields of sociology; (4) to explore groundbreaking and distinctive research areas; (5) to promote collaboration with domestic and international sociological institutions and to enhance the academic status of Taiwanese sociology.

The **International Institute for Asian Studies (IIAS)** is a global humanities and social sciences research institute and knowledge exchange platform. It aims to contribute to a better and more integrated understanding of present-day Asian realities as well as to rethink "Asian Studies" in a changing global context. IIAS acts as a global mediator, bringing together academic and non-academic institutes in Asia and other parts of the world, including cultural, societal and policy organizations. Originally established in 1993 by the Dutch Ministry of Education as an inter-university institute, IIAS today is based at Leiden University, where it works as a globally oriented interfaculty institute with strong connections throughout the Netherlands, Europe, Asia and beyond.

Citizens, Civil Society and Heritage-Making in Asia

Edited by

Hsin-Huang Michael Hsiao
Hui Yew-Foong
Philippe Peycam

ISEAS YUSOF ISHAK
INSTITUTE

中央研究院
社会学研究所
Institute of Sociology, Academia Sinica

IIAS
International Institute
for Asian Studies

First published in Singapore in 2017 by ISEAS Publishing
30 Heng Mui Keng Terrace
Singapore 119614
E-mail: publish@iseas.edu.sg
Website: <http://bookshop.iseas.edu.sg>

Co-published with

Institute of Sociology
Academia Sinica
128 Sec. 2 Academia Rd.
Nankang
Taipei 11529
Taiwan

International Institute for Asian Studies
Rapenburg 59
2311 GJ Leiden
the Netherlands

The responsibility for facts and opinions in this publication rests exclusively with the authors and their interpretations do not necessarily reflect the views or the policy of the publishers or their supporters.

ISEAS Library Cataloguing-in-Publication Data

Citizens, Civil society and Heritage-making in Asia / edited by Hsin-Huang Michael Hsiao, Hui Yew-Foong and Philippe Peycam.
1. Citizenship—Asia.
2. Civil society—Asia.
3. Asia—Civilization.
4. Xiao, Xinhuang.
5. Hui, Yew-Foong.
6. Peycam, Philippe.
DS12 C58   2017

ISBN 978-981-4786-15-7 (soft cover)
ISBN 978-981-4786-29-4 (e-book, PDF)

Typeset by Superskill Graphics Pte Ltd
Printed in Singapore by Markono Print Media Pte Ltd

Contents

Contributors

Yoshihisa AMAE is Associate Professor, Graduate Institute of Taiwan Studies, Chang Jung Christian University.

CAI Yunci is a PhD Candidate in Museum and Heritage Studies, UCL Institute of Archaeology.

Han-Hsiu CHEN is Assistant Professor, Department of Taiwan and Regional Studies, National Dong Hwa University, Taiwan.

Min-Chin CHIANG is Assistant Professor, Graduate Institute of Architecture and Cultural Heritage, Taipei National University of the Arts.

Gareth HOSKINS is Senior Lecturer, Department of Geography and Earth Sciences, Aberystwyth University, UK.

Hsin-Huang Michael HSIAO is Distinguished Research Fellow, Institute of Sociology, Academia Sinica, Taiwan; Professor of Sociology, National Taiwan University and National Sun Yat-sen University; Chair Professor of Hakka Studies, National Central University.

Li-Ling HUANG is Associate Professor, Graduate Institute of Building and Planning, National Taiwan University.

Shu-Mei HUANG is Assistant Professor, Graduate Institute of Building and Planning, National Taiwan University.

HUI Yew-Foong is Associate Professor, Department of Sociology, Hong Kong Shue Yan University; Senior Fellow, ISEAS – Yusof Ishak Institute.

LI Danzhou is Assistant Professor, Institute of Urban Governance, Shenzhen University.

Yi LI is Research Associate/Senior Teaching Fellow, Department of History, SOAS, University of London.

Hy Van LUONG is Professor of Anthropology, University of Toronto.

Rita PADAWANGI is Senior Lecturer, Singapore University of Social Sciences.

Adrian PERKASA is Lecturer, Department of History, Faculty of Humanities, Universitas Airlangga.

Philippe PEYCAM is Director, International Institute for Asian Studies.

Jayde Lin ROBERTS is Lecturer, Asian Languages and Studies, University of Tasmania.

Laurajane SMITH is Professor and ARC Future Fellow, College of Arts and Social Sciences, Australian National University.

Katrina Ross A. TAN is Assistant Professor, Department of Humanities, College of Arts and Sciences, University of the Philippines Los Baños.

Sheyla S. ZANDONAI is Research Associate, Laboratoire Architecture Anthropologie (LAA/ENSAPLV), France.

ZHANG Beiyu is a PhD Candidate, Department of History, National University of Singapore.

1

Introduction: Finding the Grain of Heritage Politics

Hui Yew-Foong, Hsin-Huang Michael Hsiao
and Philippe Peycam

This volume is a collection of papers from the second conference in a series of three. This series of three conferences was first envisioned to look into what we call "the cultural politics of heritage-making" in Asia. In positing the notion of "heritage-making", we foreground "heritage" as a dynamic process, a product that is unfinished and always in the making, akin to Harvey's (2001) assertion that the term is a verb, that is, something that is done. We further recognize that this process of heritage-making is embedded in contesting political interests that seek to present "heritage" as a finished product, a noun that becomes appropriated as a form of cultural capital, broadly speaking. Or to put it another way, "heritage" becomes the manifest material and symbolic anchor for culture, and one must have a "heritage" as one must have a nose and two ears (to borrow Gellner's simile) if one is to be recognized and recognizable in the international, national and sub-national arenas. Thus, "heritage" implies the process of heritage-making, and this process, when we consider the politics of recognition that is at stake, is embedded in cultural politics of multiple scales (see Harvey 2014).

These multiple scales, ranging from the local to the national and international levels — which we do not assume are discrete arenas of social action — involve different players with different degrees of agency and interests. In a generic way these players include the state, local actors at the grass-roots level, and international organizations and experts. Again, we do not assume that these actors or the arenas that they operate in are discrete. Often we may find actors reprising roles across the different scales, which hints at the complex assemblages that produce what we call "heritage". Without foregoing the multi-scalar complexities involved in the process of heritage-making, but with a view to foregrounding in turn the different sets of actors involved at different levels of the heritage-making chain, each of the conferences in the series focused on one set of players respectively. Thus, the first conference, held in Singapore in January 2014, focused on the role of the state. The second conference, held in Taipei in December 2014, on which this volume is based, focused on local players at the grass-roots level. The third and final conference in the series, held in May 2016 in Leiden, focussed on the international players involved in the heritage-making process.

It was no coincidence that Taiwan was chosen as the venue for the second conference. With the lifting of martial law in 1987, political space in Taiwan was liberalized, which in turn led to the proliferation of social movements and the valorization of the local within the Taiwanese body politic. The rise of the "era of localism" in the 1990s (see Chiang et al., this volume) saw local grass-roots actors articulate that which was historically and culturally distinct of their respective locales — in other words, they were involved in the process of heritage-making from the ground up. Of course, these actors were often acting with or against different levels of the state, or borrowing ideas from across national borders (such as from Japanese heritage activists), but what was distinctive was that the initiatives were often from local communities acting in their own interests. To avoid over-romanticizing the democratic extent of heritage activism in Taiwan, suffice it to say that, relatively speaking, Taiwan was an apt place for reflecting on and considering the role of local players in the making of heritage.

Who, indeed, are the local players that we seek to define and locate in this volume? The official theme for the second conference was "Citizens, Civil Society and the Cultural Politics of Heritage-Making in East and Southeast Asia". This directed attention to citizens and civil society actors as the local players that the conference was to focus on. However, the theme served as a guide rather than a dictum, and often contributors (to the conference and also this volume) bring to the fore actors that operate outside of the formal political arena.

This presses us to rethink the notions of citizenship and civil society, especially how they should be conceptualized in relation to the Asian heritage-making contexts examined in this volume. The Western conceptualization of citizenship and civil society takes the modern nation-state as the overriding frame of reference. Citizenship, in the narrow legal-constitutional sense, involves the assignment of membership by nation-states within a global system of nation-states. In other words, it acknowledges one's place in a world defined and delineated by nationalities, where one's identity is archived through documents such as birth certificates, identity cards and passports, the process of which is administered and adjudicated under the watchful eyes of the state. And even when we adopt a more expansive understanding of the citizen in the socio-political sense, the citizen's negotiation for meaning, interests and resources via the public sphere quite inevitably assumes the presence of the state (Brubaker 1992). Similarly, civil society, in challenging the ever-expanding capacity of the state in intervening in the everyday lives of individuals, following Tocquevillean formulation, is premised on an enduring though often adversarial engagement with the state (Tocqueville 2002). In short, the state stands as an imposing Other in conventional formulations of citizenship and civil society.

But what if there are contexts in which the nation-state does not figure? Or where it figures fleetingly, sometimes in view and sometimes out of view, sometimes as a receding backdrop and at other times returning hauntingly? Given Asia's colonial and post-colonial trajectories, how do we account for heritage-making in pre-national, post-national, trans-national and, God forbid, a-national contexts? Finally, to return to the subject of this volume, how do local actors define and position themselves, and what sort of socio-political space do they construct and operate in, where the nation-state is not necessarily an overriding element in their frame of reference?

Perhaps we can begin to think of how to define and locate local players by recalling that the word "citizen" is a historical referent for "city inhabitants" rather than members of a nation-state. That is, citizens were, in the first instance, inhabitants, or people who occupied a local space, and as such acted within the locus of their habitat, producing the complex constellation of social relations and experiences that constitute what Lefebvre (1991) calls "lived space" in the process. Heritage, then, is what local actors do when they relate to the past and discover meaning for the past in the present (see Smith, this volume) within the context of their "lived space".

Now that we have begun to de-nationalize the process of heritage-making, it is important to address the question of how local actors relate to this process. The relationship, as Smith (this volume) argues, can be an instrumental one, where the past is appropriated for the present through a calculus where recognition is apportioned or withheld. In this respect we can consider the Taiwanese Chinese rendition of "heritage" as "*wenhua zichan*" (文化資產), literally "cultural assets", where heritage can be construed as a form of asset, property or even capital in the Bourdieuian sense, and be put to work to generate more capital in various forms (Bourdieu 1986). To conceptualize heritage as a form of capital, then, is to locate social actors as subjects employing heritage as part of their economistic strategy to improve their social positions.

On the other hand, the relationship between local actors and heritage-making can be a non-instrumental one. Perhaps one way to begin to reflect on such a relationship is to consider the more general Chinese rendition of "heritage" as "*wenhua yichan*" (文化遺产), that is, as "cultural legacy" or "inheritance", something passed down to us by our forebears. The relationship between social actors and heritage construed in this sense takes on a more passive tone, where the emphasis is on that which is inherited, that was created by earlier generations and not by the heirs. Of course, heritage in this sense can still be appropriated to generate more wealth, but it can also be wealth that is simply enjoyed in and of itself. It is akin to air, breathed freely for one's sustenance — that is, the process of heritage-making can be part of social actors' everyday lives, a part of existence that need not necessarily be bound to interest.

The foregoing arguments, in positing that the process of heritage-making can take or not take the nation-state as an overriding point of reference, and can be defined or not defined by interests, are not presented in order to privilege any particular position. Instead, they are presented to sensitize the reader to heritage-making as practice, and as practice what it may mean to the social actors involved, so that our interpretation need not be unduly burdened by preconceived notions of what heritage entails. It is on this basis that we present the chapters in this volume, ranging over different Asian national contexts without being confined to the national framework, ranging over different historical eras without privileging a particular historical point of departure, and ranging over different local actors without discounting their interest or disinterest in relation to the process of making heritage. In so doing, we hope to engage with a reading of heritage practice on the ground, and determine the fine grain of heritage politics.

Indeed, it is because heritage is intertwined with identity and power that heritage is political. As Laurajane Smith's chapter argues, heritage is both inclusive and exclusive — it defines both identity and difference, and the process is a contested one. In reviewing the debates around the concept of heritage, the chapter provides some conceptual handles for engaging with the cases discussed in this volume. In particular, it makes explicit the relationship between heritage, identity and power through the articulation of heritage as cultural performance. Through such performances that produce and accrue meaning and emotional investments, Smith demonstrates how actors engage in the politics of recognition, legitimizing social inclusion and exclusion through the idiom of heritage.

The rest of the chapters in this volume shift the focus to more specific cases from East and Southeast Asia. They depict forms of civil society heritage-making agency, based on empirical and culturally sensitive field research, experienced "from the ground up", by anthropologists, sociologists, geographers and historians, among others. They go beyond the generic, reflecting the diversity and malleability of heritage-making processes within different Asian social environments, and with them, the infinite creativity of their members. As a result, readers should expect to encounter the grain of heritage politics in all sorts of spaces and among different kinds of communities, from the symbolic centres of nations to peripheries, among the urban poor, rural communities, regional vernacular communities and the Chinese diaspora, and of course, in Taiwan, where the conference that inspired this volume was held.

The Nation

The nation is not exactly an unexpected place to encounter processes of heritage-making. Indeed, as argued at the beginning of this chapter, heritage has become a cultural prosthesis that nations cannot do without. Yet, when we consider not the official narratives on heritage but how civil society groups and grass-roots actors apprehend and define "national heritage", especially in terms of lived experiences, the nation becomes decentred and heritage narratives take unexpected twists.

With Yangon, the former capital of Myanmar, the question of heritage emerged when the military regime moved the capital to the newly constructed city of Naypyitaw in 2005–6, thus freeing numerous colonial-era buildings formerly occupied by the government. What to tear down and what to retain, and what to do with what is retained, became pressing questions for a city thriving with foreign firms and NGOs, all competing to get a foothold in the commercial capital of a country that had recently become more open to international influences and investments.

Jayde Lin Roberts documents these recent changes and in the process points to the sharp sociological and cultural divide that exists between the views on urban physical "aesthetic" heritage preservation held by a tiny fraction of the city's civil society made up of foreign-educated Burmese and returned members of the diaspora and the concerns of the majority of the local population inhabiting the derelict city centre. The Yangon Heritage Trust, an internationally supported elite organization, seeks to preserve the British-era "modernist" architectural legacy of the former capital through its engagement with the state and also through a discourse of commodification to lure foreign investors. To Roberts, this seems at odds with the everyday anxieties of an impoverished urban population, and bears the risk of perpetuating a state of entrenched social inequality and alienation. Here, heritage politics involves not just the engagement between elite civil society actors and the state but also the disjuncture between the vision that the elite has for the city's heritage-scape and the "lived space" as experienced by the common city inhabitants. What Burmese-ness entails, against the backdrop of Yangon's increasing cosmopolitanism and corporate cityscape, is not a finished product narrated through an official script endorsed by the state, but remains a matter of symbolic struggle among these actors, often subtly embedded within the fine grain of everyday life.

Appreciation for "lived space" and the role of heritage in everyday life is articulated by Adrian Perkasa and Rita Padawangi through the notion of living heritage, explored in the context of Trowulan residents living with and off the ruins of the ancient Majapahit kingdom. Living heritage entails evolving sociocultural practices that continue to resonate meaningfully with the lived reality of local actors. It allows for the appropriation of the built environment to continue to embody meaningful social relationships and practices, such as the transformation of Majapahit ruins into Muslim cemeteries. Juxtaposed against such sites that evolve organically with the symbolic and material needs of local inhabitants, state-sponsored heritage sites that draw on this "glorious" past in the narration of the nation, in privileging the material monument over the lived reality of residents in the environs, do not exude the same kind of social vibrancy. In fact, heritage projects driven by state or market interests tend to become detached from the lives of local actors. Here, the grain of heritage politics is found not in contesting representations but in the practice of everyday life. In this banal rhythm of everyday existence, the past and present are continuously remade to meld with interests that are negotiated from day to day. In the case of these residents who live, so to speak, at the symbolic centre of Indonesia's pre-colonial past, the ruins left by their ancestors are meaningless unless they can build their own lives upon them, and in so doing make heritage on a daily basis.

The "Periphery"

Beyond the geographical and symbolic centres of nations, living heritage manifests itself wherever the past is intermeshed with the present in the performance of everyday life. Such performances can occur among "peripheral" communities, that is, communities that are usually considered to be beyond the political centre or national imaginary, such as rural and indigenous communities, or regional language groups and post-colonial entities.

Hy Van Luong's chapter moves beyond cities to focus on rural-based, community-initiated forms of heritage practices through a comparison of post-war, post-communist reconstitution of local religious festivals in the rural areas of North (Red River delta region) and South (Mekong River delta region) Vietnam. Village communities made use of new opportunities brought about by the *doi moi* government reforms of the late 1980s and the subsequent removal of strict atheist policies to organize themselves quite free from state intervention or from the new forms of commercialism engendered by the country's integration into global capitalism, such as tourism. The chapter shows how these local heritage-making initiatives — including performances of public rituals at communal houses, village and neighbourhood shrines or Buddhist pagodas — can differ in terms of the intensity of people's support. This, according to Luong, owes much to "the importance of regionally varying local dynamics", with communities in the north appearing sociologically better equipped than their southern counterparts to perform these modes of collective heritage-making, which the author attributes to a greater sense of communal identity and local social capital.

Cai Yunci's chapter examines another set of communities that is usually marginalized, or exoticized, in the official narratives of nations, namely, indigenous communities. Here, Cai interrogates the instrumentalization of heritage by comparing two indigenous cultural villages in West Malaysia that serve as outposts of heritage tourism. The Mah Meri Cultural Village was a state venture that sought to preserve and showcase Mah Meri cultural heritage. Through the commodification of handicrafts (originally embedded within the tribe's ritual economy) and cultural performances, these indigenous people were able to convert their heritage capital into a form of income to sustain them within the national market economy. However, in the process they had to contend with the state-endorsed cultural broker's infringement on their monopoly over the interpretation of their own customs as well as the profits of the cultural village. The Orang Seletar Cultural Centre, on the other hand, is an independent cultural village established through the efforts of local activists and funding from an international non-profit organization. The aim of the centre is to promote community-based eco-tourism as an alternative means of livelihood for villagers whose traditional habitat has been encroached upon by neoliberal developments. At the same time, through this spatial exhibition of their cultural heritage, the Orang Seletar lay claim to their indigenous identity and rights, and seek the state's recognition of their associated territorial heritage. In both cases the state could not be evaded, and the indigenous peoples' relationship with heritage was instrumental in nature. But in the latter case the pronounced autonomy from the state gave room for cultural change in tandem with evolving questions of livelihood and political recognition, approximating what could be articulated as living heritage.

Film-making, as an artistic medium for rendering heritage, allows "a community of artists, managers and technicians" to define new spaces of collective cultural imagination. In Katrina Ross A. Tan's chapter, a little-known yet thriving and consciously framed heritage-making process takes place through alternative regional film-making and film festivals organized in the vernacular languages of numerous regions of the Philippines. These initiatives are not just reacting to the conventional dominance of commercial films in Tagalog from Manila or Hollywood films. They result from local efforts aimed at including hitherto peripheral communities and their regional languages in the nation's film-scape through the use of digital technology and the organization of regional cultural events and networks. The Filipino state, through its cultural institutions, is recognizing these non-commercial community-based initiatives as contributing to the country's national heritage. In turn this is also recognition that such cultural and linguistic diversity is constitutive of the country's national identity. This is a rare case where the state includes heritage-making processes emanating from the country's periphery in representations of the nation.

With Sheyla S. Zandonai's study, we are brought to the fringe of the Chinese nation where the inhabitants of Macau, a former Portuguese colony now returned to Chinese sovereignty, sought to appropriate their colonial heritage as part of their post-colonial identity. The chapter first documents the political economy of post-handover Macau and the overwhelming impact the casino industry has on the city and its built heritage, with its numerous UNESCO-nominated buildings and sites, and this against the unique political background of Macau's Special Administrative Region (SAR) status. Zandonai then focuses on a transformative incident where members of the local community, mainly of Chinese origin, sought to prevent a Portuguese-built lighthouse from being blocked by high-rise developments, even when local authorities and UNESCO showed no interest. After pointing to the post-colonial ambiguity of the action — Macau residents of Chinese origin defending a colonial-era relic — the author shows how the different political entities associated with Macau, such as the Macau SAR government, the Beijing central government and UNESO, had to accommodate such unprecedented civil society action coming from Macau's inhabitants.

Diaspora

Diasporas, by dint of their transnational trajectories, often exist and subsist in the spaces between nations. While their heritages are unlikely to take centre stage within national narratives, they do usually form part of the multicultural fabric of countries in today's globalized world. The Chinese diaspora, in particular, can be found in almost any part of the world, and their heritage, in different shades and hues, do augment the cultural landscape of places they had trod. More importantly, through the notion of diasporic heritage, what comes to the fore is that, beyond business ties and networks, diasporas facilitate the translation of cultural heritage across borders, and therefore demonstrate the cultural dimension of what scholars have articulated as Chinese transnationalism (Ong and Nonini 1997).

Li Yi's chapter on the heritage-making efforts of the Chinese community in post-war Myanmar reflects the vicissitudes of articulating and preserving heritage in diaspora. Central to this tale is the Chinese community's relationship to their "homeland" and language, negotiated through a classical Chinese poetry society and a Chinese library, both established in Yangon. Where the poetry society catered to the fancies of the Chinese-educated elite and intelligentsia, the library took on the role of promoting Chinese literacy on a more general level among the Yangon Chinese. Through language, the cultural umbilical cord was maintained with the Chinese homeland, which, on the one hand, was imagined as an ancestral land steeped in timeless tradition and an immemorial past, and on the other hand, related to through a state that claimed legitimate representation of the Chinese nation. This dualism in identification among the Chinese diaspora then bespoke a complex transnationalism emerging in the interstices between polities that, post-independence or post-civil war, were still in the process of becoming nation-states. Aside from this the chapter also foregrounds how social actors, in particular members of the poetry society, relished the reciting and writing of Chinese poetry as Chinese gentry of the past would do, and in the process found a way of connecting with Chinese high culture. Their engagement in the art of heritage-making through poetry was a part of their everyday life inasmuch as it was part of their leisure.

Also dealing with the dynamics of heritage in diaspora is Zhang Beiyu's chapter on the perception of Chinese street opera in Singapore in the 1970s and 1980s. Under the rubric of a modernizing state, opera was first seen as a folk cultural practice in need of being disciplined and regulated, and then as a "dying art" in need of being resuscitated as heritage. Nostalgic representations of street opera mourns the loss, not only of this performance art-form, but also of the mode of everyday living associated with opera, in particular the sociality common to the familial experiences and neighbourly street life of that era. Besides the role of street opera in the life of the Singaporean nation, the chapter also dwells on Teochew opera as a family heritage from the perspective of practitioners. For these social actors, Teochew opera was considered a form of de-territorialized culture that involved the flow of ideas and people across geographical boundaries, spanning China, Hong Kong, Malaya and Siam. Although the performance of opera as peripatetic practice eventually became unviable through the reification and reinforcement of nation-state boundaries, the chapter was able to recover a historical perspective that recalls a pre-national context where what opera practitioners inherited from their predecessors was very much part of their everyday work and practice.

Taiwan

In this volume there are four chapters dealing with Taiwan's experiences. The first introduces, reconstructs and provides an overview of Taiwan's heritage policy formation and transformation, demonstrating how policy change has been both the consequence of civil society action and the cause of further citizens' engagement in heritage movements. This is followed by three case studies of a colonial heritage site, a military veterans' village, and a tobacco settlement. The three case studies vividly illustrate the diverse heritage-scape that has emerged in Taiwan since political liberalization in the late 1980s and 1990s, leading to extensive "Taiwanization" of the polity, growing indigenous consciousness, and the valorization of collective memories of Taiwan's past.

The chapter by Min-Chin Chiang, Li-Ling Huang, Shu-Mei Huang and Hsin-Huang Michael Hsiao traces the historical evolution of Taiwan's cultural heritage policies from the early China-centred authoritarian period to the current Taiwan-centred democratization era. This evolution is marked by shifts from the distorted cultural policies of the 1950s–70s to the authorized official heritage-making in the early 1980s, to heritage-making in tandem with new identity-formation in the late 1980s, to community development and the proliferation of local museums in the 1990s, and finally to the revised heritage policies since 2000. The revised heritage policies with the onset of the twenty-first century are characterized by the following features: replacement of Chinese cultural dominance with a multicultural paradigm; decentralization of bureaucratic mechanisms for heritage designation and registration; protection of potential heritage sites; offering of incentives to private heritage site owners to preserve the sites; and enhancement of access to and use of public heritage sites. The authors attribute such significant changes to increasing democratization, the emergence of a Taiwan-centred identity, and the corresponding awakening of civil society.

Yoshihisa Amae's chapter brings into the spotlight the Wushantou Reservoir, built during the Japanese colonial era by Japanese civil engineer Hatta Yoichi. The site is one of Taiwan's most important historical constructions and is designated as one of eighteen potential World Heritage sites in Taiwan. Although such a site is emblematic of Taiwan's colonial past, this past and its memories are not shrouded in shame or construed as a taint on Taiwan's national imaginary that need to be erased or altered. Instead, it is articulated not only as local heritage but as national and international heritage through a "circuit of culture" that involves a process of cultural production and consumption, facilitated by collaboration between the government and the public. This appropriation of the colonial past as part of Taiwan's heritage bespeaks a different kind of decolonization — not a disentanglement from the Japanese colonial past but a relinquishing of the script of pan-Chinese nationalistic history that reads the Japanese era as an encroachment on Chinese sovereignty. This discursive move, using heritage as a vehicle, projects a distinct Taiwanese identity.

Li Danzhou's chapter unveils yet another perspective on Taiwan's past through the study of the naval veterans' village in Zuoying, Kaohsiung. Such villages housed Kuomintang soldiers and their families who had retreated from mainland China between 1945 and 1953, and served as a humiliating reminder of the defeat of the nationalist army by the Communists. As a result, these villages were often hidden or exclusive, and set apart from mainstream Taiwanese society, even as their inhabitants were beneficiaries of preferential treatment from the nationalist government. Interestingly, with the liberalization and democratization of Taiwan, these villages and their history became incorporated as part of Taiwan's collective memory. This was in no small part due to the efforts of academics, intellectuals and citizen groups to "culturalize" these veterans' villages in the 1990s. Such valorization of "village culture", though contested, ascribed a sense of "place" to the villages. Consequently, even as inhabitants of the villages were relocated, some of the veterans' villages were preserved as heritage sites, serving as indelible parts of Taiwan's cultural landscape and collective memory.

The chapter by Han-Hsiu Chen and Gareth Hoskins explores Taiwan's tobacco agricultural landscape as heritage sites amidst shifting public attitudes towards tobacco smoking. The case in question is Fonglin, a former tobacco cultivation village esteemed in Taiwan since the Japanese colonial era. Chen and Hoskins considers the conflicting ideas surrounding the tobacco industry and its cultivation landscape and buildings and how this was reconciled by distilling the history of the local agricultural economy and associated collective memories from the now disreputable image of tobacco smoking. On the ground, this was negotiated by local residents, which led to an exhibition on tobacco cultivation in the Hakka Cultural Museum and the preservation of many tobacco buildings, including one that exhibited the Tudor style. At the same time, as Fonglin is not as famous as the Meinong tobacco settlement in southern Taiwan, the township also highlights its Japanese colonial legacy to attract Japanese tourists. Here, the local community had to claim authority over the identification and interpretation of what is "local heritage", and in so doing re-contextualize their relationship with tobacco and the colonial past.

* * * * *

The Taiwanese cases suggest that heritage may not always be drawn from official scripts that narrate the "glorious past". With the democratization of society and the ascendency of localism, what becomes more salient is the intimate past, which may be mundane or a cause for embarrassment, but an indelible part of a community's collective memory nonetheless. It is not surprising then to find that when grass-roots actors are involved in the cultivation and representation of their *own heritage*, it can be laced with what Herzfeld (2005) calls cultural intimacy. Likewise, the other cases selected for this volume, in highlighting the experience of grass-roots actors, puts the spotlight on their struggles over what heritage means at an everyday level, including the tensions and conflicts, the banal and the exceptional. The intimate, close-up view presented through this volume will, we hope, bring into focus the fine grain of heritage politics.

References

Bourdieu, Pierre. "The Forms of Capital". In *Handbook of Theory and Research for the Sociology of Education*, edited by J. Richardson. New York: Greenwood, 1986.

Brubaker, Rogers. *Citizenship and Nationhood in France and Germany*. Cambridge: Harvard University Press, 1992.

Harvey, David. "Heritage Pasts and Heritage Presents: Temporality, Meaning and the Scope of Heritage Studies". *International Journal of Heritage Studies* 7, no. 4 (2001): 319–38.

———. "Heritage and Scale: Settings, Boundaries and Relations". *International Journal of Heritage Studies* 21, no. 6 (2015): 577–93.

Herzfeld, Michael. *Cultural Intimacy: Social Poetics in the Nation-State*. New York: Routledge, 2005.

Lefebvre, Henri. *The Production of Space*. Oxford: Blackwell, 1991.

Ong, Aihwa, and Donald M. Nonini. *Ungrounded Empires: The Cultural Politics of Modern Chinese Transnationalism*. New York: Routledge, 1997.

Tocqueville, Alexis de. *Democracy in America*. London: Folio Society, 2002.

2

Heritage, Identity and Power

Laurajane Smith

My colleague Yujie Zhu recounted a tea ceremony he had attended in Canberra, Australia. At the ceremony was a student from Taiwan, a Chinese mainland tea expert, and a Japanese scholar. The Taiwanese student said, "Every time I drink this, it make me feel like I am back at home. It is like I am in Taiwan. I am feeling Taiwanese." The Japanese scholar responded, "Yes, I can understand, but you know, this tea was actually influenced from Japan." The tea expert then said, "Oh, interesting, because the tea is now sold as a Chinese tea."

What this story tells us is that heritage-making is always fraught and contested. Indeed it is always political, not simply because its interpretation or history may be disputed, but because any assertion of inclusive heritage must also include an implicit assertion of exclusion — "this is who I am, and you are different from me".

One of the significant assumptions that underpins both heritage management practices and heritage scholarship is that heritage is about identity. Heritage, in either its intangible or tangible form, is intuitively understood to be about the assertion and reinforcement of identity — be that associated with social, cultural, national, ethnic or other forms of identity.

The link between heritage and identity is often simply taken for granted, and there is very little work that takes as its central task an analysis of the linkages between expressions of identity and heritage.

In attempting to reveal these links, I want to develop my argument that heritage is a cultural performance, in which the meaning of the past for the present is continually recreated and reinterpreted to address the political and social needs and problems of the present. Contra to the writings of David Lowenthal (1986, 1996) and Benedict Anderson (1991), heritage is neither a cult nor is it imagined or simply invented; rather it is part of a cultural and political performance and set of negotiations that has material consequences for a range of contemporary social problems. Indeed, worrying about the authenticity of origins, as Anderson and Lowenthal do, misses the point entirely — heritage is about the present, and about how certain interpretations of the past are used in and *for* the present. Thus, the origin of the tea, which was of concern to the Japanese scholar in that tea ceremony in Canberra, is less important than how drinking that tea made the Taiwanese student feel.

These issues of identity and citizenship may be played out between individuals, as it was in the Canberra tea ceremony, or they may be played out between and within community groups or between nations as, for example, the controversy that erupted over the 2005 listing of the Dano-je Dragon Boat Races on the UNESCO Intangible Heritage List by Korea. This listing was hotly contested by China, who accused Korea of appropriating Chinese heritage. These issues become controversial, they matter, because heritage is a political resource that helps to legitimize or delegitimize claims to cultural and material capital.

This chapter reviews recent debates within heritage studies to identify the complexity of ideas and practices that occur around the concept of "heritage", and in doing so provides a context for other chapters in this collection. In reviewing these debates my aim is to illustrate the interrelationship between conceptualizations of heritage, identity and power, and to argue that understanding heritage as simply a subject of technical matters of management or urban planning entirely misunderstands the nature and value of heritage in the present.

An Anglophone History of Heritage

The Anglophone and wider European origins of a concern with "heritage" are traditionally traced back to the development of European legislation concerned with the protection of material objects or places considered to have historical and inheritable value (Lowenthal 1985; Murtagh 1997; Choy 2001; Carman 2002; Swenson 2014; Betts and Ross 2015 for overviews). The European history of this concept may appear to have little relevance in a book on heritage-making in Asia; however, it is the European conceptualization of this concept that had tended to dominate much of both international debate and, more significantly, international policy and practices, through the work of UNESCO and ICOMOS. Early European understandings of the concept have done much to obscure and deny the interrelationship between heritage, identity and power, by focusing on the material aspects of heritage to the extent that "heritage" became conceptualized as important "things" with innate and immutable historical and cultural value. This emphasis on the innate value of material heritage worked to underscore the naturalness of European social hierarchies and European nationalism, and heritage conservation practices in turn reinforced the idea of heritage as "found" objects and places whose historical meanings were assumed and unquestioned.

Nineteenth century European debates within Western European architecture, archaeology and art history, that fetishized issues of material authenticity and aesthetics, were important in facilitating this understanding of heritage. Within these debates material culture deemed to be of heritage value, that is those objects and places identified as both "old" and as representative markers of national history, were infused with a sense of innate value and meaning. Their preservation was stressed in terms of a desire to preserve the past in the face of two interlinked and increasing threats to, firstly, a particular sense of aesthetic; and secondly, and most importantly, an understanding of both the past *and* contemporary cultural and social experiences valued by a particular socio-economic stratum of European society. Thus, we get the development of a particular understanding of heritage that becomes closely tied into developing concepts of nationalism and the political strategies of the social and economic elite to maintain political influence through an appeal to their historical and cultural significance, demonstrated by the newly minted concept of national heritage. This led to the development of an Authorized Heritage Discourse (AHD), which not only cemented this nineteenth-century conceptualization of heritage as naturalized common sense, but also identified experts such as architects, art historians and archaeologists as the stewards for a supposedly fragile, finite and non-renewable past (see Smith 2006 for fuller discussion).

The AHD grew in influence and persuasive power during the twentieth century and was taken up in not only European national but also, and most importantly, international documents, treaties and conventions. Indeed, UNESCO and the professional body ICOMOS are two of the authorizing institutions of this discourse, their charters, conventions, and management and planning practices continually working to reassert the "common sense" value of this discourse. The AHD led to an understanding of heritage as largely a technical concern, that is, it stimulated research into technical issues to support and enhance what was often vaguely defined as "best practice" in conserving and managing what had become a "finite" resource. Indeed, even today, research into technical issues of management and conservation remain dominant in heritage studies.

However, during the 1980s heritage studies broadened to become more than simply a concern with management and conservation, and to a certain extent began to examine heritage itself as a social phenomenon. The publication of David Lowenthal's *The Past is a Foreign Country* heralded the commencement of what we may define as a recognizable academic field of heritage studies, but it also marks what may be defined as the so-called "heritage industry debate" led by academics from within Britain. This, and following publications by historians Robert Hewison (1981, 1987) and Patrick Wright (1985), and the archaeologist Kevin Walsh (1992) among many others, were heavily influenced by Thatcherite reactionary uses of heritage, and argued that heritage was primarily used to uphold conservative social forces. Indeed, I would argue they were reacting against the AHD — although they would not themselves have expressed it this way. These debates in the United Kingdom were echoed by similar debates in the 1980s and 1990s in the United States and Australia (see Smith 2006). While these authors and the debate overall raised important issues, how the debate was framed restricted the development of heritage studies considerably. The framing of the debate, which owes much to Lowenthal, was very much a reaction against heritage that was driven by presumed epistemological threats to historical and archaeological knowledge. In large part this was a conservative reaction against the idea of heritage, despite apparent claims to the contrary by Lowenthal (1985). It is conservative in the sense that heritage was then defined as something "popular"; to be consumed by what was defined in the "heritage industry" debate as mass tourism and a profit-driven industry — in short as something that is used in an unthinking fashion. A further issue emerges in following the roots of the arguments within this debate, and particularly the arguments by Lowenthal, arguments that also appear in his later work (1985, 1996, 2009). In following the roots of the argument, we get back to what is almost a knee-jerk reaction against heritage that draws on nothing more than established epistemological verities in history, geography or archaeology. What this does for heritage studies is constrain analysis and, as the historian Raphael Samuel pointed out in 1994, the wider social and political diversity of the way heritage is used and understood within Europe is misunderstood and neglected. As I have argued elsewhere (Smith 2006, 2011), this debate, while reacting against the AHD, did not in fact challenge it, and tended to reinvest in much of the same conceptual frameworks.

More recently we can chart the development of a critical turn in heritage studies, marked most recently by the development of the Critical Heritage Studies movement. This turn argues that the cultural phenomenon of heritage, however we may define it, is itself a subject worthy of study. This debate develops out of critical work being done by a number of authors working in interdisciplinary contexts throughout the 1990s, though I prefer to date its commencement with the work of Raphael Samuel, but lamentably he remains largely ignored in heritage studies (Gentry 2015). It also grows out of increasing criticism of the Eurocentric nature of UNESCO, which in turn led to the recognition of the concept of "intangible heritage". The work of the geographers Brian Graham, John Tunbridge and Greg Ashworth (2000), and anthropologists Kirshenblatt-Gimblett (1998) and Michael Herzfeld (1991, 2005) have been particularly influential. In addition, it is also marked by growing attempts during the last ten years to define heritage as an area of cultural production or process, and a corresponding loss of commitment to the idea that heritage can most usefully be conceived as a material phenomenon. Kirshenblatt-Gimblett (1998) has argued that heritage is a form of meta-cultural production, a process in which the meaning of the past is continually reproduced. Dicks (2000) has also argued that heritage may be understood as a communicative act, while David Harvey (2001) defines the term as a verb, that is, heritage is something that is done. These are ideas I have also developed in my own work, which has argued that heritage is an embodied performance in which the meaning of the past is continually reworked and negotiated for the needs and concerns of the present. I have argued that all heritage is intangible, because heritage is itself an embodied act, performance or practice (Smith 2006, 2011).

Heritage is not reducible to sites or places, or the things we collect in museums. It is more usefully understood as a performance or practice concerned with utilizing the past to help nations, sub-national communities, interests or groups, and individuals and their families negotiate the cultural and social values and meanings that have resonance and meaning for the present. It is a process intimately tied up with the legitimation of identity, belonging and sense of place, but it is a negotiated process in which heritage meanings or heritage-making are constantly made and remade for the needs of the present. Heritage is thus not something that is found, but is continually re-made.

Heritage-making and the continual re-negotiation of meaning that occurs with it are undertaken at any number of different social and cultural levels. For example, they occur at national and international levels over what is or is not chosen to be listed in UNESCO or national heritage lists, or what is or is not collected and displayed in museums. Heritage lists, such as the World Heritage List maintained by UNESCO, represent a continual performance of World Heritage-making. Heritage-making and negotiation also occurs around the practices of management and interpretation of certain sites, places and artefacts. Individual heritage performances can occur across the dining room table, as we glance through photo albums, talk to each other about familial histories, and so on. They can also occur in the more formal settings of those places officially defined as museums and heritage sites. While institutions such as government heritage agencies and museums work to guide and influence the heritage-making of visitors to sites and museums by carefully designing and constructing exhibitions and interpretive material, they cannot always control the meaning or understanding that visitors take away. This is because individuals themselves are often engaged in their own form of heritage-making.

James Wertsch (2002; see also Wertsch and Billingsley 2011) argues that the processes of remembering do not simply spontaneously happen, and that we will use individually or collectively a range of cultural tools to help us to remember. In the processes of remembering there will be an associated forgetting, but also as individual or collective remembering occurs the meaning of the past for the present is continually remade (Connerton 1991; Urry 1996; Wertsch 2002). Drawing on Wertsch's arguments, I contend that those things traditionally identified as "heritage" by organizations such as UNESCO or ICOMOS are more usefully conceived as cultural tools that facilitate the process of heritage-making, a process that requires both remembering and forgetting (Smith 2006). This definition also rejects the boundary often drawn between museums and heritage sites as both become theatres of memory (Samuel 1994), that is arenas or locales in which the processes of remembering and associated meaning-making occur. Sharon Macdonald (2013), in her study of memory networks and complexities in the way the past is remembered and forgotten in Europe, has defined what she calls "past presenting". She argues, similarly to myself, Harvey (2001), Dicks (2000) and Byrne (2009), that the past is brought to the present to legitimize and make sense of not only the present but, more importantly, making the past present affords opportunities to reflect and to consider new aspirations for the future (Macdonald 2013).

The reconceptualization of heritage as something that is done, rather than simply something that is possessed and managed, and a turn to analysing heritage as a cultural phenomenon, has been part of a concern to re-theorize heritage that underpinned the development of the Association of Critical Heritage Studies in 2012. The manifesto of this association explicitly aims to challenge the hegemony of the AHD, and in doing so also aims to facilitate dialogue between practitioners and academics to assist the development of democratic and inclusive policy and practice (Campbell and Smith 2011). The manifesto also argues that a critical heritage studies should also identify the range of ways and contexts in which heritage is used and the cultural, social, economic and/or political work that it does within and between different social and cultural contexts (see Campbell and Smith 2011; Smith 2012a; and for critique Witcomb and Buckley 2013).

A range of themes has developed under the umbrella of "critical heritage studies", not least of which have been debates about the interdisciplinary and international nature of studies of heritage, the latter point I will return to shortly. However, of concern to the aims set out in the manifesto is an increasing turn to New Materialism and the post-human in attempts to re-theorize heritage as a cultural phenomenon. This has been marked in particular by work led by Rodney Harrison (2013), which aims to use "Actor Network theory" (ANT) to both understand the nature of heritage and its consequences (see also Weston 2012; Felder et al. 2015); and non-representational theory to understand the affective moments of heritage (Waterton and Watson 2013). Harrison, drawing on ANT, notes that "heritage is not the inscription of meaning onto blank objects", but rather heritage is produced "as a result of the material and social possibilities, or 'affordances', of collectives of human and non-human agents, material and non-material entities, in the world" (2013, p. 217). Thus for him heritage is not "an intellectual endeavour, something that exists only in the human mind, but is one that emerges from the *dialogue*, or practices of people and things" (2013, p. 217, emphasis in the original). Rather than heritage objects and places being understood as cultural tools in the processes of negotiating the meaning of the past, heritage "things" are re-privileged as active agents, or "actants", in the heritage-making process. ANT, conceived as a methodological tool which is "not intended to add anything substantive to an explanation" (Sayes 2014, p. 9), has been justly criticized for its obfuscating language (Fischer 2014) and its focus on "what can be composed anew", and thus explicitly omits attention to the material, political and power-laden consequences of the dialogue between human and so-called non-human agents (Fortun 2014, p. 317). Similarly, Non Representational Theory (NRT) has also been critiqued for its abstruse language (Creswell 2012) and focus on the "affective moment". What is worrying about this emphasis is that in both ANT and NRT the moment becomes the focal point of analysis and many important elements of context are stripped away and disregarded. As context is removed from the analysis, and issues of class, gender, ethnicity and so forth are no longer perceived to matter, androcentric and Eurocentric assumptions of the researcher are allowed, if not encouraged, to creep back into analysis (Tolia-Kelly 2006; Fortun 2014; Leys 2011; Wetherall 2012). The consequence of this is that issues of power and politics become either redundant or dealt with idiosyncratically in post-human and New Materialist accounts, which seems to me entirely problematic for a critical heritage studies that aims to challenge the Eurocentric AHD.

The international claim of the critical heritage studies movement is itself also worthy of some critical attention. Europe has, to date, been a particular focus of the critical turn in heritage studies in two important ways. Firstly, Europe, as the home of the original authors of the AHD, has been put under intense scrutiny in terms of how this discourse tends to not only reinforce particular understandings of European nationalism, but more importantly how it helps to maintain national and a pan–Western-European historical narrative that places Europe at the centre of human history (see, for example, Byrne 1991; Labadi 2007; Meskell 2002; Meskell et al. 2015). This criticism has been particularly stark in terms of a long-term and ongoing critique of Eurocentrism in the UNESCO World Heritage List; indeed we can describe the World Heritage List as a neo-colonial

European project that has seen the spread of the European AHD across the globe, albeit sometimes more successfully than others.

Secondly, the increasing recognition of the dominance of European understandings of heritage, both in terms of international practice and theoretical development, has begun to be challenged. Michael Herzfeld (2010), Denis Byrne (2009) and Tim Winter (2013) have, amongst other commentators, led attempts to draw attention to non-European conceptualizations of heritage and called for global and pluralizing theoretical and policy debates. Their collective work has tended to focus on Southeast Asian contexts. However, the point here is that for European and Anglophone heritage practices and debates in general to meet this pluralist challenge, heritage studies needs to turn a critical and reflexive eye back on to European and wider Western contexts to understand how heritage is used to address multicultural and cosmopolitan issues. While, yes, this makes European and Anglophone concerns the focus of debate and study once again, I do think, if we are to meet the critical challenges being offered by non-European conceptualizations of heritage, any analysis of Anglophone or Western practices that aims at understanding how heritage practices either do or do not engage with cosmopolitan issues are important for opening up the arena of ongoing debate. With this point, I want to turn to an aspect of the work I am currently doing in heritage studies in which I aim to understand the political consequences of the linkages made between heritage and identity.

Heritage and the Politics of Recognition

Heritage-making, as I note above, is a process that may occur at a number of levels or, as Harvey argues, scales (Harvey 2015; see also Graham et al. 2000). To date, much of my work has been concerned with documenting heritage-making at individual levels, through the visiting of heritage sites and museums. I have been concerned to see how what Raphael Samuel (1994) defines as theatres of memory are used in the process of heritage-making. I have documented how visitors to English sites such as historic houses and labour history museums are engaged in an embodied and affective performance of remembering, and the social and political work that was done during those visits in terms of constructing and negotiating a visitor's sense of physical and socio-economic place in British society (Smith 2006). Similar work is being conducted by Rouran Zhang at the

World Heritage site of West Lake, Hongzhou, Zhejiang Province, China. Zhang (2014) is interviewing a woman about West Lake and asks:

> Rouran Zhang: What experiences do you value on visiting this site?
> WL089: on the Broken Bridge and Leifeng tower. I am thinking [of] the moment Su Dong Po and Baijuyi were writing poetry, and I am right there drinking [tea] with them (laugh).
> (WL089, tourist, female, 35–44, staff from airline company, from Shanghai)

As the woman is standing on the Broken Bridge she thinks about the poets who had written about the lake — she is engaged in a process of remembering and constructing a sense of place and connection to the past. In doing so she is affirming her sense of identity and is making heritage. West Lake becomes a site of heritage through this process of remembering and connection — not because it is inherently valuable or inherently historical, but because it has been given meaning by, at an international level, UNESCO when they placed it on the World Heritage List, by China's government when they identified it as important to the nation's national narrative, and by the individuals who visit. The site becomes a cultural tool in collective and individual processes of remembering. West Lake becomes a theatre of memory — its role is not only to facilitate remembering, but to mark that remembering and the meanings that process creates as important. As Macdonald (2009, 2013) also notes, it is the embodied performance of visiting that gives the moments of reflection of the past heightened meaning. The effort of going to the site in effect reinforces the legitimacy of the meanings thus constructed for the visitor (Smith 2006, 2012b). This is not to say that the meanings so constructed come from an "agency" or "affordance" in or of the material objects or sites she is visiting, as Harrison (2013) may suggest. Indeed there has been research that suggests visitors to heritage sites tend to possess certain narratives or understandings of history and culture prior to their visit that are frequently left intact by their visit, and draw them to visit (or not visit) particular sites (Pekarik and Schreiber 2012; Smith 2015). Through a process of remembering, the site or museum exhibition gives both space and time to reflect and to mark that reflection as legitimate.

The moment of heritage-making provided by Zhang's informant at West Lake may be interesting in and of itself, but analysis cannot simply stop at that moment — this moment has consequences. In extending the analysis I made in the book *Uses of Heritage* (2006), one of the issues I am analysing is what do claims to identity do, and to consider what consequences they have. The critical heritage studies literature has often stressed that heritage is political, but what exactly is meant by this? To answer this question I have drawn on political philosophy and the concept of politics of recognition to consider how claims for recognition, or identity claims, may be played out with regard to heritage-making.

Recognition of difference has become, during the last decades of the twentieth century, an identifiable arena of political conflict (Kymlicka and Norman 2000; Lovell 2007). Claims for the recognition of difference and identity have become a recognized platform from which to engage in struggles for social justice, and parity in negotiations over the distribution of resources of power (such as finance, welfare, housing, education). Coincidently, this growth in claims for recognition has occurred simultaneously with an increasing national and international interest in heritage. This coincidence highlights two issues. Firstly, it underscores the intensity often identified in heritage conflicts over whether or not to preserve certain heritage places, or how such places should be valued and interpreted, by placing these conflicts within a wider understanding of the political consequences that identity claims can have. Secondly, the desire and need by states and their heritage agencies to control and regulate identity claims acquires a certain urgency in the context of increasing demands for the political recognition of cultural and identity claims.

Comprehending the way heritage may be taken up in claims for recognition does two things. Firstly, it reveals the "politics" of heritage, by identifying the structures of power heritage sits within and the ways in which heritage may become not only a cultural tool but also a political resource. Secondly, it answers some of the criticisms levelled at the way the politics of recognition is conceived as neglecting how the mechanics and specifics of struggles or negotiations over recognition can be played out (McNay 2008). I am not making grand claims that the heritage process is the only way the politics of recognition can be pursued; only that it is one way. However, understanding heritage in this context provides a useful analytical framework for understanding not only the political power of heritage but also its emotional consequence.

There is a great deal of debate, and varying conceptualizations of the politics of recognition, in political philosophy. Both Charles Taylor (1994) and Axel Honneth ([1995] 2005) define claims to recognition as a particular human and emotional need, and Taylor in particular tends to argue that when misrecognition occurs this act of injustice is separate from other forms of inequality or oppression (Young 2000, p. 105). As Nancy Fraser argues, recognition needs to be approached "in the spirit of ... pragmatism" (Fraser 2003, p. 45) and conceived as a remedy for social justice that is explicitly linked to struggles over the distribution of resources. Claims for the recognition of difference and identity are linked to demands and calls for restorative justice, social inclusion and greater equity in policy negotiations over the distribution of resources such as finance, welfare, housing, education and so forth (Fraser, 1995, 2000; Young 2000). Appeals to the past lend historical and cultural legitimacy to claims to difference and particular claims to identity. As Young notes, this is a project of cosmopolitan governance, where the self-determination of self-identified peoples is the aim, rather than a homogenization of policy responses (Young 2000, p. 9), in that claims to recognition are usually "a means to undermining domination or wrongful deprivation" (2000, p. 83). This is separate to what is sometimes defined as "identity politics". As Young argues, identity politics is an attempt to "cultivate mutual identification among those similarly situated" (Young 2000, p. 107). These claims may generate conflict, but are differentiated from claims to recognition, as claims to recognition, unlike identity politics, are "rarely asserted for their own sake" and are part of claims for political inclusion and equal economic opportunity (Young 2000, p. 106). In addition, claims to recognition may include or centre on, as Andrew Sayer (2007, p. 96) notes, more broad appeals to "someone's moral worth as a person" rather than their worth as a person of a particular identity. The significant point for heritage studies is that heritage and memory, as Macdonald (2013) argues, makes the past present; moreover, the idea that heritage is a negotiated process in which meaning and narrative are affirmed and remade suggests that heritage is implicated in the way claims for recognition are made and legitimized. Further, heritage also becomes an arena where misrecognition may occur and be further propagated, as the ways in which hegemonic groups construct understandings of both themselves and "the other" are significant potential acts of recognition or misrecognition.

Two further issues that emerge from the debate on recognition are important here. The first is Honneth's argument that recognition meets a human need, and although it is also about more than this, Honneth does point out that recognition and misrecognition intersect with emotional issues. As he argues, misrecognition or experiences of disrespect are always accompanied by affective sensations which may compel individuals to act and make claims that attempt to generate self-esteem ([1995] 2005, p. 136). While, like Fraser and Young, I take the position that a search for self-esteem is not in itself where the politics of recognition stops, it does alert us to the issue of emotions. Heritage is a highly emotive phenomenon. As Yaniv Poria et al. (2003) demonstrate, heritage sites are places where people go to feel. The emotional nature and consequences of heritage have not been well researched in heritage studies, as emotions are often simply dismissed as subjective and unreliable (Ahmed 2004; Wetherell 2012). However, emotion is a form of evaluative judgment of matters that affect our well-being (Sayer 2007, pp. 90–91). While of course emotions are fallible judgements, so too are judgements made on the supposedly unemotional basis of reason — emotions, necessarily non-rational, can nonetheless often facilitate "perceptive and reasonable judgments about situations and processes" (Sayer 2007, p. 91). Indeed, Eva Illouz (2007, p. 2) makes the point that while emotions are not action per se, they provide an inner energy that "propels us towards an act". This act may be to seek recognition, but equally it can be about offering recognition.

Following this observation, the second point to emerge in this debate for me is the issue of self-recognition. This issue is informed by an understanding of cosmopolitanism in which cosmopolitanism encompasses both an obligation to others and a celebration of difference (Appiah 2006, p. xiii). In the politics of recognition, recognition is both being sought and then either conferred or withheld by other social and cultural groups, and ultimately by policymakers. For this process to occur, an ability to understand, and historically situate your own social and cultural identity, is necessary. For example, the ability to recognize oneself as an inheritor of a particular colonial de-privileging legacy, or of gender, ethnic or class discrimination, and to understand the pragmatic consequences of that, is necessary. Equally, before a cosmopolitan politics of recognition can be achieved, it is important for those from hegemonic groups to recognize themselves as the inheritor of particular historically situated privileges. This is not to say that hegemonic groups have to take responsibility for past wrongs, only the contemporary legacies of those wrongs (Young 1990, 2000), so that the recognition of difference needs to be grounded in a reflexive recognition of self. Self-reflection is vital, so that self-recognition acknowledges the power structures within which people sit, and offers of recognition do not cultivate new misrecognitions (Butler and Athanasiou 2013, p. 76). It is also important that such recognition moves beyond discourses of "tolerance" that are thinly veiled appeals to assimilation.

The issue of self-reflection links back to the idea of emotional judgements, in particular to the emotion of empathy. Empathy, linked to an imaginative ability to place yourself in another's position, is crucial, as Carol Johnston notes, to imagine "alternative futures and presents" where social justice is addressed (2005, p. 42). However, the issue of emotion and imagination, when linked to the past, must involve memory. Emily Keightley and Michael Pickering (2012) outline the idea of "mnemonic imagination" to help us understand how remembering and imagination work together. They argue that through mnemonic imagination it is possible to achieve an interactive duality between "the constitution of selfhood and the commission of social action" (2012, p. 7). This conceptualization helps to highlight the interplay between not only imagination and memory but also emotion. However, for emotion to have a transformative effect on understanding, to allow the possibility of recognition and/or the overturning of misrecognition, it has to be expressed and mediated against a measure of emotional intelligence. Here I define emotional intelligence as the skill to recognize an emotional response and to be active in the way that it is used in making judgements (Mayer et al. 2008; Illouz 2007, p. 65). These are all concepts, like the concept of heritage itself, that interestingly have been dismissed as subjective and thus unreliable (Illouz 2007; Sayer 2007; Kalela 2012; Keightley and Pickering 2012). However, they can be usefully understood as phenomena that interact to have a consequence, and their unreliability rests not in opposition to abstract notions of objectivity but rather because together they work to continually make and remake particular understandings and relationships of self and other, to either uphold or challenge established social relations and interactions.

The various debates about the politics of recognition have been criticized as too abstract, as philosophers have not grounded their discussions in the everyday, and thus the question that arises is how does such a politics play out in day-to-day activities (McNay 2008). To address this I draw on the work I have been doing with visitors to heritage sites and museum exhibitions that aims to explore the identity and memory work that visitors undertake at a range of different genres of museums and heritage sites. Overall, the project has interviewed visitors at forty-five heritage sites and museums or exhibitions of history and culture in

Australia, the United States and England, representing just over 4,500 visitor interviews.

There are a range of themes that have emerged from the data, different types of heritage-making or heritage performances that visitors engage in, either singularly or in combination, can be identified:

1. Managing and expressing emotions about the topics being visited.
2. Passing on family memories and values. Sites and museums were used for intergenerational communication and as a setting for passing on family histories, narratives and values.
3. Individual remembering and affirmation of personal or collective social or political values.
4. Asserting, negotiating or making a connection to familial identity and/or history. This differs from performance two, above, in so far as this was often a connection grown children were making with their ancestors.
5. Reinforcing what visitors already knew, understood or felt about national, regional or ethnic identity and narratives and the collective memories and values that underpinned these.
6. Offering recognition and respect or misrecognition.
7. Educational resource. Education is often seen as the main use of heritage sites and museums. The work shows that education was actually an infrequent use, and was not something many tourists or visitors engaged in. However, when learning was done, what was being learnt was often not what heritage experts or curatorial staff may have had in mind. (Smith 2015)

The first focuses on the management and expression of emotions. Heritage sites and museums become locations in which people find it permissible, or perhaps appropriate or safe, to experience and express or experiment with certain emotions. Importantly, the performative act of managing or negotiating emotional responses to the past then worked to facilitate and frame the way other heritage performances were expressed. The performance of recognition and misrecognition is discussed below.

Recognition occurs in one of four ways within the interview data. Firstly, as recognition of self, in which the visitor recognizes themselves as either the inheritor of discrimination or of privilege. Secondly, it occurs in the offering of recognition or respect. Thirdly, in the continuation of misrecognition. And finally, museums/heritage sites may be used as a barometer by some groups to measure the extent to which the museum or site — and its role representing wider societal debate — is offering or not offering recognition. The issue of recognition was found, in various ways and degrees, in all museums and exhibitions included in the study.

Examples of recognition of self, one of the most frequent ways in which museums are used, is to affirm a person's or family's sense of self and belonging. This example comes from the Tenement Museum in New York:

> As an immigrant, myself, and this is the people who really built New York, and by connotation America. Those stories are never told.
> (TM5: male, 55–64, bank regulation, African American; Hard Times tour)

In this example the speaker is asserting self-respect and self-esteem. Indeed, this form of recognition is fundamental to most heritage-making. However, in the following examples from the Pequot Mashantucket Museum in the United States, the speakers are recognizing uncomfortable aspects about their national or ethnic identity, they are self-recognizing their position as privileged people, as the invaders of Native American lands:

> Well, you know, you would say sadly like you guys [Australians], you know, we as the white people, we're the people that were the invaders. You know, brought the disease, brought the killings and all that stuff.
> (PM39: female, 45–54, teacher, Caucasian American)

> It makes me feel good that they [the Pequot] were able to do something and not lose it [their culture]. Sometimes it makes me feel ashamed as a white man for what Europeans did.
> (PM43: male, 55–64, retired human services, Caucasian American)

In this next example, from the Immigration Museum in Melbourne, Australia, the speaker moves from self-recognition to recognition of others, and illustrates the emotional strength of this process:

> I'm very fond of this museum because, I think it's, I'm going to cry, people think of museums as being sort of stuffy, artificial places and this one deals with real people and, I am going to cry.... It's because it's really powerful because it's the history of real people and the white settlers of Australia, both[,] you know[,] the immigration side which is an enormously powerful story anyway having immigrated from England myself and knowing

what it's like to leave your entire family behind and come over. That's the connection I have with that. But the cameleers [Afghan Australian community] for example, there's a little bit of history and as the film says upstairs, they[,] you know, they left no trace but their importance to the exploration and development of this country is phenomenal and these are just the little bits of history that get lost and I think this museum's really important in preserving these little bits of social history that often, in the great global scheme of political history, often get lost[,] so I think it's very important, especially in this electronic age, that we hang on to as much of this as we possibly can.

(IMM106: female, 55–64, retired radio producer, White Australian)

Both positive and negative emotions are used in these examples to reflect on self-identity. In some cases shame was used to mediate and recognize self and their place in a hierarchy of political and social experience. In the last example empathy was the emotion that was used firstly to recognize self and then to extend that recognition to the Afghan camel drivers, an often unacknowledged and ignored immigrant population in nineteenth century Australia. Moving to the second expression of recognition, that of offering recognition and respect to others, it was often facilitated by the ability of a visitor to not only feel empathy but also to have the emotional intelligence to utilize that empathy in imaginative ways. Recognition was made not only in terms of appreciating others but also in recognizing the importance of certain values, such as multiculturalism. In these examples the speakers at the Immigration Museum Melbourne are not only recognizing others and the ethnic diversity of their society, but also negotiating the nature of their civil society and their own place within that:

But yet it's diverse and it does show that people with diverse backgrounds, diverse ethnicities, languages whatever can actually live together in peace and can form an integrated community.
(IMM072: female, 55–64, nurse, Australian)

Yes, yes there are. There were a whole bunch of people in Australia before I was and they're all different.
(IMM103: male, 18–24, student, Australian)

Yes, it's [Australia is] extremely diverse, I mean you know from the Kurdish to the American for every influence in Australia. It's not better, worse or, it's just different from what we grew up with.
(IMM111: male, over 65, retired high school principal, Australian)

Another example of recognition, and the complex emotions that can underpin it, comes from the site of Montpellier, Virginia, in the American South. Montpellier was the home and plantation of James Madison, the fourth U.S. president. Madison is often referred to as the "father" of the U.S. Constitution; he not only drafted the U.S. Constitution but was also an author of the U.S. Bill of Rights — and he was a slave owner. The interview was with a white, middle-aged woman who purposely sought to distress herself, to make herself uncomfortable. Near the house was the plantation's railway station which was used to ship people and goods to and from the house. On the station were two waiting rooms — one marked "colored" and the other "whites".

The woman, herself from the American South, informed me she had explicitly walked through the "colored" door so she could both remember and prosthetically experience what her black childhood school friend had experienced as a child growing up in the South. She outlined, through her tears, how her experience walking through that door was intense and affective, and she used this to reflect on the racism in her family that had prevented her from bringing her friend home after school and what limitations being white, from a racist family, placed on her friendship. That affective moment, a moment she actively sought, also reaffirmed her resolve to continue to question her own racism.

> I'm a southerner (sighs). We rebelled against our own nation to preserve state's rights. Slavery was a big part of my family's heritage and to see it abolished is a great joy. But to learn how it was conducted, you see very little of that in any other tour you get. This shows you the degrees of slavery and the Jim Crow Museum down there at the train station (sighs) I go through the coloured door. I lived that. My dearest friend in high school was a black girl and my mother wouldn't let her come to my house (sobs).
> LS: Sorry. I'm so sorry.
> JMM85: Well, but she does now.
> LS: She does now?
> JMM85: [Name given] has been my friend since we were fifteen years old. I've lived slavery and I'll die to make sure nobody else has to live it. This isn't [unclear, crying], you'd die to get rid of these feelings to people. I've got my family, some of them they still won't ... Civil War isn't ... I'm only third generation on my mother's side from the war and believe me we were raised to know that we were different and to fight that, coming here helps you do that.
> (JMM85: female, 55–64, retired teacher, Caucasian American)

This example, and the previous examples where recognition is being offered to other people, involves a negotiation of a sense of citizenship. Here the woman is identifying and reinforcing her moral responsibility as a citizen to guard against the racism of her familial and regional upbringing.

The third example of recognition is misrecognition. A visit often indeed appears to be an embodiment of emotional commitment or investment in certain values and understandings of self and/or others. When cognitive dissonance is experienced, that is when visitors meet with a narrative that they do not expect or do not agree with, a range of emotional and discursive strategies have been identified that visitors use to close down negative emotions such as shame and reinforce more positive emotions. Most commonly, these strategies come into play when a visitor is asked to reassess an understanding of self as a member of a hegemonic group that has benefited from historical injustice (see Smith 2010). In some cases cognitive dissonance and a refusal to surrender both consensus narratives and understandings of self can result in either the continuation of, or the creation of, new forms of misrecognition. In this next example the speaker is at an exhibition mounted by the National Museum of African American History called "Slavery at Jefferson's Monticello: Paradox of Liberty". It was about Thomas Jefferson, another American Founding Father, and the so-called paradox that was created by the fact he wrote the Declaration of Independence yet owned slaves, the exhibition detailing new evidence that he had fathered several of his own slaves:

> Yes, he gave the slaves a chance and that is what this country is about, giving people a chance and creating equality.
> (J68: female, 35–44, hospice nurse, American)

The fourth and final way in which museums are used by visitors in the politics of recognition centres on groups and individuals using the museum or heritage site as a form of social barometer. Some visitors utilized their visit to assess how an exhibition is either recognizing or misrecognizing themselves or their community. This is a particularly interesting use of museums, and illustrates the degree to which communities or ethnic groups are concerned by how they are portrayed in such an authoritative cultural institution. Furthermore, it illustrates the self-conscious ways in which visitors perceive heritage sites and museums as playing an active role in the politics of recognition. This example comes from African Americans commenting on the exhibition on Jefferson and slavery:

I think it just spreads — I think for some people that don't know anything about slavery it would probably be good. But for people that are educated and have learned something about slavery they would know that this is more of a — this is like a setback to me in relation to me, I think this is a setback.

LS: Right. Setback in what way?

J20: Because it's just another thing saying "oh, you were slaves. So you're still only expected to do certain things." So instead of telling people about how they were slaves, how about telling them about how they can be doctors, can be lawyers or, you know, people like from the 1940s that went through a lot to be a doctor or be a lawyer. Because there were African American doctors and lawyers. So I think that's what I came to see. I didn't come to see about slavery.

(J20: male, 35–44, army officer, Native and African American)

This seeking of recognition can also, it is important to point out, be done not only by those seeking social justice, but also by dominant groups who feel that their status is being threatened. Here are examples from a site in Australia that celebrates rural Australian history. Historically, rural Australia is often seen as representing the rest of Australia, and this has meant that, in hard economic times, governments have given rural communities special treatment and special access to resources. However, rural Australians represent less than twelve per cent of the contemporary Australian population, and their special treatment is not always seen as democratic:

If you're off the land, yes [this place has meaning]. I think if you're from the city, I think um ... minor [meaning], but I think the city people still need to know [that] the heritage of Australia or the bush feeds our nation as well you know and I think, yes, they need to be told and we need to be seen ... um, we need to promote ourselves really, yeah.

(LR22: Male, 45–54, farmer, Australian)

Ah definitely. I think um ... I think modern day Australia needs to, probably come out of the cities if you like, and come and make a pilgrimage here and really appreciate what made modern Australia.

(LR116: male, 55–64, Pastor, New Zealand–Australian)

Conclusion

The concept of the politics of recognition allows us to explicitly understand heritage sites and the processes of heritage-making as resources of power.

What conceptualizing heritage like this does is that it identifies why heritage conflicts matter so much, why they generate so much emotional energy, and the consequences they have, not only for a person's or a collective's own self-esteem but also the consequences they have for the respect and esteem that is granted or withheld from others. Rendering heritage as simply the subject of technical management and urban planning that focuses on concerns about material authenticity, aesthetics or inherent values, misunderstands the nature of heritage and ignores the wider social and political contexts within which it is given meaning and made to "do" work in legitimizing and recognizing social inclusion and exclusion. The focus on heritage as simply a technical issue of planning or conservation removes it from its political context, and this is not an innocent act, as what this does is to deny the social and political debates with which that heritage intersects.

To return to the story I started with about the tea ceremony held in Canberra — many heritage scholars would worry about the issue raised by the Japanese scholar and the tea expert, that the tea may not have been what they call "authentic". We may say that the whole moment of heritage and cultural connection felt by the Taiwanese student was delegitimized because it was an invented tradition; the ceremony was an inauthentic made-up pastiche, a ceremony held in Canberra away from its geographical and cultural origins, origins in any case disputed by some of those involved. However, this misunderstands the act of very real self-recognition felt by the student; he affirmed his identity in a foreign place as Taiwanese. What is described is a personal and subtle single moment, but no less a powerful moment of self-recognition. The accumulative effects of such moments have not only personal but wider political consequences.

References

Ahmed, S. *The Cultural Politics of Emotion*. London: Routledge, 2004.

Anderson, B. *Imagined Communities*, 2nd ed. London: Verso, 1991.

Appiah, K.A. *Cosmopolitanism: Ethics in a World of Strangers*. London: Penguin Books, 2006.

Betts, P., and C. Ross. "Modern Historical Preservation — Towards a Global Perspective". *Past and Present* 226, supplement 10 (2015): 7–26. doi: 10.1093/pastj/gtu023.

Butler, J., and A. Athanasiou. *Dispossession: The Performative in the Political*. Cambridge: Polity, 2003.

Byrne, D. "Western Hegemony in Archaeological Heritage Management". *History and Anthropology* 5 (1991): 269–76.

―――. "A Critique of Unfeeling Heritage". In *Intangible Heritage*, edited by L. Smith and N. Akagawa. London: Routledge, 2009.

Campbell, G., and L. Smith. "Manifesto for the Association of Critical Heritage Studies". 2011 <http://archanth.anu.edu.au/heritage-museum-studies/association-critical-heritage-studies>.

Carman, J. *Archaeology and Heritage: An Introduction*. London: Continuum, 2002.

Choay, F. *The Invention of the Historic Monument*. Cambridge: Cambridge University Press, 2001.

Connerton, P. *How Societies Remember*. Cambridge: Cambridge University Press, 1991.

Cresswell, T. "Nonrepresentational Theory and Me: Notes of an Interested Sceptic". *Environment and Planning D: Society and Space* 30 (2012): 96–102.

Dicks, B. *Heritage, Place and Community*. Cardiff: University of Wales Press, 2000.

Felder, M., M. Duineveld, and K. Van Assche. "Absence/Presence and the Ontological Politics of Heritage: The Case of Barrack 57". *International Journal of Heritage Studies* 21, no. 5 (2015): 460–75.

Fischer, M.M.J. "The Lightness of Existence and the Origami of 'French' Anthropology: Latour, Descola, Viveiros de Castro, Meillassoux and Their So-called Ontological Turn". *Journal of Ethnographic Theory* 4, no. 1 (2014): 331–55.

Fortun, K. "From Latour to Late Industrialism". *Journal of Ethnographic Theory* 4, no. 1 (2014): 309–29.

Fraser, N. "From Redistribution to Recognition? Dilemmas of Justice in a 'Post-socialist' Age". *New Left Review* 212 (1995): 68–93

―――. "Rethinking Recognition". *New Left Review* 3 (May/June 2000): 107–20.

―――. "Social Justice in the Age of Identity Politics: Redistribution, Recognition, and Participation". In *Redistribution or Recognition? A Political-Philosophical Exchange*, edited by N. Fraser and A. Honneth. London: Verso, 2003.

Gentry, K. "'The Pathos of Conservation': Raphael Samuel and the Politics of Heritage". *International Journal of Heritage Studies* 21, no. 6 (2015). doi: 10.1080/13527258.2014.953192.

Graham, B., G. Ashworth, and J. Tunbridge. *A Geography of Heritage: Power, Culture and Economy*. London: Arnold, 2000.

Harrison, R. *Heritage: Critical Approaches*. London: Routledge, 2013.

Harvey, D.C. "Heritage Pasts and Heritage Presents: Temporality, Meaning and the Scope of Heritage Studies". *International Journal of Heritage Studies* 7, no. 4 (2001): 319–38.

―――. "Heritage and Scale: Settings, Boundaries and Relations". *International Journal of Heritage Studies* 21, no. 6 (2015). doi: 10.1080/13527258.2014.955812.

Herzfeld, M. *A Place in History: Social and Monumental Time in a Cretan Town*. Princeton, NJ: Princeton University Press, 1991.

―――. *Cultural Intimacy: Social Poetics in the Nation-State*. Routledge: New York, 2005.

————. "Engagement, Gentrification, and the Neoliberal Hijacking of History". *Current Anthroplogy* 51, supplement 2 (2010): S259–67.

Hewison, R. *In Anger: Culture and the Cold War 1995–60*. London: Weidenfeld and Nicolson, 1981.

————. *The Heritage Industry: Britain in a Climate of Decline*. London: Methuen, 1987.

Honneth, A. *The Struggle for Recognition: The Moral Grammar of Social Conflicts*. Cambridge: Polity, [1995] 2005.

Illouz, E. *Cold Intimacies: The Making of Emotional Capitalism*. Cambridge: Polity, 2007.

Johnson, C. "Narratives of Identity: Denying Empathy in Conservative Discourses on Race, Class, and Sexuality". *Theory and Society* 34 (2005): 37–61

Kalela, J. *Making History: The Historian and Uses of the Past*. Basingstoke: Palgrave Macmillan, 2012.

Keightley, E., and M. Pickering. *The Mnemonic Imagination: Remembering as Creative Practice*. Basingstoke: Palgrave Macmillan, 2012.

Kirshenblatt-Gimblett, B. *Destination Culture: Tourism, Museums and Heritage*. Berkeley: University of California Press, 1998.

Kymlicka, W., and W. Norman. "Citizenship in Culturally Diverse Societies: Issues, Contexts, Concepts". In *Citizenship in Diverse Societies*, edited by W. Kymlicka and W. Norman. Oxford University Press, 2000.

Labadi, S. "Representations of the Nation and Cultural Diversity in Discourses on World Heritage". *Journal of Social Archaeology* 7 (2007): 147–70.

Leys, R. "The Turn to Affect: A Critique". *Critical Inquiry* 37 no. 3 (2011): 434–72.

Lovell, T., ed. *(Mis)recognition, Social Inequality and Social Justice: Nancy Fraser and Pierre Bourdieu*. London: Routledge, 2007.

Lowenthal, D. *The Past is a Foreign Country*. Cambridge: Cambridge University Press, 1985.

————. *The Heritage Crusade and the Spoils of History*. Cambridge: Cambridge University Press, 1996.

————. "On Arraigning Ancestors: A Critique of Historical Contrition". *North Carolina Law Review* 87 (2009): 901.

McNay, L. *Against Recognition*. Cambridge: Polity, 2008.

Macdonald, S. *Difficult Heritage: Negotiating the Nazi Past in Nuremberg and Beyond*. London: Routledge, 2009.

————. *Memorylands: Heritage and Identity in Europe Today*. London: Routledge, 2013.

Mayer, J.D., P. Salovey, and D.R. Caruso. "Emotional Intelligence: New Ability or Eclectic Traits?" *American Psychologist* 63, no. 6 (2008): 503–17.

Meskell, L. "The Intersections of Identity and Politics in Archaeology". *Annual Review of Anthropology* 31 (2002): 279–301.

Meskell, L., C. Liuzza, E. Bertacchini, and D. Saccone. "Multilateralism and UNESCO World Heritage: Decision-Making, States Parties and Political Processes". *International Journal of Heritage Studies* 21, no. 5 (2015): 423–40.

Murtagh, W.J. *Keeping Time: The History and Theory of Preservation in America*. New York: Wiley, 1997.

Pekarik, A.J., and J.B. Schreiber. "The Power of Expectation". *Curator: The Museums Journal* 55, no. 4 (2012): 487–96.

Poria, Y., R. Butler, and D. Airey. "The Core of Heritage Tourism". *Annals of Tourism Research* 30, no. 1 (2003): 238–54.

Samuel, R. *Theatres of Memory*, vol. 1, *Past and Present in Contemporary Culture*. London: Verso, 1994.

Sayer, A. "Class, Moral Worth and Recognition". In *(Mis)recognition, Social Inequality and Social Justice: Nancy Fraser and Pierre Bourdieu*, edited by T. Lovell. London: Routledge, 2007.

Sayes, E. "Actor-Network Theory and Methodology: Just What Does it Mean to Say That Nonhumans Have Agency?" *Social Studies of Science* 44, no. 1 (2014).

Smith, L. *Uses of Heritage*. London: Routledge, 2006.

———. *All Heritage is Intangible: Critical Heritage Studies and Museums*, Reinwardt Memorial Lecture. Amsterdam: Reinwardt Academy, 2011.

———. "Editorial: A *Critical* Heritage Studies?" *International Journal of Heritage Studies* 18, no. 6 (2012a): 533–40.

———. "The Cultural 'Work' of Tourism". In *The Cultural Moment of Tourism*, edited by L. Smith, E. Waterton, and S. Watson. London: Routledge, 2012b.

———. "Theorising Museum and Heritage Visiting". In *The International Handbooks of Museum Studies*, vol. 1, *Museum Theory*, edited by A. Witcomb and K. Message. Chichester: Wiley-Blackwell, 2015.

Swenson, A. *The Rise of Heritage: Preserving the Past in France, Germany and England, 1789–1914*. Cambridge: Cambridge University Press, 2014.

Taylor, C. "The Politics of Recognition". In *Multiculturalism: Examining the Politics of Recognition*, edited by A. Gutmann. Princeton, NJ: University of Princeton Press, 1994.

Tolia-Kelly, D. "Affect — An Ethnocentric Encounter? Exploring the 'Universalist' Imperative or Emotional/Affectual Geographies". *Area* 38 (2006): 213–17.

Urry, J. "How Societies Remember the Past". In *Theorising Museums*, edited by S. Macdonald and G. Fyfe. Oxford: Blackwell, 1996.

Walsh, K. *The Representation of the Past: Museums and Heritage in the Post-modern World*. London: Routledge, 1992.

Waterton, E., and S. Watson. "Framing Theory: Towards a Critical Imagination in Heritage Studies". *International Journal of Heritage Studies* 19, no. 6 (2013): 546–61.

Wertsch, J.V. *Voices of Collective Remembering*. Cambridge: Cambridge University Press, 2002.

Wertsch, J., and D.M. Billingsley. "The Role of Narrative in Commemoration: Remembering as Mediated Action". In *Heritage, Memory and Identity*, edited by H. Anheier and Y.R. Isar. Los Angeles: Sage, 2011.

Westin, J. "Towards a Vocabulary of Limitations: The Translation of a Painted Goddess into a Symbol of Classical Education". *International Journal of Heritage Studies* 18, no. 1 (2012): 18–32.

Wetherell, M. *Affect and Emotion: A New Social Science Understanding*. London: Sage, 2012.

Winter, T. "Clarifying the Critical in Critical Heritage Studies". *International Journal of Heritage Studies* 19, no. 6 (2013): 532–45.

Witcomb, A., and K. Buckley. "Engaging with the Future of 'Critical Heritage Studies': Looking Back in Order to Look Forward". *International Journal of Heritage Studies* 19, no. 6 (2013): 562–78.

Wright, P. *On Living in an Old Country*. London: Verso, 1985.

Young, I.M. *Inclusion and Democracy*. Oxford: Oxford University Press, 2000.

———. *Justice and the Politics of Difference*. Princeton, NJ: Princeton University Press [1990] 2011.

Zhang, R. "World Heritage Listing and Tourism in China: Case Study in West Lake Cultural Landscape of Hangzhou", unpublished conference paper, Heritage & Healthy Societies: Exploring the Links among Heritage, Environment, and Resilience, University of Massachusetts Amherst, 14–16 May 2014.

3

Heritage-Making and Post-coloniality in Yangon, Myanmar

Jayde Lin Roberts

In a nation where the post-independence, military-led governments saw their people as potential enemies who threatened the territorial integrity of Myanmar,[1] heritage-making has been deployed as an exclusive technique of the state to manufacture a unitary national identity. That identity has been Burman (the dominant ethnic group), Buddhist, and, until recently, staunchly anti-colonial, with the Shwedagon Pagoda standing as its ultimate monument. Since 2012, educated elite in Yangon have begun to rewrite the narrative of colonial oppression to incorporate the modernity implanted through British rule as represented by the grand facades of institutions such as Grindlays Bank and the Secretariat. This foregrounding of aesthetic modernity has been spearheaded by Thant Myint-U (grandson of U Thant, the third UN secretary-general), who has returned to Myanmar from a cosmopolitan life in the West. With the assistance of foreign-educated Myanmar architects, Thant has founded the Yangon Heritage Trust (YHT) to safeguard the physical and aesthetic integrity of colonial-era buildings. In the words of Thant, "If we can make Yangon the most attractive, beautiful and liveable city in Southeast Asia, this is an asset worth billions of dollars" (Linthicum 2014).

This chapter investigates the influence of Myanmar's elite, a small segment of the city's civil society, in redefining Yangon's heritage during a time of unprecedented change. National reforms initiated in 2011 followed by the lifting of international sanctions have ushered in fast-paced real estate development that threatens to alter the face of Yangon before the local population has a chance to reflect on what they value. In the haste to save turn-of-the-century architecture from the irreparable damage of wrecking balls, critical questions about the history of Yangon and how residents live in the city have been left barely examined. The YHT's efforts to save colonial-era buildings, though important for maintaining the traces of history in the built environment, run the risk of erasing colonial abuses and masking entrenched urban inequalities. These inequalities were largely introduced by British rule, even if paradoxes, exclusions and segmentations are always a part of urban organization and city form (AlSayyad and Roy 2006). By defining Yangon as an asset with international aesthetic value, the YHT is mediating in the trade of cultural commodities in world capitalism. Kwame Anthony Appiah (1991) labels this practice a condition of "postcoloniality" and challenges the "comprador intelligentsia", the relatively small group of Western-trained thinkers, to reflect on their complicity in enabling capitalist exploitation. Specific to Yangon, initiatives from civil society do not necessarily represent the concerns of everyday people, particularly as organized by the elite. Unlike the 2011 protests against the Myitsone Dam, when Burmese people regardless of ethnicity or class rallied to save the Irrawaddy River,[2] the work of the YHT has yet to gain broad-based support.

As the YHT diligently promotes colonial architecture as Yangon's heritage, their preservation efforts serve as a case study of the contradictions and contestations inherent in the forms and functions of cities. It also reminds us of the pitfalls in designating the design and materiality of architecture as the starting point for heritage conservation, because the tangible, aesthetic qualities of buildings can easily override the less traceable practices of everyday life.

The YHT's elite position has enabled them to successfully appeal to the highest level of Myanmar's government, under former president U Thein Sein and the current government led by the National League for Democracy (NLD), and to court international funding agencies, thereby distancing them from the *yoyotha* (everyday people). However, their insider position has also afforded them an opportunity to counter the discourse of militant anti-colonialism that has been a core ideology among Burma's ruling generals. This opportunity could allow the YHT to refashion the once imposing and exclusive buildings, such as the headquarters of the Irrawaddy Flotilla Company, into a set of inclusive national symbols, representations that allow for rather than erase ethnic and religious differences. They could also serve as a platform to define architecture and heritage in Myanmar as a set of intersecting material and cultural practices that explicitly recognizes how buildings learn and how people give life to buildings (Brand 1994).

This chapter examines the heritage of Yangon as an evolving process through three historical phases: (i) Colonial Rangoon (1852 to 1947), when the British vision of a modern city set the course for its future; (ii) Independent and Military Burma (1948 to 2010), when the parliamentary and military governments repurposed colonial buildings as utilitarian spaces for ruling the nation; and (iii) Myanmar in reform (2011 to the present), when changes in political and economic policies have enabled explicit and international campaigns to preserve Yangon's built heritage. This periodization is only a preliminary framework to outline changing attitudes towards British colonial buildings and focuses on the opinions of the elite. Although Yangon is the home of a growing and increasingly more-effective civil society, there has yet to be a popularly led movement in the conservation of colonial Yangon.[3]

Scholarship on Yangon is limited. Very few scholars have examined the city in depth, leaving only minor studies and two major works as references: Bertie Reginald Pearn's *History of Rangoon* published in 1939, and Sarah Maxim's unpublished dissertation, *Resemblance in External Appearance: The Colonial Project in Kuala Lumpur and Rangoon*, submitted in 1992. Burmese scholars Than Than Nwe (1998) and U Thein Maung (1966) have also written about the city, but indigenous intellectuals have not challenged the colonial conception of Rangoon. That is, Rangoon as a praiseworthy city was created by the British. Educated Yangon residents often described their city as a once cosmopolitan gateway through which modernity first entered Burma.[4]

Colonial Rangoon: Fashioning a Modern City

Although images of Rangoon have proliferated in international popular media since 2011, portrayals of the city remain romanticized and touristic. This is because Rangoon appears to be entering the world stage anew, recalled into the global memory after decades of fading into the past.

Based on the limited scholarship, Rangoon was a loosely organized town that had grown organically around the swamps and hills in the area and suffered periodic fires. Historically, this town was ruled by the Mon, an ethnic group in Lower Burma, and was known as Lgung or Dagung, which became "Dagon" in Burmese. In 1755, Alaungphaya, a Burmese king, conquered the town and renamed it Rangoon, meaning "the end of strife" in the Burmese language, to mark the cessation of warfare between the Burmans and the Mon. Although Rangoon served as a port for the Konbaung dynasty (the last Burmese kingdom, 1742–1885), it never rose to prominence as a regional port because it was prone to flooding, and because the trade of silk and spices bypassed Burma, going directly from Java and Malacca to Calcutta (Pearn 1939, pp. 41–49). In addition, the town was never significantly built up because ports and trade towns in Southeast Asia were generally conceived of as temporary places that expanded and contracted according to the vagaries of trade (McGee 1967, pp. 31–36).

Rangoon and Lower Burma as a whole were seized by British forces during the Second Anglo-Burmese War in 1852. Soon after, Colonel Arthur Purves Phayre declared all land in and around Rangoon government property, citing the destruction of the town before the 1852 war as just cause for assuming state ownership. Through British eyes, the native topography appeared wild and devoid of value. Company men such as F.O. Oertel and painters such as Colesworthy Grant described Rangoon as a place of flimsy huts and dishevelled markets, sadly unimpressive with nothing to recommend it but the Shwedagon Pagoda (Grant 1995). Much like the Black Town of Calcutta, the native landscape did not deserve careful attention because there was nothing important in the native town (Chattopadhyay 2005). Only *after* colonial intervention and through their pure analytic vision would places such as Rangoon and Calcutta become worthy of notice.

On this conveniently "blank slate", Colonel Phayre and Lieutenant Alexander Fraser designed a rational Cartesian city composed of straight wide streets and rectilinear lots. Phayre and Fraser, like other elite in the empire, saw the need to discourage the spread of bodily disease (illness) and societal disease (crime) through the proper planning of their conquered territories. Straight and wide streets were seen as the primary instrument to flush out Rangoon's miasma-filled swampland and inculcate proper English civility in its residents. A hierarchical grid of streets — major streets at a hundred feet wide, intermediary streets at fifty feet, and minor streets at thirty feet — were systematically mapped out in central Rangoon. The planned city was divided into twenty-five blocks that were then subdivided into 172 lots per block, resulting in 4,300 lots that became available for sale, taxation and regulation.

Under colonial rule, ethnic Burmans were excluded from the city through economic and political measures. The 4,300 lots devised by Phayre were divided into five different classes, with the lots closest to the river, along Strand Road, commanding the highest prices. The riverfront, the most valuable property, was reserved for official buildings that would present a majestic facade to Europeans arriving by sea. The next three classes of property were valued according to their distance from the river and proximity to existing wharves. In addition, specific requirements were dictated for different classes. All buildings in first class lots near Strand Road and in the business district had to be made of brick with pukka or tiled roofs.[5] Regardless of class, all owners of all lots had to build "a good and substantial bona fide dwelling house or warehouse" within one year of purchase or the property would be confiscated.[6] This latter regulation was initially implemented to prevent land speculation, but also served to mandate a particular kind of physical and social environment. Only the wealthy could afford to both buy a lot and build on it according to regulation. Brick was not a common material in Rangoon and required significant skill and investment to produce. Under these regulations, Burmans were excluded from the planned city because the pricing of the lots combined with the building requirements and taxation rendered the properties prohibitively expensive. In theory the parcels in the northernmost area near Montgomerie (now Bogyoke Aung San) Road were priced for commoners, but no Burman could afford to buy lots within the planned city. Instead, they squatted on unoccupied land (Pearn 1939, pp. 190–94).

The above regulations, coupled with the ease of entry for Indian and to some extent Chinese migrants, made Rangoon a foreign city. Burma was ruled as an outpost of British India and Indians could enter and work in Burma freely without official permission. By the 1940s, Indian firms controlled about fifty per cent of Burma's import trade and operated large shops and industries throughout the country (Chakravarti 1971, pp. 78–79). Within Rangoon they owned the largest share of property, surpassing the British, even though the British dominated in the most lucrative businesses such as oil and banking (Taylor 1987, p. 122). Chinese merchants found it difficult to compete with Indian moguls, but some managed to buy lots in the Chinese Quarter, known as *Tayout Tan* in Burmese.[7] Indeed, other than the imposing institutional buildings erected by the British, Indian merchants have left a more enduring mark on Rangoon's built environment than any other population.[8]

By the early part of the twentieth century, Rangoon was usually described by British officials as "the only large Indian city which has grown up on a scientific plan" and was rated as "a study of modern urban development" (Maxim 1992, p. 322). However, through the eyes of the colonized, Rangoon was a doubly colonized city that was artificially implanted. Passing through the city in 1916, Indian Nobel laureate Rabindranath Tagore wrote,

> This city has not grown like a tree from the soil of the country …[it] floats like foam on the tides of time.… I have seen Rangoon, but it is mere visual acquaintance, there is no recognition of Burma in this seeing … the city is an abstraction. (Tagore 1940)

He lamented the fact that colonial commerce had dominated and determined the character of the city and noted that Indians, as the overwhelming majority, had essentially colonized the Burmese once more, almost in lockstep with the British Raj. The Indian population not only dominated numerically, they dominated economically and spatially. "The Indian middle class had the strongest hold on foreign [and domestic] trade of any group in Burma" (Taylor 1987, p. 135). By 1911, over half of the urban population was Indian (Chakravarti 1971, p. 19).

As in other British territories such as Calcutta and Singapore, the design of Rangoon was intended to be comprehensive and permanent. On the base of the Cartesian street grid and orderly lots, Phayre and his successors erected imposing institutional buildings in the architectural style of their day to declare British superiority and to reform the native population and landscape. Initially, neo-classical architecture, as seen in the Court House completed in 1868, was deployed to proclaim the British right to rule. The British Empire was projected as the heir to the Roman Empire, but nobler and with a more defined sense of moral purpose (Chattopadhyay 2005). This relationship was proudly claimed in the use of neo-classical architecture, which was supposed to represent British power in the empire. "The distinctive European architectural vocabulary enabled one to recognize the space occupied by the colonizers, setting out in easily observable material terms distinctions between the rulers and the ruled" (Chattopadhyay 2005, p. 29). As an outpost of British India, governed through Calcutta and then New Delhi, architecture in Rangoon was noticeably influenced by stylistic developments that were filtered through

India. Although a thorough analysis of Rangoon's colonial-era buildings is only in its formative stage, it is already evident that the grand architecture in the city followed India's trajectory from blunt British imposition to more local hybridization. From the Queen Anne–style High Court building designed by James Ransome, consulting architect to the Government of India, to the Rowe and Company Department Store designed by Charles F. Stevens based in Bombay, the built environment was not meant to make manifest the genius loci of Rangoon, but to propagate the British vision of modernity.

A more localized architecture did not appear until construction began on Rangoon's city hall in 1925. Although the need for a larger city hall was recognized in 1903 and a competition was held in 1913 — with the design by L.A. McClumpha chosen as the winner — progress stalled until 1925. The First World War broke out in 1914, which led to economic and bureaucratic constraints that delayed construction. By 1925 the rising tide of nationalism had become more organized and nationalists demanded that the city hall incorporate Burmese architectural features (Rooney 2012). U Ba Pe, a Burmese politician, spoke at the Burma Legislative Council calling for a new design for the city hall that would feature the ornamentations of the ancient capital Pagan. European members of the council disagreed, citing the inappropriateness of religious-inspired architecture for a civic building. U Ba Pe responded, "No civic architecture in the world can be found that is not founded on either ecclesiastical, monumental or other religious architecture" (Rooney 2012, p. 41). He won the debate and a Burmese architect Sithu U Tin was selected for the redesign. U Tin had worked in the Public Works Department and been apprenticed to an engineering firm in Bombay. As a product of the colonial architectural curriculum, his redesign only added a veneer of Burmese-ness through the application of traditional iconography such as peacocks and *nagas* (serpents), and the three-tiered *pyatthat* roofing.[9] Construction began in 1925 and the city hall that was completed in 1940 remains a fundamentally neoclassical building with Burmese appliqué.

Two years after the city hall was completed, the Japanese invaded Burma and occupied the country until 1945. Bombing devastated the country and destroyed strategic jetties and stockades in Rangoon. Surprisingly, monumental colonial buildings were mostly left intact. Indian, Chinese and European residents, who constituted the majority of the urban population, hurriedly fled. Based on Chinese sources, Rangoon was a ghost town during the Japanese Occupation (Huang 1990). Hundreds of thousands of Indians evacuated on foot and thousands died on their long march to Assam. Of those who survived, many if not most could not return to Burma, because the restored British Government altered regulations for Indian migration into Burma. Whereas before 1942 Indians could move freely between India and Burma as residents travelling between one district and another, after 1945 they had to acquire official approval (Taylor 1987, p. 274). The Chinese population seems to have returned en masse and even grew in number, because internecine warfare in China made their fatherland inhospitable (Lin 2004). However, the exodus of the foreign residents removed much of the capital, commercial know-how and professional skills needed to rebuild a war-torn Burma, leaving the urban landscape of downtown Rangoon almost unaltered from the turn of the twentieth century onward.

However, there must be subtler stories in the built environment that have yet to be uncovered. Research on the city is just beginning and little is documented about Rangoon between 1945 and 1990.[10] This yawning gap of knowledge explains the current elite practice of referring back to colonial Rangoon in order to define contemporary Yangon. After all, the grand institutional buildings of the British Empire remain the most conspicuous monuments in the city. The lack of alternative discourses due to an immature field of research limits our understanding, but it should not preclude other representations of Yangon. The legacy of modernity imposed by the British does not have to be the heritage of the city. The British Government of Burma departed over seven decades ago, and their exclusive vision of Rangoon should not be revived unexamined, even as a tool for international recognition or foreign direct investment. Although our understanding of Rangoon between the Second World War and 1990 is severely limited, the available fragments of information need to be placed at the forefront to question the teleological project of modernity and make room for local action that might also be defined as progress. As a step towards destabilizing the discourse of modern Yangon, the developments of the city as the capital of independent Burma are sketched out below.

Rangoon as the Capital of Independent Burma

Although the British Government of Burma returned in 1945 to begin reconstruction, they made little progress as Burmese nationalists pressed for self-rule. On 4 January 1948 the Union of Burma declared its independence under the leadership of Prime Minister U Nu. As the war-torn economy had yet to recover and the terms of the new nation-state were hastily cobbled together, the first government of independent Burma faced armed rebellion by several ethnic and ideological groups. For a period the government of U Nu was known as "the Rangoon government", as that was the only part of the country it effectively controlled. Under these dire circumstances, Rangoon, as left by the British, became the capital of the new nation-state. Unlike Jakarta and Chandigarh, where high modernist architecture was used to declare the founding of a new nation, Burma had to content itself with its colonial urban fabric.

In this discussion of heritage-making, the political and military history of Burma cannot be addressed in detail, even though conflicts between the dominant Burman population and ethnic minority groups have largely shaped the history of post-colonial Burma.[11] What is directly relevant for our understanding of Yangon is that the primary techniques for governing deployed by the British — "scientific classification" of different "races", both indigenous and foreign, coupled with differing methods of control for different groups — directly affected the form and welfare of the city.

Rangoon was the centre of Ministerial Burma, also known as Burma Proper, and was ruled directly by the British Government of India (British Government of Burma after separation from India in 1937). The Frontier Areas, which included the Shan State, Chin Hills and Kachin Tracts, were designated as a separate zone and ruled indirectly through local chiefs.[12] Under this divided structure, Burmans were separated from other ethnicities, and Rangoon saw very few ethnic minorities except for Shan royalty and the Chin, Kachin and Karen soldiers recruited to fight for the British. Under colonial rule, most Burmese, regardless of ethnicity, were excluded from the city.

This changed dramatically after the Second World War as internal migrants sought refuge from the poverty throughout Burma and armed conflict in the Frontier Areas. Neither the restored British nor the independent parliamentary governments were able to provide housing for these refugees. They squatted along the streets and railways and clustered at the edges of the gridded downtown core, stretching the carrying capacity of Rangoon's infrastructure (Than Than Nwe 1998). Slums and other sanitation problems remained until General Ne Win assumed control from U Nu and established the Caretaker Government in 1958.

Between 1958 and 1960, the Caretaker Government initiated anti-corruption and clean-up campaigns that resettled a third of Rangoon's population — about 170,000 squatters — in three satellite towns (Than Than Nwe 1998). The government also established a people-powered sanitation system in which thousands of residents and soldiers marched through the streets to remove garbage and stray animals (Charney 2009, pp. 95–99). The temporary military-led government managed to scrub Rangoon clean, but their efforts were insufficient in accommodating the increasing urbanization and infrastructural needs of a capital city run by a fledgling nation-state that was contending with insurgencies and economic challenges on multiple fronts.

In 1960 U Nu was returned to power by popular election but lost his post again in 1962. The military was concerned that U Nu's push for Buddhism to become the state religion and his ongoing discussions with Shan State leaders who advocated federalism would threaten the territorial unity of Burma. Therefore, General Ne Win and his allies staged a coup d'état, establishing the Revolutionary Council that sought to reduce foreign influence and create a new socialist economy based on *The Burmese Way to Socialism*. Unfortunately, the Revolutionary Council — that later transformed into the Burmese Socialist Programme Party (BSPP) — was ill-equipped to implement its vision of a self-sufficient Burma. Between 1962 and 1988 Burma was cut off from the world and experienced precipitous declines in the national economy, standard of living and education.

Throughout this period, Rangoon as designed by the British remained almost unaltered. Imposing institutional buildings were repurposed as headquarters for various government departments: the Irrawaddy Flotilla Company became the Inland Waterways Department, Grindlays Bank became the Burma Agricultural Development Bank, and others such as the Port Authority and Telegraph Office continued to function as government offices. For Burmese people the government has been at best a source of inconvenience and at worst a menacing force. They often say, "There are five natural disasters: floods, fires, kings, thieves, and ungrateful heirs."[13] This concise statement clearly communicates the degree of distrust in politics pervasive in Burmese culture, not only under the various troubled and unjust governments in modern Burma, but also during the reigns of Burman kings. Therefore, government buildings were places to be avoided, not centres for civic participation. Although further research is necessary and perceptions of everyday residents are still particularly hard to ascertain, Yangon's residents do not appear to feel any connection between themselves and the grand institutional buildings still standing on streets such as Pansodan.[14]

Beyond the colonial downtown core, the Revolutionary Council and BSPP constructed government housing blocks and additional satellite towns. New towns such as Thuwanna were planned in the peri-urban area to encourage Rangoon residents to resettle in the periphery. As part of the socialist campaign, they were promised the right of home ownership (not land ownership) if they built their houses with their own hands. Some Burmese scholars have begun to analyse the growth of the city beyond the colonial plan, but to date that analysis has been quantitative. The character and heritage of Yangon do not include these utilitarian settlements. However, those who built their own houses talk about their homes with feeling and attachment, emotions that are not present when discussing the grand colonial buildings in the downtown core.[15] Only the elite are sentimental about the institutional colonial buildings.

By 1987 the economy had plummeted to such lows that the United Nations placed Burma in the category of least developed country. Years of inflation, severe shortages in basic goods, and political oppression pushed Burmese people to rise up in mass protest. In August 1988 the people's uprising forced the socialist government out of power, but soon a military junta took over, continuing the rule of the generals. Initially there was hope for transition towards a democratic government, as the junta, named the State Law and Order Restoration Council (SLORC), promised and delivered popular elections. However, after the NLD led by Aung San Suu Kyi won the election in June 1990, the SLORC refused to hand over power. The struggle for a democratic Myanmar is well known. International media periodically featured Aung San Suu Kyi's quiet determination and discussed the influence of Buddhism on Myanmar's national politics. The opposition and the generals in control both called upon Buddhism to assert their right to rule.

In Myanmar the connection between the institution of Buddhism and the right to rule is commonly recognized and seldom contested. The narrative of pre-colonial Burma is that successful kingdoms were destined to flourish by the proclamation of the Buddha. The king who founded Yangon even declared himself to be a future Buddha by adopting his regnal name, Alaungpaya, a synonym for Meitreya. Pre-colonial kings and their royal families built, gilded and refurbished pagodas as acts of merit-making to maintain their right to rule, and the pagodas stand as reminders of their reigns. In post-colonial Burma, heads of state have continued this tradition by re-gilding the Shwedagon Pagoda and building new pagodas. U Nu, the first prime minister of independent Burma, constructed the Kaba Aye Pagoda in 1952 in preparation for the Sixth Buddhist Council held from 1954 to 1956. General Ne Win erected the Maha Wizaya Pagoda in 1980 to commemorate the convening of the First Congregation of All Orders for the Purification, Perpetuation and Propagation of Sasana, which formed the State Sangha Maha Nayaka Committee, a governmental regulatory body of Buddhist monks. Senior General Than Shwe, who succeeded Ne Win in 1988, ordered the building of the Swal Daw (Great Tooth Relic) Pagoda in 1994 to house a replica of the Buddha's tooth relic. These acts of merit-making have been criticized by scholars and pundits as being disingenuous, but have nonetheless become a part of Yangon's built heritage (Than Than Nwe and Philp 2002). In fact, with the exception of the Maha Wizaya Pagoda, which is referred to as the "dictator's pagoda", Kaba Aye and Swal Daw Pagodas are recognized as religiously significant places (Kyaw Phyo Tha 2014).[16]

For the post-independence rulers of Burma, and indeed for the Burman ethnic majority, reinstituting the centrality of Buddhism has been a way to reject British colonialism. They have looked back to a pre-colonial past to assert Burma's national sovereignty and the legitimacy of Burman rule. The colonial government had intentionally dismantled the Buddhist political order so as to dominate Burma. The Buddhist monastic system was not only closely associated with the monarchy, it was also integrated into the lives of everyday people through the rural monasteries that served as the religious, cultural and educational centres of all villages. Under the guise of rational rule and modernization, the British instigated a new government and educational system that significantly altered Burmese society. This imposition was such a threat that Burmese people rallied together to save Buddhism through lay monastic societies (Turner 2014). Organizations such as the Young Men's Buddhist Association (YMBA), formed in 1906, became a pillar for promoting Burmese nationalism.[17] This entanglement between Buddhism and nationalism is highly problematic and has fuelled ethno-religious tensions and even violence.[18]

In the context of Yangon, heritage-making centred on Buddhism is an attempt to reproduce the pre-colonial past, a past that is somehow more indigenous, more purely Burmese. Its ultimate symbol is the

Shwedagon Pagoda, which embodies both religious sanctity and political authority.[19] Buddhism as the national norm is also evident in the form of the Dhamma halls (Dhammayon) that have been built in every ward, even in predominantly Muslim neighbourhoods.[20] The significance and effect of these more mundane Buddhist structures have yet to be determined, but their prevalence suggests a form of religious colonization. By publically and consistently calling for the protection of architecture designed and built by the British, Indians, Armenians and others, the YHT is broadening the definition of Burmese belonging to include foreigners and their legacies in the built environment.

Myanmar in Reform: Yangon as Cosmopolitan City

As represented by the YHT, Yangon is a cosmopolitan city because it was once an international port with residents, merchants and visitors from all around the world. They claim cosmopolitanism as a part of Yangon's heritage in the hopes of the city becoming cosmopolitan again. In *30 Heritage Buildings of Yangon: Inside the City That Captured Time*, a book sponsored by the YHT and the Myanmar Architecture Association, the authors and editors celebrate the international sophistication of old Rangoon with passages such as:

> With its Italianate flourishes, [the Sofaer's Building was] once one of the city's most prestigious business addresses. Built by a Baghdadi Jewish trader whose passion was architecture, it remains a tantalizing symbol of Yangon's cosmopolitan past.

> Here, Yangon residents once purchased Theadoro Vafiadis Egyptian cigarettes, Lighthouse Munich Beer, and candies imported from England. Though the building also housed legal and financial offices such as the China Mutual Life Insurance Company, it was best known for its purveyors of fine liqueurs and commodities...

> Other tenants of the building who illustrate the cosmopolitanism of Yangon at that time include Mr. J.D. Pappademitriou, a Greek leather merchant, and Mr. M. D'Cruz, a Filipino hairdresser who first came to the city with Harmston's Circus, a travelling menagerie of performing wild animals. (Roony 2013, pp. 81–82)

This upbeat prose suggests that foreign residents and trade in premium products are highly desirable and should be revived as the character of Yangon.

However, as already discussed, the worldly city of colonial Rangoon was decidedly unequal and exclusive. Foreigners lived, worked and passed through Rangoon because it was a foreign city — a city doubly colonized by the British and the Indians. The legacy of these market-dominating minorities is still apparent in the form of colonial-era architecture and the numerous properties owned by Indian and Chinese families.[21] The call for inclusiveness is admirable, but for the average resident, day labourer or street vendor, the appeal of the colonial architecture remains to be seen.

Nonetheless, much has happened since the Europeans and many Indians left Burma between the 1940s and 1960s. The Yangon of today might look like the Rangoon of the past, but life in the city has changed dramatically in the intervening decades. As research on Yangon is still in its formative stages, both current and recent demographic patterns are not clear. Yangon-*tha* (native Yangon residents) usually designate particular neighbourhoods as Indian, Chinese and Burmese, but note in the same breath that these different ethnic groups live throughout the city, and often side-by-side on the same street.[22] Yangon is no longer cosmopolitan, but it remains diverse.

This diversity is noteworthy but does not indicate equal rights to the city for all its residents. Much as in the colonial era, Indian and Chinese families own many of the properties in the gridded downtown. If heritage is that which is passed down from one generation to the next, Burmese residents have inherited little that would tangibly improve their lives. They rent homes and shops from Indian and Chinese families in a city that is in the midst of a real estate bubble, with little or no legal recourse should landlords decide to raise the rent or evict a tenant. In this context, heritage-making as an act of remembering and commemorating could hardly benefit the residents whose parents and grandparents migrated to Rangoon after the foreigners left. In many interviews, residents in old shop houses know that the owner of the property is Indian or Chinese but have never interacted with these absentee landlords because the landlords live overseas.[23]

Understood as a city that is diverse, vibrant, and open to the world, the call to cosmopolitanism is a hopeful slogan for the future of Yangon. It has the potential to write the foreign influences of the colonial era into the history of Yangon, to render them local. Indeed, the lives within the colonial-era buildings are already local and the streets are unmistakably Burmese. The built environment designed and left by the British, Indian and Chinese has made space for a diversity of lives. Daily interactions have rubbed and scrubbed Burmese-ness into the buildings and street corners.

However, slogans often ring hollow, and the inequities hidden behind cosmopolitanism must be investigated. Scholars such as Pheng Cheah (2006), Kathryn Mitchell (2007) and Brenda Yeoh (2004) have cautioned against the elitist, universalizing tendencies of cosmopolitanism, reminding us that it can heighten nationalism even as cosmopolitanism is cast as the humanist counterpart of globalization. This warning is particularly pertinent in contemporary Myanmar, where multiple forces are at play. The country is more open to the world than ever before, but rising Burman Buddhist nationalism is threatening to derail social, economic and political reforms. Ethno-religious conflicts have flared up since 2012 and hate speech continues to spread across Myanmar's social media despite explicit sanctions from the state.[24]

Conclusion

With the world knocking at Myanmar's door, Yangon residents are becoming increasingly aware of both the costs and benefits of entering the global economy. Regional and international companies have entered the country bringing consumer goods such as affordable cell phones, Coca-Cola and Kentucky Fried Chicken. However, the post-2011 reforms and the new NLD government have brought little improvement to the built environment. The most obvious signs of globalization have been a growing number of high-rise towers and streets choked with vehicular traffic. In this rapid and unmanaged marketization and urbanization, Yangon residents have voiced concerns about the loss of Burmese culture. During my most recent fieldwork in 2015, some respondents asked for advice about how to preserve Burmese-ness. What is this Burmese-ness that they are afraid of losing, and do they conceive of Burmese-ness in terms of heritage or the history of their built environment?

The Myanmar government has been vigilant about protecting Burmese-ness since at least the 1990s and continues to promote a unified national identity. Their propaganda is well known and mostly well worn, rendering their rhetoric less potent, and therefore less worrying, at least in cities such as Yangon. However, if everyday residents are pondering their identities in response to the influx of foreign goods, companies and expatriate workers, will those identities become synonymous with the nation-state or make room for difference? Myanmar is a country of multiple ethnicities, and many ethnic groups have fought for independence from the Union of Burma/Myanmar. Therefore, Burmese-ness is fraught with potential conflict and could become a core of contention if it is defined along the lines of exclusion.

Yangon as the subject and site of heritage-making will require many more years of study. At present, the YHT's framing of heritage around colonial architecture could serve as the basis of an inclusive Burmese identity that allows for what one might call naturalized foreign artefacts and people. However, this inclusiveness must not be a naive embrace of abstract universal humanity, but an honest acceptance of differences that recognizes, not masks, past abuses. The physical, socio-economic and legal structures imposed by the British disenfranchized the average Burmese, and those structures have the strong potential of exacerbating existing inequalities. Many entangled issues are on the horizon: colonial era property laws that have yet to be updated, incomplete records of official property documents, established if slippery informal practices in the property and rental markets that have yet to be analysed, little or no means for everyday residents to advocate for themselves in front of the state, lack of trust between the people and the state, crony business practices, and others. International funding agencies and both local and international non-governmental organizations are tackling these various issues from perspectives such as land rights, human rights, social justice, law reform, public sector reform, and responsible business practices. However, in Yangon these various initiatives have yet to intersect with heritage-making. Indeed, if the press releases and reports available on YHT's website were used as a valid indicator, the YHT's strategy has been apolitical and non-confrontational. This is understandable given the current, precarious state of political reform and the obvious need for large sums of money to save the colonial-era architecture. The state and capitalism seem like natural partners.

The challenges are indeed great and the threat of losing the history in the urban fabric of Yangon is real. However, to transform the colonial-era built environment into a heritage that belongs to contemporary Yangon will require more than the *savoir faire* of the comprador intelligentsia. Marketing colonial architecture as cultural commodities cannot generate a shared sense of history and pride. A broadening of heritage needs to be pursued consciously and consistently, not as a pleasant side effect of the call to cosmopolitanism. It requires inviting the opinions of the less worldly who might see little or no connection between themselves and cosmopolitan Rangoon. It also requires a more radical value system that does not dismiss the messiness of wet markets, vendors and other undesigned spaces and practices. The YHT has taken some steps in this direction. Through collaborative and internationally funded projects such as Heritage Works Yangon, Yangon Flyover Project, and Yangon Living Streets, the YHT has begun to reach out to the residents of Yangon to get a sense of their concerns and desires. However, these efforts at public participation are extremely difficult in a country where authoritarian rule has long suppressed public expression and conceptions of good governance are just beginning to be defined. There is no clear path through the entangled and entrenched issues. The YHT has the unenviable task of having to help the municipal government establish viable and responsive governance systems so as to apply those systems to their work of saving the colonial-era downtown. They have done an admirable job championing their cause, but it is time to bring more people to the table.

Notes

1. In *Making Enemies: War and State Building in Burma* (2003), Callahan convincingly argues that the leaders of Burma saw its people as potential enemies. Although her analysis ends in the 1960s, that trend is still evident today.

    In 1989 — at the same time that the State Law and Order Restoration Council (SLORC) renamed the country "Myanmar" — the junta assigned new Romanizations for what it considered more "authentic" names for cities (e.g., Rangoon became "Yangon", Maymyo became "Pyin-Oo-Lwin"). Although the usage of these "new" names was once viewed by activists and scholars as political statements, the controversy surrounding nomenclature has largely died off. For clarity, I will use Myanmar and Yangon for the post-1989 nation-state and city, and Burma and Rangoon for all previous periods. In addition, I will refer to the people and culture as Burmese rather than Myanmarese.

2. The Irrawaddy became the definitive symbol of Burma, galvanizing the entire country against China's encroachment.

3. Of course, one could argue that architectural conservation in most cities has been led by the elite, roughly defined as professional architects and those who have sufficient wealth and comfort to be concerned about the preservation of history through the built environment. However, in the case of Yangon the concerns of the elite are more exclusive because the country is just beginning to emerge from decades of economic stagnation and decline.

4. Education in Burma declined precipitously from the late 1960s onward. The attribution of "educated" in front of Yangon residents and all Burmese in general is not meant as a critique but as a matter-of-fact statement. Many of the Burmese I interacted with only finished fourth grade. Those from better-off families finished the tenth standard. The educated I am referring to have earned bachelor's degrees and some have studied abroad in Singapore,

Australia, or Thailand. Those who have studied abroad are the elite and have a significantly different perspective from the average Burmese.

5. *Pukka* or *pucka* was a term borrowed from British India that meant solid, substantial, or properly constructed.

6. Phayre to Govt., "Rules for the Grant of Town and Suburban Allotments within the Limits of the Jurisdiction of the Town Magistrate of Rangoon", IPP/200/40, 21 Oct. 1853, no. 104, as quoted in Maxim 1992, p. 66.

7. For a more thorough discussion regarding the Chinese in Yangon, see *Mapping Chinese Rangoon* (Roberts 2016).

8. During my fieldwork between 2006 and 2009 and further research in 2014 and 2015, many residents in Yangon said that their properties are owned by Indians, even though they are not sure where the landlords actually reside. This anecdotal evidence is supported by the Indian names on many buildings, such as Rasulbewanj Building, 1925 on Sint Oh Dan Street. Furthermore, current research by Elizabeth Rhoads, a doctoral candidate at Kings College London, indicates that Indians own a majority of the properties in Yangon (conversation on 4 February 2017).

9. *Pyatthat* is the name for the multi-tiered and spired roof found in Burmese royal and Buddhist architecture. There are three primary types of *pyatthat*: three-tiered, five-tiered and seven tiered, with the greater number of tiers representing greater sanctity.

10. The departure of the British Government meant that their extensive bureaucracy for ordering and documenting Burma was also removed. Although British records of their territories constitute a practice of governmentality, their records serve as invaluable sources. The absence of extensive and catalogued records for post-colonial Burma has rendered research on Rangoon more difficult. To date, I have not been able to locate Burmese records that document changes in the city after 1948. I have seen some geological analyses and plans drawn by American experts, but those documents only provide one snapshot in time.

11. There is often confusion about the terms *Burmese* and *Burman*. In general, Burma scholars use *Burmese* to refer to all of the people who reside within the nation-state boundaries of the Union of Myanmar. In comparison, *Burman* is the dominant ethnic group among the 135 so-called ethnic nationalities in Myanmar.

12. Leaders of the ethnic minority groups in this region (Shan, Chin and Kachin) and some in Burma Proper (Karen) understood themselves to have a different and more autonomous relationship with the British Government. Unlike the largely Burman population in Ministerial Burma, whose king was deposed and exiled to India, Shan, Chin and Kachin chiefs maintained control of their princely states. This sense of autonomy would be the basis for their assertion for self-rule in post-colonial independent Burma.

13. This saying was repeated to me by many Burmese people, but no one could

cite a specific source. Nick Cheesman (2002, p. 43) refers to a sermon by
Mingun Sayadaw which includes discussion of these five dangers.

14. However, there is a notable exception. Everyone I have interviewed and
    spoken with casually, even cab drivers, point to the Secretariat as an important
    building complex that should be saved. They identify the Secretariat as the
    building where General Aung San, the father of the country, was assassinated.

15. Interviews, September 2008 and November 2014.

16. In addition to the cited newspaper article, I lived near the pagoda between
    2006 and 2008 and never saw anyone entering the Maha Wizaya Pagoda
    complex.

17. Of course, a similar series of events occurred in Sri Lanka with the Theosophical
    Society and local Buddhists deploying the strategies of the Christian
    missionaries to argue against proselytization.

18. The anti-Muslim sentiments, particularly the plight of the Rohingyas, is beyond
    the scope of this chapter. However, their untenable position needs be noted,
    even in passing.

19. The Shwedagon Pagoda is the most sacred stupa in Myanmar and is said to
    contain eight strands of hair from the Buddha. It is also a centre of Burmese
    political action and has been the site of numerous student and monk protests
    from the colonial period onward. Famously, General Aung San and his daughter
    Aung San Suu Kyi have both given political speeches at the Shwedagon
    Pagoda.

20 I am currently researching the building and placement of Dhamma halls. My
    survey to date indicates that there are Dhamma halls in every ward. Yangon
    is divided into thirty-three townships, with several wards in each township.

21. See note 8. Also, my own research on the Sino-Burmese suggests that Chinese
    families also own many properties; see Roberts 2016.

22. Doctoral fieldwork between 2007 and 2009; interviews in November 2014 and
    January 2015.

23. Ibid.

24. In the middle of 2016, Yangon Chief Minister, U Phyo Min Thein, publically
    criticized the ultra-nationalist Buddhist group Ma Ba Tha. Ma Ba Tha pushed
    back but was unsuccessful in obtaining support from the NLD. These events
    were covered extensively. See, among others, Aung Kyaw Min 2016, Palatino
    2016, and Swan Ye Htut 2016.

References

AlSayyad, N., and A. Roy. "Medieval Modernity: On Citizenship and Urbanism
in a Global Era". *Space and Polity* 10, no. 1 (2006): 1–20.

Appiah, K.A. "Is the Post- in Postmodernism the Post- in Postcolonial?" *Critical
Inquiry* 17, no. 2 (1991).

Aung Kyaw Min. "Could This Be the End of Ma Ba Tha?" *Myanamr Times*, 12 July 2016 <http://www.mmtimes.com/index.php/national-news/21327-could-this-be-the-end-of-ma-ba-tha.html>.

Brand, S. *How Buildings Learn: What Happens after They're Built*. New York: Viking, 1994.

Callahan, M.P. *Making Enemies: War and State Building in Burma*. Ithaca: Cornell University Press, 2003.

Chakravarti, N.R. *The Indian Minority in Burma: The Rise and Decline of an Immigrant Community*. London: Oxford University Press, 1971.

Charney, M.W. *A History of Modern Burma*. Cambridge: Cambridge University Press, 2009.

Chattopadhyay, S. *Representing Calcutta: Modernity, Nationalism, and the Colonial Uncanny*. Abingdon: Routledge, 2005.

Cheah, P. "Cosmopolitanism". *Theory, Culture, and Society* 23, nos. 2–3 (2006).

Cheesman, N. "Legitimising the Union of Myanmar through Primary School Textbooks". MA thesis, University of Western Australia, 2002.

Grant, C. *Rough Pencillings of a Rough Trip to Rangoon in 1846*, vol. 2. Bangkok: White Orchid Press, 1995.

Huang, C. *Huang Chouqing Shiwen Xuan* 黃綽卿詩文選 [A collection of Huang Chouqing's prose and poetry]. Beijing: China Overseas Chinese Publishing Co. 中國華僑出版公司, 1990.

Kyaw Phyo Tha. "Burma's Lonely 'Dictator Pagoda'". *The Irrawaddy*, 31 January 2014 <http://www.irrawaddy.org/feature/burmas-lonely-dictator-pagoda.html> (accessed 22 November 2014).

Lin, Q.-F., ed. 緬華社會研究 [An analysis of Sino-Burmese society], vol. 3. Macao: 澳門緬華互助會 [Macao Sino-Burmese Mutual Aid Association], 2004.

Linthicum, K. "Myanmar's Untold Stories: A Scholar is Racing to Save Colonial-era Buildings as Change Sweeps the Country. *Los Angeles Times*, 7 January 2014, p. 4.

Maxim, S. "Resemblance in External Appearance: The Colonial Project in Kuala Lumpur and Rangoon". PhD dissertation, Cornell University, 1992.

McGee, T.G. *The Southeast Asian City: A Social Geography of the Primate Cities of Southeast Asia*. New York: Praeger, 1967.

Mitchell, K. "Geographies of Identity: The Intimate Cosmopolitan". *Progress in Human Geography* 31, no. 5 (2007): 706–20.

Palatino, M. "Myanmar's Radical Buddhist Group Gets Rebuked". *The Diplomat*, 20 July 2016.

Pearn, B.R. *A History of Rangoon*. Rangoon: American Baptist Mission Press, 1939.

Roberts, J.L. *Mapping Chinese Rangoon: Place and Nation among the Sino-Burmese*. Seattle: University of Washington Press, 2016.

Rooney, S., and Association of Myanmar Architects. *30 Heritage Buildings of Yangon*. Bangkok: Serindia Books, 2012.

Swan Ye Htut. "NLD Refuses to Heed Ma Ba Tha's Request. *Myanmar Times*, 11 July 2016 <http://www.mmtimes.com/index.php/national-news/nay-pyi-taw/21297-nld-refuses-to-heed-ma-ba-tha-s-request.html>.

Tagore, R. "Japane-Parashye". In *Japan and Persia*. Calcutta: Granthalay, 1940.

Taylor, R.H. *The State in Burma*. Honolulu: University of Hawai'i Press, 1987.

Than Than Nwe. "Yangon: The Emergence of a New Spatial Order in Myanmar's Capital City". *SOJOURN: Journal of Social Issues in Southeast Asia* 13, no. 1 (1998): 86–113.

Than Than Nwe, and J. Philp. "Yangon, Myanmar: The Re-invention of Heritage". In *The Disappearing "Asian" City: Protecting Asia's Urban Heritage in a Globalizing World*, edited by W. Logan, pp. 147–65. Oxford: Oxford University Press, 2002.

Turner, A. *Saving Buddhism: The Impermanence of Religion in Colonial Burma*. Honolulu, Hawaii: University of Hawai'i Press, 2014.

U Thein Maung. *A History of Rankon (Rangoon)*. Yangon, 1966.

Yeoh, B.S.A. "Cosmopolitanism and its Exclusions in Singapore". *Urban Studies* 41, no. 12 (2004): 2431–45.

4

Living Heritage of Ruins? Contesting the Paradox in Trowulan's Majapahit Heritage

Adrian Perkasa and Rita Padawangi

Widely recognized from school history books in Indonesia, the name Trowulan is most familiar to Indonesians as the ancient capital of the glorious Majapahit Empire. The official narrative of Indonesia's national history features the kingdom of Majapahit with the notion of archipelagic unity as one nation, "Nusantara", through the Palapa Oath made by its first minister Gajah Mada. Recently though, historians have been increasingly questioning the appropriation of Majapahit in the nation-building narrative due to the mixture of myth and reality in the construction of Majapahit as the root of Indonesian nationalism. The reality of present-day Trowulan is that it resembles more a village than a city. According to the 2010 Census, the population of Trowulan was 68,154, which puts it far from being a "city". It is under the regency of Mojokerto, which is about sixty kilometres from Surabaya, the second-largest city in Indonesia.

Majapahit buildings in Trowulan are now largely ruins. Except for those that have been appropriated and altered as shrines, residents of

Trowulan are not using these ruins in their daily activities. Yet, they live with the ruins and often utilize them as resources, such as in producing new bricks (although the practice of using old Majapahit bricks to produce new bricks is unacceptable under official heritage preservation norms). The Ministry of Culture and Tourism of the Republic of Indonesia had proposed Trowulan as a World Heritage site, and it has been on UNESCO's tentative list since 2009.[1]

Trowulan's Majapahit heritage has been subjected to the invention and reinvention of later societies according to their own agendas. Applying the term *living heritage* to Trowulan would therefore appear to be a contradiction, especially since there is no evidence that the current residents have continued through the generations the cultures of the Majapahit Empire. Yet, we argue that living heritage exists even in an ancient heritage site like Trowulan that has gone through many years of contestations and appropriations for political and cultural legitimacy. How does living heritage relate to the everyday realities of historical ruins? By bringing together the historiography and the voices of residents, scholars and heritage enthusiasts, we find that living heritage is by no means an idealistic practice. Trowulan's histories of preservation, destruction and contestation are part of its living heritage that may also initiate social learning, community empowerment and meaningful interactions.

Living Heritage in Ruins

Ruins represent societal changes that led to the abandonment of man-made places that were no longer relevant to changing paradigms or needs. Volcanic eruptions, disasters, environmental change, defeat in war, economic change, and religious shifts have been cited as possible causes for great temples and magnificent sites falling into disuse, despair, and eventually ruins (Chapman 2013). Over time the original function of these buildings are no longer relevant to the subsequent societies that reside in the area. While some places may retain their religious or cultural significance, most are unused or underutilized. They are structures "caught in-between" their time and the buildings of the present (Chapman 2013, p. 31). In recent histories many ancient sites that exist as ruins are venerated as symbols of a glorious past in order to legitimize current identities, most prominently the sense of nationhood and nationalist pride (Harvey 2003).

Living heritage conveys a contrasting idea that heritage is in the realm of the living. While ruins provide the beauty of a hollow physical structure and architecture, living heritage emphasizes meaningful sociocultural practices that evolve continuously (Lenzerini 2011). One manifestation of the concept of living heritage is UNESCO's intangible cultural heritage (IHC), referring to the immaterial heritage of diverse cultures. The preservation of living heritage, however, is still subject to debate, since blending the notion of preservation and sociocultural practices may contradict the idea of ongoing evolution as a possible characteristic of living heritage. Michael Herzfeld (2014) argues that intangibility is a myth and that assigning the status of intangible heritage has often been used to legitimize politically defined cultural boundaries. The intangible–tangible dualism in UNESCO's heritage categorization has often been criticized and is considered to have perpetuated the intangible–tangible dichotomy of heritage and, to a certain extent, culture.

Such dualistic thinking produces a contradiction between ancient ruins and living heritage. The dichotomy between the tangible and the intangible fades in importance when social agency comes into the picture. The problem with the current discourse on heritage is the dissociation between heritage-making and the empowerment of societies as agents of change, often surrendering to place commodification and/or state domination (Tunbridge and Ashworth 1996). Although practice has come into the picture by acknowledging the intangible, the notion of change in heritage is subject to much debate, and again sounds contradictory. The presence of human agency in the heritage of ruins and living heritage means that members of society have a role to play in shaping and practising heritage. The social construction of meaning would clearly be one aspect, in which the meanings of places, rituals and practices are subject to continuous construction and reconstruction.

Another aspect would be the appropriation of the built environment along with current cultural practices, which touches on the considerably sensitive understanding of heritage. Rather than taking these re-appropriation practices as vandalism or as destroying heritage, there are aspects of reshaping the built environment that are manifestations of the evolving heritage. This means that living heritage is not just the intangible or immaterial; living heritage is also the material embodiment of meaningful social relationships and practices. These processes are inseparable from the street politics, development pressures, urban–rural divide and inequalities of access, as well as more encouraging processes of social learning and community empowerment.

The Political Construction of Trowulan's Ruins

Many historians, archaeologists and scholars believe that Trowulan (Figure 4.1) was the capital city of the Majapahit Empire in the fourteenth century.[2] In the kingdom's golden age, Trowulan was a prosperous city that attracted many visitors, particularly for reasons of trade and diplomacy. These visitors came from other parts of Java and other islands in the region, such as Bali, Buton, Dompo and Suwarnadwipa. Others, as documented in Prapanca's contemporary account in *Desawarnana*, came from continental Southeast Asia, Campa, Siam, Khmer, Burma and China (see also Muljana 2006).[3] After the fall of the *Kraton* (Royal Palace) of Majapahit in the Paregreg civil war, the capital city moved to Daha. By the early sixteenth century the Majapahit Empire had vanished and Trowulan had become ruins. According to *Kidung Pamancangah*, written at the beginning of the nineteenth century, many rulers of the Kingdom of Bali had conducted pilgrimages to the ruins of Trowulan since the seventeenth or eighteenth century, particularly to the remnants of royal sites such as Kedaton, Manguntur, Segaran and Alun–Alun (Gomperts, Haag and Carey 2010).

The framing of the Trowulan ruins as evidence of the glorious past for contemporary political motives was first demonstrated by Thomas

FIGURE 4.1 Aerial view of Trowulan, with the centre of Majapahit's capital city.
Source: Balai Pelestarian Cagar Budaya Jawa Timur 2010.

Stamford Raffles. In his book, *History of Java*, Raffles documented with illustrations the remnants of Hindu-Buddhist monuments in Java. From the idea of a glorified past, Raffles believed that Javanese natives could be persuaded to work with the British government to return to a golden age such as that of the Majapahit Empire. Raffles was not able to realise his idea because the Dutch retook control of Java in 1819 (Quilty 1988).[4] Nevertheless, Raffles was the first person to initiate conservation efforts in Trowulan. He ordered Captain Engineer J.W.B. Wardenaar to map and draft a plan of the area, which was still surrounded by a teak forest at the time. The whereabouts of Wardenaar's site plan of Trowulan was unknown for two hundred years until it was finally rediscovered in the British Museum in 2007.

After the departure of Raffles, the Dutch authorities continued the initiative to document Trowulan. In the early twentieth century the Dutch government established the Commissie in Nederlandsche-Indie voor Oudheidkundig Onderzoek op Java en Madoera (Archaeological Commission in Netherlands-Indies for Java and Madura) to oversee ethical and aesthetic concerns about the deterioration of the archaeological remnants, especially Borobudur Temple in Central Java. The commission later changed its name to Oudheidkundige Dienst (Archaeological Service) and extended its concern to many other Hindu-Buddhist monuments in Java. Trowulan was one of the sites where the Oudheidkundige Dienst undertook research and conservation. Many scholars under the service, such as Hendrik Kern, R. Ng. Poerbatjaraka and Willem Frederik Stutterheim, tried to make reconstructions of the area.

Nevertheless, the social and political constructions of Majapahit's glory through Trowulan research was not a monopoly of the authorities, as powerful private entities began to grow. During the same period, sugar factories mushroomed in East Java, as after 1870 the Dutch authorities enacted regulation to give land rights to European private individuals to build and operate factories. Sugar was one of the main commodities of the Netherlands East-Indies at that time. Many sugar factories were built around Trowulan, and many of them used neglected ancient bricks from the Majapahit era, which were of higher quality and stronger than new bricks. The builders transported the old bricks to factory sites to build structures such as chimneys and storage facilities. The sugar-driven economic development induced migration and settlement around the factories and sugarcane fields, leading to a significant population growth for Trowulan.

Despite their use of ancient bricks, the owners of sugar factories near Trowulan decided to fund an organization called Oudheidkundige Vereeniging Majapahit (OVM; Majapahit Archaeological Association). Members of the association conducted research about Majapahit heritage and history. Their main research project from 1924 to 1926 was to reconstruct Trowulan as Majapahit's capital city. This research produced a more comprehensive picture of the Majapahit ruins (*Pusat Penelitian dan Pengembangan Kebudayaan*, 2008). The members and initiators of this association were not only archaeologists and historians but also included Adipati Ario Kromodjojo Adinegoro, the *Bupati* (regent) of Mojokerto, where Trowulan is located, and Henry Maclaine Pont, a famous Dutch architect in the region. Both men were also collectors of Hindu-Buddhist Javanese artefacts.

The OVM's board of directors had a unique composition that included state power, the economic power of relatively big businesses, and the ability to engage experts in the field. The key office holders were part of a new generation of plutocrats in the sugar business of the time. The chairman, J.M. Ackett, was the representative of sugar factories owned by the Eschauzier family, one of the wealthy sugar-industry families with close government connections. J. Verboom, the secretary and treasurer, was an important figure in the Consortium of Netherlands-Indies Sugar Enterprises in Surabaya. Compared to Oudheidkundige Dienst's work on Trowulan, the activities and output of the OVM was much greater. The OVM collected many artefacts from local people, built an in-situ open museum, published their own newsletter for members, conducted fundraising for conservation efforts, and even had an ambitious project, led by Maclaine Pont, to reconstruct the ancient capital city of Majapahit in Trowulan based on the book *Nagarakretagama* and archaeological findings.

The role of Maclaine Pont was not limited to documenting and making reconstructions from archaeological findings; he also had an influence on the local economy. In addition to bringing attention to archaeological and heritage conservation in Trowulan, Maclaine Pont also influenced local residents to produce arts and crafts. Sabar, a villager from Bejijong in Trowulan who worked on Maclaine Pont's archaeological projects, became a famous sculptor following Indonesia's independence. Maclaine Pont had supported Sabar to continue his sculpture work, particularly in metal, since the worker helped him to craft a statue of Jesus for a church in Mojowarno, Jombang, East Java. To date, Sabar's descendants still live in Trowulan and continue the family sculpting business. The business has also influenced other villagers to become sculptors. It remains unclear whether the training of locals in Majapahit-related arts and crafts was the initiative of Maclaine Pont alone or of the OVM as an organization. Yet it was obvious that Maclaine Pont was the one who engaged with the locals to affect their aspirations and economic and cultural practices through the promotion of Majapahit-related arts and crafts.

The engagement of local residents in the social construction of Majapahit greatness in Trowulan is broader than merely arts and crafts; locals were also involved in treasure hunting. In the OVM era, treasure hunting — in addition to brick factory labourer, archaeological worker, and artist — became one of the popular professions in Trowulan. There are no records to say when exactly treasure hunters around Trowulan first appeared. Many of them lived around Trowulan in villages such as Bejijong and Jatipasar. Initially, Maclaine Pont worked with local villagers to excavate several sites that were thought to be part of Majapahit city. Maclaine Pont's supervision of this work was curtailed when he was imprisoned by the Japanese during the Second World War.[5] After their patron was incarcerated, the villagers continued to dig the soil near their houses or ancient monuments around Trowulan like Brahu temple, Wringin Lawang temple, and Kedaton temple, and some started selling the artefacts they found.

Treasure hunting therefore represented the intersection between embracing the belief in Trowulan as a representation of Majapahit's glorious past and economic rationality to accumulate personal wealth. A former staff member of the current Suaka Peninggalan Sejarah Purbakala (Archaeological Artifact Sanctuary) under Indonesia's Ministry of Education and Culture, Pak Nuriyadi, conveyed in an interview in 2013 that many treasure hunters were previously farmers of Trowulan who changed their profession to get more income. Almost all of them who found precious artefacts made of gold, silver or bronze became very rich. Most of the treasures found were jewellery, boxes of golden paper, small-size linga or yoni, and gold or bronze kris. The valuable artefacts mentioned in Nuriyadi's interview are consistent with written records by Odorico da Pordenone, a Franciscan missionary who came to Majapahit city in the fourteenth century:

> This is thought to be one of the largest islands in the world, and is thoroughly inhabited; having great plenty of cloves, cubebs, and nutmegs, and all other kinds of spices, and great abundance of provisions of all kinds, except wine. The king of Java has a large and sumptuous palace,

the loftiest of any that I have seen, with broad and lofty stairs to ascend
to the upper apartments, all the steps being alternately of gold and silver.
The whole interior walls are lined with plates of beaten gold, on which the
images of warriors are placed sculptured in gold, having each a golden
coronet richly ornamented with precious stones. The roof of this palace
is of pure gold, and all the lower rooms are paved with alternate square
plates of gold and silver. The great khan, or emperor of Cathay, has had
many wars with the king of Java, but has always been vanquished and
beaten back. (Portenau 1996)

Treasure hunting stopped suddenly after the Gestok[6] incident in 1965, not
because of any implementation of heritage law but because of the mass
killings in Indonesia at the time — one of the most extensive mass murders
in the twentieth century. In several areas of East Java such as Kediri, Blitar,
Banyuwangi, Malang and Jember, many people suspected of involvement
with Partai Komunis Indonesia (PKI; the Indonesian Communist Party) or
organizations affiliated with it were brutally slain by the masses and the
army (Anonymous 1990). According to Teguh,[7] the Kepala Desa Bejijong
(Head of Bejijong Village) at that time, vigilante groups and the army also
arrested many treasure hunters. They were accused of being members or
supporters of Barisan Tani Indonesia (Indonesian Farmers Legion), which
was affiliated with the PKI. Some of them really were supporters but many
were not involved in any political activities, yet all were arrested. Seeing
the situation as very dangerous, the remaining hunters decided to return
to farming and lost interest in treasure hunting.

State Domination in the Heritage Discourse

The role of the state in the political construction of Trowulan heritage
became more prevalent following independence, in particular through the
association of Indonesia's nationalism with Majapahit's "Nusantara" and the
promotion of cultural tourism as an official national development agenda.
The first president, Sukarno, who was in power from 1945 to 1966, coined
the term *pariwisata* as the Indonesian translation for the word "tourism".
His administration introduced "Guided Tourism" that restricted the role
of the private sector — along with his idea of "Guided Democracy" — and
changed the name of Dewan Tourisme Indonesia to Dewan Pariwisata
Indonesia (headed at the time by Sri Sultan Hamengkubuwono IX, the
Sultan of Yogyakarta) (Kodhyat 1996). In the 1950s, Sukarno was also in

full support of the reconstruction of the Shiva temple in the Prambanan complex in Solo, Central Java, and created momentum for transforming archaeological sites into modern Indonesian heritage.

With regards to Trowulan, the Surabaya-born Sukarno, who trained as an architect, was familiar with the site from an early age. Hence, his attention towards Majapahit heritage in Trowulan was also influenced by the role of the Dutch, particularly the work of Maclaine Pont and the OVM in documenting the artefacts. During Sukarno's presidency, a terracotta mask that was found in Trowulan was pronounced by minister of education Muhammad Yamin as a portrait of first minister Gajah Mada.[8] Trowulan eventually gained wide public attention at the national level (Bloembergen and Eijckhoff 2011).

The New Order regime (1966–98) under President Soeharto implemented programmes to make heritage sites, including Trowulan, into tourist attractions. Several heritage conservation projects commenced from the end of the 1960s. The Suaka Peninggalan Sejarah Purbakala (Archaeological Artefact Sanctuary), the government agency responsible for heritage conservation, launched the Trowulan reconstruction project to acquire lands encompassing several heritage monuments, and constructed fences around them.

The projects were in accordance with the development policies of Soeharto's government, famously called the Rencana Pembangunan Lima Tahun I (the first Five Year Development Plan). The plan noted that "cultural heritage" should be conserved "as far as possible to maintain the culture and its environment, which is the wealth of Indonesia and the powerful tourist attraction, and to be useful to the Indonesian people themselves" (Departemen Pariwisata, Pos, dan Telekomunikasi 1990). The general focus was to develop the national economy and promote political stability. Besides economic growth, the government aimed to boost patriotism, strengthen the unity and integrity of the nation, and preserve culture and the environment. As part of this policy, many major architectural ruins were reconstructed to support tourism.

When oil exports declined around the late 1970s and early 1980s, the Indonesian government intensified the development of tourism in order to generate more state revenue and introduce the richness of Indonesia's nature and culture to the world (Departemen Pariwisata, Pos, dan Telekomunikasi 1990). The government also promoted cultural-tourism entrepreneurship in Trowulan by publishing a book titled *Trowulan, Bekas*

Ibukota Kerajaan Majapahit (Trowulan, Former Capital City of Majapahit Kingdom), in order to disseminate how to run a travel business offering tourist packages to Trowulan. In the meantime, archaeologists warned the Ministry of Culture and Education that increased tourism could cause further damage to the Majapahit heritage in Trowulan as there was no sufficient preservation efforts in place. Finally, in 1985–86 the Suaka Peninggalan Sejarah Purbakala conducted a major project to map all the heritage sites in and around Trowulan and to make a comprehensive planning framework for heritage conservation.

Trowulan's local residents in general welcomed the government's intention to promote Majapahit heritage as a tourist attraction. In a survey conducted by Lembaga Ilmu Pengetahuan Indonesia (LIPI; the Indonesian Institute of Science) in 1987, more than ninety per cent of Trowulan villagers said that they wanted the area to become a famous tourist attraction. They believed that if many tourists visited Trowulan they could earn more money and run several businesses, like restaurants, souvenir shops, or homestays (LIPI 1988). Little was revealed by the survey, however, whether respondents were aware of the contradictions within the government's plans that had the potential to undermine the aspirations of the locals.

Democratization and the Dawn of the Resistance Era

Whilst the role of the state in heritage preservation began in the colonial period, the Soeharto regime established the dominance of the national government in heritage planning and management. Combined with the suppression of political opposition, magnified by Gestok that led many treasure hunters to return to farming, the role of local residents in heritage-making has largely been reduced to seeking to obtain economic benefits from tourism. This top-down approach was sustained after Soeharto's regime ended, even after the decentralization era when local governments (at the *Kabupaten* [Regency] and *Kotamadya* [City] level) were given greater autonomy. The Mojokerto Regency, as the local government, took more control of heritage sites and exploited these sites to earn revenues through the Dinas Kebudayaan, Pariwisata, Pemuda dan Olahraga (Office of Culture, Tourism, Youth and Sports). The residents were only entrusted with relatively little things to do in heritage preservation, with the exception of the government-appointed staff of the archaeological office or museum in Trowulan and the *juru kunci* (the "gatekeeper", referring to the worker responsible for monitoring a particular, often small, heritage site). Semi-formal involvement of local residents took the form of managing vehicle parking spaces in several larger heritage sites, like the temples of Bajang Ratu, Tikus and Brahu. Like many transportation industries in Indonesia, the local branches of the Karang Taruna (Youth Organization) close to those sites were the ones responsible for managing vehicle parking.

Although the official preservation narratives and the role of the state in heritage management remained dominant and local communities seemed to be agreeable to develop heritage tourism in the Soeharto era, resistance towards the government's heritage policies began to emerge before the end of the regime in 1998. The most tenacious local resistance took place in the early 1990s when the government wanted to relocate more than a hundred Muslim graves around Wringin Lawang and Bajang Ratu Temples to make way for a new park as a tourist attraction. The temples, which were ruins back then, had been reappropriated as cemeteries by Trowulan locals. The Javanese believe that descendants should respect their deceased parents and ancestors. Consequently, graves are very important because making pilgrimages to graves is a way to honour the dead. Several smaller Majapahit shrines have also been reappropriated as Muslim burial sites on a smaller scale (see Figure 4.2), but the most obvious resistance was at Wringin Lawang and Bajang Ratu, as the government plan challenged local beliefs and practices. The governor of East Java could not prevent a deadlock in negotiations between the national government and local residents. The graves were finally evicted after long and exhausting negotiations, but some locals only relented because of military pressure.[9]

As Indonesia underwent a national regime change after the 1998 Reform Movement, which marked a significant milestone for democratization in the country, civil society voices in defence of local practices and beliefs began to wrestle the social and cultural authority over heritage preservation from the domination of the state. The reform of 1998 challenged the role of the military in government and limited the role of the military in civilian life, particularly through the abolition of the military's dual function (*dwifungsi ABRI*) that previously legitimized the army's intervention in ideological, political, economic, social and cultural activities of civilians. In the meantime the rebound in development after the 1997 economic crisis and the subsequent decentralization of planning and budgeting governance to local city governments and regencies resulted in a greater presence of

FIGURE 4.2   Relatively small Majapahit ruins that had been reappropriated by Trowulan residents to be a Muslim burial site. Photographs by the authors, 2014.

private sector operations in developments transforming urban and rural landscapes, including that in Trowulan. While the resistance in the early 1990s was mainly against government plans, post-1998 Trowulan saw both the government and private sector as targets of resistance movements, as they continued to affect heritage landscapes of the area.

Resisting the National Government Project Post-1998

The reform of 1998 was followed by a proliferation of civil society organizations across Indonesia, including those focussed on heritage preservation. Consequently, the social and political constructions of the Trowulan ruins as heritage has been subjected to the relevance of residents' current concerns. A prominent example is the case of the Majapahit Park Master Plan for cultural tourism (Kawasan Wisata Budaya Majapahit) written in 2006 by Balai Pelestarian Peninggalan Purbakala Jawa Timur (East Java Archaeological Conservation Agency).[10] The plan included a visitor centre in Majapahit Park. However, the location of the new centre would be on old brick structures from the Majapahit period, which would cause significant damage to the ancient structures under the surface.

The project became the centre of a dispute between its supporters and protestors following national media coverage in *Kompas* and *Tempo* in 2009, when the development was already under way. A special report from *Kompas* included an interview with Endro Waluyo, the head of the registration group in the Balai Pelestarian with the authority to monitor all projects in Trowulan and East Java, who was against the project. The interview pointed to the head of Balai Pelestarian, Made Kusumajaya, as the initiator, and the Ministry of Culture and Tourism as the institution that fully supported the project. A few days after receiving Endro's report on the damage, Moendardjito, a senior archaeologist with the University of Indonesia in Depok, West Java,[11] visited the construction site and was shocked to see the impact of the new construction on the ancient structures.[12] Moendardjito subsequently asked several journalists to cover the destruction of heritage and archaeological remains in Trowulan, which resulted in intensive coverage by *Kompas* and *Tempo*.

Meanwhile, local response to the project was mixed, as the ruins affected by the information centre did not immediately represent a place of cultural, social or economic significance. *Kompas* conducted interviews with several local people and found varying degrees of response. Wanito, one of the interviewees, said that he did not care about the development project. He only wanted to work and hoped that many job opportunities would be available as soon as possible in Trowulan. However, artists in Trowulan were not as welcoming towards the project. Supriyadi, a bronze sculptor, rejected the project because neither the information centre nor Majapahit Park involved any local people. Another sculptor, Ribut, agreed with Supriyadi. Ribut, a famous stone sculptor in Trowulan and member of Dewan Kesenian Mojokerto (Mojokerto Arts Council),[13] appealed to the government to stop the project and to conduct a dialogue with local residents.

The project was subsequently suspended by the minister of culture and tourism, Jero Wacik. The minister recognized "many mistakes and carelessness when the developer constructed the new building", although he stopped short of blaming the master plan. Wacik claimed that the Ministry of Culture and Tourism had already created an evaluation team consisting of various experts, including Moendardjito as a senior archaeologist, to evaluate the project before *Kompas* and *Tempo* made the dispute their headline news. Other members of the evaluation team included architects Osrifoel Oesman and Arya Abieta and representatives of non-governmental organizations (NGOs) around Trowulan, such as Anam Anis from Gotrah Wilwatikta.[14] Minister Wacik defended the government's involvement with the project as expressions of goodwill to revitalize the heritage of Majapahit, especially for the future of the younger generation (*Kompas* 2009). Baskoro Tedjo, the architect responsible for the design of the information centre justified his involvement in the project for three reasons: First, recommendations from a UNESCO conference in New Delhi in 1956 that emphasized the importance of museums and information centres in the preservation of heritage. Second, he argued that the centre would prevent massive damage at Trowulan as a heritage site, because after the centre and park were built, local people would be more likely to participate and to seek careers in the tourism and heritage industries. Third, he claimed that an earlier design for the building prior to his involvement would have created even more damage to the Majapahit-era structures (Tedjo 2009).

In spite of the suspension and the ensuing explanations, many locals, archaeologists, architects, NGOs and other interest groups insisted on halting the project. These groups held many seminars, public discussions and a "national dialogue" on the issue. The first discussion, on 14 March

2009, only two months after the dispute was first reported in the national media, featured the evaluation team, Endro Waluyo, and Anam Anis as speakers. The Indonesian Archaeologist Association and representatives of many other universities attended this discussion, which was held in Gadjah Mada University, Yogyakarta. A few months later, another discussion was held in Trowulan. The speakers at the second discussion were Totok Rusmanto from the Faculty of Architecture at Diponegoro University, Inajati from the Archaeological Department of Gadjah Mada University, and Hadi Purnomo from Ciputra University. Local people from ten villages in Trowulan were also invited as speakers to express their aspirations in response to the project.

These rounds of discussions continued in the form of a national dialogue in October 2009. Besides involving more groups and universities, the national dialog discussed new perspectives on heritage law. The debate highlighted the fact that the existing national heritage law from 1992 was unsuitable for current conservation efforts because it could not resolve many problems on the ground, especially land acquisition to prevent destruction of heritage sites. The national heritage law also could not accommodate "lay-people" — the local people who are considered non-experts — or other groups apart from the government in heritage conservation efforts. The most important recommendation to come out of this dialogue was for a new national heritage law to regulate the participation of more groups in conservation efforts. Finally, the House of Representatives in Jakarta acknowledged this aspiration and drafted a new heritage law in 2010.

Resisting Private Sector and Local Government Plans

The new heritage law represented a shifting of authority in the social construction of the Trowulan ruins. In contrast with the experience under previous regimes, in which heritage was mainly the domain of the government, the new heritage law allowed to a certain extent the participation of non-government actors. The impetus for the shift was the assessment by experts of the damage to the ruins and the critique on the lack of participation channels for locals in heritage-related decisions. The introduction of the new law has led to wider public participation in heritage preservation. The tangible–intangible dualism, however, persists. The new law still refers to heritage in terms of *benda, situs* and *area* ("artefact", "site" and "area") rather than as heritage practices in everyday life. There is, however, acknowledgement (in Chapter 56) that "everybody can participate in preserving heritage".

The law was almost immediately put to the test in a controversy regarding a planned steel factory in 2013. Hundreds of villagers stood at the main gate to the site for the planned factory shouting "Save Trowulan! Selamatkan Trowulan dari industrialisasi!" (Save Trowulan from industrialization!) The owner and director of PT Manunggal Sentral Baja, HM Sundoro Sasongko, planned to build a factory in Jatipasar and Watesumpak villages in Trowulan. Although the owner had already obtained permission from the regent of Mojokerto, the villagers around the factory strongly rejected the project. They began to mobilize protests to the head of the village, to the district head, to the company owner, and to the regent.

The factory owner had almost completed all the requirements for planning permission from the government at the local and national level. He recognized that his factory complex would be close to Wringin Lawang, one of the heritage sites of Trowulan, but he had received a recommendation from the Ministry of Education and Culture in Jakarta that suggested he should ask for another recommendation letter from the archaeological agency in Trowulan (Balai Pelestarian Peninggalan Purbakala Trowulan). There was also a letter from the head of Balai Pelestarian Peninggalan Purbakala Trowulan, dated 18 July 2012, which explained that the site of the planned steel factory was not a listed heritage monument/building (*Bangunan Cagar Budaya*), that the area is outside the main Wringin Lawang conservation area, and that Balai Pelestarian Peninggalan Purbakala Trowulan supported start-up industries around Trowulan in order to create local employment.[15]

In contrast to the earlier case of the planned information centre, where initial resistance came mostly from archaeologists and academics, resistance to the steel factory began at the grass roots. The 2009 controversy over the information centre had revived the association of the area among residents with Majapahit's glorious past, particularly through the active role of local representatives in the series of dialogues. The plan for the steel factory therefore triggered local resistance, specifically because it was seen as a violation of Majapahit identity. The inhabitants of Watesumpak and Jatipasar villages in Trowulan only became aware of the plan in July 2013, and immediately began to resist it. Together with local artists they conducted a theatrical performance as a public protest against the factory at the Mojokerto Parliament Complex. The demonstration led the parliament to open a hearing session with the people, facilitated by the chairpersons of the NGO Badan Pelestarian Pusaka Indonesia (BPPI; Indonesian Heritage Trust). The meeting resulted in a parliamentary recommendation that construction of the steel factory be postponed until the dispute could be resolved. In the same month, BPPI issued a press release advocating that construction of the steel factory be halted and that the Trowulan site be designated as a National Strategic Site and National Heritage Zone. A few days later a number of artefacts were discovered within fifty metres of the steel factory site.

Continuous observation and social exchanges with local residents revealed that the activists and residents that rejected the construction of the factory believed that they were the descendants of Majapahit residents and therefore had an obligation to oppose the destruction of the site. When the Bupati of Mojokerto supported the designation of Trowulan as a National Heritage Zone the year before the steel factory controversy, he referred to Majapahit as a venerated national heritage that was internationally recognized (*Citizen Journalism* 2012). Mojopahit Trowulan Artists, a group of local artists in Trowulan, responded to the bupati's statement as "a forced defense statement from a 'leader' who was cornered because of his own doing that was ungrateful and unappreciative of his [Majapahit] ancestors' glory".[16]

Since then, BPPI increased its push for Trowulan to be classified as a National Heritage Zone. The move was in parallel with the local resistance movement against the steel factory. During Independence Day celebrations on 17 August 2013, artists and cultural observers conducted a mass painting session to draw attention to opposition to the steel factory. In the same month, BPPI and the Majapahit Conservation Network (Jaringan Pelestarian Majapahit; JPM) initiated an online petition. This was followed by a visit by members of the national parliament to the site in response to reports about the case. Their visit led to them requesting the government of Mojokerto Regency to develop a concrete plan for the National Heritage Zone and its conservation efforts. In October 2013, the efforts of various NGOs and heritage enthusiasts led to Trowulan's inclusion in the 2014 World Monuments Watch, a list maintained by the international NGO World Monuments Fund, on the basis that it "suffered heavily from prolonged neglect". Later in the same month the minister of education and culture finally stated that the planned location for the steel factory breached an area potentially designated as a National Heritage Zone. The resistance of Trowulan residents, their alliance with the local and national parliaments, and support from the national government influenced the Bupati of Mojokerto to finally declare his commitment in October 2013 to stop the construction of the steel factory, to relocate the factory to a designated industrial zone, and to safeguard the social stability of the residents.

Social mobilization strategies, however, are not only used by one group. In the case of the steel factory, banners that supported the construction of the steel factory and at the same time rejected the designation of Trowulan as a National Heritage Zone started to appear at the end of October, followed by a public demonstration by supporters of the steel factory in early November. A few days later, on 10 November 2013, the supporters of National Heritage Zone designation, particularly local residents and the Save Trowulan Community, held a Grand Thanksgiving celebration to celebrate the 720th anniversary of the Majapahit Empire and to reiterate their commitment to preserving Trowulan.

Heritage-based Social Mobilization as Living Heritage?

While reliance on the belief and pride in being Majapahit descendants is interesting in itself as an ideological resource of resistance, finding economic relevance for heritage preservation is an important ingredient to heritage-based community empowerment. As observed in the cases of the Majapahit Information Centre in 2009 and the steel factory in 2013, the argument of job creation for locals was repeatedly cited, both to legitimize and to debunk the projects. However, there was little mention of the existing economy of Trowulan or of a linkage with the everyday lives and livelihoods of Trowulan residents. Interviews with local sculptors, whose profession could be traced back to the time of Maclaine Pont, revealed their aspirations to be able to relate their profession more closely to the Majapahit heritage of Trowulan. Many of their artworks had to be marketed to tourists in Bali rather than being sold in Trowulan.

The government's ambition to conserve heritage in Trowulan in order to boost the tourism industry took a twist by turning it into a site for religious tourism, with the establishment of Troloyo Cemetery in Trowulan as a Muslim shrine. During his short presidency, President Abdurrahman Wahid (1999–2002), who was a respected religious leader, visited the historical

Majapahit-era Muslim cemetery and induced widespread attention to the site. As buses of pilgrims regularly come to the cemetery, a small market economy began to flourish around the entrance, offering various commodities such as food, souvenirs and cell phone credits (Figure 4.3).

The vibrancy of the Troloyo Cemetery economy stands in stark contrast with the quiet open spaces of Bajang Ratu and the revised version of the Majapahit Information Centre now known as Majapahit Museum. Beautifully landscaped and rehabilitated, Bajang Ratu hardly receives visitors unless there is a special event, and the museum relies on school visits. Despite the objective of preserving Majapahit heritage, the government-led projects seem distant from the everyday reality of local people and their livelihoods. The paradox between heritage projects and the local economy means Trowulan's heritage is prone to developments that threaten the longevity of the sites — the increasing distance between the Majapahit ruins and everyday cultural, social and economic practices render the remaining fragments of Majapahit buildings

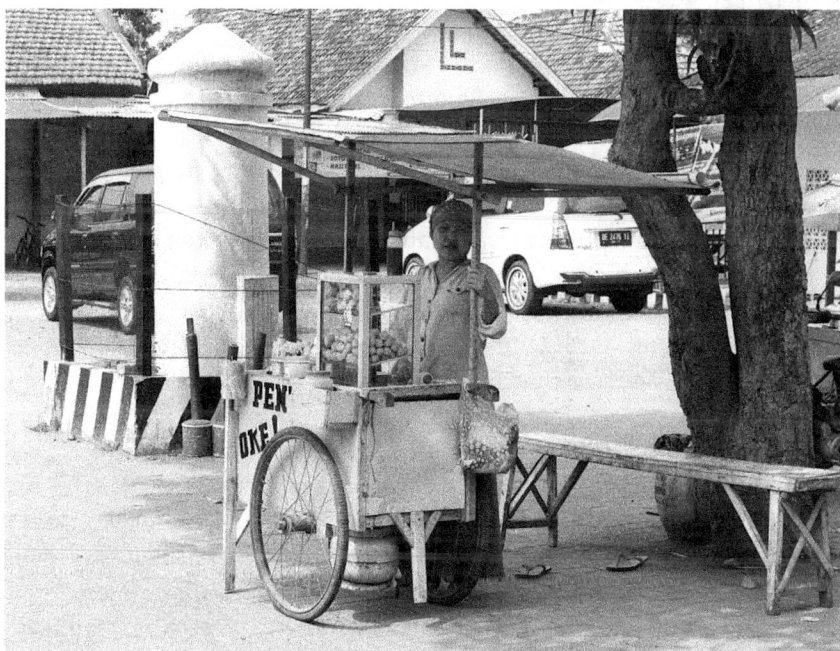

FIGURE 4.3 A food vendor at the Troloyo Cemetery entrance. Photograph by the authors, 2014.

ever more irrelevant to the social realities and livelihoods of the current population, other than the interests of heritage enthusiasts and academics.[17] The politically constructed dilemma between economic development and historic preservation as seen in Trowulan is a familiar story in developing countries in Asia (Li 2010).

By focusing on a physical reconstruction of Majapahit's splendour, the official discourse in Trowulan perpetuates the disempowerment of locals in heritage conservation and preservation. What is missing from the discourse is the recognition that the built environment gradually evolves as cultural practices do. The Trowulan case illustrates the possibility of acts of reappropriation as part of heritage, as demonstrated by the Muslim cemeteries at Wringin Lawang and Bajang Ratu. But when the reappropriation is monopolized by the state or a combination of factions of the local state and private sector — as in the cases of the Majapahit Information Centre and the steel factory — local residents may resist and form coalitions with heritage enthusiasts, academics, and factions in the local and national governments to propose their own ideas about heritage preservation.

Critics may remain sceptical about the motivation of those who supported the steel factory, but the antagonism between these groups is inseparable from the limitations in opportunities for livelihoods that exist under the current understanding of heritage preservation. "Cagar Budaya" or "Heritage Site" status in Indonesia in practice is a restriction of economic opportunities rather than a benefit, by imposing the responsibility to preserve a location's physical traits rather than treating them as a cultural resource relevant to social and economic empowerment. Consequently, tourism is often the only relevant economic activity that can be thought of for heritage sites. Dedi Gumelar, a member of the national parliament who visited the site, said that Trowulan should be developed as a cultural tourism destination rather than industries. He said, "The economic development will be accelerated if in Trowulan we develop hotels and restaurants because they are related to tourism" (*Jawa Pos* 2013*a*). This was supported by the vice chairman of the local parliament of Mojokerto Regency, Syaiful Fuad (*Jawa Pos* 2013*b*). Although support for tourism was consistent with the effort to reject the steel industry, tourism-related businesses may also come into conflict with the local economy, culture, social relationships and local solidarity. These local practices would be subjected to market-driven developments once they fully subscribe to the national and international tourism industry, and gentrification may well follow, as has been demonstrated in various World Heritage sites.

Living heritage of ruins can overcome contradictions when heritage discourse and practice recognize the following realities. First, the built environment is bound to be changed and to be reappropriated by the population along with societal change, which means that the "intangible" social and cultural practices are in fact material, including their embodiment in the changing built environment. Second, reappropriation of heritage sites by the people that occur incrementally in relevance with evolving cultural practices is different from reappropriation by the state or market-driven industries. The use of Majapahit ruins as sites of Muslim graves serves as evidence of this reappropriation to realign Majapahit's glory with current cultural and religious practices. Yet, the effort to politically acknowledge reappropriations as heritage, hence the heritage of the living, is also subject to the ability to connect with government actors and economic relevance, as these reappropriations may collide with market-driven industries in using the space.

Third, heritage-based social mobilizations are by no means unproblematic; they are bound to have complexities and are multifaceted. The process of preserving or conserving living heritage is also inevitably complex, as sociocultural practices and meanings are evolving. The meaning of Majapahit identity in the everyday lives of Trowulan residents has evolved over time, as seen to a limited extent in the various stages of recorded history in this chapter. The recent economic prominence of Troloyo cemetery as a Muslim pilgrimage site is an example of how Majapahit identity continues to evolve, although there may not be a consensus on what practices exactly represent Majapahit identity in contemporary Trowulan. Understanding living heritage would require dismantling the dichotomy between the intangible and the tangible; and critical questioning of the relationship between heritage and the obsession with prioritizing physical structures.

Notes

1. <http://whc.unesco.org/en/tentativelists/5466/>.
2. Based on a range of scholarly works since the early of twentieth century, from N.J. Krom (1916), F.D.K. Bosch (1931), W.F. Stutterheim (1948) to current research like that of Moendardjito (1986), Miksic (1995), and Gomperts, Haag and Carey (2014).

3. See also Muljana (2006).

4. According to Quilty (1988), Raffles used romanticism to raise awareness among the Javanese about their pre-Dutch history. Raffles believed that the Dutch would never benefit the Javanese because of monopolistic practices, especially in economics. He also convinced his readers in *The History of Java* that the British were going to return Java to its former glory. Seen critically, the move by Raffles was to use Javanese history to justify British colonial authority and superiority and to make a case for British rather than Dutch colonial rule.

5. Maclaine Pont was arrested by the Japanese colonial government and held in Kalisosok prison in Surabaya before being transferred to Cimahi, West Java, in 1943.

6. *Gestok* is an abbreviation for "Gerakan Satu Oktober" (First October Movement), formed in 1965. It refers to the action initiated by General Soeharto to crack down on communists after the Communist Party of Indonesia was blamed for the deaths of six generals and a high-ranking military official.

7. Interview with Pak Teguh, April 2013.

8. Gajah Mada was a celebrated first minister during the reigns of Queen Tribhuwana Tunggadewi and King Hayam Wuruk, which historians consider the heyday of the Majapahit Empire.

9. Interviews with affected family members, April 2013.

10. The new name of the Suaka Peninggalan Sejarah Purbakala (Archaeological Artefact Sanctuary) after the 1998 reform

11. Interview with Professor Moendardjito, May 2013

12. Endro's actions resulted in him being demoted (from Jakarta to Trinil Museum in East Java) because he was judged to be "harming" Moendardjito's reputation as one of the most senior archaeologists in Indonesia (*Kompas*, 5 January 2009). Moendardjito was reported to have been appalled upon hearing about Endro's demotion, and decided to contact the journalists to ask for more intensive coverage on the case. Following the media coverage, Made Kusumajaya, head of Balai Pelestarian, came under scrutiny and was consequently compelled to frame the project as having good intentions to promote and conserve Majapahit heritage. He also argued that the project was intended to make Trowulan open to the public, not only for archaeologists as it had been in the past.

13. Interview with Pak Ribut and Pak Supriyadi, June 2013.

14. Gotrah Wilwatikta is an NGO devoted to documenting instances of looting of Majapahit artefacts in Trowulan.

15. See *Jawa Pos* (2013c) for a statement by Yoko Priyono, head of the Centre for Research and Technology Development (Badan Penelitian dan Pengembangan Teknologi; BPPT) of Mojokerto Regency, that there was no evidence of any archaeological findings at the location of the planned steel factory.

16. Discussions with local artists, October 2013.
17. We are aware that there are significant numbers of small-scale brick production enterprises that operate in Trowulan as part of the local economy. These brick producers may be aware that they should avoid using any Majapahit artefacts and old bricks as production material, but there are also many who are not sensitive to heritage preservation. Whilst we do not discuss the brick producers in this chapter, it is worth noting that brick production is a form of local economic activity. The brick producers need not be in conflict with the needs of heritage preservation and conservation, but the current contradiction between such local practices and Majapahit heritage is also inseparable from the rigidity of the state-led heritage discourse and preservation/conservation practices that do not involve the local economy.

References

Anonymous. "Additional Data on Counter-Revolutionary Cruelty in Indonesia, Especially in East Java". In *The Indonesian Killings 1965–1966, Studies from Java and Bali*, edited by R. Cribb and R. Cribb, pp. 169–73. Clayton: Centre of Southeast Asia Studies Monash University, Australia, 1990.

Bloembergen, M., and M. Eijckhoff. "Conserving the Past, Mobilizing the Indonesian Future: Archaeological Sites, Regime Change, and Heritage Politics in Indonesia in the 1950s". *Bijdragen tot de Taal-, Land- en Volkenkunde* 167, no. 4 (2011): 405–36.

Bosch, F.D.K. "Welke waarde hebben de oud-javaansche monumenten voor de huidige en toekomstige javaanse cultuur?" *Djawa* 4, no. 4 (1931): 167–74.

Chapman, W. *A Heritage of Ruins: The Ancient Sites of Southeast Asia and Their Conservation*. Honolulu: University of Hawai'i Press, 2014.

Citizen Journalism. "Komisi X Dukung Mojokerto Kembangkan Situs Kerajaan Majapahit". 13 February 2012 <http//www.citizenjournalism.com/world-news/indonesia/cj-dpr-ri-news/komisi-x-dukung-mojokerto-kembangkan-situs-kerajaan-majapahit/>.

Dahles, H. *Tourism, Heritage, and National Culture in Java: Dilemmas of Local Community*. Richmond: Curzon, 2001.

Departemen Pariwisata, Pos, dan Telekomunikasi. *Sejarah dan Pembangunan Pariwisata, Pos, dan Telekomunikasi*. Jakarta: Departemen Pariwisata, Pos, dan Telekomunikasi, 1990.

Gomperts, A., A. Haag, and P. Carey. "Rediscovering the Capital of Majapahit". *SPAFA Journal* 20, no. 2 (2010): 12–15.

———. "The Archaeological Identification of the Majapahit Royal Palace: Prapanca's 1365 Description Projected onto Satellite Imagery". *Journal of the Siam Society* 102 (2014): 67–118.

Harvey, D.C. "'National' Identities and the Politics of Ancient Heritage: Continuity and Change at Ancient Monuments in Britain and Ireland". *Transactions of the Institute of British Geographers*, n.s., 28, no. 4 (2003): 473–87.

Herzfeld, M. "Resilience and the Myth of Intangibility: Muted Mutterings from the Asian Undergrowth". Keynote paper at The Resilience of Vernacular Heritage in Asian Cities Conference, Singapore, 6–7 November 2014.

Jawa Pos. "Pabrik Baja Harus Dihentikan: Komisi X DPR RI Datang ke Trowulan". 13 September 2013*a*.

———. "Sembilan Titik Aman". 2013*b*.

———. "Siapkan Raperda Cagar Budaya Untuk Melindungi Situs". 2013*c*.

Kodhyat, H. *Sejarah Pariwisata dan Perkembangannya di Indonesia*. Jakarta: Grasindo, 1996.

Kompas. "Menbudpar: Pusat Informasi Majapahit Akan Didesain Ulang". 5 January 2009 <http://nasional.kompas.com/read/2009/01/05/21390036/Menbudpar.Pusat.Informasi.Majapahit.Akan.Didesain.Ulang> (accessed 27 June 2013).

———. "Pembangunan Pusat Informasi Majapahit Niatnya Baik". 5 January 2009 <http://nasional.kompas.com/read/2009/01/05/20431372/> (accessed 27 June 2013).

Krom, N.J. "De Oudheden van Modjokerto". *Nederlandsch Indië: Oud & Nieuw: Maandblaad gewijd aan bouwkunst, archaeologies, land-en volkenkunde, kunstnijverheid, handel en verkeer, cultures, mijnbouw, hygiene*, no. 3 (1916): 1–20.

Lembaga Ilmu Pengetahuan Indonesia. *Aspek-Aspek Sosial, Ekonomi, dan Kultural Daerah Bekas Wilayah Keraton Majapahit Sebagai Daerah Pariwisata*. Proyek Penelitian Dinamika Masyarakat. Jakarta: LIPI, 1988.

Lenzerini, F. "Intangible Cultural Heritage: The Living Culture of Peoples". *European Journal of International Law* 22, no. 1 (2011): 101–20.

Li, N. "Preserving Urban Landscapes as Public History: The Chinese Context". *Public Historian* 32, no. 4 (2010): 51–61.

Miksic, John, ed. *The Legacy of Majapahit*. Singapore: National Museum of Singapore, 1995.

Moendardjito et al. *Rencana Induk Arkeologi Bekas Kota Kerajaan Majapahit Trowulan*. Jakarta: Proyek Pemugaran dan Pemeliharaan Peninggalan Sejarah dan Purbakala, 1986.

Muljana, S. *Tafsir Sejarah Nagarakretagama*. Jogjakarta: LKiS, 2006.

Pusat Penelitian dan Pengembangan Kebudayaan. *Kajian Integratid Pengembangan Situs Kerajaan Majapahit di Trowulan*. Badan Pengembangan Sumber Daya. Jakarta: Departemen Kebudayaan dan Pariwisata, 2008.

Portenau, O.d. "Travels of Oderic of Portenau, into China and the East, in 1318". In *Java: A Travellers' Anthology*, edited by J. Rush, pp. 1–2. New York: Oxford University Press, 1996.

Quilty, M.C. *Textual Empires: A Reading of Early British Histories of Southeast Asia*. Clayton: Monash Asia Institute, 1988.

Riana, I.K. *Kakawin Desawarnnana uthawi Nagarakretagama*. Jakarta: Penerbit Buku Kompas, 2009.

Ricklefs, M. *A History of Modern Indonesia Since c.1200*, 4th ed. Palo Alto: Stanford University Press, 2008.

Soekmono. *Menapak Jejak Arkeologi Indonesia*. Jakarta: M3 books, 2002.

Stutterheim, W.F. "De kraton van Majapahit". *Verhandelingen van Het Koninklijk Instituut voor Taal-, Land-, en Volkenkunde*, vol. 7. The Hague: Nijhoff, 1948.

Tedjo, B. "Baskoro Tedjo dan Kontroversi Trowulan". 17 January 2009 <http://heptadesain.wordpress.com/2009/01/17/baskoro-tedjo-dan-kontroversi-trowulan/> (accessed 21 June 2013).

Tunbridge, J.E., and G.J. Ashworth. *Dissonant Heritage — The Management of the Past as a Resource in Conflict*. Wiley, 1996.

5

The Reconstruction of Heritage in Rural Vietnam: An Analysis of State and Local Dynamics

Hy V. Luong

We have lived not only in the era of globalization but also in the age of heritagization. More and more sites and activities have been officially designated as tangible or intangible heritage, from the local level to the international. Many scholars have attributed the making and remaking of heritage, both tangible and intangible, to globalization and state policies, specifically to the impact of the accelerating international tourist flow as well as to state efforts to shape distinctive national identities and to attract international tourists through cultural-historical heritage.

International research on the remaking of heritage in Vietnam — which has focused on major tourist attractions like UNESCO-designated heritage sites in Huế and Hội An — has similarly emphasized the impact of global forces and state policies (see Long 2003 and Salemink 2007 regarding the Huế festival). Vietnamese research has strongly centred on state policy issues, such as how to maintain or to manage heritage in the context of globalization and urbanization (Trương Thìn 1993; Bùi Hoài Sơn 2009; Đặng văn Bài 2012). However, in numerous localities throughout Vietnam, heritage is being made and remade far from the domestic and international tourist gaze, and with little state support. In this chapter, I suggest that local networks and regionally varying community dynamics play *at least* as an important role as global forces and state policies in the making and remaking of tangible and intangible heritage in Vietnam.

Focusing on rural/semi-rural festivals normally linked to sacred spaces in particular localities, I analyse why the revival of festivals as intangible heritage is much stronger in the Red River delta of northern Vietnam than elsewhere in the country. According to 2006 statistics from the Department of Community Culture (Vietnamese Ministry of Culture, Sports and Tourism), the Red River delta, although home to only 21.6 per cent of the Vietnamese population, witnessed the celebration of 3,650 festivals (46 per cent of all festivals in Vietnam in 2006). The Mekong delta of southern Vietnam, with 20.7 per cent of the Vietnamese population, had only 1,234 festivals (15 per cent of all festivals in Vietnam that year). Of the two main metropolitan areas in Vietnam, Hanoi had 1,097 festivals (14 per cent) while Hồ Chí Minh City, despite having a larger population, had only 91 festivals (1.1 per cent; see appendix).

In order to explain the differences in community festivals as intangible heritage between the Mekong and the Red River deltas, we need to take into account the differences in sociocultural dynamics between these two regions, specifically a stronger sense of village identity, tighter intra-community networks, more intense inter-village competition, less diverse ritual institutions, and less commercialization of services in the northern Red River delta than in the southern Mekong delta. I illustrate these differences on the basis of data from a comparative and longitudinal study of Hoài Thị village in Bắc Ninh province (in the Red River delta) and of Khánh Hậu in Long An province (in the Mekong delta).

The Dynamics of Rituals and Festivals as Intangible Heritage: A Comparative Analysis of Two Communities

Overview of the Two Communities

The village of Hoài Thị (pop. 955 in 2000, 1,141 in 2012) is one of six in the commune of Liên Bão, Tiên Du district, in Bắc Ninh province. At a

distance of twenty-seven kilometres from Hà Nội, it is situated near the
Hà Nội-Bắc Ninh expressway, which continues north towards Lạng Sơn
on the Chinese border. The community of Khánh Hậu (pop. 10,696 in
2000, 14,213 in 2012), located sixty kilometres south of Hồ Chí Minh City,
is on the principal highway from Hồ Chí Minh City to the Mekong delta.[1]

In comparison to Hoài Thị, Khánh Hậu is a more open and diverse
community, not only spatially but also socioculturally and in relation to
the global economy.

Spatially, the settlement pattern in Hoài Thị is nucleated, while that in
Khánh Hậu is dispersed, with households spread out along roads, rivers
and canals. This difference between Hoài Thị and Khánh Hậu is typical of
rural communities in the Red River delta and the Mekong delta.

Economically, Khánh Hậu is well integrated into the global economy,
partly through its extensive rice exports.[2] Beyond agriculture, four foreign-
capital factories were set up in Khánh Hậu in the period 2000 to 2012,
bringing the number of foreign factories to five, each of which employs a
few hundred workers. In 2012, 10.5 per cent of the Khánh Hậu workforce
were employed in enterprises with foreign capital. In contrast, in Hoài Thị,
rice was cultivated mainly for subsistence; most of the rice grown in Hoài
Thị was retained for local consumption (99 per cent in 2000 and 77 per cent
in 2012, according to our socio-economic censuses of village households).
Beyond agriculture, by 2012, 16 per cent of the adult workforce in Hoài
Thị worked in foreign enterprises, mostly in nearby industrial zones.
Despite having a higher proportion of the local workforce employed in
foreign enterprises, as Hoài Thị had a subsistence-oriented agriculture,
like most other villages in the Red River delta, Hoài Thị participated in
the global economy to a lesser extent than Khánh Hậu and most other
southern communities.

In the 2000 to 2012 period, Khánh Hậu had higher per capita net income
than Hoài Thị. Our household surveys reveal that the gap in annual per
capita income between the two communities was relatively large in 2000
(4.13 million Vietnamese dong, or US$290, in Khánh Hậu versus 2.48 million
dong, or US$174, in Hoài Thị; the former being 67 per cent higher than
the latter). By 2012, because per capita income in Hoài Thị had increased
significantly, this gap had narrowed: 31.12 million dong (US$1,482) in
Khánh Hậu versus 22.97 million dong (US$1,094) in Hoài Thị, the former
being 35 per cent higher than the latter; see Figure 5.1.[3]

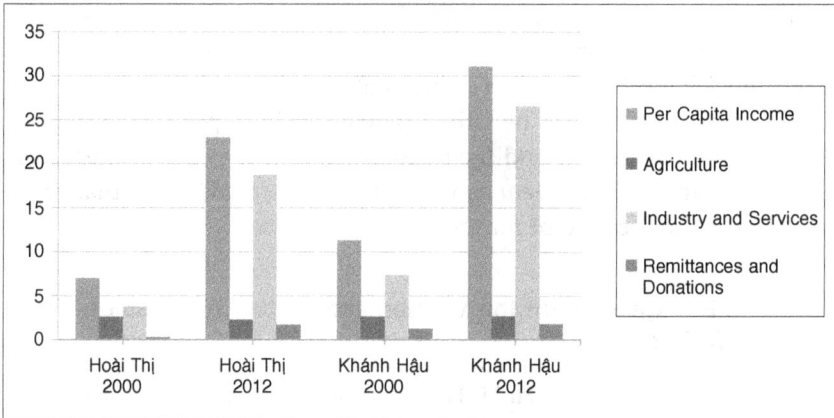

FIGURE 5.1   Per capita net income (in million dong constant 2012) and income sources in Hoài Thị and Khánh Hậu, 2000 and 2012.

The ritual landscape of Khánh Hậu is also more open and diverse than that of Hoài Thị. Hoài Thị has only one communal house (*đình*) and one Buddhist pagoda (both renovated in the mid-1990s), and one small shrine. In contrast, Khánh Hậu has two communal houses, two Buddhist pagodas, three Cao Đài temples, one Quan Công temple, the Marshal Nguyễn Huỳnh Đức shrine, as well as sixteen small shrines throughout the commune.[4] Because, in the 2000–2012 period, Khánh Hậu had ten to twelve times the population of Hoài Thị, it is not surprising that the number of public ritual sites was larger in Khánh Hậu than in Hoài Thị.

A more significant difference is the more open and diverse ritual landscape in the southern community of Khánh Hậu than in the northern village of Hoài Thị. More specifically, the three Cao Đài temples in the former locality belong to three different Cao Đài sects (Tiên Thiên, Ban Chinh Đạo Bến Tre, and Ban Chinh Đạo Đô Thành). A number of Khánh Hậu villagers also follow two other Cao Đài sects (Tây Ninh and Minh Chơn Lý) and worship at Cao Đài temples in the provincial capital of Tân An and in a neighbouring commune. Khánh Hậu villagers who follow Catholicism attend masses at the Catholic church in Tân An. Many villagers, especially female ones, also travel a few hundred kilometres to the Lady of the Realm temple in Châu Đốc province near the Cambodian border. On the other hand, many people from other communes attend the bimonthly ceremonies at the Tiên Thiên Cao Đài temple in Khánh Hậu.

The major annual event on the ninth day of the ninth lunar month at the Nguyễn Huỳnh Đức shrine attracts visitors from as far away as Hồ Chí Minh City. Khánh Hậu has two communal houses because it was formed in 1917 from the merger of two villages (Hickey 1964, pp. 1, 8). If in Hoài Thị the communal house and the pagoda serve as the central ritual sites respectively for male and female villagers, in Khánh Hậu no ritual space can serve as the focal point for the entire community.

Historical Background on the Vietnamese State's Repression of Local Heritage

The two communities of Hoài Thị and Khánh Hậu differ not only in the openness of their socio-spatial landscapes but also in the historical trajectory of state–community interaction with regard to local heritage. More specifically, the northern community of Hoài Thị experienced four decades of the state's repression of past "feudal" and superstitious vestiges, while the southern community of Khánh Hậu was affected by this for the shorter period of a decade and a half.

The public ritual space in Hoài Thị before 1945 included a communal house (đình), the tomb of the village tutelary deity (nghè), two pagodas, a village shrine, and smaller neighbourhood ones.[5] Beginning with the 1946–54 war, the public ritual space in Hoài Thị gradually contracted. The communal house was partially destroyed as part of the "scorched earth" policy of the Vietminh under the leadership of Hồ Chí Minh. The large village pagoda (Đại Bi) burned down in 1949 for reasons which are unclear. The village leadership had the front building of the đình (communal house) taken apart in 1957 to build a separate cultural house in the village, and seven years later turned the communal house area into the warehouse of the agricultural cooperative. The space of the communal house was reduced to the inner sanctum and its small front yard. According to an elderly female villager, the smaller village pagoda was destroyed in 1966–68, with only two towers remaining. Elderly female villagers subsequently held their prayer sessions in a sheltered area just in front of the tomb of the tutelary deity. Both the communal house and the new makeshift pagoda became dilapidated over the course of four decades.

In Hoài Thị, not only did ritual space but also public ritual activities contract significantly; male rituals at the communal house faced more difficulties than female ones at the pagoda. The latter's two prayer sessions every month, on the first and fifteenth days of each lunar month, have continued unabated. In contrast, from 1954 to 1958, male villagers could not conduct the usual twice-monthly worship of the village tutelary deity at the communal house. Although the worship resumed after 1958, communal house rituals were greatly simplified. For example, the major deity worship ceremony at the communal house on the village festival day (the tenth of the first lunar month) was no longer performed, although according to one elderly man, even during the period of American bombing (1965–73), a number of families still brought their offerings to the tutelary deity at the communal house on that day.

The aforementioned discontinuities and simplification in public rituals related partly to economic hardships, especially during the 1946–54 war and the period of U.S. bombings. But they resulted primarily from the post-colonial state's ideological perspective that those rituals were not compatible with modernity and science. The state also considered them a waste of resources that could be tapped for development and the war effort (see Luong 2007).

In Khánh Hậu, in terms of physical space, from 1975 to 1988 the local government undertook less radical measures than its Hoài Thị counterpart did three decades earlier. The local government in Khánh Hậu took control of both communal houses as well as the Marshall Đức shrine, the central space in the village that the local landowning elite had controlled either directly or indirectly (Hickey 1964, pp. 214–18, 248–51). The land area of the main communal house (đình Tường Khánh) was reduced by the expansion of the village school and the construction of the police building. Most communal house buildings were turned into living quarters or village offices. The rear sanctuary of the main communal house (tiền vãng house) where village founders were worshipped was turned initially into living quarters for non-village cadres and, from 1980 onwards, into the sales cooperative office. Another side building became an office for village officials to receive people. The main sanctuary of this communal house was left to deteriorate with a leaking roof. The cult committee for this communal house had to "borrow" the sanctuary from the village government for the organization of any traditional ceremony.

In the context of the new local government's control over physical and symbolic space and their dwindling private resources, the vulnerable traditional landowning elite had few choices but to curtail and simplify communal house (đình) rituals and to make symbolic accommodation to the new authorities. As early as May 1975, the socialist regime's troops stationed in Khánh Hậu criticized the waste of resources in the main ceremony of the communal house because of expenditures for the classical opera performance and the slaughter of four pigs and two cattle. Although the records of *đình* expenditures were not available for the 1975–86 period, the 1987 ones indicated that only two medium-sized pigs were sacrificed at the main communal house ritual that year. For thirteen years, between 1976 and 1988, the cult committee of the main *đình* also deleted classical opera performances from the main ceremony at this *đình*. In a dialogic accommodation to the new secular authorities' discursive emphasis, by the late 1980s the invocation to tutelary deities contained references only to Hồ Chí Minh's nation-building achievements, and no longer to deities' titles or any royal deity decrees.

In Khánh Hậu, partly in accordance with the national policy on religious freedom, the local government did not take control of the Buddhist and Cao Đài worship sites, although in the course of land reform the Buddhist pagodas were persuaded to "donate" most of their land to destitute households (none of the Cao Đài temples had any land). More importantly, the local government sought to gradually undermine the authoritative nature of potentially subversive discourse by religious leaders. It focused its attack primarily on the Cao Đài sects that had been hostile to the ideology of the new regime during the first and second Indochina wars (see Luong 1994, pp. 98–99). The local government of Khánh Hậu did not consider the village pagoda, the nuns' pagoda or the Quan Công temple major threats to the construction of a new order, apparently because of their popularity primarily with elderly and middle-aged women.

Ritual Space and Community Festivals: The Reclaiming and Reconstruction of Local Heritage

In both Hoài Thị and Khánh Hậu, as well as in numerous other communities in Vietnam, public ritual space has been renovated over the past quarter century. Community festivals have also intensified, in comparison to the 1954–90 period for Hoài Thị and the 1975–90 period for Khánh Hậu. In both communities the renovation of public ritual space and the intensification of community festivals have involved community reclaiming and restructuring of local heritage. However, these processes differed significantly between Hoài Thị and Khánh Hậu, or more generally between the northern Red

River delta and the southern Mekong delta, due to the more open and diverse socio-spatial landscape, the fairly strong centrifugal force, and the stronger commercialization in the latter than in the former.

In Hoài Thị in 1994–95 the communal house was renovated and expanded (Figure 5.2). The expenses for the renovation and purchase of ritual accessories and attire for the ritual team came to 70 million dong (over US$6,000), of which about half came from the agricultural cooperative in Hoài Thị and most of the rest from villagers' donations. A ritual team (đội tế) composed of elderly male villagers was subsequently established (Figure 5.3). This team played the key role in communal house ceremonies. In 1996 the pagoda in Hoài Thị was also reconstructed at a cost of 70 million dong (Figure 5.4). The cost of renovation of the communal house and pagoda in Hoài Thị amounted to approximately 8.5 per cent of the net incomes of all villagers in the mid-1990s. A number of elderly female villagers also established a female ritual team (đội dâng hương) before the renovation of the pagoda. They purchased their own ritual dresses and

FIGURE 5.2 Communal house in Hoài Thị, renovated in 1995.

FIGURE 5.3 Male ritual team in Hoài Thị in the communal house.

shoes and organized four annual incense-offering ceremonies to Buddhas at the village pagoda (Figure 5.5). Further renovation was conducted at the *đình* and the pagoda over the next five years at a cost of 316 million dong (US$19,610).

In 2001, for the first time in fifty-six years, Hoài Thị villagers organized a tutelary deity procession on the day of the village festival (the tenth day of the first lunar month). It was the second village in Liên Bão commune to organize such a procession in the post-colonial era. The tutelary procession in 2001 was more elaborate than those held during the French colonial period, because over a hundred villagers participated and because the procession went around the village instead of simply going from the tomb of the deity to the communal house next door.[6] In 2002, as our research team agreed to videotape the rituals on the ninth and tenth days of the first lunar month in Hoài Thị, about two hundred villagers participated in the procession. Villagers and guests donated 10 million dong (about US$700) on the occasion of the village festival

FIGURE 5.4 Hoài Thị pagoda rebuilt in 1996.

in 2001, 7 million dong (about US$500) in 2002, and 8.5 million dong (US$536) in 2005. Virtually all Hoài Thị households made donations on those occasions. The successful mobilization of two hundred villagers for the procession in 2002 was no small feat, because village households were very busy hosting guests and returning relatives at family banquets on the day of the procession and festival. The village festival day had long been the occasion for relatives living not too far away to return to Hoài

FIGURE 5.5 Female ritual team performing a ritual at the pagoda on Hoài Thị festival day.

Thị with their families (husbands, children, and grandchildren) and for the in-laws of villagers' children to visit the village. Hoài Thị youth also invited their friends and close classmates from neighbouring villages to participate in family banquets. The tutelary deity procession in Hoài Thị in 2002 took place at the time when Hoài Thị households were busy preparing for banquets and entertaining guests and returning relatives. But despite conflicting obligations, many villagers participated in the tutelary deity procession, which rendered this tenth day of the first lunar month more festive and made it a community-wide festival (see also Lương Văn Hy and Trương Huyền Chi 2012) (Figures 5.6 and 5.7). Thus, besides effectively mobilizing resources within the community for the gradual improvement of their sacred ritual space, Hoài Thị villagers also worked together to recreate at a relatively low cost an annual community festival as their intangible heritage.

In Khánh Hậu, community ritual space and rituals have also undergone a major transformation since the late 1980s. However, this transformation

FIGURE 5.6   Tutelary deity procession on Hoài Thị festival day, 2005.

FIGURE 5.7   Tutelary deity procession on Hoài Thị festival day, 2005.

process has been different from that in Hoài Thị due to the differences in historical context and local sociocultural landscape.

As far as the ritual space was concerned, in 1988 the administration of the Khánh Hậu commune returned the two communal houses to the two communal-house management committees. In 1993 the Nguyễn Huỳnh Đức shrine was also designated a national heritage site. Local ritual space began to be renovated from the early 1990s onwards.

However, whilst per capita income was considerably higher in Khánh Hậu than in Hoài Thị, the contributions of Khánh Hậu villagers to the fund for the renovation of local ritual space were more modest and slower in coming. Prior to 2001, Khánh Hậu villagers made their largest financial contribution to ritual space renovation when they donated 35 million dong (US$3,095) and two thousand labour days (equivalent to 20 million dong) for the renovation of the main pagoda in 1992 and 14 million dong (about US$930) to the repair of the pagoda fence in 2001.

The most expensive renovations in Khánh Hậu over the past two decades have been funded mainly by non-members of the community. In chronological order, they include:

1. Thiên Phước (nun) pagoda, 1994: 800 million dong (over US$70,000) (Figure 5.8);
2. Nguyễn Huỳnh Đức shrine, 2000: 350 million dong (about US$25,000) (Figure 5.9);
3. Quan Công temple, 2008: over 400 million dong (about US$25,000) (Figure 5.10);
4. Diêu Quang pagoda (main village pagoda), 2010: renovation cost estimated at almost a billion dong (about US$50,000) (Figures 5.11 and 5.12);
5. Thiên Phước (nun) pagoda, 2007–11: slightly over a billion dong (slightly over US$50,000) for the construction of guest houses for religious students;
6. Ban Chỉnh Đạo (Cao Đài) temple, 2011: about 450 million dong (about US$22,500); and
7. Tiên Thiên (Cao Đài) temple: about 1.8 billion dong by 2013 (about US$85,700).

The renovation of religious sites in Khánh Hậu was funded mainly by religious devotees from elsewhere, and the ancestral shrine for the Nguyễn Huỳnh patrilineage was renovated with funding primarily from

FIGURE 5.8 Thiên Phước (nun) pagoda, main building renovated in 1994.

FIGURE 5.9 Renovated Nguyễn Huỳnh Đức shrine.

FIGURE 5.10   Quan Công temple — old building on the left and new building on the right.

FIGURE 5.11   Renovated Diêu Quang pagoda.

FIGURE 5.12 Main worship hall of Diêu Quang pagoda.

descendants no longer residing in Khánh Hậu.[7] This reflects the more open social and religious landscape of Khánh Hậu.

In contrast to the religious sites renovated with fairly good funding were the communal houses of Nhơn Hậu and Tường Khánh (serving, respectively, the wards of Tân Khánh and Khánh Hậu). The Nhơn Hậu communal house (Figure 5.13) was renovated in 2006 at a reported cost of a hundred million dong, of which about eighty million (about US$5,000) came from Khánh Hậu villagers. This amount was modest in relation to the estimated total income of US$1.5 million in 2006 for four thousand villagers living in the domain of this communal house. In 2013 it looked nondescript, especially in comparison to the Quan Công temple nearby (Figure 5.10), of which the renovation was funded by Buddhist devotees elsewhere with the objective of converting it into a Buddhist pagoda.

The Tường Khánh communal house fared better with the major renovation in 2007 which was funded mainly by donations of approximately 500 million dong (about US$31,000) by Khánh Hậu villagers. However, as the domain of the Tường Khánh communal house had about seven thousand people with an estimated total income of US$2.9 million in 2007, the donations amounted to only about 1.1 per cent of total local income. This percentage was modest in comparison to the contributions of Hoài Thị villagers to the renovation of the Hoài Thị communal house and pagoda more than a decade earlier, which represented 8.5 per cent of total local income at the time.

Furthermore, besides donations, the communal house management committee had to borrow about 200 million dong to complete the renovation in 2007, and about 170 million dong for further work in the early 2010s; and these debts (amounting to approximately 0.6 per cent of annual local income) had not been paid off by 2013, due to unsuccessful local fundraising. In contrast, in Hoài Thị in 2007 the management committee for the communal house decided to invest 316 million dong (US$19,610) for renovation of the tomb of the tutelary deity and construction of a kitchen and guest room for the communal house. Besides donations, many villagers lent money interest-free for this project. By 2013 the communal

FIGURE 5.13 Nhơn Hậu communal house.

FIGURE 5.14   Renovated Tường Khánh communal house.

house and pagoda management committee in Hoài Thị was able to pay off this debt with the savings from annual festival donations.

The difficulties that the community of Khánh Hậu faced were not limited to the mobilization of financial resources for the renovation of its non-religious ritual space. In Khánh Hậu, community festivals (the worship of Marshal Nguyễn Huỳnh Đức and the main ritual at the communal house) had much lower rates of participation, involved community organizations to a much lesser degree, and incurred much higher expenses due to the higher degree of commercialization in the local economy. Whilst tutelary deity processions in Hoài Thị had at least 150 participants and at times even over 200 participants, all on a voluntary basis, the procession in Khánh Hậu in 2013 to bring royal decrees for the tutelary deity to the communal house had only twenty-nine participants, including fifteen hired hands.[8] And while the rituals within the communal house and the pagoda in Hoài Thị were conducted by two all-volunteer teams (a male team at the communal house and a female team at the pagoda), supplemented by the all-volunteer female ritual teams from some other communities, those at the main (Tường Khánh) communal house in Khánh Hậu had to involve six paid ritual assistants, complemented by some paid female opera singers. And while in Hoài Thị villagers actively participated in a performing arts show as part of the village festival, either as volunteer performers or as audience, in Khánh Hậu the communal house organizing committee had to hire a classical opera troupe for performances, at the cost of over US$1,000. The attendance at these opera performances in 2013 was quite small: peaking at seventy in the early evening of the first day and dropping to as low as thirty-eight. Most members of the audience were middle-aged or elderly women. The classical opera performances continued a long-standing tradition in Khánh Hậu, but they attracted fewer people in the age of television, VCRs and the Internet and amid changing tastes for performing arts of the local population. In Hoài Thị, villagers had diverse tastes too, but they showed up in a large number to support family members, relatives and friends who participated in different shows.

Festival organizers in Khánh Hậu explained the hiring of six ritual assistants, four musicians and a classical opera troupe in terms of the busy lives of community members and the forgone earning opportunities for community participants (specifically ritual team members). However, in Hoài Thị, community members engaged in wage labour to the same degree, yet they were willing to donate time and efforts to organize annually a community festival, including a festive performing arts show.[9]

In order to understand the difference in heritage reconstruction between the two studied communities and between the northern Red River delta and the southern Mekong delta in general, I suggest that we need to take into account their differences in local social networks and identities.

Social Networks and Community Festival Participation

Social networks in Hoài Thị and in Red River delta villages in general are tighter than those in the Mekong delta because of village endogamy over generations and the proliferation of intra-village voluntary associations in the Red River delta. Figure 5.15 shows that among the villagers in Hoài Thị or Khánh Hậu that had married and were still living there in 2005, the percentage of community-endogamous marriages was much higher in Hoài Thị (50 per cent) than in Khánh Hậu (24 per cent).[10] The spouses who married into the Khánh Hậu community also came from a much wider geographical area than those marrying into Hoài Thị. Figure 5.16 shows that almost 40 per cent of the marriages of Khánh Hậu residents involved spouses from other provinces, and 20 per cent involved spouses from other districts in Long An province.[11] The respective percentages were 7 per cent and 6 per cent in Hoài Thị. Because of the high rate of village endogamy over generations, two Hoài Thị villagers A and B normally had multiple kinship relations to each other (see Luong and Diệp Đình Hoa 2000, pp. 50–51).

The multiplicity of relations between any two villagers in Hoài Thị also increased because of the proliferation of intra-village voluntary associations. Hoài Thị villagers established numerous associations, the most important of which were the same-age associations (*hội đồng niên,* mainly among male villagers), the education-promotion associations (*hội khuyến học*), and the Buddhist elderly women's association. For every 100 villagers above the age of 16 in Hoài Thị, there were 112 association memberships among men and 70 among women. The respective figures for Khánh Hậu were 17 and 7.6 (see Figure 5.17; see also Luong 2016).[12]

In the process of renovating ritual space and organizing community rituals and festivals, in Hoài Thị the elderly played a crucial role through their associations based at the communal house and the pagoda and through their extensive and tight social networks in the community. In Hoài Thị it was the elderly who organized the fundraising campaign to renovate the communal house and the pagoda in the mid-1990s. They

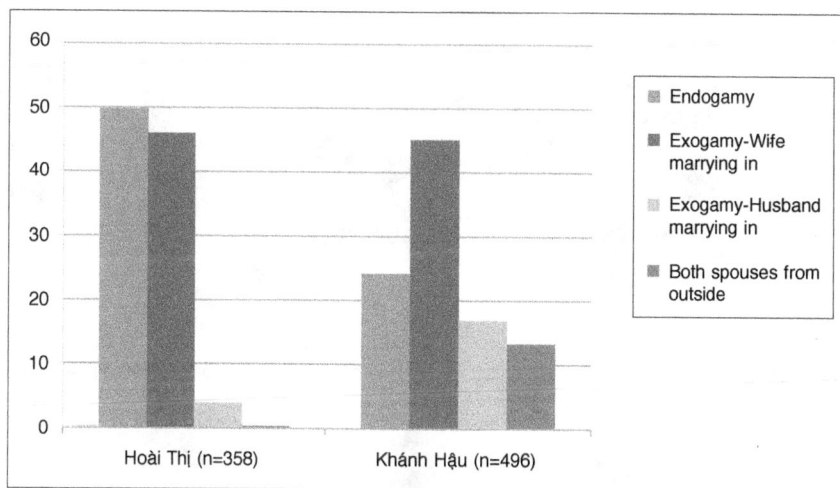

FIGURE 5.15 Percentages of community-endogamous and exogamous marriages in Hoài Thị and Khánh Hậu.

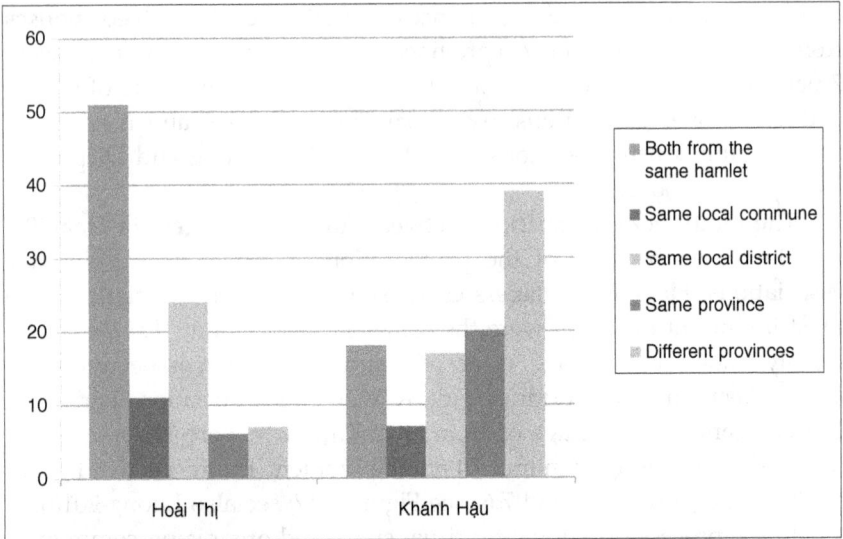

FIGURE 5.16   Native origins of spouses (percentage of couples from).

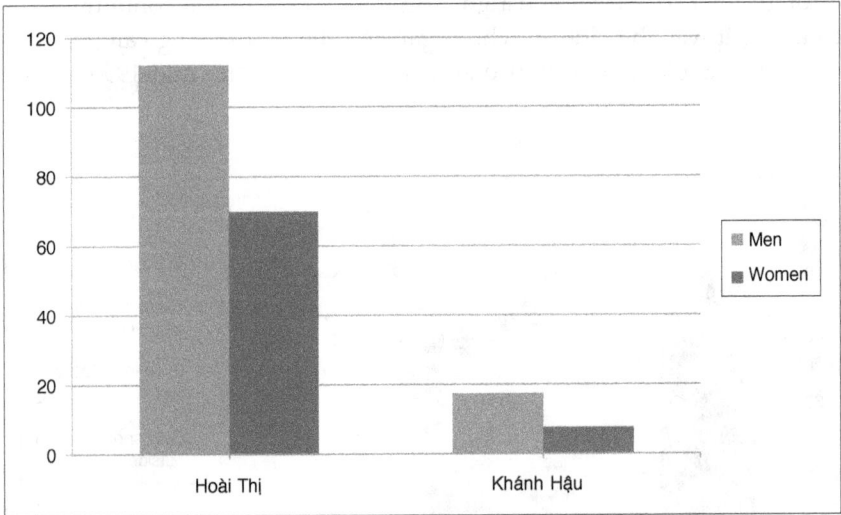

FIGURE 5.17   Voluntary association membership: Number of memberships per 100 residents above the age of 16.

also played the leading role in the reconstruction of the tutelary deity procession on village festival day in 2001 and thereafter. They were motivated by a strong sense of village identity and by competition with surrounding villages (the village of Hoài Thượng in the same Liên Bão commune resurrected its tutelary deity procession in 1994.) Furthermore, in Hoài Thị, donors' names were written on scrolls visibly displayed in the communal house and the pagoda. On the occasion of the village festival, all village households, except those in official mourning for deceased relatives, participated in one or more community event. At the approach of the festival, the village loudspeaker announced the names of donors and their donation amounts. This and the tight social network within the village made it difficult for any village household not to contribute to the village festival fund. Hoài Thị villagers mobilized one another to contribute time, labour and financial resources in order to renovate ritual space and to organize the village festival out of a strong sense of village identity and in competition with surrounding villages, not to attract tourists or for profits, because there was no expectation by any Hoài Thị villager about any domestic or international tourists coming to the Hoài Thị village festival. In contrast, in Khánh Hậu in the southern Mekong delta, the more open spatial landscape, the weaker sense of community identity, and the looser local kinship and social networks made it difficult to mobilize community members to contribute time, labour or financial resources to the renovation of the non-religious ritual space and to community events.

Conclusion

Over the last two decades the flow of domestic and international tourists have played an important role in the development and maintenance of *some* festivals in Vietnam, specifically the festivals at the Hương pagoda in the northern Red River delta, at the UNESCO-designated World Heritage sites in Hội An and Huế in Central Vietnam, and in some other localities (see Long 2003 and Salemink 2007 regarding the Huế festival). But festivals attracting tourists make up a very small number among the almost eight thousand festivals held in Vietnam in 2006. In this chapter I have argued that the improved economic conditions in most households in Vietnam have helped the reconstruction of local heritage, specifically the organization of community festivals, as well as the renovation of ritual space linked to these festivals. But community festivals as local intangible heritage have intensified not for the motives of profit. The differences between the northern Red River delta and the southern Mekong delta in the reconstruction of community festivals have had nothing to do with state policies either, since state policies were formulated at the national level and have remained the same for the different regions of Vietnam. In order to explain the differences in the reconstruction of festivals between the northern Red River delta and the southern Mekong delta, I argue that we need to take into account the differences in sociocultural dynamics at the community level. More specifically, Red River delta communities have tighter intra-community networks, a stronger sense of village identity, more intense inter-village competition, and less diverse ritual institutions. All of these factors help to make ritual institutions like the communal house and the village pagoda the focal points for community activities and facilitate the organization of community-wide village festivals in the Red River delta. They help to explain why the intangible heritage of community festivals is stronger in rural communities in the Red River delta than in those in the Mekong delta. It would be problematic to reduce the economic and sociocultural changes to only globalization and international capital or to a state scheme, and to overlook local sociocultural dynamics.[13]

Appendix
Festivals and Population in Six Regions of Vietnam (2006)

Region	Type of Festival			Population	No. of Administrative Units		
	Community	Other	Total	(millions)	Ward	Town	Commune
Red River Delta	3,502 (49.8%)	148	3,650 (46%)	18.2 (21.6%)	284	103	1,861
including present Hà Nội	1,070 (15.2%)	25	1,097 (14%)	5.9 (7%)	147	22	408
Bắc Ninh	421 (6%)	21	452 (5.7%)	1.01 (1.2%)	9	7	109
Northern Midlands & Highlands	1,339	62	1,401	12.1	157	145	2,399
Central Coast	802	90	892	19.5	244	145	2,497
Central Highlands	147	75	222	4.9	61	47	579
Southeast	244	169	413	12.1	327	42	484
including Hồ Chí Minh City	24 (0.3%)	67	91 (1.1%)	6.1 (7.2%)	259	5	58
Mekong Delta	854 (12.1%)	380	1,234 (15%)	17.4 (20.7%)	157	115	1,288
including Long An	50 (0.7%)	2	52 (0.65%)	1.4 (1.7%)	9	15	166
Total	7,039	927	7,966	84.2	1,230	597	9,098

Note: In the 2006 statistical yearbook by the General Statistics Office of Vietnam, Ninh Thuận and Bình Thuận provinces are considered to belong to the Southeast. In this table they are considered to belong to the Central Coast, as they have been for a long time in Vietnam.
Sources: Việt Nam, Cục văn hóa cơ sở 2008, pp. 11–14; and Vietnam, Tổng Cục thống kê 2007.

Notes

1. In 2006 the commune of Khánh Hậu was divided into two urban wards, Khánh Hậu and Tân Khánh, both within the municipality of Tân An. I will use the phrase "the community of Khánh Hậu", given the administrative change from "commune" to "ward" in the 2000–2012 period under focus. The population of Khánh Hậu grew significantly from 2000 to 2012 because boarding houses had been constructed by 2012 to accommodate students at a new university located in Khánh Hậu, as well as workers from elsewhere employed in Khánh Hậu factories.

2. Most of the rice grown in Khánh Hậu was sold for export (94 per cent in 2000 and 98 per cent in 2012). The local rice retained for consumption in Khánh Hậu averaged less than fifteen kilograms per person per year, and Khánh Hậu villagers purchased less-expensive rice from the Plain of Reeds (Đồng Tháp Mười) for their own consumption.

3. The data on household incomes in Hoài Thị and Khánh Hậu are from the census of all Hoài Thị households and a panel study of 14 per cent of Khánh Hậu households which were chosen by random probability sampling in December 2000 and restudied in November 2012. By 2012, the net incomes from agriculture (including animal husbandry), accounted for only 9.8 per cent of the incomes of Hoài Thị households and 8.5 per cent of those in Khánh Hậu.

4. Marshal Nguyễn Huỳnh Đức, a native of Khánh Hậu, assisted King Gia Long (1802–20) in regaining the throne and became an influential mandarin during the latter's reign. Cao Đài is a syncretic religion — the pantheon of which includes Buddha and Jesus, among other figures — that emerged in southern Vietnam in the 1920s. It has many sects (see Smith 1970a, 1970b; Werner 1981; Hoskins 2015). Quan Công was a deified Chinese general in the Three Kingdom period.

5. The communal house of Hoài Thị is for the worship of Princess Đống Long of the Lý dynasty, who lived in the twelfth century. Elderly villagers have mentioned that during the 1946–54 war with the French the village still had two pagodas. Đại Bi pagoda (inside the village, next to the communal house) reportedly had a five-room principal building, a five-room bell tower, and possibly as many as eighteen rooms for receiving guests. Ngô Linh pagoda, located outside the village settlement, had a two-room building and two small towers. The village shrines reportedly are for the worship of miscellaneous female deities and ghosts.

6. Elderly informants reported that in the 1940s only about forty male villagers participated in the tutelary deity procession.

7. An informed member of the Nguyễn Huỳnh patrilineage reported that the principal donor to the Nguyễn Huỳnh Đức shrine renovation fund was a

long-lost lineage member working in business in the city of Cần Thơ in the Mekong delta. Khánh Hậu villagers also reported that some other members of this lineage living overseas made fairly important financial contributions.

8. The second procession to return the tutelary deity decrees to their storing place at an official's house had only twenty-five people, including fourteen hired hands.

9. In Khánh Hậu, the only two community organizations besides the communal house management committee that donated their time were the Diêu Quang pagoda prayer group and a Cao Đài temple group. Since the renovation of the main communal house in 2007, both groups have performed two new rituals at this communal house.

10. If the unit of analysis was taken as Hoài Thị village or a hamlet in Khánh Hậu, not the commune of Khánh Hậu, the percentage of marriages involving village/hamlet endogamy would be 18 per cent in Khánh Hậu and 50 per cent in Hoài Thị.

11. The high percentage of spouses in Khánh Hậu coming from other provinces reflects the fact that Khánh Hậu is located next to Tiền Giang province. Khánh Hậu's percentage of spouses from other provinces is much higher than those in most other Mekong delta communities.

12. Both Hoài Thị and Khánh Hậu also had government-established mass organizations, such as Women's, Peasant, Elderly, Youth Associations, and in the case of Khánh Hậu, trade unions. Among women above the age of sixteen, the percentage joining the Women's Association was 44 per cent in Hoài Thị and 11 per cent in the Dinh hamet of Khánh Hậu. For every 100 villagers above the age of sixteen, there was an average of 84 mass organization memberships among Hoài Thị men and women, and 14 memberships among men and 9 memberships among women in Khánh Hậu.

13. See also Yang (2000) regarding the ritual economy in rural China and her questioning of reductionist analyses emphasizing the role of capitalism.

References

Bùi Hoài Sơn. *Quản lý lễ hội truyền thống của người Việt* [Managing Vietnamese traditional festivals]. Hanoi: Nhà xuất bản Văn hóa dân tộc, 2009.

Đặng Văn Bài. "Vấn đề bảo tồn và phát huy giá trị văn hóa của lễ hội truyền thống" [The issue of conserving and promoting cultural values through traditional festivals]. In *Bảo tồn và phát huy lễ hội cổ truyền trong xã hội Việt Nam đương đại* [The conservation and promotion of traditional festivals in contemporary Vietnamese society], edited by Việt Văn hóa nghệ thuật Việt Nam [Vietnam Institute of Cultural and Arts Studies], pp. 38–47. Hanoi: Nhà xuất bản Văn hóa thông tin, 2012.

Hickey, Gerald. *Village in Vietnam*. New Haven: Yale University Press, 1964.

Hoskins, Janet. *The Divine Eye and the Diaspora*. Honolulu: University of Hawai'i Press, 2015.

Lê Hồng Lý. *Sự tác động của kinh tế thị trường vào lễ hội tín ngưỡng* [The impact of market economy on rituals, festivals, and beliefs]. Hanoi: Nhà xuất bản Văn hoá thông tin and Viện Văn hoá, 2006.

Long, Colin. "Feudalism in the Service of the Revolution: Reclaiming Heritage in Hue". *Critical Asian Studies* 35, no. 4 (2003): 535–58.

Luong, Hy V. "The Marxist State and the Dialogic Re-Structuration of Culture in Northern Vietnam". In *Indochina: Social and Cultural Change*, Keck Center for International and Strategic Studies, monograph No. 7, edited by D. Elliott, H.V. Luong, B. Kiernan, and T. Mahoney, pp. 79–117. Claremont: Claremont McKenna College, 1994.

———. "The Restructuring of Vietnamese Nationalism, 1954–2006". *Pacific Affairs* 80, no. 3 (2007): 439–53.

———. "Dòng quà tặng và vốn xã hội trong 2 cộng đồng nông thôn Việt Nam" [The flow of gifts and social capital in two rural Vietnamese communities]. In *Hiện đại và động thái của truyền thống ở Việt Nam: Những cách tiếp cận nhân học* [Modernities and the dynamics of tradition in Vietnam: Anthropological approaches], vol. 1, edited by Lương Văn Hy, Ngô Văn Lệ, Nguyễn Văn Tiệp, and và Phan Thị Yến Tuyết, pp. 397–424. Hồ Chí Minh City: National University of Hồ Chí Minh City Press, 2010.

———. "Social Relations, Regional Variation, and Economic Inequality in Contemporary Vietnam: A View from Two Rural Vietnamese Communities". In *Connected and Disconnected in Vietnam*, edited by Philip Taylor, pp. 41–72. Canberra: Australian National University Press, 2016.

Luong, Hy V., and Diệp Đình Hoa. "Bốn cộng đồng nông thôn và thành thị Việt Nam: Cảnh quan kinh tế, xã hội và văn hoá" [Four rural and urban communities in Vietnam: Economic, social, and cultural landscapes]. In *Ngôn từ, giới, và nhóm xã hội từ hiện thực tiếng Việt* [Discourse, gender, and social groups: Vietnamese reality], edited by Hy V. Luong, pp. 39–97. Hanoi: Social Science Press, 2000.

Luong, Văn Hy (Hy V. Luong) và Trương Huyền Chi. "Thương thảo để tái lập và sáng tạo "truyền thống": Tiến trình tái cấu trúc lễ hội cộng đồng tại một làng Bắc bộ" [Negotiation to re-establish and to invent "tradition": The re-structuring of a community festival in a North Vietnamese village]. In *Những thành tựu nghiên cứu bước đầu của Khoa Nhân học*, pp. 235–79. Hồ Chí Minh City: National University of Hồ Chí Minh City Press, 2012.

Mellaissoux, Claude. *Maidens, Meal and Money: Capitalism and the Domestic Economy*. Cambridge: Cambridge University Press, 1981.

Salemink, Oscar. "The Emperor's New Clothes: Re-Fashioning Ritual in the Huế Festival". *Journal of Southeast Asian Studies* 38, no. 3 (2007): 559–82.

Smith, Ralph. "An Introduction to Caodaism 1: Origins and Early History". *Bulletin of the School of Oriental and African Studies* 33, no. 2: (1970*a*): 335–49.

―――. "An Introduction to Caodaism 2: Beliefs and Organisation". *Bulletin of the School of Oriental and African Studies* 33, no. 3 (1970*b*): 573–89.

Taylor, Philip. *Goddess on the Rise: Pilgrimage and Popular Religion in Vietnam.* Honolulu: University of Hawai'i Press, 2004.

Trương Thìn. "Báo cáo sơ kết ba năm thực hiện quy chế mở hội truyền thống" [A preliminary report on the three-year implementation of regulations on traditional festivals]. *Hội nghị hội thảo về lễ hội* [Conference on festivals], pp. 9–20. Hanoi: Bộ Văn hóa –Thông tin, Vụ Văn hóa quần chúng và thư viện, 1993.

Vietnam, Tổng cục thống kê. *Niên Giám Thống Kê-Statistical Yearbook 2006.* Hanoi: Nhà xuất bản Thống kê, 2007.

―――. *Kết quả khảo sát mức sống hộ gia đình năm 2006* [Results of household living standard survey in 2006]. Hanoi: Nhà xuất bản Thống kê, 2008.

Vietnam, Cục Văn hóa cơ sở. *Thống kê lễ hội Việt Nam* [Statistics on festivals in Vietnam]. Hanoi: Cục văn hoá cơ sở, Bộ văn hoá, thể thao, và du lịch, 2008.

Werner, Jayne. *Peasant Politics and Religious Sectarianism: Peasant and Priest in the Cao Dai in Vietnam.* New Haven: Yale University Southeast Asian Studies, 1981.

Winter, Tim. "The Political Economies of Heritage". In *Cultures and Globalization: Heritage, Memory, and Identity,* edited by Helmut Anheier and Yudhishthir Raj Isar, pp. 70–82. Los Angeles: Sage, 2011.

Yang, Mayfair. "Putting Capitalism in Its Place: Economic Hybridity, Bataille, and Ritual Expenditure". *Current Anthropology* 41, no. 4 (2000): 477–509.

6

Performing Cultures, Negotiating Identities: The Cultural Politics of Indigenous Cultural Villages in West Malaysia

Cai Yunci

Influenced by transnational indigenous rights movements and heritage activism, indigenous peoples in Malaysia are actively engaging in the display and performance of their tangible and intangible cultural heritage. This has manifested in demonstrations of traditional crafts, customs and rituals, as well as the recent establishment of indigenous cultural villages, a form of living museum or open-air museum which aims to preserve the "living" traditions and customs of cultural peoples by exhibiting collections of buildings and expressions of cultural heritage in an open-air setting. In this chapter, I explore how indigenous cultural heritage is being instrumentalized by different actors for different agendas, and the cultural politics of this instrumentalization, through a comparative study of two indigenous cultural villages in West Malaysia; namely, the Mah Meri Cultural Village on Carey Island and the Orang Seletar Cultural Centre in Johor Bahru.

A comparative perspective was adopted as I was drawn to the contrast between the two indigenous cultural villages, despite the fact that they were both established to showcase the cultural heritage of the indigenous peoples of West Malaysia. At the Mah Meri Cultural Village, which was established by the government and features a large tourism complex with modern facilities, the Mah Meri villagers felt disenfranchised by the development. In contrast, the Orang Seletar Cultural Centre, which features a small wooden hut constructed by the Orang Seletar villagers from modest funding provided by an international organization, the development played a significant role in the assertion of local indigenous rights.

The comparison of these two indigenous cultural villages offers insights into the workings of a state-initiated "top-down" heritage project represented by the Mah Meri Cultural Village, and those of a community-initiated "bottom-up" heritage project represented by the Orang Seletar Cultural Centre. This chapter attempts to shed light on the implications of UNESCO's recent mandate for the instrumentalization of culture for development and the gradual decentralization of aid provision through intermediary agencies and entrepreneurs in the current age of neo-liberalism. While UNESCO has a laudable mandate to integrate culture and heritage as part of human development strategies aimed at community development, the instrumentalization of culture for development seems to produce uneven outcomes.

My objective is to examine how indigenous cultural heritage has been instrumentalized by the different stakeholders for different agendas in the establishment and management of the two villages, and the cultural politics of the instrumentalization, in order to illuminate how and why there have been different outcomes at these two sites. In what follows, I will provide brief background information about the government policies towards the indigenous peoples of West Malaysia before delving into the cultural politics of the two indigenous cultural villages. I conclude with some observations on the relationship between cultural heritage and indigenous self-determination.

Primary data for this study were derived using ethnographic research methods such as participant observation, unstructured and semi-structured interviews, and visual analysis carried out during a three-month immersion at each of the two field sites, as well as interviews with non-profit organizations (NGOs) and government officials. As my research concerns indigenous communities, I follow the strict ethical guidelines that govern such research, including adherence to the principle of free, prior and informed consent as outlined in the UN Declaration on the Rights of Indigenous Peoples, which means that I secured prior signed consent of my interviewees and research subjects for documenting any conversation, interview or activity. I will make extensive use of informant quotes as an ethnographic method, to allow the issues to emerge in my informants' own words so as to facilitate a better appreciation of the local contexts as experienced by the indigenous peoples.

Background Context: The Indigenous Peoples of West Malaysia

The indigenous peoples of West Malaysia, collectively known as the Orang Asli, are the earliest known inhabitants of the region (Carey 1976; Nicholas 2000). Based on the 2011 census, they constitute about 0.6 per cent of the total population of West Malaysia, and can be considered a minority. Historically they have been associated with subjugation by the later settlers in the region, such as the Malays (Dentan et al. 1997). The Orang Asli are not a homogenous people but are widely treated as a single community due to their shared social histories and socio-economic status (Nicholas 2000). For administrative purposes, the Orang Asli have been classified into eighteen ethnic sub-groups under three categories of Negritos, Senoi and Proto-Malays (Carey 1976; Nicholas 2000). Nicholas (2000) suggests that this perception of Orang Asli as a homogenous group was the result of outsiders' perceptions and ideological impositions on the Orang Asli, rather than one based on their own self-identification, although over time the Orang Asli began to adopt this common identity as a form of strategic essentialism over the social, economic, cultural and environmental stresses that they were — and continue to be — confronted with.

The Department of Orang Asli Affairs (JAKOA) is the government agency responsible for Orang Asli affairs in West Malaysia under the guise of development and eradicating poverty (Denton et al. 1997; Nicholas 2000). It has been argued, however, that the covert aim of JAKOA is to regulate and control indigenous peoples, largely through resettlement efforts and encouraging them to adopt sedentary livelihoods, as well as converting them to Islam, the official state religion, through positive discrimination (Denton et al. 1997; Nicholas 2000). The Orang Asli remain marginalized, as the decision-making powers within JAKOA lie with the ethnic Malays, and the indigenous Orang Asli hold only low-level positions within the agency (Nicholas 2000). With little political agency, customary lands belonging to the Orang Asli are frequently taken away by the Malaysian government and sold to private developers, with little or no compensation to the Orang Asli. The loss of their lands and resources has led to the displacement of Orang Asli and the loss of their livelihoods (Denton et al. 1997; Nicholas 2000; Nobuta 2008; Nicholas et al. 2010).

A key policy that has been undermining the status of indigenous peoples in post-colonial Malaysia is the New Economic Policy (NEP), also known as the *bumiputera* or "sons of the soil" policy. Conceived in 1969 following racial riots between Chinese and Malay populations over economic disparities in Malaysia, and officially implemented in 1971 (Andaya and Andaya 2001), the NEP extends preferential policies to Malay-Muslims and other indigenous peoples in wide-ranging areas such as university admissions and access to civil service jobs, mainly to counter the economic dominance of the Chinese and Indian populations (*The Economist* 2013). However, due to their non-Islamic religious affiliation, the Orang Asli are considered second-class *bumiputeras*, and they continue to be marginalized by the Malay-Muslims regarding access to economic and social privileges under the NEP policy. The dominant social imaginary of Malaysia's indigenous peoples as traditional, backward and in need of modernization is still actively deployed by the Malaysian state to justify its appropriation of their customary lands for logging, dam construction and other development projects (Nicholas 2000).

Heritage Dissonance at the Mah Meri Cultural Village

The Mah Meri people, also known as *Besisi* by early researchers, are one of the Orang Asli groups under the category of Senoi that resides mainly in Selangor Mainland and Carey Island (Karim 1981). Although the Mah Meri people believe they originate from Indo-China, they are known to have occupied areas in the south of Selangor, mainly in Johor and Malacca, over the last two centuries (Karim 1981). While the Mah Meri ancestors were mainly fishermen and mangrove hunter-gathers, the Mah Meri people now undertake small-scale sedentary agriculture and wage labour as a source of their livelihoods (Rahim 2007; Chan 2012).

The Mah Meri Cultural Village (Figure 6.1) was established in July 2011 on the traditional lands of the Mah Meri people at Kampung Sungai

FIGURE 6.1 Mah Meri Cultural Village on Carey Island, West Malaysia. Photograph by the author.

Bumbun on Carey Island in the state of Selangor, to serve the triple objectives of capitalizing on the economic potential of heritage tourism, preserving Mah Meri cultural heritage, and improving the livelihoods of the Mah Meri people by creating employment through tourism. According to the then minister, Datuk Seri Dr Ng Yen Yen, the Mah Meri Cultural Village is to be promoted as an artisan village to "attract high-end tourists who are willing to fork out thousands of ringgit for the unique pieces" (*The Star Online*, 2 February 2012). Developed through a public–private–people partnership, the infrastructure of the Mah Meri Cultural Village was implemented by the Ministry of Tourism and Culture with funding of RM3 million (US$900,000) and built by the Corporation Asli Selangor Private Limited, a government-linked company run by the indigenous peoples from the state of Selangor. Once it had been built, it was handed over to a government-endorsed ethnic Malay cultural broker to oversee and to manage the day-to-day operations.

The Mah Meri Cultural Village has on site an exhibition gallery showcasing the history and cultural traditions of the Mah Meri people, a room to display the Mah Meri woodcarvings that are for sale, a community hall for cultural performances and staged ritual demonstrations, as well as life-size models of a wooden boat, a spiritual altar, and a spirit house used by the Mah Meri people. The cultural village runs a full-day cultural tour for visitors at a charge of RM85 (US$25) per person, which includes a guided tour of the exhibition gallery, detailed explanations of Mah Meri rituals and customs, cultural performances, a staged wedding ceremony, and craft demonstrations that aim to introduce visitors to the cultural traditions of the Mah Meri people.

At the conceptualization of the project it was intended that the cultural broker would train the Mah Meri villagers during the first three years of operation in order to prepare them to take over management of the village and run it as a community-owned project from 2014. While the Mah Meri Cultural Village was intended to benefit all the Mah Meri people living on Carey Island, only two out of nine villages — Kampung Sungai Bumbun and Kampung Rambai — have been involved in the day-to-day workings of the cultural village, while a third village, Kampung Sungai Judah, shared information about their cultural heritage with the cultural broker. According to a village headman whose village was not involved with the Mah Meri Cultural Village:

> When the idea of a cultural village was first raised, all the Tok Batins [village headmen] of the Mah Meri villages on Pulau Carey were invited for a meeting. It was discussed that each village would take turns to perform at the cultural village. But later, when I found out that the management of the cultural village was an outsider, I did not want to be involved.

Mired by a complex web of local politics, the initial contract held by the cultural broker came to an end in 2014 but there is currently no handover plan in sight. No one seems to know the government's future plans for the Mah Meri Cultural Village. The Mah Meri villagers at Kampung Sungai Bumbun, where the cultural village is located and whose cultural heritage the cultural village is based on, are dismayed with the situation. One member of the Committee of Village Development and Security, known colloquially as the JKKK (Jawatan Kuasa Kemajuan dan Keselamatan Kampung), lamented:

> We have plans to take over the management of the Mah Meri Cultural Village, but we have no government support and we are not ready due to the lack of training. He should give us training, but he only make us low-pay workers. The JAKOA can't take action, because the Mah Meri Cultural Village is under another government agency.

Meanwhile the cultural broker has alternative plans for the cultural village. Since late 2014 he has been making presentations to the Ministry of Tourism and Culture to rebrand the Mah Meri Cultural Village as a "discovery centre". He is confident of retaining management of the cultural village, as he said to me:

> I have many years of experience running such cultural villages. I used to manage a similar cultural centre at Bukit Lagong in Perak that was bigger than the Mah Meri Cultural Village. The communities thought they could run the centre on their own. They took over and converted it into a training camp for youths, and it failed miserably. If they [the government authorities] want me to leave, they can come up with many reasons to make me leave, but they didn't.

He added that it would be a colossal task to decide who within the Mah Meri villagers would be a suitable party to take over the management of the Mah Meri Cultural Village, as there were different factions among the villagers who could not get along with one another.

A major source of tension between the cultural broker and the villagers of Kampung Sungai Bumbun lies in the representation of Mah Meri cultural heritage, leading to heritage dissonance. The cultural broker claims his authority based on thirteen years of cultural interaction with the Mah Meri people, while the villagers claim authority to represent their own cultural heritage by right of their ancestry. The cultural broker had sought permission from the village headman and had consulted with the Mah Meri villagers on the proposed location of the various facilities within the cultural village, such as the placement of the spiritual altar and the spirit house, as well as consulted academic resources on Mah Meri culture where they were available. But the final authority on the representation of Mah Meri cultural heritage in the cultural village lies with the cultural broker. Much of the interpretation of Mah Meri cultural heritage presented at the cultural village is also derived from his own research and his interactions with the Mah Meri people over the years.

There is some dissonance in the interpretation of Mah Meri cultural practices between the cultural broker and the Mah Meri villagers of Kampung Sungai Bumbun. According to one villager, the traditional Mah Meri game of *jerat tupai*, or "squirrel game", has been misrepresented by the cultural broker:

> According to our tradition, we carry it when we go into the forest, and try to solve the puzzle to calm ourselves when we get lost in the forest. But he

tells the tourists that this is used to test the intelligence level of the groom. These are games we play, but they are not part of our marriage rituals.

In another instance the cultural broker has misrepresented the divorce procedures of the Mah Meri people. According to the same villager:

He tells the tourists we wear a coconut around the neck, and go to each house to declare that the marriage is now over. This is not true at all. According to our tradition, couples who wish to divorce should consult the *Tok Batin* [village headman] and *adat* [customs] community to decide on the payment of the fine. We will meet in the community house to discuss. Who and how much to pay is based on the fault of the marriage. If the husband beats the wife, the husband will have to pay the fine. The *Tok Batin* decides on the payment after consulting with everyone.

Due to incidents such as these, the Mah Meri villagers feel that their cultural heritage has been misrepresented by the cultural broker and they have not been given sufficient authority to represent their own heritage at the village.

Despite the villagers having conveyed to the cultural broker that some of his interpretations of Mah Meri cultural heritage are not correct, he maintains that these are authentic representations based on his observations:

The Mah Meri are shy and timid people. The Mah Meri people, like the other Orang Asli groups, have a deep mistrust for people. They develop the mask tradition, so that they can take on different personas. They also have two names, an ecological name and a given Malay name. They may disagree with you in their hearts, but they will say yes to you. They have this internal system, and they will not tell you everything about their cultural heritage. I have lived with the communities for many years, and I observe them and decipher their cultural heritage. And I found out that there is a reason for them to do things. The Mah Meri has this game called the *jerat tupai* that they play for fun. After interacting with them, I learn that this game can be categorized as an IQ test for their in-law to-be since the game will reflect on the ability of their would-be son-in-law.... Also for the divorce procedures, many people think that the Mah Meri cannot divorce. Actually they can. I observe that when they divorce, the husband wears a coconut around his neck, goes to each house, knocks on the door, and tells everyone in the house that he is divorcing.

As such, it can be observed that the cultural broker considers such misrepresentations of Mah Meri cultural heritage as a source of what

Steinmeiz (2008) calls "ethnographic capital", a symbolic capital that he has accumulated through his long-term interactions with the Mah Meri people.

Although widely speculated to generate additional income for the Mah Meri villagers, the Mah Meri Cultural Village did not significantly increase the villagers' incomes from the levels prior to the establishment of the cultural village, as it merely changed their income sources. As a villager noted:

> Each month, we take home about RM900 [US$202] from the performances at the Mah Meri Cultural Village, and doing some weaving on the side. Due to the sporadic nature of the performances, we cannot take up other more stable jobs, so there is an opportunity cost to us.

Meanwhile, the cultural broker also had reservations about the villagers from Kampung Sungai Bumbun. A source of challenge he identified in the management of the Mah Meri Cultural Village was the craft centre located opposite the Mah Meri Cultural Village, as he complained:

> The craft centre opposite the Mah Meri Cultural Village, which the villagers set up on their own with JAKOA funding, poses competition to the Mah Meri Cultural Village. I mean, if the government is interested to set up another cultural village, they should choose another Orang Asli group elsewhere to work with, not crowd in Pulau Carey.

However, the villagers at Kampung Sungai Bumbun expressed surprise when asked whether the craft centre was set up to challenge the Mah Meri Cultural Village. As one villager clarified:

> The craft centre was built in 2009/2010 by JAKOA, before the Mah Meri Cultural Village. In fact, we have been doing cultural performances for a long time, and our cultural group, *Tompoq Topoh*, has been coordinating the dances for quite some time. The craft centre was not affected by the Mah Meri Cultural Village, as business was brisk anyway prior to the establishment of the Mah Meri Cultural Village.

Due to the tensions between the cultural broker and the villagers of Kampung Sungai Bumbun, for craft demonstrations, visitors to the Mah Meri Cultural Village would be driven to the craft centre at Kampung Rambai, located ten minutes away by car from the Mah Meri Cultural Village.

The local realities about who from among the Mah Meri people should take over the management of the cultural village, who should be given the opportunity to work at the village, and whose version of Mah Meri cultural heritage ought to be represented there, point to the problems of conceptualizing the Mah Meri people as a collective community with a common purpose. Indeed, the notion of community has been criticized in anthropological literature to be too vague to be useful as an analytical framework (Bauman 1996; Amit and Rapport 2002). What is deemed as the collective Mah Meri people is made up of different groups of social networks which cut across different situations, categories and allegiances, each existing in its own right and operating in a distinctive manner (Amit and Rapport 2002). This complicates the working dynamics of the Mah Meri Cultural Village.

Despite the tensions with the cultural broker, the villagers continued to work at the village, albeit with less motivation and a lacklustre attitude, as they saw value in generating awareness about their cultural heritage and asserting their indigenous cultural identity through the project. According to one villager who served as a liaison with the cultural broker for the cultural performances:

> We still support Mah Meri Cultural Village because it is located in our village, and it is showcasing our cultural heritage. We have no other income. It is not from the willingness of our hearts, but we still do it.

The Mah Meri villagers, however, developed several coping strategies, or what Scott (1985) considered "weapons of the weak", highlighting that they were not passive agents in the unequal relationship, but were negotiating their marginalized positions with creativity and agency. When asked whether there was any difference to them between performing at the Hari Moyang (Ancestor's Day) festival — the villagers' own ritual ceremony — or at the Mah Meri Cultural Village, a villager replied:

> The feeling is not the same. At Hari Moyang there are lots of food and blessings from the ancestors, so we perform with more energy. But at the Mah Meri Cultural Village, we are less motivated, so the music is less spirited and slow.

The villagers' lacklustre attitude towards working for the cultural village was also keenly felt by the cultural broker, who complained that the villagers were very unreliable in the provision of their services. He once said to me:

> I hope you will maintain some distance from the communities. Once they get too close to you, it may affect their work. There was once an occasion when the communities did not turn up for work, in order to celebrate

the visit of a foreign researcher whom they know. This cost me a lot, because I had already taken bookings for cultural performances on that day and I had to refund all the visitors because the communities didn't show up to perform.

Besides trivializing their work commitments at the Mah Meri Cultural Village, the villagers also developed other coping strategies to deal with their dissatisfaction towards the cultural broker. One strategy was to laugh off the misinterpretation of their culture, as another villager employed at the cultural village, said:

> Sometimes we feel angry. Sometimes we feel funny. Like when he tells the tourists how we grind our teeth as part of our marriage rituals to look like Dracula, the tourists ask us why we are laughing. We just smile. We dare not explain to them why we are laughing. And the tourists believe what he said. Because we already told him this is not the way, but he just does it his way.

Another strategy was to accept that the misrepresentation by the cultural broker was something beyond their control and to recognize that the tourists would be rational enough to judge for themselves. According to the same villager:

> We are a bit confused because the Mah Meri Cultural Village does not follow Mah Meri customs. Actually, he can tell the tourists the truth, but he doesn't want to. He knows the truth. It doesn't matter to us if he doesn't tell the truth. But we prefer him to tell the truth because it is a centre that shares our heritage with tourists. It will affect people's perception of Mah Meri if the truth is not told. But it also depends on the tourists what to believe in the Mah Meri Cultural Village. If the tourists are interested, they can ask the villagers.

Although this involved the commodification of their traditional rituals, the villagers did not perceive authenticity of the cultural performances to be problematic for their cultural beliefs, as they had rationalized the re-enactment of their performances within their belief systems. As another villager said:

> Moyang [Ancestors] understand that we need to make money. A local tourist guide who visited the Mah Meri Cultural Village once told me: we need to create something to find food and income. It is fine to make fake wedding, but at Hari Moyang, you must perform at least three songs for the Moyang if you can't perform seven songs for them. So the cultural

performances at the Mah Meri Cultural Village do not affect our beliefs. But for us, we cannot participate in the fake marriages as grooms and brides ourselves, as this will affect us in the future.

Similar to what Doolittle (2004) had observed for the rural development projects in Sabah, the Mah Meri villagers self-consciously conformed to their expected roles in order to receive the benefits from the Mah Meri Cultural Village, however meagre these were, albeit with some resistance and negotiations.

Indigenous Activism at the Orang Seletar Cultural Centre

The Orang Seletar Cultural Centre (Figure 6.2) is an independent cultural village constructed by the Orang Seletar people themselves within Kampung Sungai Temon to preserve and showcase their cultural heritage. In 2011 a Malaysian-Chinese marine biologist and environmental activist from the Malaysian Society of Marine Science, who conducted research on seahorses in the Johore Strait and was inspired by the Orang Seletar people

FIGURE 6.2   Orang Seletar Cultural Centre at Johor Bahru, West Malaysia. Photograph by the author.

living in the area, lobbied an international NGO, the Global Environment Facility, for funding of RM60,000 (US$18,000) to establish the 2,500 square feet Orang Seletar Cultural Centre with the villagers (Yap 2011).

Managed by the family of the village headman since the activist passed on, the Orang Seletar Cultural Centre features a collection of photographs by British photographer, naturalist, ethnologist, documentary film-maker and medical doctor, Dr Ivan Polunin, who lived in Singapore and Malaysia from the 1950s until his death in 2010. The centre presents maps and photographs showcasing the cultural heritage of the Orang Seletar, replicas of hunting tools and traditional boats used in their daily lives, and photographs of marine wildlife found in the area. It also has a wooden stage for cultural performances, which take place mainly on Saturday nights. Even though the Orang Seletar Cultural Centre only has on offer the Orang Seletar cultural performance to complement the museum exhibits, it exudes the feelings of a "living museum" because a significant component of the exhibits at the centre deal with contemporary issues such as news reports of community involvement in the establishment of the cultural centre and their ongoing court case with JAKOA and the developers of the Danga Bay waterfront development that encroached on their customary lands. According to the village headman, Salim Palun, the centre has a number of objectives, including ensuring that "the traditional Orang Seletar culture is preserved", that "the younger generation do not forget their roots", showing that the Orang Seletar "have stayed in this area for many generations", and that "development should not come at [their] expense or encroach on this land" (Yap 2011).

The Orang Seletar are a sea people who were known to roam the lands and waters around Singapore and the Johore Strait in the nineteenth century. Skeat and Blagden (1906, p. 88), citing an account from Thomson published in 1847, noted that "they numbered in all 200 people, or 40 boats, and were subject to a *Batin* or petty chief, under the sovereignty of the Sultan of Johor", but had taken their name from the Seletar river, a mangrove creek on Singapore island. By 1971 there were three settlements of Orang Seletar, two settlements in Johor and one in Singapore, numbering about three hundred people in total (Carey 1976). Today there are nine Orang Seletar villages located along the southern coast of Johor, of which seven are located within the Iskandar Development Region (IDR) (COAC 2014). Amongst them, only two villages — Kampung Bakar Batu and Kampung Simpang Arang — have been partly gazetted as Aboriginal Reserves under the Aboriginal Peoples Act 1954 (Act 134) (COAC 2014). The other villages do not have secure land titles and are at best tenant-at-will, which means their continued occupation of the lands is dependent on the will of the state, and they can be evicted if the state needs the lands for development (Nicholas 2000).

Since 2010 the Danga Bay area and its surroundings, where the Orang Seletar villages are located, has gradually been alienated to private developers for massive reclamation and the development of high-rise waterfront properties as part of the IDR vision. The class action lawsuit proposed by Eddy bin Salim, Salim bin Palon and Mat bin Inder on behalf of themselves and another 185 Orang Seletar villagers sought to stop the Iskandar Development Region Agency's development on their traditional lands and waters, even though much of the surrounding natural environments had already been destroyed by the development, severely threatening their subsistence as fishermen and their traditional ways of life (COAC 2014).

The Orang Seletar turning to the courts for the assertion of their indigenous rights follows a trend that has gained much popularity since the late 1990s. Brought about by increased awareness by the indigenous peoples of their rights, the exhaustion of other avenues such as dialogue and negotiation to make their concerns heard, and the successes of indigenous peoples in seeking compensation for infringement of their native rights through legal jurisprudence, indigenous peoples in Malaysia began to turn to the courts to address alleged breaches of their land and resource rights (Nicholas 2000; Idrus 2010; Aiken and Leigh 2011).

As part of the court proceedings, the judge, in order to understand their cultural heritage, was brought on a tour of the Orang Seletar Cultural Centre situated within Kampung Sungai Temon and other sites of customary significance in the vicinity. This is significant, as indigenous peoples could acquire native customary rights to their traditional lands, territories and resources by showing evidence demonstrating their continued practice of indigenous cultural heritage that indicated a connection to the lands and territories (Bunnell and Nah 2004; Nah 2008; Idrus 2010; Aiken and Leigh 2011). By articulating their historical connections to the lands, made visible through geographical landmarks such as ancestors' graves and culturally significant geographical features connected to their indigenous cosmologies, as well as evidence of their material cultural heritage displayed in the Orang Seletar Cultural Centre, the Orang Seletar villagers and their lawyers sought to stake their customary claims through "place-based imaginaries" (Cooke 2013) that were "realised historically *in* and *through* place" (Bunnell and Nah 2004, p. 2459, italics in the original).

By alluding to indigeneity as grounded in time and space from time immemorial, Malaysian law has embraced an antiquated anthropological notion of indigeneity based on primordiality and autochthony, which is argued to produce an essentialized notion of indigeneity by extending it legal legitimacy, a process that also reifies cultures and cultural differences as ontological (Barnard 2006; Birrell 2009). This incompatibility in the conception of indigeneity between judiciary narratives as a bounded entity and literary imaginaries as a fluid entity has produced a conundrum where "the indigenous subject is created by and remains *within* the law, impenetrable, whereas indigeneity remains *outside* the law, *before* the law and *beyond* the law" (Birrell 2009, p. 235, italics in the original). Despite its epistemological incongruity, the recognition of native titles and proprietary rights in and to native lands within Malaysian law offers a channel for indigenous peoples to redress their historical marginalization and dispossession by instrumentalizing an essentialized notion of their cultures to assert their native claims to traditional lands and territories.

Even as the Orang Seletar villagers await the outcome of the court proceedings on Kampung Sungai Temon and Kampung Bakar Batu, the wider development of the IDR elsewhere continues unabated, and the large-scale land reclamation and urbanization are affecting their livelihoods as fishermen. A member of my host family spoke about the extent of their hardships:

> Since the development of Danga Bay in 2010, the fishery catch has been severely affected. The farming of green mussels is also severely affected. Twelve years ago, we can get 30 to 40 kg of green mussels every half a year due to the rich nutrients in the waters of Johore Straits. Now, in one year, we get perhaps 1 to 3 kg of green mussels, certainly less than 5kg.

In the aftermath of the declining harvests from the sea due to pollution and the destruction of the natural environments in Danga Bay, the Orang Seletar Cultural Centre serves as a basis for the development of ecotourism as an alternative means of livelihood for the Orang Seletar villagers. Since 2014 the villagers of Kampung Sungai Temon have been running ecotourism tours around their village, aimed at increasing awareness of their cultural heritage and natural environments in partnership with a

Malaysian ecotourism outfit known as "Nature Classroom". The ecotourism programmes enable the Orang Seletar villagers to draw on their cultural heritage and tacit knowledge of the seas and lands surrounding their living environments for their livelihoods.

I had the opportunity to attend one of the tours in the company of a child from my host family, whom I had sponsored for the tour. The full-day ecotourism tour at Kampung Sungai Temon began with a morning briefing on the history and lifestyles of the Orang Seletar people through a tour of the Orang Seletar Cultural Centre, followed by the pairing of an Orang Seletar child with the participants, who had been asked to sponsor a young villager to accompany them on a boat trip around the mangrove swamps of the Johore Strait, guided by the villagers of Kampung Sungai Temon. During the boat-trip, participants were introduced to the fauna and flora in the area by the Orang Seletar villagers. They were also asked to collect natural materials that they would use for a craft-making session later. After a home-cooked buffet meal prepared by the villagers, the participants adjourned to the cultural centre for a craft-making session, before the day ended with a gift presentation session and the sharing of thoughts among the participants with the villagers.

The ecotourism programmes are intended to increase awareness of the Orang Asli people in Malaysia and break down any preconceived notions that non-indigenous Malaysians have of the indigenous peoples. As the organizer, Yun, said:

> I would like to facilitate better understanding of the Orang Seletar people, and to get people engaged with the natural environments, especially the lush mangrove habitats. Many people in Malaysia still don't know about the Orang Asli. They think that the Orang Asli live in the forests in very backward and primitive conditions. I want to bring people to interact with the Orang Seletar to let them know that they are just like one of us.

The ecotourism tour with the Orang Seletar villagers garnered many accolades from the participants, mainly Malaysian Chinese living in Johor Bahru, who said that they had enjoyed the tour, and the experience had changed their views of the Orang Seletar people:

> The Orang Seletar children are so brave. The Orang Seletar girl was only five years old, yet she jumped into the mangrove swamps to chop down the leaves for our crafts with a cleaver without fear. I think they can take

care of themselves at such a young age, because they are exposed to these dangerous tasks. Comparatively, my children are so protected.

I am very envious of their childhoods of being close to nature, so carefree. In Malaysia today, it is hard to find this kind of lifestyle.

The ecotourism programmes at Kampung Sungai Temon serve to promote a better understanding of the Orang Seletar people and their culture, seeking to break down the prejudiced views towards Orang Asli as a backward and underdeveloped people, demonstrating how indigenous cultural heritage can be instrumentalized for the promotion of multicultural tolerance and diversity. However, it is argued that this constitutes a form of "zoological multi-culturalism" in which the diversity of Malaysia's multicultural heritage is put on display for the consumption of the urban elites — in this case the economically superior ethnic Chinese Malaysians — which masks the economic, social and political inequalities between the indigenous and non-indigenous peoples in Malaysia (Graham et al. 2000; Harrison 2013).

The Orang Seletar Cultural Centre resembles an indigenous museum, a form of cultural development that has gained popularity in the Pacific region since the 1980s (Mead 1983; Stanley 2007). Established for the display of indigenous cultures, indigenous museums share these characteristics: having known "publics", usually small in scale and restricted by category; with different manner of contemplation of the museum's contents; a privileged role for oral traditions; a focus on the transmission of traditions rather than display and conservation; and contemporaneity, which is to use collections and museums to address contemporary issues (Stanley 2007). They rely on indigeneity and customs as "a source of authority and power" to help indigenous peoples prosper in the face of a rapidly changing world (Stanley 2007, p. 16).

During my fieldwork at Kampung Sungai Temon, I became acquainted with Ah Chek, an ethnic Chinese Malaysian who ran a provision shop in the village. Ah Chek offered a contrasting perspective on the Orang Seletar Cultural Centre, which cast doubt on the idealized view of the external sponsorship of community-run cultural institutions as a tool for development. In his opinion, the Orang Seletar Cultural Centre was merely an economic opportunity for the Orang Seletar people. As he explained:

When Choo was setting up the cultural centre, he also sought my views. I felt that the effort put in by the Orang Seletar villagers did not justify the funding given to the project. Do you know that wages were paid to the Orang Seletar villagers to gather the materials and set up the cultural centre? The villagers did not set up the cultural centre for free, but they were later given the cultural centre for free. It was such a good deal for the villagers, but they did not value it by keeping it in a tip-top condition. Instead, they allow it to languish. Given the lack of care of the villagers over the cultural centre, I did not think it was a worthwhile effort.

Ah Chek also cast doubt on the authenticity of the heritage represented by the cultural centre:

> The cultural centre was not authentic, as this was based on research and not their everyday lived experiences. Ten to twenty years ago, the Orang Seletar villagers would hang out and dance every evening — those were the authentic Orang Seletar dances. To understand their lives in the past, you should consult the oldest Orang Seletar women, who were still alive in Kampung Bakar Batu. The cultural dances performed at Kampung Sungai Temon were not authentic; they were recently invented.

As Ah Chek had rightly highlighted, the Orang Seletar cultural dances performed by the villagers at Kampung Sungai Temon are not part of traditions handed down by their ancestors, but rather were the brainchild of an individual Orang Seletar man who served as the songwriter cum dance choreographer for the villagers. Being modern creations, the Orang Seletar cultural performances speak of their current lives in twenty-first-century Malaysia and of a sense of community spirit and resilience to cope with the raft of changes they have experienced over the years. There was a performance about their plight as a community faced with dwindling resources due to rapid urbanization and land reclamation that has affected their traditional lands. There was another piece that spoke of the carefree lifestyle they have had with the sea, interacting with the sea creatures, which were and still are so central to their lives.

Musical instruments and dance movements were also frequently renewed based on the inspirations of the lead songwriter and dance choreographer. Although the Orang Seletar cultural performances were modern creations, this did not stop them from winning the first prize in the national dance competition at the Orang Asli Entrepreneur Carnival 2014, suggesting that these were generally accepted as an authentic cultural heritage of the Orang Seletar people. This alluded to the dynamism of indigenous cultural heritage in the everyday lives of the Orang Seletar people, which contrasted with the essentialized notions of Orang Seletar cultural heritage portrayed in the court case and in the displays of material culture at the Orang Seletar Cultural Centre.

At its core, however, the Orang Seletar Cultural Centre is no different from other museums or heritage institutions, as it reifies an essentialized representation of indigenous cultural heritage based on past cultures and traditions, against its dynamic manifestation in the everyday lives of indigenous peoples. As Nicholas, an activist with the Centre of Orang Asli Concerns (COAC) in Malaysia, who served as an expert witness for the Orang Seletar villagers in their court case for the assertion of their native customary rights, said:

> What you see in the cultural centre of the Orang Seletar is what they used in the past. It is like a museum piece. Now, you go to the museum, you see things in the past. Because society is always changing, culture is never static. Because the government's effort to modernise you, assimilate you and integrate you into the mainstream, you naturally change your way of life. The things you no longer use are relegated to the museum. You don't find a motorboat in the museum because it's still being used. It's only when you don't use it anymore, then you put it there, but it doesn't mean just because it's not being used, the culture stop being practised. It's modified. Before, you use the wooden boat, now you use the fibre-glass boat.

At my last visit to Kampung Sungai Temon in August 2016, the Orang Seletar Cultural Centre was in a dilapidated condition. Its lights were no longer working and the wooden hut looked worn down. The status of the Orang Seletar Cultural Centre is in limbo pending the outcome of the court judgement, but there is little doubt that it will eventually be dismantled when the villagers move to a new settlement. The village headman assures me that it will be rebuilt in their new village if they relocate to a new settlement as a community. Kreps (2007) suggests that the larger concern over indigenous museums is whether they have contributed to sustaining the indigenous peoples' cultural lives and their socio-economic development. Despite its short-lived existence in Kampung Sungai Temon, the Orang Seletar Cultural Centre has made a useful contribution to the political, cultural and social lives of the Orang Seletar villagers, and in this sense it can be deemed a successful indigenous museum.

Conclusion

Through my comparative study of the Mah Meri Cultural Village and the Orang Seletar Cultural Centre, I have demonstrated how indigenous cultural heritage has been instrumentalized in different ways by two Orang Asli groups for their respective agendas. Both the Mah Meri and the Orang Seletar villagers recognize the roles played by the respective indigenous cultural villages in generating awareness for their cultural heritage, and the importance of such awareness for asserting their cultural identity and self-determination in mainstream Malay-Muslim Malaysian society. However, these indigenous cultural villages have produced different outcomes for the two Orang Asli groups due to the different levels of agency and stewardship extended to the villagers.

At the Mah Meri Cultural Village, which is a "top-down" heritage project initiated and funded by the Malaysian state, and managed by a government-endorsed ethnic Malay cultural broker, the Mah Meri villagers lack the full agency and authority to represent their cultural heritage, leading to heritage dissonance. However, they continue to work for the cultural village despite their dissatisfaction with the cultural broker, as they see value in the role of the cultural village in generating awareness for their cultural heritage. Nonetheless, they are less successful in instrumentalizing their cultural heritage for developmental needs due to the lack of community stewardship. At the Orang Seletar Cultural Centre, which is a "bottom-up" heritage project established and managed by the local villagers, under the initiation of a non-indigenous activist who sought funding from an international NGO for the development, the Orang Seletar villagers have full agency over the representation of their cultural heritage, and tend to be more successful in instrumentalizing their cultural heritage for their development needs.

Although both the Mah Meri and the Orang Seletar peoples have established indigenous cultural villages to showcase and preserve their cultural heritage, the level of success enjoyed by the villagers in instrumentalizing their cultural heritage for the reassertion of their identity and self-determination hinges on the level of agency and authority extended to them in managing their own indigenous cultural villages. While UNESCO has a laudable mandate to integrate culture and heritage as part of the human development strategies aimed at improving the living conditions of less-developed and marginalized peoples, the success of such community programmes often hinges on their stewardship.

The decentralization of developmental aid provision through intermediary agencies and entrepreneurs, a trend popular in the current age of neoliberalism, may be futile in addressing the developmental needs of the intended recipients. As Ferguson (1994) had observed, rather than alleviate local poverty, developmental projects which work through social actors and cultural structures have tended to expand the bureaucratic power of the state and sidestep local issues by casting aside local resistance to the politics of land, labour and resources as obstacles to development. Perhaps bottom-up approaches to the delivery of aid premised on the full ownership and agency of the local peoples concerned can deliver better outcomes for the intended recipients.

Acknowledgements

I would like to thank my Orang Seletar and Mah Meri informants for their warm hospitality and generous sharing of information, without which this chapter would not have been possible. I would also like to acknowledge the assistance and advice of Dr Colin Nicholas from the Centre for Orang Asli Concerns (COAC) and Dr Yogeswaran Subramaniam for the insightful discussions that informed this article. In addition I would like to express my sincere gratitude to my supervisors, Professor Paul Basu from the School of Oriental and African Studies (SOAS) and Professor Rodney Harrison from the UCL Institute of Archaeology, for their guidance and advice towards my research. I would also like to acknowledge the financial support offered by the UCL Overseas Graduate Scholarship and the UCL Graduate Research Scholarship for funding my studies at the UCL Institute of Archaeology, as well as the UCL External Training Fund for the sponsorship towards my Malay language training at the University of Malaya. Importantly, I would like to express my gratitude to Academic Sinica, Institute of Sociology, for funding my participation at the "Citizens, Civil Society and the Cultural Politics of Heritage-Making in East and Southeast Asia" conference from 11 to 13 December 2014 in Taipei, Taiwan, during which an earlier version of the paper was presented. Lastly, I would like to thank the two anonymous reviewers for their helpful comments on my earlier drafts.

References

Aiken, S.R., and C.H. Leigh. "Seeking Redress in the Courts: Indigenous Land Rights and Judicial Decisions in Malaysia". *Modern Asian Studies* 45 (2011): 825–75.

Amit, Vered, and Nigel Rapport. *The Trouble with Community: Anthropological Reflections on Movement, Identity and Collectivity*. London: Pluto Press, 2002.

Andaya, B., and L.Y. Andaya. *A History of Malaysia*, 2nd ed. Basingstoke: Palgrave.

Barnard, Alan. "Kalahari Revisionism, Vienna and the 'Indigenous Peoples' Debate". *Social Anthropology* 14, no. 1 (2001): 1–16.

Bauman, G. *Contesting Culture: Discourses of Identity in Multi-ethnic London*. Cambridge: Cambridge University Press, 1996.

Birrell, Kathleen. "Indigeneity: Before and Beyond the Law". *Studies in Law, Politics, and Society* 51 (2009): 219–58.

Bunnell, Tim, and Alice M. Nah. "Counter-global Cases for Place: Contesting Displacement in Globalising Kuala Lumpur Metropolitan Area". *Urban Studies* 41, no. 12 (2004): 2447–67.

Carey, I. *Orang Asli: The Aboriginal Tribes of Peninsular Malaysia*. Oxford University Press, 1976.

Centre for Orang Asli Concerns (COAC). "Court Battle against Big Time Developers Continues over Ancestral Territories. 2014 <https://www.facebook.com/notes/707485839295345/> (accessed 30 January 2017).

Chan, C.S.C. "Heterogeneity in the Musical Acquisition of Orang Asli Children from the Mah Meri and Semai Groups". *Malaysian Music Journal* 1, no. 2 (2012): 1–19.

Cooke, F.M. "Constructing Rights: Indigenous Peoples at the Public Hearings of the National Inquiry into Customary Rights to Land in Sabah, Malaysia". *SOJOURN: Journal of Social Issues in Southeast Asia* 28, no. 3 (2013): 512–37

Dentan, R.K., K. Endicott, A.G. Gomes, and M.B. Hooker. *Malaysia and the "Original People": A Case Study of the Impact of Development on Indigenous Peoples*. Boston: Allyn and Bacon, 1997.

Doolitte, A.A. "Resources, Ideologies, and Nationalism: The Politics of Development in Malaysia". In *Development Brokers and Translators: The Ethnography of Aid and Agencies*, edited by David Lewis and David Mosse, pp. 51–74. Bloomfield, CT: Kumarian, 2004.

The Economist. "A Never Ending Policy". 27 April 2013 <http://www.economist.com/news/briefing/21576654-elections-may-could-mark-turning-point-never-ending-policy> (accessed 2 March 2016).

Ferguson, J. *The Anti-Politics Machine: Development, Depoliticization and Bureaucratic Power in Lesotho*. Minneapolis: University of Minnesota Press, 1994.

Graham, B., G.J. Ashworth, and J.E. Tunbridge. *A Geography of Heritage: Power, Culture and Economy*. London: Arnold, 2000.

Harrison, R. *Heritage: Critical Approaches*. Abingdon: Routledge, 2013.

Idrus, R. "From Wards to Citizens: Indigenous Rights and Citizenship in Malaysia". *PoLAR: Political and Legal Anthropological Review* 33, no. 1 (2010): 89–08.

Karim, W.B. *Ma'Betisek Concepts of Living Things.* New Jersey: Athlone, 1981.

Kreps, Christina. "The Theoretical Future of Indigenous Museums: Concept and Practice". In *The Future of Indigenous Museums: Perspectives from the Southwest Pacific*, edited by Nick Stanley, pp. 223–34. Oxford: Berghahn, 2007.

Mead, S.M. "Indigenous Models of Museums in Oceania". *Museum* 138 (1983): 98–101.

Nah, A.M. "Recognizing Indigenous Identity in Postcolonial Malaysian Law: Rights and Realities for the Orang Asli (aborigines) of Peninsular Malaysia". *Bijdragen tot de Taal-, Land- en Volkenkunde* 164 (2008): 212–37.

Nicholas, C. *The Orang Asli and the Contest for Resources: Indigenous Politics, Development and Identity in Peninsular Malaysia.* Kuala Lumpur: Centre for Orang Asli Concerns, 2000.

Nicholas, C., J. Engi, and Y.P. Teh. *The Orang Asli and the UNDRIP: From Rhetoric to Recognition.* Subang Jaya: Center for Orang Asli Concerns, 2010.

Nobuta, T. *Living on the Periphery: Development and the Islamization of the Orang Asli.* Kyoto: Kyoto University Press, 2008.

Rahim, R. *Chita' Hae: Culture, Crafts and Customs of the Hma' Meri in Kampung Sungai Bumbun, Pulau Carey.* Kuala Lumpur: Centre for Orang Asli Concerns, 2007.

Scott, James C. *Weapons of the Weak: Everyday Forms of Peasant Resistance.* New Haven, CT: Yale University Press, 1985.

Skeat, W.W., and C.O. Blagden. *Pagan Races of the Malay Peninsula*, vol. 1. London: Macmillan, 1906.

Stanley, N., ed. *The Future of Indigenous Museums: Perspectives from the Southwest Pacific.* Oxford: Berghahn, 2007.

The Star Online. "Ministry to Promote Mah Meri Cultural Village". 2 February 2012 <http://www.thestar.com.my/News/Nation/2012/02/02/Ministry-to-promote-Mah-Meri-cultural-village.aspx/> (accessed 8 May 2014).

Steinmetz, G. "The Colonial State as a Social Field: Ethnographic Capital and Native Policy in the German Overseas Empire before 1914". *American Sociological Review* 73, no. 4 (2008): 589–612.

Yap, Sean. "Seletar's Cultural Heritage". *The Star Online*, 2 August 2011 <http://www.thestar.com.my/Story/?file=%2F2011%2F8%2F2%2Fsouthneast%2F9210213> (accessed 8 May 2014).

7

Constituting Philippine Filmic and Linguistic Heritage: The Case of Filipino Regional Films

Katrina Ross A. Tan

Heritage-making is, more often than not, a task taken by the national government to bind its peoples and to make them recognize representations of national history, culture and identity. In this case the state becomes a source of what Laurajane Smith calls the "Authorized Heritage Discourse or AHD", where heritage is seen as "nationally significant" (2014b). In this instance heritage-making entails processes that at times homogenize naturally diverse cultures; at times impose a national character to tangible and non-tangible artefacts that may not necessarily represent something meaningful to some people in other parts of the country. This practice of heritage-making invokes a collective experience, a shared culture that erases differences within the nation-state. In its recognition of what is a "national heritage", it misrecognizes others' heritage in the periphery. This is especially problematic in the context of the Philippines, an archipelagic country composed of 7,107 islands populated by various ethnic groups, and that makes processes of nation-formation complicated. The diversity of the country's cultures challenges the homogenized notion of a "national culture" and "national heritage" that the state espouses in its cultural policies.

A clear example of this cultural politics in the Philippines is the declaration of Filipino as the official language, a language that is primarily based in a regional language called Tagalog. This is despite the fact that 183 languages exist in the country that includes other major regional languages like Cebuano spoken widely in the Visayas and Mindanao islands, Ilocano in northern Luzon, Kapampangan in central Luzon, Hiligaynon in Panay and Negros islands, Bicol in Southern Luzon, and Waray in Samar and Leyte islands, among others. The said islands are among the largest and most populous in the Philippines. On the other hand, Tagalog is widely spoken in Manila, the capital city, and other nearby provinces and islands in Luzon.

When Tagalog was declared as the basis for the national language in 1937, the country was a commonwealth under the United States but essentially still a colony. Prior to this, in 1934, a Constitutional Convention was called to formulate the constitution for the commonwealth government to prepare for the colony's self-governance, which was to begin in 1935. A Committee on Official Language was created after one Felipe R. Jose, a delegate from Mountain Province in the northern Philippines, spoke in Tagalog and raised the need for a national language in order to be fully considered an independent nation.[1] The committee was tasked to study the native languages and survey the populace in order to arrive at a national language. According to the committee's subsequent report, one of their findings was the "wide diffusion of Tagalog in provinces not speaking it, notwithstanding the absence of encouragement of its use" (Almario 2014, p. 24). In another explanation by the Commission on the Filipino Language, the 1934 committee also based their choice on the expert opinion of Najeeb Mitry Saleeby, a Lebanese-born naturalized American based in the Philippines. His services were contracted by the colonial power mainly due to his research work on the Moro in the Southern Philippines (Marr 2014, p. 78). Saleeby, a surgeon by profession but also a linguist and ethnologist, remarked in 1924 that "[o]n theoritic and scientific grounds, no one hesitates to give preference to Tagalog as the best developed and fittest dialect to be selected as a common national language" (Najeeb Mitry Saleeby, quoted in Almario 2014, p. 28). He cited as reasons Tagalog's geographical relation to the capital as well as its historical relation to Filipino revolutionaries who spoke the language and used it in their writings (Almario 2014, p. 24). In addition, Trinidad A. Rojo, a Filipino researcher, cited other reasons for choosing Tagalog as the basis for the national language. In his study, *The Language Problem in the Philippines*, Rojo said that Tagalog "has the most highly developed literature of all dialects", and it is the language used more popularly in general publications like newspapers and magazines (Almario 2014, p. 35). The 1935 Commonwealth Constitution, however, does not specify Tagalog as the national language.

On 30 December 1937, Manuel L. Quezon, the Philippine Commonwealth's first president, read his Executive Order 134 over the radio declaring Tagalog as the basis of the national language. Quezon chose to announce the decision on this day due to its symbolic meaning: the country was commemorating the anniversary of the martyrdom of Jose Rizal, the unofficial national hero of the Philippines. His novels *Noli Me Tangere* (Touch Me Not) and *El Filibusterismo* (literal translation, The Filibuster, but it is also known as The Reign of Greed in English), written in Spanish, stirred the hearts and minds of the revolutionaries by exposing the 300-year oppression of the *indios*, or natives, at the hands of the Spanish colonizers, particularly the clergy and officials. His execution ordered by Spanish officials was said to ignite the armed revolution led by Andres Bonifacio and the members of the revolutionary group, Katipunan.

Quezon's decision to select Tagalog as the basis for the national language was made based on the recommendation of a group of language experts and scholars convened by the National Language Institute (NLI) to research the issue. Voltaire Tupaz reported that the members of the NLI were experts from different ethnolinguistic groups: Santiago A. Fonacier (Ilocano), Filemon Sotto (Cebu Visayan), Casimero Perfecto (Bicol), Felix S. Salas Rodriguez (Panay Visayan), Hadji Butu (Moro), and Cecilio Lopez (Tagalog). The group was headed by Jaime C. De Veyra (Samar-Leyte Visayan) (Tupaz 2012). The resolution submitted on 9 November 1937 by these experts recommending Tagalog as the official language states:

> This conclusion represents not only the conviction of the members of the Institute but also the opinion of Filipino scholars and patriots of divergent origin and varied education and tendencies who are unanimously in favor of the selection of Tagalog as the basis of the national language as it has been found to be used and accepted by the greatest number of Filipinos not to mention the categorical views expressed by local newspapers, publications, and individual writers. (Tupaz 2012)

In all the succeeding versions of the Philippine Constitution after 1935, varying provisions relating to the national language were put in place. Most notably, the 1943 Constitution implemented during the Japanese Occupation cited Tagalog as the eventual national language. Article 9 sec. 2 states that, "The government shall take steps toward the development and propagation of Tagalog as the national language." After the Japanese left the country the 1935 Constitution was again put into effect, but the constitution that was in place during the Occupation essentially solidified the place of Tagalog in national linguistic consciousness (Tan 2014). In the 1973 Constitution, however, the provision on the national language took a different turn. The Constitution no longer explicitly stated that Tagalog was the basis of the national language; instead, it said that the state would work on the development of a common national language to be called "Filipino". In a news article, Nigel Tan reported that this was brought about by heated debate on the national language, even questioning the idea of having one, during the Constitutional Convention in 1971. The result was a carefully worded provision in the 1973 Constitution. This was carried over into the 1987 Constitution and is still in place today (Tan 2014). Article 14 sec. 6 of 1987 Constitution states, "The national language of the Philippines is Filipino. As it evolves, it shall be further developed and enriched on the basis of existing Philippine and other languages."

Despite the openness of the 1987 Constitution relating to the continuing development of Filipino as the national language, it cannot be denied that it is still primarily based on the grammatical rules and conventions of Tagalog. Some critics even say that it is just a formalized form of Tagalog. In the 2000 census on languages spoken in the country, Tagalog was said to have 21,500,000 speakers, mostly found in Luzon, including the National Capital Region (Lewis 2009). It must be noted, however, that despite this number, Tagalog is not spoken as first language in many parts of the country outside Luzon, the largest island in the country. Instead, Cebuano is used by people in the Visayas and Mindanao islands.

This constitutional provision on language has broad implications in heritage-making. In the literary arts, for example, Tagalog novels, short stories and poems suddenly take on a "national" character. Literary works written in other major regional languages are consequently labelled as "regional literature". The once regional language — Tagalog — is transformed into a national one by virtue of an executive order, and any text that uses it is endowed with a national character. This is admittedly a

Tagalog-centric mindset, but it is precisely this mindset that made possible the domination of Tagalog culture in the discourse of national culture.

The same can be said in the case of Filipino films. For so long, Tagalog cinema has dominated the film industry. Eventually it came to be regarded as the national cinema (Deocampo 2007, p. 20). Interestingly, Deocampo pointed out that Tagalog cinema was initially a regional/local form that only later took on a national character. He raised an intriguing question: how did such a regional/local culture became national? (2007, p. 21). While language experts were able to provide explanations for why Tagalog was used as the basis for the national language, very few film scholars have come up with explanations comparing Tagalog cinema with Cebuano cinema, a cinema that is equally as vibrant and far-reaching as the one from the capital, with its base of operation in Cebu City in central Philippines, known as Queen City of the South. Filipino film historian Nick Deocampo in his book *Cine: Spanish Influences on Early Cinema in the Philippines* offered an explanation on how Tagalog cinema came to be regarded as the national cinema. As the seat of Spanish colonial power since the sixteenth century, Manila asserted its dominance over the rest of the country as the capital city, and consequently its Tagalog culture, including cinema, came to dominate the rest of the country (Deocampo 2007, p. 20). This domination was systematically carried out through the political and cultural hegemonic forces of Manila, primarily that of the state and the succeeding colonizers, the Americans and the Japanese. While Deocampo's book did not intend to answer the question of how a regional culture became national, raising it means questioning the basis and validity of the idea of "national" that is based on only one regional culture among many others.

The present essay precisely challenges the established notion that Tagalog cinema is the only one that constitutes the filmic heritage of the Philippines. Through a discussion of early and contemporary regional cinemas, the study illustrates how regional films reconstitute the country's filmic heritage through the combined efforts of film-makers, cultural workers and the audience. The discussion covers the key characteristics of regional films, particularly their deliberate use of vernacular languages. Given the latter characteristic, regional films have also been discussed in the context of the country's language politics and how regional films engage in the making of its linguistic heritage. Lastly, as contemporary regional film-making emerged beyond the capital where the base of operation of the film industry is located, its alternative film practices are presented as part of the heritage-making process of film-makers, cultural workers and audiences in the nation's periphery.

Heritage-Making from the Periphery

Film productions in the regions are practices of contemporary heritage-making, following Smith's formulation of heritage as "a cultural process" or a "practice of cultural production" (Smith 2014b). This implies that heritage is not only about the past but more importantly about the present. Specifically, it is "about the present, and about how certain interpretations of the past are used in and *for* the present" (Smith 2014a). In filmmaking, then, heritage is made every time a film is finished, since the directors offer their interpretation of social realities, past and present. However, the director is not the sole heritage-maker — there is a whole network of artists, managers and technicians. In the case of Philippine regional films, also included in the process are festival organizers and the local audience, which is usually composed of students.

While there is no agreement as to what definitely constitutes a regional film, one established characteristic is their use of regional languages. They are usually shot on location in a region by film-makers based in the region. The film-makers will likely hire local talent as cast and crew, although in recent years Manila-based actors have been seen in regional films. In some instances, film-makers with roots outside the capital who have migrated to other areas also make films in their mother tongue. In regional films, the familiarity of the language and unfamiliarity of the faces on the screen make it seem like the film is a documentation of the local culture. Consequently, the audience experiences these films differently than those produced in Manila.

A key example of contemporary regional film is the Cebuano film *Damgo ni Eleuteria* (Eleuteria's Dream, 2010) directed by Remton Zuasola. The film was shot entirely on Olango Island in Cebu and used the Cebuano language. It also employed local cast and crew. The film was funded by Cinema One Originals, an annual film competition in Manila funded by a cable channel owned by ABS-CBN, the country's biggest broadcasting network.

Damgo documents the day of departure of Eleuteria to Germany to marry a stranger in exchange for a fee. The money she will get from the arranged marriage will be used by her family to ease their life on the island. Shot in one long take, *Damgo* depicts the conflict in the lead character's decision to leave: if the decision only affected her, she would not leave the island; however, the survival of her family rests with her. In the end Eleuteria leaves her family, friends, neighbours, lover and life on the island to take a chance at a better life. The film depicts the extent of government neglect on the island that causes misery for its poor inhabitants. *Damgo's* portrait of poverty stands in juxtaposition to images of urban poverty in films produced in Manila. The pristine waters of Olango Island provide a stark contrast to the uncertain lives of the island's residents.

Damgo became a landmark regional film because of the national recognition it garnered, most important of which was winning the Best Film award at the 2011 Gawad Urian, awarded by the Manunuri ng Pelikulang Pilipino (MPP; Critics of Filipino Films), whose members include a national artist, university-based film scholars and critics, and film journalists. In the televised awards ceremony of Gawad Urian, Roland Tolentino, then chair of the MPP, announced the arrival of regional films in Philippine cinema. Additionally, *Damgo* competed in international festivals and brought home the Jury Prize from the Jeonju International Film Festival.

Indeed, regional films have been creating their own space in the landscape of Philippine cinema. After *Damgo*, another regional film received the Best Film at the 2013 Gawad Urian, this time a film from Davao City in Mindanao, a region that has been scarred by war for decades due to the presence of rebel Muslim and communist groups on the island. Arnel Mardoquio's *Ang Paglalakbay ng mga Bituin sa Gabing Madilim* (The Journey of the Stars in the Dark Night, 2012) brought to the fore the longstanding conflict in Mindanao between government forces and rebel groups from the perspective of locals who knew the history and root causes of the conflict. Other film-makers will not readily adopt the theme of war in Mindanao due to the complexity of the subject, but for a Mindanaon film-maker the war is a reality he cannot escape. It has become part of the daily fabric of life in Mindanao.

The film tells the story of Faisal, a boy whose rebel parents are killed early in the film. He is left in the care of his Aunt Amrayda and another female, Fatima. The three travel to escape the seemingly peaceful landscape of Mindanao, but behind the silences of the fields and the hills lies the enduring conflict in the land. Once in a while American soldiers appear on screen and it seems like an ordinary fact of life. The locals do not seem startled by their presence in the area, but this ordinariness communicates the tension of the fragile peace in Mindanao. Along the way the three travellers stop over at the house of Bapa, an older male, presumably a member of a rebel group. Faisal is journeying with a bag given to him by his mother. Bapa discovers that the bag contains a lot of American dollars, and he knows where the money comes from. He later explains to Amrayda that the order for Faisal's parents to be killed was issued because of rumours they were involved in kidnapping for ransom. Disillusioned, Amrayda gives up on the revolution. While crossing the sea at night to finally escape to the city, the three end up in an ambush, though there is no indication for the audience as to who has fired the shot. The film ends on a note of uncertainty as to whether or not the characters survive.

Aside from Cebu and Davao, two highly urbanized cities, other cities and provinces are also sites of regional film-making. Pampanga in Luzon, for example, has produced many films in the Kapampangan language; namely, *Ang Magkakabaung* (The Coffin Maker, 2014) by Jason Paul Laxamana and *Ari: My Life with a King* (2015) by Carlo Catu. The former is about a father who loses his child dues to poverty. He administers the wrong medicine to his daughter because he is unable to bring her to a doctor for a check-up. The film depicts the deadly consequence of poverty aggravated by the exploitative schemes of those better off. *Ari*, on the other hand, problematizes the fading local culture among the young generation through the story of Tatang Haspe, the King of Poets, and Jaypee, a young male who can only speak in Tagalog and not the native Kapampangan. Jaypee shows interest in learning Kapampangan through the poems of Tatang Haspe, but it is not until the end of the film that he learns to speak the language. Catu's *Ari* sends the message that the younger generation need not adapt and practice traditional culture in order to show appreciation, but the young should recognize the culture of their roots while living in a globalized society. Both these Kapampangan films received recognition in various international film festivals.

Prior to the advent of these relatively big regional productions, self-financed short and even some feature films were already being made, usually by non-professional film-makers, including students. The emergence of many regional film festivals attests to the growing number of short film productions in the regions. Some of these short films competed in national and international film festivals, such as the case of Anj Macalanda's *Wawa* (Mouth of a River, 2014). This film is a piece of visual poetry shot in Rizal province but adapted from a poem about a burial practice in Samar where the dead are wrapped in a straw mat and a procession takes place on the river to send the dead to their final destination. It won the Jury Prize in the Exground Film Festival, a festival of short films in Wiesbaden, Germany, and in the Cinemalaya Philippine Independent Film Festival. I consider these short film directors to be critical to the development of regional film-making because they are the ones who regularly produce films, and this is possible because of the practicality of the short film format. It must be noted that the production of short films is also considered important in the development of Philippine independent film-making in general (Deocampo 1995).

Examples of locally funded feature films in the region include Catu's *Ari* produced by a university in Pampanga and Mardoquio's first film, *Hunghong sa Yuta* (Earth's Whisper, 2007), produced as an advocacy film for Brothers of the Sacred Heart and the Loradzen Foundation as part of their "mobile peace education campaign" (Lumbera 2008). *Hunghong sa Yuta* depicts the consequences of the government's war against rebels in a fictional remote town called Hinyok, where all children are deaf and mute. The war has silenced its inhabitants and robbed its future generation of the ability to live peacefully. When the character Vigo arrives in Hinyok as a volunteer teacher, not everybody welcomes his presence for fear he is a spy. The people eventually come to trust the outsider and are able to learn from him how to read and write. Their newfound knowledge provides them an alternative to the decades-old war in achieving peace. Gigi Alfonso, a member of the MPP, remarked that "the Mindanao story can only be well articulated by a Mindanaoan as proven by *Hunghong sa Yuta*" (Alfonso n.d.).

Aside from demonstrating a successful model for local film production, *Hunghong sa Yuta* was also successfully distributed in the Davao region. The film was screened, not inside commercial cinema houses, but in the auditoriums of various schools throughout Davao, and even in Manila. According to Mardoquio, the film, which was produced for 800,000 pesos (less than US$20,000), earned approximately 2 million pesos (around US$45,000).[2] This shows the commercial viability of regional film-making made possible by a synergy between the efforts of film-makers and educational institutions. The success of *Hunghong sa Yuta*'s alternative distribution conveys the idea that film-makers need not be dependent on the traditional mode of distributing films where big companies provide the capital and distribute in commercial theatres. A new mode of film-making requires a new mode of producing and distributing films.

Meanwhile, the emergence of regional films can also be attributed to factors external to the desire of film-makers to create films. One of which is the advent of digital technology. The availability and accessibility of digital video cameras have made it possible for independent film-makers to create their films. While commercial cinema in Manila was declared to be dead, independent cinema, not only in the capital but also in many regions outside it, have risen. Like the surge of independent film-making in Manila, regional film-making has also benefitted from the advent of digital film technology. Other factors include the availability of short film courses or workshops to hone skills needed in film-making (Gutierrez 2011, p. 54). One such long-running film workshop is held outside Manila — the Negros Summer Film Workshop in Bacolod City. It was founded by film-maker Peque Gallaga in 1991. Gallaga is known for *Oro, Plata, Mata* (Gold, Silver, Death, 1982), *Scorpio Nights* (1985), and his horror film series in the 1990s, *Shake, Rattle and Roll*. Independent film-making has also benefitted from production grants given by film festivals, government agencies, and even international funding agencies. Feature films from the regions, for example, depend highly on them. In addition, the relative ease and lower costs of post-production processes now allow film-makers to edit their films using their own laptops or desktop computers (Deocampo 2007, p. 21).

From another perspective, the emergence of regional filmmaking can also be attributed to the rise of urban areas outside Manila. According to the Philippine Statistics Authority, the country has thirty-three highly urbanized cities (HUC), or cities with a population greater than 200,000 and a 50 million pesos (US$1 million) income (L.G.S. Bersales 2016). A number of these HUCs are found outside the capital region. Urbanization in the regions brought along with it increased economic activity, resulting in expanded job opportunities for residents. Consequently, it gave people disposable incomes that could be spent on leisure and other personal uses, such as purchasing electronic gadgets like digital video cameras. In addition, urbanization opened up access to technology and the ways of the modern world, as what likely happened during the development of Tagalog cinema in Manila in the late nineteenth century (Deocampo 2007, p. 20). Indigenous cultures gradually fade into the background of sweeping global culture, causing alienation among locals.

Linguistic Turn in Filipino Films

In all of the mentioned examples of regional films, the use of a local language is their regional characteristic mark. In a country of 7,107 islands and 183 living languages, to use one's own language in a film makes it distinct from other film productions. By using their native languages, film-makers are able to achieve a deeper level of connection with the audience through the shared culture and identity articulated through it. The connection created through language adds a layer of emotional connection to local audiences, propelling them to engage more deeply with the local films. Local audiences appreciate films more when the dialogue is in their local language because they fully understand its idioms and nuances. It is also possible that they subsequently appreciate their language more or see it in a different light. As film-maker Laxamana communicated to me, when Kapampangan films began earning recognition abroad, Kapampangan audiences and film-makers began appreciating local films more.[3] In the process, the audience becomes part of the creation of local film heritage.

The use of a local language in regional films reinforces the vitality of the language. Moreover, it clearly identifies the film-maker's ethnolinguistic background and it gives them a certain cultural capital when it comes to national film competitions. This identification marks their cultural difference from other film-makers. From the point of view of festival programmers, regional films create diversity under the banner of Philippine cinema. There are some current instance though where regional film-makers have elected to use Tagalog in their regional films, especially when they use Manila-based actors or when they want to compromise for the commercial release of their films.

Regional films also become the medium to document languages that are seeing diminished use. Manny Magbanua, a film-maker from Antique, directed a short film called *Handum* (Dream, 2010) that used his native Kinaray-a language, which according to him is no longer widely spoken.[4] Another example is that of Christopher Gozum from Pangasinan province. In his films — such as *Anacbanua* (Child of the Sun, 2009) which is narrated through poetry in Pangasinan, and *Lawas Kan Pinabli* (Forever Loved, 2011) based on a popular local folk song — he introduces the cultural texts of his mother tongue to the medium. It should be noted that even written literature in Pangasinan is very seldom practised. Although not endangered or dying, the languages mentioned have never been used previously in film. In these cases the film-makers advocate the popularization and contribute to the development of their local languages through the medium of film.

The decision to use non-Tagalog languages in films from the regions directly challenges the legitimacy of Tagalog as the language of Philippine cinema. With regional films, other Philippine languages gain legitimacy as languages of cultural texts. This has redefined the concept of a Tagalog-centric national cinema. Moreover, regional films become a medium to popularize and therefore preserve the country's multilinguistic heritage. As such, regional films have not only filmic but also linguistic value.

Regional film festival organizers also contribute to spreading the use of local languages by including their use in the competition rules. Laxamana, a film-maker and festival director of Cine Kabalen Film Festival (CKFF) in Pampanga, related that his insistence on including the use of the Kapampangan language in CKFF's competition rules is intended to spread its use through this effective medium. If it were not for this rule, he believes that Kapampangan film-makers would most likely use Tagalog due to their exposure to Tagalog films and their "illiteracy in their own language". He added that the use of the Kapampangan language seemed odd to local film-makers, especially the younger ones, and only a few initially joined the CKFF. As the years went by, however, Kapampangan films have been recognized both nationally and internationally, and local film-makers have been encouraged to use their mother tongue in their films. Laxamana hopes that the CKFF "will inspire the local film-makers [to make]... Kapampangan films, and the local audience to patronize and be proud of Kapampangan films".

Early Regional Films

Contrary to the common notion, regional film-making in the Philippines is not only a product of contemporary times. While Tagalog cinema dominated Manila and the other nearby provinces during the first decades of the country's film industry, Cebuano cinema dominated the islands in the central and southern Philippines. In fact, an industry on a par with the one in the capital is in place in Cebu City, emerging just a few years behind its counterpart in Manila. Three years after Jose Nepumoceno, considered the Father of Philippine Cinema, made *Dalagang Bukid* (The Country Maiden) in Manila in 1919, Florentino Borromeo, a Cebuano film-maker, made *El Hijo Disobediente* (The Disobedient Son) and screened it in Cebu and other neighbouring Cebuano-speaking provinces in the Visayas (Deocampo 2005).

The history of Cebuano cinema parallels that of Tagalog cinema. For instance, film studios in Manila and Cebu were established at almost the same time. Nick Deocampo, who wrote a monograph on the history of Cebuano films, reported that in 1938, Estudio Americo-Filipino, the first film studio in Cebu, was established by Dr Virgilio Gonzales. The big studios in Manila, such as Sampaguita pictures and LVN, were established in 1937 and 1938, respectively. Another parallel is that both Tagalog and Cebuano cinemas had their heydays in the 1950s. By this time the big three studios in Manila — LVN, Sampaguita and Premiere — had produced genre films throughout the year. Down south, as many as eight films per year were produced by thirteen film studios, eight in Cebu and five in Davao City in Mindanao. Co-productions were also done with sugar barons from Negros province, Teves and Arnaiz (Deocampo 2005).

In addition, Visayan cinema also produced commercially successful and artistic films. One of these films is *Salingsing sa Kasakit* (Sprigs of Sorrow, 1955), which was so good it was dubbed in Tagalog and shown in theatres in Manila. This is the first documented account of a regional film being shown in the capital, although not in its original language. Nonetheless, it is an important milestone in regional films penetrating the Manila market. Another Cebuano film shown in Manila in the mid-fifties was *Dalagang Pilipinhon* (Filipino Women), starring Cebu's "greatest actress" Gloria Sevilla and her future husband Mat Ranillo Jr.

Given the relative success of Cebuano cinema, it is surprising that many Filipino film history references do not include it. The history of Philippine cinema needs to be rewritten to recognize early Cebuano cinema's place in the country's filmic heritage. Deocampo is one of the few who has written about it. His monograph *Films from a "Lost" Cinema: A Brief History of Cebuano Films* was published only in 2005. In his discussion of Cebuano films, Deocampo referred to newspaper and magazine articles of Resil Mojares, a Cebuano cultural scholar and historian, written in the early 1990s when the Visayan film industry was in decline. One of the latter's articles refers to Visayan cinema as a "lost chapter in Philippine movie history", and indeed it is. Fortunately, a recent initiative by Paul Grant and Misha Annisimov, Cebu-based film scholars, to reconstruct the history of Cebuano cinema has led to the publication of archival photos and documents in *Lilas: An Illustrated History of the Golden Ages of Cebuano Cinema*. In this coffee-table book, Grant and Annisimov cover seventy full-length films from their three-year research and conclude that Cebuano cinema had two "Golden Ages" — the 1950s and the 1970s (J.R. Bersales 2016). Despite some debate over whether the 1970s can be considered a golden age for Cebuano cinema (since only seventeen films were produced from the late 1960s to the 1970s), this publication is a welcome development in revaluating Philippine cinema history and in reconstructing its filmic heritage.

Contemporary Regional Films

The initial emergence and growth of regional film-making can be attributed to the initiatives of the regional film-makers themselves who funded their own films, local producers, and festival organizers and the academe that provided venues to showcase regional films. Later on, regional film-makers were able to make feature films with external funding from competitive film festivals in Manila. These provided the opportunity for the dramatic growth and recognition of regional film-making at the national level. As early as its second edition in 2006, Cinemalaya, the prime film festival for Filipino independent films, funded partly by the Philippine government, resulted in films depicting stories from outside the national capital region. One such film is *Batad: Sa Paang Palay* (Batad, 2006), which tells the story of a young Ifugao boy living in Batad who works hard at different jobs in order to buy the pair of shoes he wants despite his family's financial hardships. When he eventually gets the shoes he wanted, albeit a bigger size, he decides to leave his Ifugao town in order to experience the city. While *Batad* can be considered to be a regional film, the fact that it is directed by a Manila-based film-maker originally from Davao City makes it a little complicated to categorize as such. Add to that the fact that the film is in Tagalog and not the indigenous or vernacular language of Ifugao province.

In the same year, Cinema One Originals produced Sherad Anthony Sanchez's *Ang Huling Balyan ng Buhi* (The Last Priestess of Buhi, or Woven Stories of the Other). It was reported that in order to make the film the twenty-two-year-old director had to immerse himself in an indigenous tribe in Compostela Valley in Mindanao, where he learned about the slow death of the practices of the *balyan*, or tribal priestess, due to creeping modernization in the area (IMDb n.d.).

The film tells woven tales of communist rebels, soldiers, siblings looking for their mother in the forest, and a village healer in a changing Mindanao. It depicts the various wars in the region and the threat of extinction to the Buhi tribe and its *balyan*. These tales were all situated in the Arakan Valley in North Cotabato. The film took the prize for Best Film in the First Features section of the ninth Osian's Cinefan Festival of Asian and Arab Cinema. The synopsis of the film in the programme of that event describes it as follows:

> This is a tale about an inter-tribal war and the threat of extinction hanging over the Buhi tribe. Its over-protective Balyan (tribal shaman/village healer) provides the backdrop for parallel tales, about the changing landscape of southern Philippines. Spoken entirely in Mindanao Bisaya and starring local people, *Woven Stories of the Other* is a revelatory look at a culture in flux. Manay, a priestess and bearer of stigmata, is at the center of several incidents that touch upon themes of identity, loss, and change. While the Balyan rails against her disappearing Buhi traditions, a group of guerrillas studies Marxism in the forest, and two children go on a search. A haunting score complements rich, tableaux-like images to create a vivid and sometimes conflicting portrait of a people. Beautifully shot and sparsely scored, this film is a masterful first attempt to tackle history of colonialism and imperialism in the director's country. (Tolentino 2012)

Outside the country, *Huling Balyan* was screened at the Hong Kong International Film Festival, Singapore International Film Festival, Asian Hot Shots Berlin Festival for Film and Video Art, Festival Paris Cinema and other festivals in Europe. Back home it was the frontrunner in Cinema One Originals in 2006, bagging Best Film, Best Director, Best Screenplay and a Special Jury Citation (IMDb n.d.).

Between *Batad* and *Huling Balyan*, the latter comes closest to what a regional film is because it is directed by someone with roots in the region where the story comes from; he therefore has access to local knowledge. This was made possible because of the Bisaya language widely spoken and understood in Mindanao that Sanchez shares with the indigenous tribe members. In addition, its narrative of local stories provides viewers with images of local issues that are of enduring national concern: conflict with the communist rebels, militarization, and fading indigenous cultures in the light of modernization. Essentially, the film articulates a discourse on issues specific to regional identity, politics, and economy.

On the other hand, *Batad* does not share *Huling Balyan*'s characteristics of regional film. Because *Batad*'s director is not originally from Ifugao where the story is set, his access to the local culture is limited. While it may be true that he can conduct research and immerse himself in the indigenous culture of the North, the language barrier restricts him from gaining a nuanced understanding of the northern tribe's culture. As noted, the film was not produced in the region's vernacular language, therefore affecting the Filipino audience's perception of the authenticity of the narrative. For some, the story seems generic, not rooted in the local experiences. It appears like a narrative transposed from Manila, or any other area for that matter, shot against the backdrop of the world-famous rice terraces. In short, it seems that the story of the young Ifugao male obsessed with owning a pair of shoes could occur anywhere in the country. An element of authenticity to the regional culture is absent from this film.

The regular production of films from the regions requires a continuously updated understanding of what constitutes a regional film. To provide a specific definition would be limiting, so conventions are only set when it comes to discussing characteristics. In this case, constant appraisal of regional film outputs is a must. Perhaps it is useful to say that a local audience would know a regional film if it saw one. The local audience can see through the director's intention and understand the discourse his film is trying to make in relation to regional issues.

Notwithstanding the ongoing debates over what constitutes a regional film and, by extension, national cinema, these films are now part of the country's filmic heritage and have changed the face of Philippine cinema. While foreign audiences may not appreciate the variations in the Philippine languages used in Filipino regional films — since they would not be able to discern the difference and rely on English subtitles — the cultural specificity embedded in the languages differentiates them from those produced in Manila. Some foreign film programmers appreciate this difference. For instance, for several years now Philip Cheah, programmer of the annual Southeast Asian Film Festival held in Singapore, has been programming regional films. In its 2015 edition the festival featured two films made by Davao-based film-makers: Charliebebs Gohetia's *Gukod sa Hapak sa Balud* (Chasing Waves, 2015) and Mardoquio's *Ang Mga Tigmo sa Akong Pagpauli* (Riddles of My Homecoming, 2013). The former tells the story of Sipat, a young boy whose family lives in the mountains. When their landlord forces them to leave the land, he and his family migrate to the unfamiliar terrain of a seaside community. The film documents the last days before their departure and shows the pristine landscape of Mindanao as a fitting backdrop to the narrative. On the other hand, *Riddles* is a silent experimental narrative film whose premise is based on the indigenous tribe's belief that the soul of a dead person returns to his/her homeland. When Alfad's soul returns to the land of his birth, he witnesses the suffering the community has experienced: hunger, poverty, exploitation, death. The silence of the film speaks volumes about the enduring issues in Mindanao through the montage of images throughout the film.

Other film festivals based in Manila that later emerged have also produced regional films. For instance, at the 2016 edition of the QCinema International Film Festival funded by the Quezon City government, four of the seven films presented in its main competition were regional ones. These were Bagane Fiola's *Baboy Halas* (Wailings in the Forest) from Davao, Kristian Cordero's *Hinulid* (The Sorrows of Sita) from Naga in Southern Luzon, Victor Villanueva's *Patay na si Hesus* (Jesus Christ is Dead) from Cebu, and Sheron Dayoc's *Women of the Weeping River*, which was the festival winner, from Zamboanga in Mindanao. All these films used the vernacular languages of the regions. With this regular presence at national film competitions, it can be said that in less than a decade regional films have made their mark on Philippine cinema and have allowed for a reconfiguration of traditional notions of national cinema.

Government programmes have contributed to the development of regional film-making, although these were not instituted solely for the latter. A case in point has been the competitive grants programme of the National Commission for Culture and the Arts (NCCA), which can provide partial funding for film production. The Film Development Council of the Philippines (FDCP), the agency tasked to develop the nation's film industry, established its flagship Sineng Pambansa (National Cinema) programme, "whose basic mission is to revitalize the Filipino film industry by encouraging and supporting the production [of] high quality films, and by promoting the works of Filipino film-makers to a wider public through national and international film festivals" (FDCP n.d.-*b*).

A film programme specific to regional films would not be instituted until 2009, when the NCCA launched its flagship Cinema Rehiyon project, a non-competitive festival of regional films. This launched in February

2009 at the Cultural Center of the Philippines in Manila, with the theme "Films from the Other Philippines". Twenty-seven film-makers attended and over forty short and feature films were presented (Cinema Rehiyon 2012). According to Teddy Co, who was the programmer of the first three editions of Cinema Rehiyon, it was difficult to locate regional films at that time. He had to travel from island to island, literally knocking on the doors of film-makers or anybody who could give him a lead in finding regional films. With its non-competitive nature, Cinema Rehiyon provides a friendly and relaxed atmosphere for these alternative voices and images so that stories of the "other" Philippines can be experienced. In his message for the maiden edition of the festival, Dr Miguel Rapatan, then chair of the NCCA Cinema Committee, said that in the regional films programmed, "one encounters a startling and stirring variety of alternative perspectives that remind us that the national culture defies easy or parochial definitions" (Rapatan 2009, p. 4). Since 2011, Cinema Rehiyon has been conducted outside Manila — the regions take turns to host it. It has been held in Davao, Bacolod, Los Baños in Laguna, Cagayan de Oro, Cebu, and Dasmariñas City in Cavite. Each year more films from the regions are programmed and more film-makers are "discovered".

To support this flagship project, the NCCA has also established the Cinemas in the Regions programme. This programme provides funds for regional film festivals, which serves the dual purpose of providing venues for regional film-makers to screen their films and making it easier to gather films for Cinema Rehiyon. As a result of this programme, several existing regional film festivals have been sustained and new ones established. On Luzon, the biggest island in the Philippines, some of these festivals include Cine Kabalen in Pampanga and Pelikultura and Pasale in Southern Luzon. In the Visayas regions in central Philippines, there is Bacollywood in Bacolod City in Negros Oriental, the Lutas Film Festival on the other side of Negros island in Dumaguete, Cine Kasimanwa in Iloilo City, and Binisaya and Lilas Binisaya in Cebu City. In the southern Philippines, Mindanao is home to one of the earliest regional film festivals — the Mindanao Film Festival, already in its thirteenth year. It started as an initiative of film enthusiasts based in Davao City. Held annually in December, the festival is a competition of films from all over the island of Mindanao competing in several categories. Other film festivals in Mindanao include Cinemagis in Cagayan de Oro City, Nabifilmex in Nabunturan, Compostela Valley, and Lantawan Film Festival in General Santos City. Outside the Cinemas in the Regions programme are other festivals based in the regions; one of which is the Salamindanaw International Film Festival in General Santos City. The latter illustrates the fact that cultural workers in the regions also work independently to participate in the development of local film communities and, consequently, that of the national. It must be noted as well that although NCCA funded the aforementioned film festivals, the funding is only partial and the festival organizers had to seek further support from local government, universities and schools, and private institutions. The festivals, in this sense, become an expression of each stakeholder's participation in heritage-making that strengthens local film culture.

While it is important to recognize the efforts of individual film-makers to redefine the country's filmic heritage, it is equally important to recognize the cultural workers based in the regions that organize film festivals and the audiences that attend them. In a regional film festival, a film competition is usually conducted to gather works made by local film-makers. These festivals feature short films made by student and amateur film-makers because of the form's practicality — they are a more realistic proposition to make than feature-length films, considering the context of regional film-making. Some festivals also programme feature-length films as their opening and/or closing film. The best short film is chosen from the finalists and awarded a cash prize. Some festivals also give out special awards, such as a Jury Prize, Best Actor, Best Actress, Best Cinematography, Best Screenplay, among others.

By organizing regular regional film festivals, cultural workers contribute not only to the development of regional film-making but also to the constitution of the country's filmic heritage. They provide critical support and encouragement to regional film-makers, and the regional festivals they organize allow local film-makers to gain experience and the confidence to participate in national film competitions. These festivals, including Cinema Rehiyon, sustain the growth and development of regional films because they provide venues for local film-makers to exhibit their work, especially younger film-makers and students. Scattered across the different regions of the country, the short film competitions of these festivals have produced a new breed of film-makers. Local film-makers are encouraged to remain in their home regions to make films and benefit from local production grants. In the past those interested in making films would tend to go straight to Manila, but today they have the option to stay and use the advantage of being able to tell stories of their regional culture. In some instances the cultural specificity of their films also becomes their ticket to international film festivals.

(The Lack of) Policies Relating to Film

Despite these developments, the issue of sustainability of regional film-making rests on the shoulders of every one involved. Funding for productions is volatile and uncertain, no distribution system for regional films exists, and no laws or policies exist to safeguard regional film productions. One initiative in Davao City has been started — most probably inspired by the quality of film outputs, the recognition received by Davao film-makers, and regular film activities in the city. In 2013, Peter Lat, former FDCP Davao Coordinator, stated that he received orders from then chair Briccio Santos — who is a Dabawenyo, a native of the city — to start dialogues with private institutions and the local government unit to create a film council in the city (*Edge Davao*, 1 September 2013). Interestingly, film-makers and cultural workers were not included in Santos' directive. This implies a number of things about how the government perceives film-making, the most obvious of which is the non-recognition of practitioners as stakeholders but perhaps only as workers in the industry. Film has always been seen as a commercial enterprise by the government, a steady source of state revenue through the thirty per cent entertainment tax being withheld from films that eventually benefits the FDCP. It can be inferred then that this directive is only aimed at expanding the commercial industry and not really at developing regional cinema.

Since Davao City is a regional city with one of the most active film scenes — having produced award-winning films and film-makers and being home to a thirteen-year-old regional film festival — it is but fitting for the city to have its own film council. *Edge Davao*, an online publication, reported that the FDCP-proposed film council would formulate guidelines and policies relating to film in the city. It reported that the Davao film council would also "extend grants and conduct trainings for the education and development of Dabawenyos who show intense interest and extraordinary talents to become players in the industry" (*Edge Davao*, 1 September 2013). In January 2014, *Mindanews*, a local newspaper, reported that the city council had already begun hearings for the ordinance that would create the film council (*Mindanews*, 2 January 2014). The report stated that Councilor Leonardo Avila III, the proponent of the ordinance, wanted the leadership of the film council to be composed of the film-makers themselves. In Avila's proposal, a cinema evaluation board was also to be established in the city, "to evaluate and grade films submitted to the council subject to the rules under Republic Act 9167, or the Act creating the Film Development Council of the Philippines (FDCP)". In the hearings that were held, film-makers and cultural workers attended and participated to ensure that the film council would not only promote film as entertainment but provide job opportunities to make the city film industry sustainable. *Mindanews* reported that the ordinance had been endorsed by the city's committee on education, culture and arts. But in December 2015 *Sunstar Davao* reported the passing of Avila (Canedo and Tejano 2015). In 2016 the country held national and local elections and a new set of Davao city officials was elected. No news on the final approval of Avila's film council ordinance has been reported to date.

At the national level, most film policies pertain to the taxation and classification of films. As already mentioned, all films, considered by the state to be entertainment products, are taxed a hefty thirty per cent. Senate bills proposing to lower the entertainment tax have yet to be debated by legislators. Because of this constraint, producers are only encouraged to make films that will have assured box office sales. As a result, Filipino film releases are usually genre films that are rated G (general patronage) or PG (parental guidance) by the Movie and Television Review and Classification Board so as to reach as broad a paying audience as possible. Many of these films follow the generic formulas that the Filipino audience is used to. It is not surprising then that the blockbuster Filipino films fall into the comedy and romantic comedy genres.

Independent films, both from Manila and the regions, could not compete with commercial films in terms of distribution in cinemas. The pull-out policy of commercial theatres —referring to the practice of pulling films from theatres even during the first day of showing if it does not achieve the targeted sales quota — does not encourage a healthy environment for independent films to thrive. This points to the fact that the independent films produced should establish their own distribution system, just as the regional film *Hunghong sa Yuta* did. A group of film-makers in Davao has recently formed a group called Pasalidahay (screening or showing), whose main concern is distribution. Still in its infancy, the group aims to develop a viable model for distributing films in Mindanao, including those produced in the region itself. We see here another initiative from film-makers-turned-cultural-workers aiming to cement the place of regional films in the country's filmic heritage.

At present there is high hope that regional film-making will finally flourish with the support of the government. In 2016 the newly elected president, Rodrigo Duterte, who was a former mayor of Davao City, declared his intention to develop the regions primarily through federalism, which would entail a change in the system of governance. It remains to be seen whether Filipinos would adapt federalism; nonetheless, the president's mandate to focus on developing the regions would reverberate in the FDCP when its new chair, Liza Diño, adopted the policy in the context of developing regional film-making. On her first day as newly appointed chair, Diño announced her three-year plan, which includes the empowerment of regional film communities (FDCP n.d.-*a*). Since 2016 the FDCP has provided funding to NCCA's Cinema Rehiyon and regional film festivals like Binisaya in Cebu City.

The new FDCP chair's pronouncement is a welcome development because it means the national government has finally recognized the regional film movement that was begun by local film-makers and supported by local governments, cultural workers in the academe and industry, and the audiences. Without the bold initiatives of the local stakeholders, the national government would continue to have a Manila-centric view of Philippine cinema.

The Heritage of Philippine Regional Films

Film historians like Deocampo and Mojares recognized the role of regional film productions in the development of national film culture, one that is not centred on the film industry in the capital. Mojares, in discussing the revival of Cebuano cinema, suggested that "in building a strong national culture, the rise of alternative regional centers of cultural production is something we should not only welcome but actively promote (Mojares 1991). Picking up from the points raised by these two historians, regional cinemas as "centers of cinematic productions" and as "alternative regional centers of cultural production" (FDCP n.d.-*a*) and, if I may add, cultural distribution are thus necessary in the constitution of a national filmic heritage that is more inclusive and that recognizes the plurality of our cultures as expressed filmic narratives. What is considered "national" is not only what is in the capital or what uses the mandated national language — for it is limiting, homogenizing — but also a recognition of our diverse cultures as Filipinos. As Teddy Co, film archivist and present chair of the NCCA Committee on Cinema, said, regional films define a truly national cinema culture (Co 1987). This manifests in the various regional film communities that have emerged, with their own film-makers, audiences, festival programmers and organizers, and critics. Film-making at this point is no longer monopolized by those in the capital. Regional film-making completes the picture of Philippine cinema and it is only possible because of the combined efforts of regional film-makers who choose to make films about their home regions. Co claimed that the "maturation of regional film-making" is one reason why Philippine cinema is back on the upswing. Regional films "can now legitimately claim [their] position as the third leg in the triad of Philippine film-making: mainstream, independent, and regional" (Co 2013, p. 18).

In addition, regional film-makers introduce a "new" national consciousness in Philippine cinema through their films and cultural work, decentralizing film-making and redefining film-making practices. Film-making in the country has become democratized. This new national consciousness captures the various regional sensibilities, with all their complexities, cultures and identities, albeit partially, for perhaps no national cinema can wholly capture these aspects. It opens up a space for filmic expressions of variegated images of the country.

A Truly National Film Culture

The steady increase in the number of film productions in the regions, the growth of regional film festivals, the development of regional audiences, and the support of government and private agencies have all contributed to the strong presence of regional cinema in both local and national film culture. Regional films demonstrate the power of citizens to make a heritage that is meaningful to them. On the other hand, the value of regional films with respect to building a national filmic heritage lies in the plurality of filmic expressions, not only dependent on the dominant culture in the capital. Its value also lies in the unique cultural expression of film-makers from the regions. They use films to articulate how issues of national concerns are experienced in local contexts. In this way they expand our understanding of the "national" and connect regional issues with those in the capital and other regions.

Contemporary regional films represent a Philippines unlike that presented by commercial and independent films centred on stories from Manila. These regional films present a culturally rich country and celebrate our multilingual, multi-cultural cultures. They welcome the seemingly chaotic idea of forging a national identity based on this diversity. Philippines' filmic heritage, then, is becoming both multilingual and multicultural.

Regional film communities help to spread the use of regional Philippine languages by using a popular medium and consequently elevating the cultural value of the languages. The same goes for the insistence of film festival organizers of accepting only films employing the local language. In addition, the deliberate employment by regional film-makers of their mother tongue in their films keeps their languages in circulation, keeping them alive despite the fact that many in their regions no longer use them. In such cases, films become a medium to reintroduce the local language and to re-educate the population on their mother tongue.

At the same time that regional films constitute a national film culture in contemporary times, they also constitute the country's filmic and, by extension, linguistic heritage. Contemporary national film culture, which now legitimately includes regional films, articulates cultural differences and variations in the country and, at the same time, considers these varied articulations necessary in the making of a more inclusive Philippine national filmic heritage. In all of these, the role of the citizens that make up the regional film communities is crucial to the reimagining and constitution of the country's filmic and linguistic heritage.

Notes

1. Committee on Official Language Report by the Constitutional Convention on 28 September 1934. Quoted in Almario (2014), p. 23.
2. Arnel Mardoquio (film-maker), in discussion with the author, May 2015.
3. Jason Paul Laxamana (film-maker), Facebook message to the author, 6 May 2015.
4. Manny Magbanua, open forum at Cinema Rehiyon, Davao City, 9–13 February 2011.

References

Alfonso, Gigi. "Hunghong sa Yuta: The Ghosts of War". Manunuri ng Pelikulang Pilipino (MPP). n.d. <http://www.manunuri.com/reviews/hunghong_sa_yuta_the_ghosts_of_war> (accessed 5 February 2017).

Almario, Virgilio S. *Madalas Itanong Hinggil sa Wikang Pambansa/Frequently Asked Questions on the National Language*. Translated by Marne Kilates. Manila: Komisyon ng Wikang Filipino, 2014.

Bersales, Jobers R. "Celebrating Two Golden Ages of Cebuano Cinema". *Cebu Daily News*, 17 August 2016 <http://cebudailynews.inquirer.net/101841/celebrating-two-golden-ages-of-cebuano-cinema.> (accessed 1 February 2017).

Bersales, Lisa Grace S. "Highlights of the Philippine Population 2015 Census of Population". Philippine Statistics Authority, 16 May 2016 <https://www.psa.gov.ph/content/highlights-philippine-population-2015-census-population> (accessed 1 February 2017).

Cañedo, Dax. "Message". *Cinema Rehiyon Davao 2011* catalog. Davao City, 2011, p. 5.

Canedo, Karina V., and Ivy C. Tejano. "Davao Councilor Passes Away". *Sunstar* (Davao), 20 December 2015 <http://www.sunstar.com.ph/davao/local-news/2015/12/20/davao-councilor-passes-away-448072> (accessed 5 February 2017).

Cheah, Philip. "War Indeed is a Tender Thing". In Southeast Asian Film Festival 2014 festival programme. Singapore: Singapore Arts Museum, 2014, p. 8.

Cinema Rehiyon. "Cinema Rehiyon: A Brief History", 2012 festival programme. Bacolod, 8–12 February 2012.

Co, Teddy. "In Search of Philippine Regional Cinema". *Movement* 2 no. 1 (1987): 17–20. Quoted in Deocampo 2005.

———. "Found! New Cinemas from the Regions". In Cinema Rehiyon 2009 festival programme. Manila: National Commission for Culture and the Arts, 2009, pp. 6–7.

———. Introduction to Cinema Rehiyon 2011 festival programme, edited by Richard Bolisay. Davao City: National Commission for Culture and the Arts, 2011, pp. 6–7.

———. "Cinema Rehiyon: Crossing Over". In Cinema Rehiyon 2013 festival programme, edited by Richard Bolisay. Laguna: National Commission for Culture and the Arts, 2013, pp. 18–21.

Deocampo, Nick. *Short Films: Emergence of a New Philippine Cinema*, edited by Alfred A. Yuson. Manila: Communication Foundation for Asia, 1995.

———. "Films from a 'Lost' Cinema: A Brief History of Cebuano Cinema". Manila, 2005.

————. *Cine: Spanish Influences on Early Cinema in the Philippines*. Pasig City: Anvil, 2007.

Edge Davao. "FDCP to Create Davao Film Council". 1 September 2013 <http://edgedavao.net/the-big-news/2013/09/01/fdcp-to-create-davao-film-council/> (accessed 5 February 2017).

Film Development Council of the Philippines (FDCP). "An Empowered and Educated Film Community Envisioned by New FDCP Chair Ms. Liza Diño". n.d.-*a* <https://www.fdcp.ph/contents/news%3Fid%3DNew%20FDCP%20Chair%20Liza%20Di%C3%B1o> (accessed 5 February 2017).

————. "Sineng Pambansa". n.d.-*b* <http://fdcp.ph/contents/view?id=Sineng Pambansa> (accessed 4 February 2017).

Gutierrez, Jose C. III. "For the Youth: Pursuing Sustainability in Filipino Indie Filmmaking". *Plaridel* 8, no. 2 (2011): 53–70.

IMDb. "Huling Balyan ng Buhi". n.d. <http://www.imdb.com/title/tt0829198/?ref_=tttr_tr_tt> (accessed 4 February 2017).

Lewis, Paul M. "Tagalog". *Ethnologue: Languages of the World*. 2009 <http://archive.ethnologue.com/16/show_language.asp?code=tgl> (accessed 27 January 2017).

Lumbera, Bienvenido. "Film Review: Hunghong sa Yuta: A Mindanao Film for the Nation". *Mindanews* (Davao City), 8 May 2008 <http://www.mindanews.com/c68-films/2008/05/film-review-hunghong-sa-yuta-a-mindanao-film-for-the-nation/> (accessed 5 February 2017).

Marr, Timothy. "Diasporic Intelligences in the American Philippine Empire: The Transnational Career of Dr. Najeeb Mitry Saleeby". *Mashriq & Mahjar* 2, no. 1 (2014): 78–106 <http://lebanesestudies.ojs.chass.ncsu.edu/index.php/mashriq/article/view/27> (accessed 4 February 2017).

Mindanews (Davao City). "Davao City Wants a Film Council". 2 January 2014 <http://www.mindanews.com/top-stories/2014/01/davao-city-wants-a-film-council/> (accessed 5 February 2017).

Mojares, Resil. "Lost Chapter in Philippine Movie History". *Philippine Graphic*, 28 October 1991. Quoted in Deocampo 2005.

National Commission for Culture and the Arts. "Cinema Rehiyon: A Brief History". In Cinema Rehiyon 2012 festival programme. Bacolod City: National Commission for Culture and the Arts, 2012, p. 6.

Rapatan, Miguel. "Welcome Message". In Cinema Rehiyon 2009 festival programme. Manila: National Commission for Culture and the Arts, 2009, p. 4.

Smith, Laurajane. "Heritage and the Politics of Recognition and Misrecognition: Implications for Citizenship and Social Justice". Presentation at the International Conference on Citizens, Civil Society & the Cultural Politics of Heritage-Making in East and Southeast Asia, Taipei, Taiwan, 11–12 December 2014*a*.

————. "Uses of Heritage". In *Encyclopedia of Global Archeology*, edited by Claire Smith. Springer, 2014*b*.

Tan, Nigel. "What the PH Constitution Say about the National Language". *Rappler*, 11 August 2014 <http://www.rappler.com/newsbreak/iq/65477-national-language-philippine-constitutions> (accessed 4 February 2017).

Tolentino, Rolando B. "Huling Balyan ng Buhi: Pagkatangi ng Huling Balyan at ilang isyu mula rito". *Roland Tolentino* (blog), 9 May 2012 <https://rolandotolentino.wordpress.com/2012/05/09/huling-balyan-ng-buhi-pagkatangi-ng-huling-balyan-at-ilang-isyu-mula-rito/> (accessed 4 February 2017).

Tupaz, Voltaire. "How Filipino Became the National Language". *Rappler*, 30 December 2012 <http://www.rappler.com/nation/18809-how-filipino-became-the-national-language>.

8

Encounter and Counter-Narratives of Heritage in Macau

Sheyla S. Zandonai

At dusk, from the outer rim of Macau's Reservoir edging the Pearl River Delta, one can see the casino cluster on the opposite bank gradually light up, illuminating the darkening sky and projecting itself as a colourful sequin pattern over the still water. Next to it, a hill shrouded in darkness bears a solitary spot radiating a moving beam of light. Somewhat outshined by the LED panels and glittering signs that separate by a few hundred metres the casino district from the city's highest geographical point hosting one of its World Heritage sites, the Guia Lighthouse continues, nevertheless, to glow. This urban scene embodies the contrasting nature of struggles over space ensuing from Macau's drastic transformation over the last ten years. Materialized in this setting, the adjacent position of gambling and heritage is a powerful representation of the forces, complementary, but also uneven, which have marked their relationship throughout the integration of the Macau Special Administrative Region (SAR) into China. To some extent it signals the seemingly irreversible connection between the realization of capital and the (im)possibility of the social (cf. Bissell 2005: pp. 221–22). The ambivalences they evoke can, thus, be easily grasped in binaries, the old and the new, the colonial and the post-colonial, the past and the future — the latter of which carries the particular connotation in China that it can only be attained with the demise of the past (Zhang 2006). In this chapter, I argue that the relationship between the political economy of gambling and the emergence of "heritage" as a new cultural narrative of place in Macau is, however, multiple, claiming their striking opposition, rather than casting the invalidation of the social, acts as a catalyst for change.

In light — literally — of modern, extravagant and dominating structures over the cityscape, it is tempting to surrender to that mental construct of antinomies. Despite the fact that they hold true to some extent — a casino erected in 2008 is irrefutably *new* compared to an eighteenth century church — the processes these phenomena represent cannot be seen simply as a matter of the new replacing the old or the past succumbing to the future. As an economic activity, gambling is as old as some of Macau's historical sites and buildings, arguably older than many.[1] As a whole the city is a complex amalgam of different periods of urbanization, architectural styles, attempts at planning, and the lack thereof, underlying the battles and ideologies that have shaped their times and materialized differently in space. It is modern and old, highly contemporary and traditional, dense and congested, "spectacular" and low-key, with all these features coexisting more or less in harmony or in incongruity, yet rarely in a conventional manner (Park 1915, p. 578; Zandonai 2014; Chu 2015).

James Ferguson argued that it is rare that novelty enters the world in the mode of replacement: "Much more common, it does so by addition and layering. The new sits alongside the old, rearranging existing ways of doing things, but rarely simply erasing them" (2011, p. 196). In this process the past is written anew, memories are reactivated as buildings disappear, and novel, timely or frustrated appropriations of the city arise, responding to operations of urban replacement as well as *addition* that push people to pick their cultural struggles. It is over this process of addition, primarily physical, and the frictions and adjustments that have emerged therein, that I have tied my efforts to reflect upon the ways "heritage" has integrated the perception and experience of place in Macau in a novel way, against what has been voiced by residents and activists as the "ruthless" pressure of private interests following extraordinary conditions of a "gambling-led" economic growth.

In addition to infrastructure development at sites in Macau and in the Cotai — the SAR includes the Macau peninsula and the islands of Taipa and Coloane, connected by the Cotai landfill — destined to host casino projects or integrated resorts (IR), as the industry itself might refer to them, other commercial and residential properties have been part of the moving picture of urban restructuring in the city. The Guia Lighthouse, which I will deal with more specifically here, came under pressure under these conditions. The emergence of new developments responding both to private and public plans in the vicinity of this monument of Portuguese architecture has been highly contested by residents. Triggering scepticism and popular discontent about the ways economic policies have been handled with regard to the protection of classified sites, it has prompted various sectors of Macau's society to stand in opposition and demand accountability from the government (cf. Liu 2008; Chung 2009). In so doing, I argue, they have engaged in the production of counter-narratives to incumbent economic uses of space and to perceived threats to the city's material legacies, suggesting different cultural understandings of place that are worth examining.

The material I present here derives from long engagement with field observations resulting from ethnographic research conducted intermittently in Macau since 2006.[2] I was conducting fieldwork for my doctoral studies when the Guia case unfolded and actions by activists started, so I could follow part of the story in situ in 2006 and in 2007. After that I kept track of it for a while, mostly by reading the local press online, until I returned to the city the following year, 2008. In 2014, when I was once again in Macau, I revisited the data I had collected in my previous stays and conducted new interviews. The information gathered and analysed in this chapter results, therefore, from periods of immersion and from learning with local sources and informants (Agar 2008). It is complemented by newspaper reports, online information collected from social media platforms, government documents and statistical data, as well as relevant legislation.

The Political Economy of Gambling: Heritage on the Line

On 17 July 2005, UNESCO inscribed Macau's Historic Centre as the thirty-first World Heritage site in China (UNESCO 2005, p. 130). The campaign, led by the People's Republic of China (PRC), drew on the city's blend of Portuguese and Chinese material legacies, harnessing the rhetoric of "East and West encounter" and the "multicultural dimension" of Macau's historic roots (World Heritage Convention 2002). Yet, the conditions that enabled the candidacy to UNESCO harked back to the work of classification and preservation initiated in the 1950s by the former Portuguese administration, followed later by the involvement of China, through the Luso-Chinese Liaison Office, and UNESCO's scientific agency, the International Council on Monuments and Sites (ICOMOS), as early as the 1990s.[3]

Championing Portugal's historical presence as shared legacy, China's national programme for Macau has entailed the transformation of the city into a major tourist destination, backed by the expansion of the gambling sector, which was liberalized in 2002. Although in Macau the activity is far from being new — it was first legalized in 1849 (Pina-Cabral 2002, p. 94) — it gained momentum in 2006, when the city became the world's richest gambling centre. Macau currently remains the only legal gambling locality in the PRC, where the activity was banned in 1949 following the Chinese Communist Party's (CCP) rise to power (Fifoot 1994, p. 54).[4] Six gambling companies operate in Macau today, following the termination of the forty-year monopoly contract of Stanley Ho Hung-sun's Sociedade de Turismo e Diversões de Macau (STDM), marked by opaque transactions implicating the former secretary for Land, Transport and Public Works (DSSOPT), Ao Man Long, in illegal concessions of land and construction contracts (Liu 2008, p. 120) which enabled the doubling of the original gambling licences from three to six.[5]

This unforeseen change in the original liberalization act laid out several administrative irregularities. First, it overlooked the 1986 law, revised in 2001, which stated the liberalization could allow up to a maximum of three gambling licence holders, with no amendments to date (Law no. 10/86/M; Law no. 16/2001). Secondly, while tolerating that the owners of "sub-concessions" — as they are commonly known in Macau — paid rights of cession to the original concessionaires,[6] and not to the government, it converted government-controlled gambling licences into commercial sales. Misdeeds notwithstanding, the newly liberalized political economy of gambling and tourism has produced an important economic boom. Macau's stunning growth rates since the liberalization[7] have followed the trend of urban development and gentrification that has marked China's economic rise. The country's position as the second world economy, with growth rates close to ten per cent in the last decade, and the ways foreign Chinese and transnational investments have been involved with the *relocalisation* of capital in Asia — through direct investment and the development of financial institutions (Arrighi 1996; Smart and Smart 1999; see also Abu-

Lughod 1989) — all have had an impact in Macau through revenue increase due to the development of casino businesses and connected services and activities, such as hotels and real estate.

China's industrialization and rapid development since the launching of the 1978 reforms have been discussed at length with regard to the country's monumental, if unsettling, urban achievements and restructuring (Chang et al. 2000; Liu 2002; MacKenzie 2002; Zhang 2006; Smart and Li 2006; Nonini 2008). Akin to mainland China, where many cities have undergone deep urban renewal or been erected at a rapid pace nearly from scratch, from modest villages to thriving metropolises (Chang et al. 2000; Koolhaas 2000; Zhang 2006), construction sites in Macau have for a while been, following the liberalization, a constant rather than a temporary feature of place.

Since 2004, when the first casino ensuing from the liberalization, the Sands Macau, opened its doors, a rapid pace of construction has deeply transformed parts of the city's landscape and morphology. Along with massive infrastructure and property development came transnational and foreign capital, in addition to an important influx of populations, both immigrant workers and tourists.[8] Land reclamation, an old practice of Macau's urban development (Karakiewicz and Kvan 1997; Edmonds and Kyle 1998; Daniell 2015) has continued to alter the shape of its exiguous territory in attempts to cope with increasing demands for casino development, housing and infrastructure. Admittedly, political and economic elites, which are often the same in Macau (Lo 2009), have either constantly claimed that land and space are scarce resources in a city under great development pressure or pushed development regardless of law constraints, as the Guia case turned out to so clearly reveal.

In the meantime, many of the people to whom I spoke in Macau — regardless of ethnic origin — often recollected that places of their childhood or young adult life have vanished. The stories of Henrique de Senna Fernandes,[9] a well-known Macanese (土生) lawyer and writer who passed away in 2010, portray an old, laid-back city and atmosphere that belong, in many parts of the city today, to the memories of its people and the history and stories of place. Exerting pressure over prices, existent infrastructures and demographics, the political economy of gambling began, for instance, pushing small and medium enterprises out of business — a situation similar to the impact of new casino developments in the United States (e.g., Joliet, Illinois), where small businesses have disappeared due to corporate competition (Hannigan 1998, p. 152). In Macau, many had to close their doors due to changing needs in consumption, to the loss of the labour force to the casinos,[10] as well as prohibitive leasing prices.[11]

The rise in real estate prices, which I have discussed elsewhere and can only briefly introduce here (Zandonai 2017), constitutes but one phenomenon highlighting the strong forces at work worth considering in the study of Macau's contemporary urban formation. Overall, economic growth has often driven private interests, and to some extent the government, through a path that has engendered hectic change to people's lived spaces and the city's protected sites to the point of unrest. Several scholars have shed light on the increasing contestations that unfold from an urgent embrace of modernity into "living historical spaces" (Zhang 2006, p. 465), in China and elsewhere, which have engendered the destruction of protected areas in the name of "progress" (Chan 2005; Smith 2006; Herzfeld 2006; Brumann 2014). Drawing on the case of Kunming, the capital of Yunnan Province in southwestern China, Li Zhang argued that this kind of "development narrative" has often encouraged the formation of pro-growth coalitions between local governments and real estate developers, stirring "business-state clientelism" as a powerful force in the rise of a cadre-capitalist class in Chinese city politics today (Zhang 2006, pp. 464–65, 468; cf. Nonini 2008, p. 160). One of the contentious effects ensuing from this in China, Zhang noted, is that local governments have turned a blind eye to existing norms that classified urban sites and neighbourhoods for protection when the reforms started pushing heavily towards economic development and urban restructuring — the State Council designated Kunming as a "renowned historical cultural city" nearly ten years before the city's Master Plan was defined (1993–2010) (2006, pp. 465–66). The case of the Guia Lighthouse shows how popular forces have emerged against the political economy of gambling, revealing a multivocal and multi-scale involvement that has eroded ethnic lines often tied to the colonial stamp of "heritage", while resituating the narrative of a divided city more in line with a shared legacy.

The Guia Lighthouse: Looking East

The Guia Lighthouse, built in 1865,[12] is considered to be the oldest lighthouse of Western-architecture style in the south of China (Teixeira 1997, pp. 378–79; Macao Heritage Net; World Heritage Convention

2002). Macau's geographical location corresponds to its exact coordinates (113° 55' East and 21° 11' North). The building sits at the city's highest geographical point, Guia Hill (91 metres), integrated in a complex that comprises the Fortress, built between 1622 and 1638, and the Chapel, built in 1622. While in the Portuguese language those edifices are all named after Nossa Senhora da Guia, which could roughly translate to as Our Lady of Guidance, its Chinese name, 東望, conveys another meaning — "looking towards the East". The complex constitutes the second of the two core zones inscribed on UNESCO's World Heritage List, formally known as the Historic Centre of Macau.[13] With sites ranging across Portuguese and Chinese, as well as "foreign" legacies (e.g., the Moorish Barracks, the Protestant Cemetery), the first core zone is, however, broader and more representative of the global history of multi-ethnic coexistence and encounter that underlines the specificities of Macau's built heritage. In addition to the sites and monuments classified by UNESCO, a long list of historical sites and buildings of architectural interest[14] and artistic value, some of which overlap with UNESCO's, constitute the "local heritage" category created over the last thirty years by the Macau Cultural Affairs Bureau — commonly referred to by its Portuguese acronym, IC, that is, Instituto Cultural.

In light of architectural and urban complexities inscribed in different historical strata, highlighting the extent to which Macau's topography is both embedded and confronted with the city's status as a major tourist destination, the Guia Lighthouse was entangled in a rather incongruent episode in the city's recent urban transformation. In 2006 the announcement of several construction projects for high-rise buildings in the area surrounding Guia Hill initiated contentious debate. One of the constructions was destined to host the CCP's Liaison Office (99.91 metres), at Avenida Rodrigo Rodrigues. For the same avenue there was a plan for a fifty-storey mixed-use commercial and residential edifice (135 metres). Another project consisted of a residential building (126 metres) located at the Calçada do Gaio. Finally, there were plans for the expansion of Macau's public hospital building (Centro Hospitalar Conde São Januário). All these construction projects raised the problem that their planned heights would compromise the panoramic view from the lighthouse and obscure it from various points elsewhere in the city. In spite of the fact that they were not located in the designated World Heritage buffer zone, they were adjacent to a "Protected area" established by law in 1992 following the approval of provisions for height control intended to preserve visual connections to Guia Hill (Decree 68/91/M, Outer Harbour Reclamation Area Urban Intervention Plan-PIUNAPE) (Chung 2009, p. 149). That same year, however, Chief Executive Order no. 248/2006 issued by Edmund Ho Hau Wah revoked the previous decree. In addition to the argument of "land scarcity", the new order claimed it was necessary to provide the conditions to allow the development and expansion of the gambling industry.

The authorization for projects that conflicted with previous height restrictions in the area — 20.5 metres for the Outer Harbour Reclamation Area (NAPE) (Chung 2009, p. 149) — and the changes on altimetry quotes that followed were closely connected to the misdemeanours of former DSSOPT secretary, Ao Man Long. Turning a blind eye to the law, Ao was involved, among others, in opaque contracts for land concessions, approvals for land reclamation plans without Beijing's consent, and construction projects that ran counter to existent urban legislation (Liu 2008; Lo 2009). Although the secretary was arrested in 2006 and sentenced in 2008 to twenty-seven years in prison, a long imbroglio with regard to the Guia area was bound to evolve from this. When irregularities in the plans for the buildings in the area adjacent to the hill began to surface in the local press at the end of 2006, several associations became involved and different activist movements emerged, with some gaining momentum in their efforts to reverse the government's decision to approve the projects (Chung 2009; Chu 2015, p. 446). In addition to the Macau Architects' Association (AAM) and the Association for the Protection of Macau's Historical and Cultural Heritage, political representatives including the New Macau Democratic Association (ANMD) and members of the General Union of the Neighbourhood Associations (街坊, gaai fong) took part in the claims to protect Guia. Residents also organized themselves, forming groups to pressure the administration; namely, the League of the Guia Lighthouse Protectors and the Guia Lighthouse Protection Concerned Group, the latter composed of residents living in buildings located in areas adjacent to the new construction sites (e.g., Associação dos Condóminos do Edifício Merry Court).

Shedding Light on Heritage

Arguably one of the most interesting movements to have emerged from the social mobilization taking place at that time was the Guia Lighthouse "march". To Romano Lobo, an architect involved with different heritage protection activities in Macau, whom I interviewed on different occasions in 2014, this was a "truly popular movement": "I remember that a grass-roots association appeared at that time, which was something that [has] never happened in Macau, because there is always some manoeuvring, always one of those groups [backed by the CCP], and it was called the Lighthouse Association." He explained that a video anonymously posted on the Internet showing the final outline of the new projects planned for the Guia area was an important incentive to action. It was one of his colleagues, a young Chinese architect, who came to his office one day to show it to him. "It was terrible and that is also why we put it on YouTube, anonymously. And in the following couple of days, it became viral. Thousands and thousands of accesses." The forty-seven-second video Lobo showed to me in 2014 was uploaded to YouTube on 24 January 2007 and is still available online.[15] Opening with a dramatic sentence, "This may be your future Macau", the silent video continues by demonstrating a 3D virtual model of a block of residential buildings that was planned to be built near Guia Hill. It closes by asking a couple of questions: "Why? Do we deserve this?"

Still according to Romano Lobo, what was amazing about the movement was that the Lighthouse Association did not have a face, since many of the people behind it worked for the government. "These people were crucial … because it was a first social conscience about identity and heritage, [though] these were people from the government … so they could not speak. But they had, let's say, a more asserted conscience about what that loss represented. Thus, they were the ones who started this communication." After that, he noted, many people got involved, "legislators, political parties, groups and associations … when they received the information, they realized that this was important, and got involved and spread the information".

The League of the Guia Lighthouse Protectors, composed of roughly fifteen members, among them architects, engineers and historians, created a webpage (guialighthouse.blogspot.com) on which they regularly informed the public and campaigned for the protection of the lighthouse against "opportunistic development" (*Hoje Macau*, 30 January 2007). At the same time that the league and the Guia Lighthouse Protection Concerned Group were voicing their disquiet to the public and the local authorities, they raised international attention to the situation of Guia Lighthouse when they addressed a public appeal to UNESCO in August and October 2007.

In their letter the members of the league claimed that the "Macao SAR government broke its promise regarding its World Heritage nomination to UNESCO ... [and] has made it easy for private developers to build more and more high-rise buildings". The letter continues: "As residents who have grown up and lived in Macao, we are frustrated to be blocked from any detailed information about plans for those lands by the government and the developers. The plan has turned into a money game by the developers, which is unacceptable in a civilised world."[16]

This appeal, it should be noted, took place after experts from UNESCO had visited Macau in August that same year and concluded that the Guia situation was worrying (Chung 2009, p. 151). The league further engaged in the organization of public debates and exhibitions to raise public awareness about the risks the proliferation of high-rise buildings would entail for other classified sites (*Hoje Macau*, 30 January 2007). Through these strategies, Lobo claimed, they were able to communicate with different groups of people, and it was then that a new movement within the movement started, a real "procession" to the hill, as he describes below:

> At first, people protested, carried posters with sayings such as "Protect the Lighthouse". Then ... people started to march to the Lighthouse, up the hill, and there were people who talked, housewives, cab drivers, kids from school, people who worked at the market, everybody ... went there and spoke in their own words ... because there was no face, no leadership, and they spoke of their own will. And what was very special about it, was that this is a building of Portuguese origin being defended by the Chinese community, who answered to no command.

The fact that the majority of the people who got involved in the lighthouse protection initiative were residents of ethnic Chinese origin was also an aspect that struck me at first. After all, why would the Chinese go through the trouble to protect a site which embodies the Portuguese historical presence in Macau, and raises several associations with "colonial" memories? William Bissell wrote about a similar experience he encountered in Zanzibar while repeatedly meeting Africans who voiced their appraisal and longing for the colonial past (2005). In keeping with his suggestion (2005, p. 217), the question to be examined here points to the task of identifying the ways in which social aspirations and frustrations lead people to embrace or contest symbolic and material aspects of their history. One important answer to this question came from an interview I conducted in

November 2014 with Jacob Cheong Cheok Kio, former president of IC's Cultural Heritage Department (2006–15). To him the apparent improbability of ethnic Chinese agency towards the safeguarding of "Western heritage" is not the central question about the Guia movement:

> The Lighthouse is a modern lighthouse in the Far East.... It sent orientations for the ships, both Chinese and Portuguese, or from other countries. A hundred years ago, there was a lot of Chinese boats, and right now, fishermen.... So it is very important to the city, not only to the Chinese or the Portuguese.... And because the lighthouse has been there for more than a hundred years, it becomes part of the life of Macau, every day.

Acquainted with the movement and the march, Cheong explained that when Macau residents became involved, back in 2007 and 2008, they were initially focused on the visual impact near the Lighthouse. But while Macau "adjusted" from being a "small town to an international city", they also became increasingly concerned about the ways these changes would affect their lifestyles. "Of course, [in] this kind of movement there are some people very interested in protection, and I think they love Macau, because, actually, that [residential] building would have a very negative impact", he concluded. Thus, other than simply highlighting an ethnic turn, the Guia case revealed that the defence of "heritage" was about drawing a line between the people of Macau and the economic forces that were already yielding important changes to their lived spaces.

Disjunctures and Adjustments

At the beginning of 2007 the CCP announced that it would reduce the planned height of its Liaison Office building, complying with public opinion and Guia Hill's altitude, i.e., 91 metres. A few months later, in July 2007, it communicated that the height, originally planned to be 99.91 metres — a number intentionally the reverse of the year of Macau's handover to China — would be reduced by nearly 11 metres to 88 metres (*Hoje Macau*, 30 January 2007). Whilst the population received the CCP's decision with a mix of applause and reserve, the declaration by the Macau SAR government in October 2007 that it would maintain the 126 metres originally planned for the residential building located at Calçada do Gaio again triggered concern and discontent. Arguing that there should be no cause for worry since the building, although quite high was also rather narrow, the then director of the DSSOPT, Jaime Roberto Carion, also claimed that it was not realistic to expect a 360-degree view from and to the lighthouse in a city where space was scarce (*Tribuna de Macau*, 25 October 2007). This position from the government, when social engagement was already in motion and people have affectively committed to protect the Lighthouse, might have been a turning point. The Guia case turned into a moment to channel further frustrations that had been building since Ao Man Long's corruption scheme was revealed.

Contested reactions to the Macau SAR government's position continued to arise from local and international agents in addition to national agencies. While popular movements in defence of the Guia Lighthouse intensified, the director of UNESCO's World Heritage Centre addressed a letter to the Macau authorities in early 2008 in which he expressed his concerns about the situation of the lighthouse in the light of recent private development projects and threatened to withdraw Macau's inscription from UNESCO's World Heritage List (*Hoje Macau*, 17 April 2008). In the meantime, conservation authorities from China, invited by local associations to produce an opinion on the Guia case, also concluded that the situation was a cause for concern (Chung 2009, p. 151). Arguably one of the most striking stances came from the Chinese central government, of which the contested Liaison Office project, contiguous with the Guia buffer zone, was itself close enough to jeopardize Macau's second heritage core zone. Later, by the end of November 2007, the PRC National Committee for UNESCO and the State Administration of Cultural Heritage in Beijing sent a "letter of concern" to the Macau SAR government in response to the World Heritage Committee's appeal to Beijing. In the letter, they requested clarifications from the Macau government about the preservation of heritage sites, with special regard to the constructions adjacent to the buffer zones, urging the implementation of measures that could attune urban development to heritage conservation (Chung 2009, p. 151).

With UNESCO's support and pressure from Beijing, grass-roots movements had an opportunity, rather than to simply voice discontent, but to make that discontent heard. Zhang (2006) pointed out that increasing concern over the demolition and misuse of heritage sites in several cities in China that were denounced in the media and by international heritage agencies (e.g., UNESCO) have also prompted the State Council to take action with regard to the situation of "renowned historical cultural cities".

In Kunming, impending inspection and re-evaluation from the council led the local government to slow down urban restructuring and increase protection initiatives, for instance, through the preservation of century-old streets and the restoration of a traditional neighbourhood (2006, p. 467). In Macau, whereas UNESCO was only in a position to alert and advise, and the central government sat in a rather ambiguous position in its attempt to save face when it went back on its initial plan for the Liaison Office, the letters and appeals and people's continuous mobilization on the ground eventually prompted change on the part of the administration.

Restoring Light to Guia

Following the conclusion of a two-year study conducted in the Guia area by the DSSOPT and the IC, the Macau SAR government, still under chief executive Edmund Ho Hau Wah, adopted and published a new decision in the Official Gazette in April 2008 ordering the protection of Guia as World Heritage (Executive Dispatch no. 83/2008). The order defined new height limits that ranged from five to ninety metres for eleven new zones immediately surrounding the hill, totalling an area of 2.8 square kilometres in addition to the already established buffer zones. Although some applauded the initiative, the population received the plan with scepticism. In fact, and though the plan for a 135-metre building was never realized (the plan had not been licensed by the administration by the time the Guia dispute began), the new decision to set a 52.5-metre height limit for constructions in the zone where the Calçada do Gaio building was located led to other problems.

First, this decision would cut the planned 34-storey building roughly by half, when the structure had already reached 80 metres of its initially planned 126 metre height. The construction was suspended and the administration offered to compensate the construction company, San Va Construções e Fomento Predial Lda. However, the league was concerned about the amount of money the government was planning to offer the company as compensation and for how long. Secondly, supported by other associations, the league contested the new limit of 90 metres established for areas adjacent to the hill, questioning the decision's "scientific basis" and indicating that it could not be subject to verification given that the government never made public the results from the study conducted in the area. Moreover, experts and the representatives of associations agreed that the measures approved were not sufficient to rectify the problem: some of the heights permitted would continue to interfere with the view of the lighthouse.[17] In July 2008, however, popular claims about the risks new urbanization projects and private development entailed for the Guia Lighthouse became somewhat muted when UNESCO published a list of endangered World Heritage sites in which Macau did not appear (Chung 2009, p. 153).

Similar to the plans announced for the expansion of the public hospital facilities, which remain uncertain today, the fate of the building at the Calçada do Gaio continues to be a blank page in Macau's recent urban history. Ten years have passed since the Guia imbroglio began and no solution has been found to date. Whereas concerns with regard to financial compensation to the construction company still echo now and then in the local press, the company has not received any official notification from the government after several letters and appeals have been sent to the Macau administration (*Tribuna de Macau*, 17 April 2013; *Tribuna de Macau*, 22 April 2015; *Hoje Macau*, 10 August 2016). In 2011 UNESCO censured the Macau SAR government for not doing enough to adopt more efficient measures to safeguard the city's World Heritage sites, threatening once again to withdraw its nomination from the World Heritage List (*Hoje Macau*, 13 July 2011). In spite of the dismaying picture, new efforts from the local government emerged in 2013–14 when a more comprehensive law for the protection of cultural heritage was approved and ratified (Law no. 11/2013) following the approval of the new laws on land use and urban planning (Law no. 10/2013 and Law no. 12/2013). Together, they constitute attempts to counter adverse costs ensuing from economic development, while responding to local, national and international pressures on heritage preservation and the management of urban sites.

Conclusion: Adding to the Future

The Guia Lighthouse case is arguably one of the most representative movements with regard to heritage protection initiatives to have taken place in Macau since UNESCO's nomination in 2005. In addition to experts, the Macau SAR government, UNESCO and Beijing, it involved residents in an unprecedented manner in efforts to define and reconsider what place heritage could be ascribed in a society increasingly subject to the pervasive effects of economic growth. It highlighted the disjunctures created from the clash of different interests, sectors and ideas, and from the differing experiences of place that are entrenched in the public-versus-private struggles that have marked Macau's development since the liberalization of gambling in 2002. It encapsulates a moment of redefinition of Macau's economy, image and society which laid out social processes involved with "heritage" in its broadest sense: what is being created and why, and what will remain to be passed to the next generations (Smith 2006).

Hence, the emergence of "heritage" as a new cultural narrative of place in Macau is entangled with at least two other processes — *belonging* and *transmission* — espousing David Lowenthal's idea that heritage is preserved and maintained only if it is continually remade by fabrication and addition. "To reshape", he claimed, "is as vital as to preserve" (1998, p. 19). The Guia case was rather exceptional in this regard. And that is also why the League of the Guia Lighthouse Protectors was discontinued. It was an ad hoc association that was put together during a critical phase. When its members deemed their demands had been heard, and partly answered, they receded, but also because other mechanisms of heritage protection have emerged in the meantime — the new law, for one. The question of transmission with regard to the Guia case is, therefore, twofold: it lies in continuity as well as cultural transformation, since it has mobilized the Chinese population who had not until then been explicitly involved with heritage claims and protection initiatives.

Back in 2007 the activism that was taking place in defence of Guia was, thus, rather extraordinary. Collective claims and civic initiatives of this type are not commonly part of people's agendas and social position in Macau. Even today the enormous pressure from soaring real estate prices, rising living costs and the serious dysfunction of public transport due to the large increase in non-resident workers and tourists entering the city, for instance, have rarely elicited similar reactions. It is, thus, interesting to examine the Guia Lighthouse case in light of this hiatus. It shows that not all attacks on the public good or interests encounter the same fate. This is not to say that popular complaint and dissatisfaction do not exist, rather that if they do find a way on to the government's agenda it is not usually through the kinds of channels that were mobilized for the protection of the Guia Lighthouse — social media–oriented, anchored on international support.

Lately, however, the government has also been conducting regular public consultations. I attended one of them in November 2014 organized by the IC to debate the "framework" for the "Safeguard and management plan of Macau's Historic Centre". The auditorium of the Macau Museum, although not big, was full. Many young Chinese residents, a few experts, journalists, and a representative of the gaai fong all listened attentively to Guilherme Ung Vai Meng, IC's then president, and to Cheong from the Cultural Heritage Department, before the public offered comments and raised concerns and questions in the final part of the session. Nevertheless, and although the government engages more often with public opinion today, there is no guarantee that dissatisfied voices are finding their way into the government's plans (Lo 2009, p. 20).

Concerns with heritage seem to be a new element in the perceptions of ordinary people about Macau's urban reality, but these concerns cut across different sectors and appear to be building progressively into a more assertive position. Until the liberalization of the gambling sector, economic forces were not as hostile to people's daily environments and urban change was rather an episodic aspect to life. Attempts at safeguarding heritage can be seen as a way to resist drastic changes to one's immediate environment, emerging as a means to keep alive memories of place that belong to a near, but already strikingly different, past. Yet, rather than yearning for the return of a colonial past while embracing (European) heritage, the position of residents in defence of the Guia Lighthouse has ultimately shown how cultural struggles tied to the production of place and channelled into narratives of attachment to Macau have been shaped against the misuse of political power, the governance of capital, and the overwhelming social impact of an economy of tourism and gambling under Chinese sovereignty. Rather than solely engaging with the protection of the city's past, it highlights an ongoing and multifaceted struggle for the city's future.

Notes

1. Indications of gambling as a popular social practice and economic activity in Macau and in the south of China can be traced back to the foundation of the city in the sixteenth century (Porter 2000; Paulès 2010). As a taxed economic activity, it was first legalized in 1849 (Pina-Cabral 2002, p. 94).
2. I conducted fieldwork in Macau in 2006 (6 months), 2007 (6 months), 2008 (2 months), 2009 (2 weeks), 2013 (2 weeks), 2014 (5 months), and 2015–16 (10 months).

3. I owe this information to Cristina Flores, an architect working at the Cultural Heritage Department of the Macau Cultural Affairs Bureau, whom I interviewed in 2014.

4. Although gambling on horses has recently been allowed on the mainland, joining then the only type of gambling permitted in Hong Kong (Spencer 2008) since the activity was forbidden by the British administration in 1844 (Eadington and Siu 2007, p. 4).

5. The three original gambling licences were granted to Wynn Resorts (United States), Galaxy Entertainment Group (Hong Kong), and Sociedade de Jogos de Macau (SJM), a subsidiary of STDM (DICJ). The following three emerged soon after the formal licences were granted, when Galaxy broke with precedent granting a licence to Sheldon Adelson's Las Vegas Sands (USA). The two other original gambling licence holders followed in Galaxy's footsteps. SJM granted a sub-concession to MGM Grand Paradise (USA) in a joint venture with Pansy Ho, Stanley Ho's daughter, and Wynn Resorts to the Australian group Melco Crown (formerly Melco PBL), which has another of Stanley Ho's successors, Lawrence Ho, as its director.

6. According to MacDonald and Eadington (n.d.), SJM sold the sub-concession to MGM/Pansy Ho for a reported US$200 million, while the PBL/Melco sub-concession was sold for US$900 million (p. 2).

7. GDP growth rates in real terms for selected years: 26.9 per cent in 2004; 8.3 per cent in 2005; 14.7 per cent in 2007, 26.5 per cent in 2011, 9.2 per cent in 2012, 11.2 per cent in 2013 (DSEC 2015, p. 358).

8. According to the latest data released by the Statistics and Census Service (DSEC), Macau's population was estimated at 647,700 people in the third quarter of 2016, while the number of immigrant (non-resident) workers reached 180,277 people for the same period. For the whole year of 2016, roughly thirty-one million people entered the city on visit purposes (DSEC 2016).

9. See, for instance, *Nam Van* and *Mong-há*.

10. Jobs as croupiers are amongst the most financially attractive in Macau for people with basic education, with salaries reaching up to MOP$15,000 (roughly US$2,000). The sector employs several thousand residents; in 2013 roughly 48,600 people worked as croupiers and cage cashiers (DSEC*b* 2013, p. 72).

11. In 2013, local rents were raised by roughly 15 per cent (*Ponto Final*, 27 November 2013) and the selling prices for housing units skyrocketed to 43 per cent on a year-on-year basis (DSEC 2013*a*).

12. The year 1885, according to the Macao advisory board document (World Heritage Convention 2002). Teixeira argues that the lighthouse was rebuilt in 1874 after a typhoon on 22 September that year damaged it. Still, according to Teixeira (1997), a new edifice was erected in 1910 (p. 378). Chung (2009) argues that the lantern's beacon was renovated and reopened in 1910, but does not mention that the building was replaced by a new one (p. 148).

13. Core Zone 1 comprises "the central area of the historic settlement of Macao ... representing the integration of Portuguese and Chinese elements along the city's primary urban route, Rua Direita, which leads from the ancient Chinese harbour in the south to the old Christian city in the north". Core Zone 2 is situated some 500 metres east of Core Zone 1 (World Heritage Convention 2002).
14. Category created in 1992, Law no. 83/92/M (Wan, Pinheiro, and Korenaga 2007, p. 19).
15. <https://www.youtube.com/watch?v=XJZV-yad1EM>.
16. <http://guialighthouse.blogspot.com/2007/09/letter-to-world-heritage-centre.htmlhttp://guialighthouse.blogspot.com/2007/09/letter-to-world-heritage-centre.html>.
17. Among the strategic points that operate as visual corridors towards the hill listed in the text ratified by the government are the Ferry Terminal, which is the main access to the city from Hong Kong; Tap Seac Square, the largest square in Macau (13,000 square metres), located in Saint Lazarus Parish; and the Mount Fortress, adjacent to the Ruins of Saint-Paul (Executive Dispatch no. 83/2008).

References

Abu-Lughod, Janet L. *Before European Hegemony: The World System A.D. 1250–1350*. New York: Oxford University Press, 1989.
Agar, Michael H. *The Professional Stranger: An Informal Introduction to Ethnography*. San Diego, CA: Academic Press, 2008.
Arrighi, Giovanni. "The Rise of East-Asia: World Systemic and Regional Aspects". *International Journal of Sociology and Social Policy* 16, nos. 7–8 (1996): 6–44.
Bissell, William Cunningham. "Engaging Colonial Nostalgia". *Cultural Anthropology* 20, no. 2 (2005): 215–48.
Brumann, Christoph. "Heritage Agnosticism: A Third Path for the Study of Cultural Heritage". *Social Anthropology* 22, no. 2 (May 2014): 173–88.
Chan, Selina Ching. "Temple-Building and Heritage in China". *Ethnology* 44, no. 1 (Winter 2005): 65–79.
Chang, Bernard et al. "PRD Pearl River Delta". In *Mutations*, edited by Rem Koolhaas et al., pp. 280–308. Éditions Actar, 2000.
Chu, Cecilia L. "Spectacular Macau: Visioning Futures for a World Heritage City". *Geoforum* 65 (2015): 440–50.
Chung, Thomas. "Valuing Heritage in Macau: On Contexts and Processes of Urban Conservation". *Journal of Current Chinese Affairs* 38, no. 1 (2009): 129–60.
Daniell, Thomas. "Artifice and Authenticity. Post-colonial Urbanism in Macau". In *Asian Cities: Colonial to Global*, edited by Gregory Bracken, pp. 69–94. Amsterdam: Amsterdam University Press, 2015.

DICJ. "História da indústria de jogos em Macau". <http://www.dicj.gov.mo/web/pt/history/index.html> (accessed 13 October 2014).

DSEC (Statistics and Census Service). "Private Sector Construction and Real Estate Transaction, 4th Quarter 2013". 2013*a*.

———. *Yearbook of Statistics 2013*. DSEC, 2013*b*.

———. *Yearbook of Statistics 2015*. DSEC, 2015.

———. "Demographic Statistics, 3rd Quarter 2016". 2016. <http://www.dsec.gov.mo/Statistic.aspx?NodeGuid=7bb8808e-8fd3-4d6b-904a-34fe4b302883> (12 February 2017).

Eadington, William R., and Ricardo C.S. Siu. "Between Law and Custom: Examining the Interaction between Legislative Change and the Evolution of Macao's Casino Industry". *International Gambling Studies* 7, no. 1 (2007): 1–28.

Edmonds, Richard Louis, and William John Kyle. "Land Use in Macau: Changes between 1972 and 1994". *Land Use Policy* 15, no. 4 (1998).

Ferguson, James. "Novelty and Method: Reflections on Global Fieldwork". In *Multi-sited Ethnography*, edited by Simon Coleman and Pauline von Hellerman, pp. 194–207. New York: Routledge, 2011.

Fifoot, Paul. "One Country, Two Systems – Mark II: From Hong Kong to Macao". *International Relations*, no. 12 (1994): 25–58.

guialighthouse.blogspot.com <http://guialighthouse.blogspot.com/2007/09/letter-to-world-heritage-centre.html>(accessed 7 November 2014).

Hannigan, John. *Fantasy City. Pleasure and Profit in the Postmodern Metropolis.* London: Routledge, 1998.

Herzfeld, Michael. "Spatial Cleansing: Monumental Vacuity and the Idea of the West". *Journal of Material Culture* 11, nos. 1–2 (2006): 127–49.

Hoje Macau. "Salvo?" 30 January 2007.

———. "Interesses à régua e esquadro". 17 April 2008.

———. "Nada de novo no panorama". 13 July 2011.

———. "Mak Soi Kun exige acção do Governo sobre caso da Calçada do Gaio". 10 August 2016.

Karakiewicz, Justyna, and Thomas Kvan. "Regaining the Sense of the City: A History of Reclamations and Public Spaces in Macau". *Proceedings of the East West Conference*. University of Hawaii, 1997.

Koolhaas, Rem. "PRD Pearl River Delta". In *Mutations*, edited by Rem Koolhaas et al., pp. 309–35. Éditions Actar, 2000.

Liu Shih-Diing. "Casino Colony". *New Left Review*, no. 50 (March–April 2008): 109–24.

Liu Xin. "Urban Anthropology and the 'Urban Question' in China". *Critique of Anthropology* 22, no. 2 (June 2002): 109–32.

Lo, Sonny. "Casino Capitalism and Its Legitimacy Impact on the Politico-administrative State in Macau". *Journal of Current Chinese Affairs* 38, no. 1 (2009): 19–47.

Lowenthal, David. "Fabricating Heritage". *History and Memory* 10, no. 1 (Spring 1998): 5–24.

Macau Guia Hill. YouTube. 24 January 2007 <https://www.youtube.com/watch?v=XJZV-yad1EM> (accessed 11 February 2017).

Macao Heritage Net, Instituto Cultural de la R.A.E. de Macau. <http://www.macauheritage.net/en/HeritageInfo/HeritageContent.aspx?t=M&hid=50> (accessed 10 November 2014).

MacDonald, Andrew, and William R. Eadington. "Macau: A lesson in Scarcity, Value and Politics". The Institute for the Study of Commercial Gaming, University of Macau <http://www.umac.mo/iscg/publication/Publications/ExternalResources/Macau%20scarcity.pdf> (accessed 16 April 2015).

Mackenzie, Peter W. "Strangers in the City: The *Hukou* and Urban Citizenship in China". *Journal of International Affairs* 56, no. 1 (Fall 2002): 305–19.

Nonini, Donald M. "Is China becoming Neoliberal?" *Critique of Anthropology* 28, no. 2 (2008): 145–76.

Park, Robert. "The City: Suggestions for Investigation of Human Behavior in the City Environment". *American Journal of Sociology* 20, no. 5 (1915): 577–612.

Paulès, Xavier. "Gambling in China Reconsidered: Fantan in South China during the Early Twentieth Century". *International Journal of Asian Studies* 7, no. 2 (2010): 179–200.

Pina-Cabral, João de. *Between China and Europe: Person, Culture and Emotion in Macao*. Continuum: London, 2002.

Ponto Final. "Os dramas do arrendamento". 27 November 2013.

Porter, Jonathan. *Macau: The Imaginary City*. Boulder, CO: Westview, 2000.

Senna Fernandes, Henrique de. *Nam Van. Contos de Macau*. Macau: Instituto Cultural de Macau, 1997.

———. *Mong-há*. Macau: Instituto Cultural de Macau, 1998.

Smart, Alan, and Zhang Li. "From the Mountains and the Fields: The Urban Transition in the Anthropology of China". *China Information* 20, no. 3 (2006): 481–518.

Smart, Josephine, and Alan Smart. "Personal Relations and Divergent Economies: A Case Study of Hong Kong Investment in South China". In *Theorizing the City: The New Urban Anthropology Reader*, edited by Setha M. Low, pp. 169–200. New Brunswick, NJ: Rutgers University Press, 1999.

Smith, Laurajane. *Uses of Heritage*. London: Taylor & Francis, 2006.

Spencer, Richard. "China to Legalise Horse Racing and Betting". *The Telegraph*, 12 January 2008 <http://www.telegraph.co.uk/news/worldnews/1575374/China-to-legalise-horse-racing-and-betting.html> (accessed 19 March 2014).

Teixeira, P. Manuel. *Toponímia de Macau*, vol. 1. Instituto Cultural de Macau, 1997.

Tribuna de Macau. "Edifício na Calçada do Gaio 'não tem impacto grave' no Farol". 25 October 2007.

———. "Cinco anos de indecisão na Calçada do Gaio". 17 April 2013.

————. "Esperança renovada na resolução de impasse na calçada do Gaio". 22 April 2015.

UNESCO. "Decisions of the 29th Session of the World Heritage Committee, Durban, 2005". WHC-05/29 COM/INF.22. Paris: UNESCO World Heritage Centre, 2005.

Wan, Penny Yim King, Francisco Vizeu Pinheiro, and Miki Korenaga. "Planning for Heritage Conservation in Macao". *Planning and Development* 22, no. 1 (2007): 17–26.

World Heritage Convention. "Advisory Body Evaluation, Macao (China) n. 1110". 31 January 2002 <http://whc.unesco.org/archive/advisory_body_ evaluation/1110.pdf> (accessed 28 May 2014).

Zandonai, Sheyla S. "La Présence Portugaise à Macao: Une Culture d'Accommodements". *Portuguese Studies Review* 22, no. 1 (2014): 205–25.

————. "'Selling Out the City': Casino Development and the Question of Ownership in Macau". *Pacific Affairs* (forthcoming 2017).

Zhang, Li. "Contesting Spatial Modernity in Late-Socialist China". *Current Anthropology* 47, no. 3 (June 2006): 461–84.

9

Cultural Activities of the Chinese Community in Post-war Myanmar

Yi Li

Heritage, community and identity remain "malleable" (Harvey 2001, p. 310) for scholars who have for years been investigating the meaning of the past (Graham and Howard 2008, p. 13). Nevertheless, it is generally agreed that things related to the past are open to interpretation and manipulation under the present political and social contexts, and it is an ever-changing, ongoing process (Harvey 2001, p. 320). "If heritage is constructionist and concerned with the selected meanings of the past in the present, this suggests that the past in general, and its interpretation as history or heritage, confers social benefits as well as potential costs in the construction and reproduction of identities" (Graham and Howard 2008, p. 5). Indeed, this particular ambiguity presents a unique opportunity to make and remake heritage "according to the needs of articulating and empowering" (Crooke 2010, p. 17), sometimes by individuals and communities at disadvantaged positions.

This chapter examines the formation, maintenance and recent development of the cultural heritage of the ethnic Chinese community in Yangon in the post-war era. It looks at two Yangon-based grass-roots institutions, a Classical Chinese poetry society and a Chinese language library, and follows their ups and downs throughout the eventful decades between the late 1940s and the present day. For an ethnic-minority, ex-migrant community in a newly independent nation state that has been dominated by the indigenous majority, communal organizations like these have to walk a fine line to reconnect the ancestral past with a volatile and demanding present, in a balanced style through careful and conscious selections, and must constantly adjust their strategies. The heritagization of certain cultural practices not only established a relationship to the community's temporally and geographically remote, sometimes imaged, past, but also faithfully reflected the changing social environment of what was permitted and what was not. Furthermore, questions such as what is to be defined the community's cultural heritage and who has the authority to define it, have been negotiated over the years and are still open to debate. It is also worth pointing out that in post-war Myanmar the awareness of preserving heritage (heritage as we understand today) has been fairly limited if not non-existent among the cultural practitioners, and the most obvious driving force often came from contemporary geopolitical pressures and personal subscriptions. Interestingly, despite competing political influences and social obstacles, both cases chose to focus on literature and language, important markers of cultural heritage and ethnic identity (Edwards 1984), to find meanings for the community.

Introduction: The Chinese Community in Post-War Myanmar

In January 1948, Myanmar declared its independence from Britain. The newly established Union of Burma (later the Republic of the Union of Myanmar)[1] became one of the newest nation states in post-war Southeast Asia. However, it was far from a smooth transition. Just six months before the birth of the new nation, the founding father and the leader of the Burmese nationalist movement, General Aung San, was assassinated (along with other cabinet members), allegedly by his political opponent. Over the following decades, civil wars were fought between the Yangon-based central government and the military forces of several ethnic minorities, not only from the mountainous borders but also, in some cases, from the capital's suburban areas. Among the country's top leaders who followed Aung San throughout the anti-colonial and anti-Japanese struggles, there was an ideological split. Rival political parties, each with its militia wings, were formed by those who were not happy with Yangon, including several forces pursuing Communism.[2]

Despite all these political instabilities, ethnic conflicts and military turmoil, the early years of post-war Myanmar did witness a certain degree of development and prosperity in a limited number of urban centres such as Yangon. Emerging from the ruins of the Second World War, Myanmar could still boast solid commercial and agricultural bases, mainly inherited from its colonial past, as well as a pool of relatively well-educated and experienced professionals from its multi-ethnic population, including a small number of ethnic Chinese who first settled in the country in large numbers since the mid-nineteenth century under British rule.[3] When the Indian and European merchants, who had traditionally dominated the commercial and industrial sectors of pre-war Myanmar, left the newborn country, the Chinese quickly filled the vacuum and profited, in the short-term, from the development of the country's nascent industry (Fan 2003). For many Chinese who settled in urban centres, it was a small-scale renaissance, not only in commercial prosperity but also in social realignment. Communal activities and traditional organizations, interrupted by the war, were resumed and expanded with great enthusiasm and sufficient funds by the Yangon Chinese in particular. To adjust to the new agenda of an independent nation state, the ethnic Chinese prepared for the fact that they were no longer travelling merchants, labourers or sojourners with mobile flexibility beyond national borders. In the years immediately following independence, the ethnic Chinese continued to rely on their communal institutions and the well-established tradition of mutual support in a migrant community. In addition they set up new associations that were atypical for a traditional Chinese migrant society. Cultural organizations such as dancing and chorus groups, often associated with Chinese-medium schools, were particularly popular among the youth who were eager to embrace modernity and seek recognition in a new country.

But any discussion of Chinese communal activities in this period should not ignore the underlying political rivalry of contemporary Chinese politics after the civil war that divided the nation between the People's Republic of China (PRC) in Beijing and the Republic of China (ROC) in Taipei. As a matter of fact, it was almost impossible to identify any Myanmar Chinese organization in this period that was not associated with either a pro-PRC or pro-ROC faction. In many cases support from the homeland (either Beijing or Taipei), in terms of material, personnel and occasionally financial aid, laid the ideological foundation for many newly established, cultural-related organizations, and influenced century-old traditional establishments too. Politics remained an inevitable element of everyday life for members of the communal organizations and participants of communal activities in the early years of independence. Although both cases discussed here are pro-PRC, political influence also worked on other factions.

Whether they were aware of it or not, Chinese communal establishments during this period made a collective effort to have their cultural, communal and ethnic heritage integrated into the official discourse of a new nation state, having at times to negotiate with and sometimes struggle against it. This was albeit without any explicit aim at heritage-making, a concept that was not fully developed until the final quarter of the twentieth century in the West (McCrone, Morris and Kiely 1995, p. 1). Many in Yangon Chinatown believed their mission was to maintain and promote the traditional culture — a tradition based on a long history and a vast imaginary land of China as ancestral home — in a new era in order to give meaning to the community. But what sort of "homeland", or heritage associated with it, did they have in mind and put into practice? It could be argued that "the contents, interpretations and representations of the heritage resource are selected according to the demand of present and, in turn, bequeathed to an imagined future" (Graham and Howard 2008, p. 2). We witness here a highly selective and resilient process being conducted by communal establishments and their members. Based on ideological conflicts and policy changes within and beyond the country, personal experiences, perspectives and communal protocols meant that "certain artefacts, traditions and memories have been selected from the near infinity of the past. The key word here is 'selected'.... therefore heritages are present-centred and are created, shaped, and managed by, and in response to, the demands of the present" (pp. 2–3). For the cases considered here, the "present" refers to the eventful decades of the ever-changing political climate of Myanmar after 1948.

It was therefore not surprising that all cultural developments and heritage-making attempts came to a sudden halt in 1967, when the anti-Chinese riot broke out in Yangon (Fan 2012). In fact, the decline had been foreshadowed by the changing policies of the previous years. After the 1962 coup, Ne Win's military regime left almost no space for private commercial and social initiatives. From 1964, private businesses were nationalized, significantly affecting the Chinese whose main incomes were from the commercial sector. Similarly, private schools teaching in and private newspapers using non-Burmese languages were forced to close.

The consequence of not being able to use the Chinese language, the medium for a distinctive ethnic group and the culture it was associated with, could not be underestimated. Language is a fundamental element underlying both cases discussed here. The poetry society used a traditional and gentrified form of the language to express a cultivated outlook of a diaspora community. The library was founded with the explicit purpose of improving the proficiency of the language among the younger generation in the community. When this key marker of ethnic identity and ancestral culture was officially prohibited, the practice of maintaining and disseminating a cultural identity looked doomed for many years.

Zhubo Yinshe (The Zhubo Poetry Society)

In 1948, the year of Myanmar's independence, a group of Classical Chinese poetry lovers set up a poetry society in the capital Yangon. They decided to name it *Zhubo Yinshe* 朱波吟社, or the Zhubo Reciting Association. The word *Zhubo* came from an eleventh-century Chinese dynastic chronicle, *Xin Tang Shu*.[4] It uses Zhubo as an ancient name for the Kingdom of Pyu, a kingdom that once existed on the territory of present-day Myanmar. Ever since the name first appeared in the eleventh century, it has been one of a fixed set of options for later Chinese scholars to choose from to refer to the land of Myanmar and its people. It was therefore natural that in the mid twentieth century a group of Yangon-based Classical Chinese poets, immersed in their historical Chinese predecessors and literary metaphors, should decide to adopt this ancient name, not only to indicate the poetry society's present-day location but also to recall the long-established and gentrified link to Myanmar from a Chinese point of view.

Without the society's official records it is hard to know the background of its members and the criteria for membership. Individual cases suggest that members were often local intellectuals such as editors and journalists of Chinese-language newspapers and teachers from Chinese-medium schools. But the society also welcomed businessmen and other professionals with considerable reputations within the community and who were themselves fans and practitioners of Classical Chinese literature. Although most of the members were male, there were at least four female poets in 1981.

The Zhubo Society celebrated its founding anniversary on the fifth day of the fifth month of the lunar year, falling on the Chinese festival of

Duanwu 端午. This festival often claims as its origin the commemoration of the death of a well-known historical figure, the patriotic poet Qu Yuan from the fourth century BC. Further development of the legend of Qu Yuan leads to special events and symbols closely associated with the Duanwu Festival, such as dragon boats, glutinous rice wrapped in leaves, and warding off of evil spirits. In the lunar calendar of the northern hemisphere, Duanwu also marks the beginning of summer, although in Lower Burma it is in the middle of the monsoon season. Even without any textual or verbal explanation from the society regarding the choice of this founding date, the connection between the Duanwu Festival and classical poetry in the Chinese tradition is obvious.

Certainly, the Zhubo Society was not the only Chinese poetry society active in the immediate years after independence. In Yangon alone there were several societies (such as the *Chenguang* 晨光, or Dawn Light; the *Simei* 似梅, or Plum-like; the *Tiannan* 天南, or South of Heaven; and the *Caiyun* 裁雲, or Cloud-Tailoring), all of which were specialized in classical poetry. At least one society, *Baihua* 百花 (literally "hundred-flowers" but its pronunciation is close to 白話, the "plain language", or vernacular Chinese as opposed to Classical Chinese), worked in the "new-style" poetic form employing vernacular Chinese. Each society was associated with one of the contemporary Chinese-language newspapers in Yangon and regularly published the work of their members in the special columns or literary supplements of the papers. According to one contemporary member, despite the different political orientations of the newspapers and the poetry societies involved, the explicit mission to promote the tradition of Chinese literature and to improve Chinese language skills was nevertheless shared (Xu 2013).

At the height of their activity, amateur Chinese poets gathered regularly in the *Shifang Guanyin Si* 十方觀音寺 (Ten-facets Guanyin Temple), a Chinese Buddhist temple at the foot of Yangon's most important Buddhist site, the grand Shwedagon Pagoda. They composed new pieces, appreciated each other's works, and enjoyed these fine moments with gentrified peers (Xu 2013). The fact that these literature gatherings were organized in this particular way was itself a deliberate nod to the long-established tradition of generations of Chinese poets and mandarin gentry. Some of the most famous poetry events in this manner were organized and recorded as early as the fourth century,[5] and they have been deliberately imitated ever since.

The Zhubo Society seemed to be particularly close to the pro-PRC camp. Its associated newspaper was the *Renminbao* 人民報, which had a similar political orientation. In addition to publishing poems in the columns of the newspaper, the Zhubo also published the collective works of its members in a special anthology series, *Yincao* 吟草 (the Drafts of the Reciting). The 1951–52 anthology, published in September 1954, invited the chief editor of *Renminbao*, Chen Lanshen 陳蘭生, to write a preface. Chen was a well-established Chinese intellectual in Yangon whose journalistic career started before the war, when he worked for the left-wing newspaper *Yangguangribao* 仰光日報. He was himself an exponent of classical literature and his poems were included in this anthology. Chen's preface acknowledged the "rich cultural heritage, based on our thousand-year-long history … inherited by members of the Zhubo" and reminded them that it was their duty to "serve our great nation [PRC] and the local overseas Chinese, to praise … the work ethics, for the country, for the co-operation in and outside of our country, for peace, for our bright future, and for the socialist construction … this is a poet's duty, and also a duty of the overseas Chinese who now benefit from a strong homeland" (Ai Wu 1986). The political influence on the cultural heritage could not be clearer here. Although this society is "Zhubo"-based, its cultural orientation — and to some extent its political aspirations if not affiliation, at least in the 1950s — was entirely towards its ancestral land of China. It might not have been the most appropriate choice for the Myanmar Chinese, as this was the last thing any new multi-ethnic nation state would have liked to see among its peoples. However, it was a viable option that attracted considerable support and, while not everyone in the Zhubo might have been as determined as Chen, they were at least not uncomfortable with it.

Fushan Temple 福山寺 was a Hokkien temple located in a suburb of Yangon. It was established in the mid-nineteenth century[6] and later became a popular destination for excursions and day trips for ethnic Chinese living in central Yangon. When the temple was undergoing renovations in the early 1960s, several Chinese-style pavilions were specially commissioned by poetry societies, each of which bore the name of its donor, such as a *Zhubo Ting* (the Zhubo Pavilion, Figure 9.1) and a *Chenguang Ting* (the Chenguang Pavilion) (Xu 2013). Inside the Zhubo Ting a banner listed the donations and expenditure for the construction of the pavilion (in 1961). A donation of 4500 kyat was made by twenty-nine individuals, almost certainly all members of the Zhubo that year. The biggest donation came from Fan Liang

FIGURE 9.1 *Zhubo Ting*, Fushan Temple, Yangon, 2014. Photograph by the author.

范良, who alone contributed 500 kyat. Fan Liang was also the calligrapher who wrote the couplet on the front of the pavilion; the text was composed by Chen Lanshen.[7] After a series of political reshuffles and policy changes in the mid-1960s, the Chinese Buddhist temple near Shwedagon Pagoda was no longer suitable for any overtly Chinese gathering. Instead, the poets moved to Fushan Temple, which was quieter and drew less attention, to continue their beloved literary activity in a low-key fashion.

With the nationalization of private newspapers in Myanmar from the mid-1960s, there would be no public space for newly composed poems. The decades of the 1970s and 1980s remain largely unknown for scholars working on the recent history of Myanmar. What we know about the Zhubo is that it maintained its poem-writing gatherings in an informal way and continued to publish the anthologies irregularly, paid for from the pockets of members and for private circulation only. The story of a head of the Zhubo in the early 1980s allows us a glimpse of the Chinese community in Yangon during these shrouded years, including persistent efforts to keep the Chinese cultural heritage alive.

Lu Shaoting 盧紹庭 (Law Shaw Tin, or U Kyaw Tin, 1908–83), a Hakka merchant, led the society in the early 1980s. Current sources do not indicate the year when Lu became the director of the Zhubo, though he must have been in that position no later than 1979.[8] Lu was born in Yongding, a mountainous county in western Fujian from which many people moved to Southeast Asian ports from the nineteenth century onwards. His father was a country doctor who loved literature and who sent his son for classical education at the tender age of four (*Shaoting xiansheng zhuanlue*, p. 1). Lu claimed to have written his first poem at the age of thirteen (ibid., p. 9) and to have left his home for Yangon in 1922. After working as a shop assistant in various towns in the Irrawaddy Delta, Lu started his own business in the 1930s, opening a medical shop in Letpadan in 1934, and a second one in Hinthada the following year. These shops traded a wide range of products, from Chinese and Western medicines and groceries, snacks and processed seafood, to stationary and books (ibid., plates showing Lu's business cards). In 1942 the family fled the Japanese Occupation and temporarily settled in the coastal Fujian city of Zhangzhou. In 1946 they returned to Myanmar via Hong Kong and Thailand. The Lus soon re-established their business in Hinthada and Pyay (two big towns in the Delta), and expanded to Yangon in 1955 (ibid., p. 2).

Despite the nationalization of his many operations in the 1960s and a significantly reduced financial proposition, Lu remained a respectable member of the Yangon community and maintained a decent level of living. A picture of a family visit in 1980 to the Kan Daw Gyi (the Royal Lake, Figure 9.2), a popular park in central Yangon, shows two cars in the background and women and children almost all in Western dress in the forefront. A poem was also composed by Lu to commemorate this excursion. In 1981 he was the head of at least eight Yangon Chinese associations, among them the Yong Jing Association (for the Hakka), the Ho Sum (a Hokkien triad society)[9] and the Zhubo Poetry Society. In the same year, he was invited, for the fourth time, to visit mainland China as a prominent representative of the overseas Chinese from Myanmar. This is generally seen as recognition by Beijing of the status and dedication to the pro-PRC overseas Chinese. For Lu and his family and friends, including those in the Zhubo Society, the trip became a great opportunity for photography and composing poems. Upon Lu's death in 1983, members of the Zhubo composed a long poem in a special format, *lianju* 聯句,[10] as an obituary for its late director.

Lu's first personal poetry anthology, *Yijiang Shicao* 伊江詩草 (The Drafting Poems of the Irrawaddy), was published privately in 1971. A second one was published no later than 1981. Both of these were distributed among members of the Zhubo to invite reviews and critiques. There is no document mentioning the reason why Lu was chosen as the director. The poems he wrote did not express any extraordinary talent compared to some of his fellow poets. However, in a close-knit and highly factious community like the Chinese in Yangon, a reputation as an impartial, warm-hearted and well-regarded character with extensive connections across the social strata might be the most sought-after characteristics for any organization, regardless of its mission. In addition, his pro-PRC orientation certainly fitted well into the Zhubo's general outlook.

From among all the poetry societies thriving in the 1950s and 1960s, only the Zhubo survives. In 1997, in its 49th anniversary special collection, a new poem was cited in the preface claiming that the society's collective "passion for the Classical Poetry was as strong as aged wines, and the enjoyment of composing and reciting was beyond limit".[11]

The connection between the Zhubo Society and traditional culture could not be more obvious. Using the finest format of literature and the best level of the language, the poets were fully aware of their efforts to

遊燕子湖即景

莊康大道任飛馳　堤岸蔭林竹數枝
塔影鐘聲連鳥語　湖平寶鏡照英姿
清風沸面鴛鴦舞　好景怡神蜂蝶知
兒女成群親友二　獎車遊罷夕陽遲

一九八〇年秋

FIGURE 9.2 A family portrait of the Lus, 1980. From *Shaoting xiansheng zhuanlue*.

continue a cultural heritage that could be dated back to the dawn of Chinese history. Although the initial outlook was somewhat ambiguous between an ancient, almost imagined, China and the modern here-and-now Myanmar, over the years it has consciously implemented a practice suitable to an ethnic minority community, one integrated into everyday lives and improvised in an ever-changing environment in order to best accommodate local demands.

The Myanmar Chinese Library

On the busy thoroughfare of Maha Bandula Street of Yangon Chinatown today, there is a Chinese library located above street shops and pedestrian hawkers, on the second floor of a seemingly anonymous building (Figure 9.3).[12] Many Yangon residents, including members of the Chinese community, might not know of its existence, let alone visit its premises. The entrance to the library is on the first floor, marked by a very obscure sign, and reached by a steep, dark and narrow staircase up to its second-floor reading room. It opens daily from ten to five, except on Mondays.

Like the Zhubo Poetry Society, the Myanmar Chinese Library 緬甸華僑圖書館 traces its history to the days immediately after independence. According to its current librarian, the library started as a reading room for the Burmese Chinese Student's Union 緬華學聯 and its affiliated "Public Book and Newspaper Room" 公立書報社 in 1948. The reading room was originally set up on 16th Street in a room rented from the Burma branch of the China Democratic League 中國民主同盟, one of the pro-CCP Chinese political parties that survived after 1949 in China and whose members were mostly left-wing intellectuals. After 1950 the reading room was expanded and the designation as a proper library seemed appropriate. In 1957 it rented the fourth floor of a building on Maha Bandula Street between 23rd and 24th Street; the building itself belonged to the Cantonese triad society, Hong Shun Tang (Ngee Hain).[13] In 1963 it moved again, to its current address on Maha Bandula Street. All of these addresses were a short distance from each other and at the heart of Yangon Chinatown. The current multi-floor building at the corner of Maha Bandula Street (*Guangdong Dajie* 廣東大街, or the Cantonese Grand Street as it is known by the Chinese) and Bo Ywe Road (*Wushichi Lu* 五十呎路, or the Fifty-Feet Road) was also owned by the Hong Shun Tang. The library rented a large front room on the second floor, facing the busy Chinatown thoroughfare, at a rather nominal sum, with no significant rise in rent for many years up till 2014.

FIGURE 9.3 Myanmar Chinese Library, Yangon, 2014. Photograph by the author.

There were two sources for the library's initial collection. In the 1950s and the early 1960s, as part of its expansion, the library wrote to major bookstores and libraries in Beijing, Shanghai and Hong Kong requesting donations of books, in particular Chinese and international classics and Chinese-language textbooks. The most valuable collection was said to be some hundred volumes, bound by threads in the traditional way and dated from the Qing period, on the history of Yunnan and the Nanzhao Kingdom (a multi-ethnic kingdom in present-day Yunnan between the eighth and tenth centuries) and their historical interactions with Myanmar. The second source was from local Chinese communal associations. The 1950s and the early 1960s provided a brief window for the Chinese in Myanmar to consolidate and expand commercial and social networks in a relatively peaceful environment. As a result, many pre-war communal associations resumed their activities and built new buildings (such as the above-mentioned Hong Shun Tang). Special commemorative issues were often published to celebrate these important events and a copy would be duly presented to the library —

then regarded as *the* place where local Chinese-language publications were to be kept for future reference.

In the early years, one of the key missions of the library was to help students of Yangon-based Chinese-medium schools to improve their language skills and to foster a cultural attachment to the ancestral homeland by providing extracurricular and the latest reading materials. Its intimate relationship with pro-PRC schools and other organizations in Yangon were bespoken from the day of its foundation. Furthermore, the early leadership included overseas members of the Chinese People's Political Consultative Conference and headmasters of several pro-PRC schools in Yangon. The library was perceived as an essential component of the local Chinese-language education system, as well as a contact node between the Myanmar Chinese and major cultural and educational institutions in Mainland China.

It is not known how this communal institution, with a strong and explicit ideological preference and basing itself on a foreign language and culture, managed to survive the 1967 anti-Chinese riot and the years that followed. With the closure throughout the country of the Chinese-medium schools and Chinese-language newspapers in the mid-1960s, and the Yangon riot in 1967 that led to the deaths of dozens of ethnic Chinese school teachers, it was a miracle that a communal establishment with such extensive links to the sensitive parties involved was not forced to close immediately. One account attributed this lucky escape to the cautious measures taken by the library's management body and its staff members, claiming that "we avoid any explicitly titled books bearing or remotely related to communism, revolution, and alike [*sic*]. Therefore the monitoring government agencies and visiting plain-clothes informants would have no excuse to act against us." However, this is not convincing given the complicated circumstances at the time, and it is likely there are more subtle reasons that it is still not suitable to acknowledge, perhaps due to the "cautious measurements" that obtain even in post-2011 Myanmar where censorship is no longer a top priority of the government.

The post-1967 years saw the library troubled by two major issues: a lack of income and the loss of its readers and collection. For many years it relied heavily on community donations. A group of donors would subscribe on a monthly or annual basis. They formed a donors committee (size unknown), and used the funds collected to pay staff salaries (about five) and the daily maintenance for the premises. The amount of donations and the number of donors continued to diminish. In 1988 only three members remained in the donors committee. Nowadays the major source of funds for its everyday expenditure is the *hongbao*, the "red envelope" that is given at the annual Chinese New Year celebration by the Yangon Chinese community. Occasionally there are ad-hoc donations of cash, equipment or books from well-off Burmese Chinese or foreign visitors. Using one such donation in 1998, the library managed to undertake major renovations of the premises, installed a telephone and a satellite TV, commissioned new bookshelves and bought decorative plants for the balcony. Should a financial need emerge, the library would organize a special banquet and invite dignitaries from the community. According to the prevailing communal protocols, guests will each have to bring a big *hongbao*, the amount of which must significantly exceed the costs of the food and venue. The surplus, therefore, becomes the income of the library to solve the urgent financial problem. As the current librarian acknowledges, the annual *hongbao* income is just enough to keep the library running. Ever since he took charge in 1998 there has been no sustained plan to expand the collection. In fact, the library can barely manage to keep its existing collection. New books arrive sporadically from donors with rather diversified interests and tastes.

This leads to the other issue threatening the library: the loss of books and readers. According to some estimation the library had around 30,000 books when it was established, but in a 1998 tally only 10,800 survived, of which no proper indexing or care had ever been taken. The previously mentioned pride of the library, the Qing collection, had disappeared along with the entire post-war compilations of Chinese-language newspapers published in Yangon. There were no more special commemoration issues either, because for many years the community dared not organize, nor could it afford, large-scale celebrations as it once did. These days the books are locked in dusty bookshelves with glass windows. Some are clearly outdated, such as the Chinese encyclopaedic books dating from the 1950s aimed at imparting general knowledge to students. These are mixed with a few Burmese-language books on general topics from the same period. Later additions include odd titles of popular romance and martial-art novels from the mainland, Hong Kong and Taiwan from the 1970s to the present-day, and the occasional sets of reprinted Chinese classics and Chinese language textbooks, perhaps donated through the official governmental channel. With no proper plan for management and expansion, the library simply accepts any new books that are brought in by local residents back from overseas trips, therefore the selection is random and the standard varies greatly.

The chief librarian has tried at least twice, when he travelled to China in the late 1990s and the early 2000s, to receive pledges for donations of newer books. However, a persistent communication problem under the military regime had been Myanmar's unreliable international postal services. On one occasion, he recalled, a shipment of books from China, procured through his own personal connection, arrived at the Port of Yangon but failed to reach its designated recipient. The official notification from the Post Office said the goods were lost. But the librarian later found that the parcel was dumped at a recycling station not far from the Post Office, and he had to buy it back. This, however, was not uncommon under the junta. Many residents of Myanmar have similar stories to tell, regardless of their ethnicity or the nature of the parcels. Subscriptions to Chinese-language newspapers is another problem. Local Chinese newspapers have seen their ups and downs over the last few decades, even though the ban on non-Burmese language newspapers is no longer as strict as it used to be. In late 2014 the library subscribed to a weekly newspaper edited and published in Yangon, and a Yangon edition of a Bangkok-based daily newspaper. A subscription to a Singapore-based daily newspaper is sponsored by a group of sympathizers in Singapore, but there is no long-term plan beyond this one-off donation. No other newspapers from major centres in the Greater China region are available here, unless one counts the occasional, and often back, issues brought by travelling residents and visitors.

The institutional foundation of the library had been almost completely uprooted since the mid-1960s. The disappearance of Chinese-medium high school students immediately reduced its readership, and in the long term the disappearance of a generation who can read Chinese challenges the very existence of the library. Staff members willing and capable to work in the library are increasingly difficult to find, as fewer people in Yangon Chinatown have the necessary level of language to handle daily operations. In the 1970s and 1980s, one of the female poets from the Zhubo Society was the chief librarian. The current librarian was born in China and arrived in Yangon after the war. None of the librarians in post-war Myanmar have been locally educated.[14]

For many years the only visitors to the library have been a small group of ageing ethnic Chinese who come to watch a Hong Kong–based pro-PRC satellite channel (Phoenix TV), browse the newspapers, regardless of how inadequate they are, and play Chinese chess with their peers. It feels more like a seniors' common room than a library. There is hardly any need to open the dusty bookshelves and take out old books — or perhaps these regular visitors have already read all the books a long time ago. While the collection was initially set up to improve the language proficiencies of a younger generation, the current situation is completely the opposite.

Hanging on the inner wall, in a significant position, is a banner bearing the calligraphic work of the Chinese name of the library, written by a notable Chinese politician and writer, Guo Moruo 郭沫若. Guo was renowned for his left-wing literary works and had a prominent political career after 1949. The calligraphy was perhaps written when he led a PRC delegation to Myanmar in the summer of 1961. Back then this overseas Chinese community in a friendly, neighbouring, new Asian country must have been seen as promising and prosperous, and Guo would have been happy to accept an invitation from local intellectuals to write the name for a well-furnished Chinese communal library.

Compared to the Zhubo Society, which focused on a refined genre of literature and an elite membership, this language-based communal establishment took a different approach to disseminate the language and culture to the widest possible audience at the grass-roots level. But similarly we witness here efforts made to preserve Chinese culture. Among the strategies the library has taken, a less conventional yet notable one is the collection of *hongbao* during the communal festivities. Indeed, this communal protocol represents an essential, albeit mundane, aspect of the community's well-established everyday practice. In this regard, both the explicit mission and the daily maintenance of this community institution are "ingrained in the unspoken traditions and habits of everyday life" (Harvey 2001, p. 326).

Post-2011 Developments

Both the poetry society and the library work for "the demonstration or preservation of the identity of particular voices and cultures" (Graham and Howard 2008, p. 6), but the communal practice could not be separated from the bigger environment, even though neither of them, from their post-war experience, made explicit efforts to go beyond the inwardly looking community and push for a wider engagement with the general public. Up to the first decade of this century, like many other communal organizations in Yangon Chinatown, they have faced inevitable decline despite years of negotiation and struggle.

But if the formation of cultural and communal identity represents a constant adjustment, the ancestral past can always be selected and interpreted to reflect the new demand. This is particularly true for post-2011 Myanmar, where the country has been witness to an unprecedented series of political, social and economic change. Recent developments in cultural activities in the Chinese community has once again confirmed that heritage is a process subject to change and anything but a static entity.

The latest challenge to the library is imminent and almost unavoidable. In October 2014, Hong Shun Tang, the library's long-term landlord, wanted to take back the space, claiming there was never any official agreement signed regarding the rental. In response the library cited a "friendly" agreement and informal transactions between earlier leaders of both parties (once again a well-accepted protocol that has been widely used in this migrant community for decades). The dispute escalated and entered the legal stage in late 2014 and the library tried to solicit moral support by publishing articles, written in Chinese, on the community's online forum.[15] At the heart of the dispute, as anyone with a basic knowledge of the current property market in Yangon could easily point out, is the huge financial potential of a large space like this at the most premier location in central Yangon.

The recent changes in Myanmar have brought both challenges and opportunities for communities and their institutions. For instance, the renewed interest in Chinese-language education from the general public, this time for a very straightforward commercial purpose, could be an excellent chance to reclaim and expand the library's readership beyond the limited scope of the Chinese community. This could eventually lead to funding prospects. On the other hand, free access to the outside world through modern information technology could point to the library to expand its collection from paper to multimedia and increase its exposure to the rest of the world without going through the difficulties of traditional communication channels. This may make itself more appealing to a new generation of Chinese-language students. The possibilities are evident but, after all, it has to be the community's own initiative to move to the next stage, as it did half a century ago.

The abundance of possibilities in the post-2011 era introduces yet another layer of tension to the community and its heritage-making efforts;

that is, who is "entitled to make decisions about what is (or is not) heritage" (Waterton and Smith 2010, p. 10). In 2013 a young ethnic Chinese journalist from northern Myanmar visited the Myanmar Chinese Library and afterwards wrote an article for the Singapore-based *Lianhe Zaobao* (Duan Chunqing 2013). It faithfully described the decline of the library being "a place only people above 60 will go", and asked "What will become of it?" Being a young Myanmar Chinese with reasonably good Chinese-language education, the journalist was not lacking in nostalgia and sympathy. The question raised by the young Myanmar Chinese from outside Yangon, blunt as it may be, directly challenges the continued authority of the group of Yangon-based Chinese intellectuals from the 1950s. This is a group that was active in the post-war years, with access to community resources and heavily engaged in community activities. It inevitably means that some other members of the community, who were geographically or temporally disconnected from the above-mentioned group, were under-represented and therefore excluded from the heritage-making of the community to which they also belong.

Unsurprisingly, alternative interpretations and practices began to emerge to voice the "internal unease, disappointment, conflict or power" of other members of the community, who may decide against being part of "a blander, homogenous collective" (Waterton and Smith 2010, p. 10). A recent instance took place in March 2015 when the Pen Club of Southeast Asian Chinese Poetry Writers held its eighth congress in Yangon. It was the first time that this event had been organized in Myanmar. The congress was hosted by the Pentagon Poetry Society, a Myanmar Chinese poetry society writing "new-style" poems in vernacular Chinese (SEACPW n.d.). The Pentagon was founded by four young Myanmar Chinese in 2012 and has developed rapidly ever since. Almost all of its current members were born in the 1980s, grew up and received education in northern Myanmar, and are now living in various countries in Asia. Back in the 1950s there was just one notable Chinese poetry society to focus on the "new-style" poems. However, for the young Myanmar Chinese cultural practitioners in the 2010s, this particular literature genre was selected to best represent their own connections to the language and the culture.

Yet the relationship between "old" and "new" groups competing in heritage-making is subtler than being mutual exclusive. In the process of heritageization, each stage has its own merit and often prepares for the next. One may reasonably doubt the future of the Zhubo Society and its elderly members, but certain commonalities are easy to spot. The Pentagon members have often benefited, directly or indirectly, from the earlier cultural practitioners in Yangon Chinatown, as students and as readers. And like their predecessors, many Pentagon members in Myanmar, while writing poems in their leisure time, are full-time teachers in Chinese-medium schools or part-time journalists for Chinese-language newspapers. However, to adjust to the post-2011 era, this new generation of Myanmar Chinese poets is eyeing for a regional and international stage to "facilitate close exchange between Myanmar and the rest of Southeast Asia" (ibid.) through a modern Chinese-language literature genre. They are comfortable utilizing information technology for publicity far beyond the Myanmar Chinese community. Although the language remains a key issue here, it is now a linking point to the rest of the Chinese-speaking regions, instead of a cultural identifier that has faced many crises over the last decades.

Conclusion

This chapter looks at the complicated relationship between heritage, community and identity through two cases from post-war Myanmar. For the Chinese community seeking cultural identity and social recognition during the last six decades, the heritage has been "constructed and reconstructed according to time and place; on each occasion heritage is redefined according to what is most expedient" (Crooke 2010, p. 17). Over the years the community witnessed the birth of a nation-state newly emerged from its colonial past, the Cold War conflicts and anti-Communist movements in the region, long-term political isolation and, very recently, rapid and unexpected development. In response to all these changes, the "resurgence and reinvention of ethnic heritage is integral to the preservation process, as they are grounded on the existing social and political structure of society" (C. Li 2015). Both the poetry society and the library — by taking up certain cultural activities and preserving certain aspects of heritage with explicit missions and integrated everyday practice — renewed and redefined the community's relationship to its ancestral homeland and shared past. Yet, as the recent developments sufficiently indicate, the process of heritage-making is always an open book inviting new chapters and new readings. Indeed, against all odds, the Chinese community in Myanmar has constantly adapted to the changing environment in its interpretations of the past, and no effort has been spared to make it relevant to the present.

Notes

1. For the change of the official name of the country, see Chapter 3, note 1 of this volume.
2. For a brief history of post-war Myanmar, see Taylor (2009).
3. For the Chinese in colonial Burma, see Li (2017).
4. Original text in Chinese: 驃，古朱波也，自號突羅朱，闍婆國人曰徒裏拙。在永昌南二千裏，去京師萬四千裏。東陸真臘，西接東天竺，西南墮和羅，南屬海，北南詔。地長三千裏，廣五千裏，東北袤長，屬羊苴咩城. From "Nanman xia" (南蠻下), *Xin Tang Shu* (新唐书) (Beijing: Zhonghua Shuju, 1975).
5. One of the most famous gatherings happened in southern China in AD 359. Forty-one renowned literati joined this event near a hillside pavilion, *Lan Ting*, and composed thirty-seven poems. All the poems were recorded on the spot and a preface was composed. The preface was written by one of the best Chinese calligraphers of all time, Wang Xizhi. It has been the best known and most imitated pieces of Chinese calligraphic work ever since.
6. For the establishment of the Fushan Temple, see Li (2017, p. 129).
7. Banners and couplets of the *Zhubo Ting*, visited in November 2014. The front couplet reads: 朱樂品味撩鄉思，波影浮金洽綺懷.
8. Based on a farewell poem dedicated to the Chinese Embassy staff in *Shaoting xiansheng zhuanlue* (n.d.).
9. A couplet written by Lu is still in the Ho Sum Society in Hinthada, a town that played an important role in the early years of his commercial activities. Another couplet, written by his two sons, is also there.
10. In this format, each contributor composes four pairs of seven-character sentences using a predefined rhythm.
11. Original text in Chinese: 八仙過海顯神通，各有千秋氣魄雄；驃國詩情濃似酒，吟哦揮洒趣無窮, quoted in Xu (2013).
12. Most of the information cited in this section, unless otherwise indicated, comes from the author's interview with the chief librarian in May 2014, a private article written by the chief librarian in 2013, and the author's personal observations between 2007 and 2014.
13. For history of the Ngee Hain, see Li (2017, p. 162).
14. For post-war Chinese-language education in Myanmar, see Y. Li (2015, pp. 9–16).
15. For example, see several online articles on the Mianhuawang (缅华网) (Mianhuawang, 17, 23, and 25 October 2014).

References

Ai Wu (艾芜). "Ji yangguang huaqiao Chen Lansheng" (记仰光华侨陈兰生). *Xinwenxue shiliao* (新文学史料) 4 (1986): 42–45.

Crooke, Elizabeth. "The Politics of Community Heritage: Motivations, Authority and Control". *International Journal of Heritage Studies* 16, nos. 1–2 (2010): 16–29.

Duan Chunqing (段春青). "Huaqiao tushuguan" (华侨图书馆). *Lianhe Zaobao*, 19 March 2013.

Edwards, John. "Language, Diversity and Identity". In *Linguistic Minorities, Policies and Pluralism*, edited by John Edwards, pp. 277–310. London: Academic Press, 1984.

Fan Hongwei (范宏伟). "Miandian dulihou huaqiao jingji de bianhua (1948–1962nian)" (缅甸独立后华侨经济的变化 (1948–1962年). *Southeast Asian Affairs* (南洋问题研究) 2 (2003): 48–55.

———. "The 1967 Anti-Chinese Riots in Burma and Sino–Burmese Relations". *Journal of Southeast Asian Studies* 43, no. 2 (2012): 234–56.

Graham, Brian, and Peter Howard, eds. *The Ashgate Research Companion to Heritage and Identity*. Burlington, VT: Ashgate, 2008.

Harvey, David C. "Heritage Pasts and Heritage Presents: Temporality, Meaning and the Scope of Heritage Studies". *International Journal of Heritage Studies* 7, no. 4 (2001): 319–38.

Li, Chuo. "Heritage and Ethnic Identity: Preserving Chinese Cemeteries in the United States". *International Journal of Heritage Studies* 21, no. 7 (2015): 642–59.

Li, Yi. "Yunnanese Chinese in Myanmar: Past and Present". *Trends in Southeast Asia* 12 (2015).

———. *Chinese in Colonial Burma: A Migrant Community in a Multiethnic State*. New York: Palgrave Macmillan, 2017.

McCrone, David, Angela Morris, and Richard Kiely. *Scotland–the Brand: The Making of Scottish Heritage*. Edinburgh: Edinburgh University Press, 1995.

Mianhuawang (缅华网). "Mianhua Tushuguan he Lizhanrao xiansheng" (缅华图书馆和李焜尧先生). 17 October 2014 <http://www.mhwmm.com/Ch/NewsView.asp?ID=7070> (accessed 5 November 2014).

———. "Dashui Chongle Longwangmiao" (大水冲了龙王庙). 23 October 2014 <http://www.mhwmm.com/Ch/NewsView.asp?ID=7188> (accessed 5 November 2014).

———. "Miandian huaqiao tushuguan yanzheng shengming" (缅甸华侨图书馆严正声明). 25 October 2014 <http://www.mhwmm.com/Ch/NewsView.asp?ID=7207> (accessed 5 November 2014).

Shaoting xiansheng zhuanlue (紹庭先生傳略). Yangon, n.d.

Southeast Asia Chinese Poetry Writers (SEACPW) (東南亞華文詩人網). "Dibajie dongnanya huawen shiren dahui zai yangguang chenggong juban" (第八届东南亚华文诗人大会在仰光成功举办). n.d. <http://seacpw.com/tin_tuc/-59.html> (accessed 8 April 2015).

Taylor, Robert. *The State in Myanmar*. Singapore: NUS Press: 2009.

Waterton, Emma, and Laurajane Smith. "The Recognition and Misrecognition of

Community Heritage". *International Journal of Heritage Studies* 16, nos. 1–2 (2010): 4–15.

Xin Tang Shu (新唐书). Beijing: Zhonghua Shuju, 1975.

Xu Junquan (許均銓). "Diaoling de mianhua shishe" (凋零的緬華詩社), personal blog, 3 February 2013 <http://www.myanmarchineseliterature.com/home.php?mod=space&uid=13&do=blog&id=45> (accessed 5 November 2014).

10

Chinese Street Opera in Singapore: Heritage or a Vanishing Trade

Zhang Beiyu

Chinese street opera has had an active presence among Nanyang diaspora since the early 1900s. Initially, they were transplanted into Nanyang as an indispensable part of Chinese migrants' religious life. Later on, from the 1930s, colonial societies like Singapore and Penang began to exhibit unprecedented cosmopolitan features, one of which was the emergence of a vibrant entertainment culture. Over a long period, sojourning Chinese communities in pre-war Nanyang had witnessed the thriving of Chinese street opera for temple celebrations and the staging of commercial opera in theatres, cinemas and amusement parks. They formed an important part in the collective social memory of many diasporic Chinese. It was when they entered the post-independence era that the overall scene of traditional Chinese street opera began to decline. They became increasingly associated with ideas of a "dying art" and cultural heritage.

In this chapter we have placed Chinese street opera in the context of Singapore's nation building of the 1960s and 1980s. It was a critical time, in that immediately after independence the new nation-state was both embarking on a new phase and searching for cultural continuity.

The contentions and compromises that characterized this ambiguous transition could be appropriately mirrored in the ways in which Chinese street opera was hotly debated in public discourses. Significantly, the process of turning street opera into cultural heritage can be seen through a kaleidoscope of the different competing forces in the nation building of Singapore: the state, the citizens, and local diasporic/de-territorialized opera community.

However, Chinese opera is such an all-embracing category that it hardly imparts any meaningful understanding for a particular historical context. Yet, in this chapter we will focus on the earliest, most primitive and enduring form of the performing culture in Nanyang (later in Singapore): the street opera. Chinese street opera 街戏/大戏 (*jiexi/daxi*) was also sometimes rendered in local Malay terms as "Chinese wayangs". Both terms underline a fundamental feature of this performing culture: its socio-spatiality of "streets". Yet, by *street* it did not mean any street; rather, it was a sacred space with religious significance, such as the temple grounds often used for ritual celebrations for Chinese deities. Put simply, when we talk about street opera, we are referring to the sacred occasions whereby Chinese dialect opera were staged in the vacant streets near to a Chinese temple as part of ritual processions to entertain the spiritual beings. Their association with the religious and traditional practices of diasporic Chinese made them easily fall victim to the nation building of Singapore.

Secondly, Chinese street opera in Nanyang were mostly performed by four major dialect opera troupes — including Hokkien opera, Teochew opera, Cantonese opera and Hainanese opera — in accordance with the major ethnic-linguistic groups that migrated from South China to Nanyang. While we acknowledge there were great variations in performing styles and operations of the different dialect opera troupes, we have elected to focus on one particular form of dialect opera: the Teochew opera and troupes. When we come to the micro-history of a particular group of opera practitioners in the last section of the chapter, we will also zoom in on specific Teochew opera troupes. Part of the consideration for this is that in the post-independence era it was the Teochew opera troupes that were most actively engaged in and best known for their street opera performances. Moreover, the life histories of Teochew opera practitioners were not uncommon in depicting the struggles of people involved in this fading trade. Hence, exploring the individual memories of Teochew opera practitioners has enabled us to penetrate the contradiction between heritage and diaspora, one that is entangled with a unified national narrative and people's lived transnational diasporic experiences. Teochew opera troupes and practitioners were representative of the large group of people whose voices were marginalized and overlooked.

Street Opera and Troupes on the Road: Diasporic Mobility in Pre-war Nanyang

Roughly around the 1850s, early colonial accounts testified the existence of the earliest and the most enduring shape of Chinese theatrical spaces in the Straits Settlement: temple-theatres. Architecturally, temple-theatres refers to a sacred performing space constructed specifically as a semi-attached compartment to the main building of the temple for the purpose of street opera during ritual celebrations. Therefore, the textual and archaeological remains of numerous temporary and permanent temple-theatres in pre-war Nanyang best illustrated the indispensable role played by Chinese street opera and opera troupes in the history of Chinese migration. For example, Jonas Daniel Vaughan, who had served in the government of the Straits Settlement since 1846, was especially interested in the Chinese community in the territories. He observed that the Chinese gods were particularly fond of drama, as in front of the temple one would see "a large flagged square surrounded by a high wall, in which temporary stages are erected for theatrical performances" (Vaughan 1971, p. 52). Vaughan noted how Cheang Hong Lim 章芳琳, a wealthy Chinese businessman, had built a theatre opposite the gateway of the temple[1] so that when dramas were performed on the stage they could be fully enjoyed by Mah Choh Poh — sometimes rendered as Mazu 妈祖 (the Goddess of Sea) — and her attendant gods through the gateway (p. 58). Vaughan's account attests to the fact that the earlier phase of Chinese opera activities in Nanyang was closely linked to the religious practice of the diasporic Chinese; the ritual function of Chinese street opera had a major role to play in helping Chinese theatres take root in Nanyang.

More importantly, street opera in pre-war Nanyang was in such demand that there two distinct structures of temple-theatres to house the staging of a variety of opera performances developed simultaneously: one was referred to as *xipeng* 戏棚 (theatre shed), a kind of temporary shed with a wooden stage that could be dismantled easily; the other was referred to as *xitai* 戏檯 (theatre stage), indicating the construction of a permanent stage (Ling 2010, p. 226; Chen and Chen 1975, pp. 67–68). The availability of such flexible theatrical spaces in pre-war Nanyang further enhanced the mobility of opera troupes. They often made full use of the extensive networks of these temple-theatres, travelling from one locality to another, fully contracted with local temples all year round.

Yet it should be emphasized that the popularization of Chinese street opera and their accompanying temple-theatres (such as the ones of Thian Hock Temple 天福宫 in Singapore, Cheng Hoon Temple 青云亭 in Malacca, and Kong Hok Keong 广福宫 in Penang) in various forms was actually a product of the connectedness of the pre-war Nanyang region afforded by the especially mobile and resourceful diasporic Chinese merchants. Scholars have agreed that the construction of these earliest Chinese temples in Singapore and Penang should be attributed to important Malacca Strait Chinese. For example, it was Tan Tock Seng 陈笃生, a Hokkien-speaking ethnic Chinese born and raised in Malacca, who initiated the construction of Thian Hock Temple in Singapore. His family was involved in agricultural plantations in Malacca, but he chose to move to Singapore after Raffles made it a free port (Ling 2010, p. 19). These diasporic merchants used their acute sense for business to move between Malacca, Penang and Singapore to mobilize resources and maximize profit. In the process of their travels they brought along business practices, culture, lifestyles and, most importantly here, religious affiliations, which are evident at the Thian Hock Temple in Singapore and Kong Hok Keong in Penang (Lin 1986, p. 54). Put simply, in the single act of temple/temple-theatre building, we have seen multidirectional flows of people and capital, circulating to and among the important trading ports of Nanyang, from Malacca to Penang and Singapore (Frost 2005, pp. 43–48).

Following the ritual needs of the diasporic Chinese, an increasing number of opera troupes flocked to Nanyang for commercial opera tours. The booming entertainment market in Nanyang and the development of many cosmopolitan port cities kept luring Chinese opera troupes to seek profit and fame. Teochew opera troupes that had successfully toured Nanyang returned to Shantou not only with more money but also full of excitement at having discovered a niche market craving for "homeland opera". According to Wen Shu, when a troupe was considering the risk of venturing into the diaspora market in Bangkok, the *banzhang* 班长, the acting "diplomat" of the troupe, would send letters to the diasporic side expressing interest in touring the troupe there (Lin 1993, p. 23). Having received the messages about the planned tour, interested Bangkok Chinese merchants would mobilize into joint ventures to invest in it. Such investment usually included one-way travelling expenses and a fixed monthly salary for the troupe ranging from 2,500 to 3,000 baht (p. 23). The contracts were usually valid for four months, after which the troupe might receive a renewal if their performances were profitable. If not the troupe might have to look for other opportunities, either by turning to other diaspora societies or returning to their homeland (p. 23). Such ventures were deemed investments for diasporic merchants, and they entailed financial risk. If the performances generated profits in excess of the capital invested, the merchants might make a good fortune from the margin, but they ran the risk of losing money should the revenue from ticket sales fail to cover the salaries of the troupe. In other words, the troupe was not involved in the financial risk of the venture, as they received their fixed monthly salaries no matter how many tickets were sold. With more performing opportunities, better and more stable incomes and less risk, opera troupes swarmed into the region, hence travelling opera troupes began to be increasingly involved in the diasporic trading communities.

Examining the historical development of Chinese street opera, temple-theatres and commercial opera tours in pre-war Nanyang also illuminates the larger picture of Nanyang as a connected diasporic region and the kinds of roles Chinese migrants and their cultural religious and business practices had to play in it. For one thing, the emergence of temple-theatres and street opera in pre-war Nanyang cannot be separated from two significant historical processes: first, the flow of Chinese migrants and the accompanying cultural religious practice from *qiaoxiang* 侨乡 (native places) to the diaspora and second, the multi-directional circulation of people, ideas and practices among the Nanyang diaspora. Philip Kuhn helpfully theorized the process of Chinese emigration with his concepts of "ecologies" and the idea of a "corridor" (2008, p. 2). By "ecologies" he was referring to a specific natural, social and economic environment where the Chinese migrants lived and worked and where they developed ways of coping. By "corridor" he was referring to the two-way interaction and communication between the homeland and the sojourning society. Through the migrant "corridor", people, ideas, practices and goods were in constant exchange across geographical boundaries (pp. 43–52). However, the migrant "corridor" was often unstable due to changing "ecologies" — especially the new political and historical conditions of each diasporic society. Post-independence Singapore was definitely one such society that had effected a tremendous change on the nature of the diasporic/ de-territorialized migrant culture of Chinese street opera.

Street Opera, from Dying to Reincarnation: Nation Building and Heritagization, 1960s–1980s

The underlying diasporic/de-territorialized practices of the diasporic mentality — connectedness, mobility and regional interaction — were deemed essential to the very existential being of a performing culture like Chinese street opera. What then was the fate of these travelling troupes when we entered the era of nation building, in which rootedness, belonging and national identity became the priority? In this section we will highlight how the Chinese street opera troupes underwent a process of struggle, being driven to the point of dying out and then being revived, despite some half-hearted endeavours under different state imperatives.

One of Singapore's pioneer minsters, S. Rajaratnam, pointed out in the 1980s that there was a "supreme indifference" about Singapore's past. The indifference should be understood as a deliberate effort to divert memory away from a traumatic past that could hinder the independence struggle of the nation-state. Separation from Malaysia in 1965 was a traumatic episode that continued to remind people of the painful past. The history of different diasporic ethnic communities was seen as a hidden danger that could trigger racial riots in the "new" multi-ethnic nation-state (Kwa, Heng, and Tan 2009, pp. 1–2). These concerns attested to the vulnerability of the emerging nation-state, making it even more urgent for Singapore to make a break from the past. In particular, the state's emphasis on economic development could be seen as a rhetoric strategy to subtly shift people's attention from the contested past. To quote the words of Chua Beng Huat: "the economic is privileged over the cultural because economic growth is seen as the best guarantee of social and political stability necessary for the survival of the nation" (Chua 1995, p. 59). What came along with such an emphasis were the ideologies of multiculturalism, developmentalism and pragmatism. Guided by these top-down state ideologies, citizens were "de-rooted" by the overwhelming forces of Westernization, whereby the promotion of English-language proficiency further sidelined the diversity of ethnic/dialect traditions and culture.

As part and parcel of economic development, the post-war state launched a series of progressive campaigns,[2] by which the remaining vestiges of the past were erased. One of the most far-reaching, while no less controversial, projects was the implementation of public housing in the 1960s. The state initiated a discourse targeted at mobilizing kampong people out of their traditional dwellings. Specifically, words such as "clearance", "emergency" and "rehousing" were collectively circulated to legitimize the state's intervention in the reordering of space (Loh 2009, pp. 613–43). "The urban *kampongs* were criminalized as places of social danger — in threatening public health, safety and order — not only to the residents themselves but to society as a whole" (p. 628). The opposite to kampongs, the new public flats were hygienic, safe, ordered and therefore able to mark a new phase in the development of the independent nation.

The drastic changes to the physical landscape, represented by the mushrooming of modern Housing Development Board (HDB) flats, raised more pertinent issues about the incompatibility of citizens' traditional cultural practices with the modern understanding of spaces. On 8 September 1970, an anonymous citizen wrote to the editor of the *Straits Times* complaining that Chinese street opera generated unbearable noise through loudspeakers; the midnight tearing down of opera stages and food stalls created more suffering for the neighbouring HDB residents (*Straits Times*, 8 September 1970). The letter resonated so well with other citizens that complaints about Chinese street opera were filed widely in both Chinese and English newspapers from 1970 to 1974. Later, an "anti-noise campaign" was set in motion to reform the practices of Chinese street opera. Importantly, during the "anti-noise campaign", one of the most frequently expressed sentiments was the desire to relocate opera stages away from HDB areas. One letter writer even complained about people misusing HDB public spaces for the worship of shrines, staging street opera and funeral observances (*Nanyang Siang Pau*, 29 July 1974). Many also complained about the inconvenience of stages taking up their parking spaces (*Nanyang Siang Pau*, 26 April 1975). The common emphasis in these narratives is that citizens saw traditional practices represented by Chinese street opera as being no longer compatible with the modern spaces represented by public housing. Xin Guang, a writer for *Nanyang Siang Pau*, observed that even though a third of the population had moved into the "new environment", their minds and spirits — traditional customs and living habits — had not changed (*Nanyang Siang Pau*, 4 May 1971).

In addition there were several reports of "untidy wayang men" being fined for littering or for failing to clean up after their performances (*Straits Times*, 30 May 1972, 12 September 1972, 19 September 1972). Incidents of robbery and brawling were also attributed to Chinese street opera troupes, creating a stereotype of opera performers as uncivil and uneducated — Chinese street opera and its practitioners had become undesirable for the modern Singaporean identity. A decade after the public housing policies began to be implemented, citizens had been gradually equipped with the idea of what a proper Singaporean identity stood for — rationality, civility, progress and modernity — features opposite to what a traditional Chinese street opera represented.

In her study of the French Revolution, Mona Ozouf pointed out that the construction of a rational space was deliberately used to educate and discipline proper modern citizens. That is, after people had been constantly exposed to the reconstructed space they were supposed to consume the symbolic meaning of the particular form of spatial arrangement (Ozouf 1991). Likewise, the underlying logic of modern public housing, as James Scott points out, lies in the "self-confidence about scientific and technical progress" and "the rational design of social order commensurate with the scientific understanding of natural laws" (1998, p. 4). In the same vein, James and Nancy Duncan warn that landscapes are dangerous ideological tools that make culture appear natural (Duncan and Duncan 1988). Therefore, the construction of landscape in a particular form is never innocent, but rather it naturalizes the power embedded in state disciplinary projects. Put simply, HDB projects helped to discipline residents into citizens with desirable characteristics, characteristics opposite to what the traditional kampongs and Chinese street opera spoke to. For example, in a speech by Dr Ahmad Mattar, minister for the environment, at an event at the Queenstown Sports Complex to enhance community spirit, he emphasized that as they moved into the high-rise flats a sense of social responsibility should enter the consciousness of each citizen.[3] For reasons of social responsibility, Dr Ahmad asked residents to change such of their unsocial habits as littering and noise pollution that could have a great impact on their neighbours. This indicated that living in HDB flats is closely tied to a healthy way of living that demonstrates greater social responsibility and community spirit.

However, the era beginning from the latter half of the 1970s witnessed a "mini-revival" of Chinese street opera in public discourses. Chinese street opera came to be increasingly rendered as a "dying art" (*Nanyang Siang Pau*, 3 September 1975). Initially, critics of local opera intended to redefine Chinese street opera by drawing on the vocabulary of "art".

They began increasingly to invoke the discourse of "art" in the hope of stopping traditional dialect opera from dying out. Huang Mushen, one of the local opera critics who published articles in the *Nanyang Siang Pau*, traced the genealogy of Teochew music back through over a thousand years of Chinese civilization. He believed that the original Teochew opera was all about elegance, rather than the unartistic sound that they now had (*Nanyang Siang Pau*, 24 January 1975). The underlying philosophy was that art is eternal — a culture that could stand the test of time proved to be an art. Accordingly, as many dialect opera had a history of over a thousand years, they ought to possess eminent artistic values that had kept them alive and vibrant over the centuries. However, it should be pointed out that street opera (as mostly performed by dialect opera troupes) had never been seen as a form of art, nor were their performances ever judged by aesthetic standards. Rather, what had always accompanied street opera had been the religious context in which rituals were conducted and sacrifices made. Using a secular aesthetic criteria to judge traditional religious performance, or even to replace the ritual street opera, was not only a misconception, but it was also an effort to circumscribe traditional street opera with a modernist rationale.

Secondly, underlying such a positive discursive turn to the preservation of Chinese street opera, lay a more profound shift in the state's cultural policies. After a decade of exuberant economic development and industrialization, excessive expressions of materialism, individualism and hedonism appeared to have developed. Meanwhile, the emphasis on English proficiency had made the younger generation become so westernized that they were easily subject to the unhealthy "yellow culture". Fearing that its citizens were undergoing deculturalization, the government appealed to the discourse of "Asian values", with Confucian ethics being promulgated as the key to economic success in the post-colonial era. Chinese street opera definitely benefited from this new "Asian renaissance" (Chong 2003, p. 464). In a speech delivered in parliament in 1976, MP Huang Shuren spoke of the role of Chinese street opera in the nation building of modern Singapore. He held that "while we forbid the performances of Chinese wayangs, our ministers were often seen enjoying the opera performances of overseas troupes; yet as a matter of fact, it is our own wayangs that have more intimate ties with the history and tradition of Chinese opera" (*Nanyang Siang Pau*, 20 March 1976). By situating the "overseas" and "foreign" performing troupes opposite to the local and national ones, Huang called for an opera performance for "our own". In this way Huang subtly redefined Chinese street opera as a tradition belonging to the national culture of Singapore. Here, efforts of going back to one's history and culture bring us to the dialects of the past and the present. "The past validates present attitudes and actions by affirming their resemblance to former ones" (Lowenthal 1985, p. 40). At this juncture, the past as embodied in Chinese street opera no longer spoke to the worthless residue of times gone by, or the antithesis of modernity; rather, they were picked up as useful resources upon which a national identity and culture could be constructed, albeit through careful selection and appropriation.

Noticeable efforts had been made in drafting new cultural policies, yet with an emphasis on the potential of culture in facilitating the process of nation building. For example, the Board of Tourism had established the Handicraft Centre where opera troupes were often invited to stage performances during traditional Chinese festivals in order to satiate the touristic gaze (*Nanyang Siang Pau*, 20 February 1978). One of the most outstanding projects was the Hong Lim Park Opera Series from April to June 1978, co-organized by the Ministry of Culture and the Board of Tourism. "Operas in Cantonese, Hokkien, Teochew and other dialects will be held during the weekends every fortnight on a make-shift stage" (*Straits Times*, 21 February 1978).

The process of making street opera into national cultural heritage shed much light on how a particular form of tradition was mobilized and appropriated by the concern for nation building. In the first place, turning Chinese street opera into heritage started with the recognition of its cultural and historical value. However, the very act of recognition — the act of identifying what should be preserved — alters the original shapes of the past. First, certain aspects of Chinese street opera had to be highlighted to make them attractive for display. Features such as antiquity became a central element the organizers attempted to promote. For example, there was a deliberate remark on the antiquity and enduring history of particular performing troupes — both Lao Yi Zhi Xiang 老一枝香 and Xin Rong He Xing 新荣和兴 Teochew troupes were particularly admired, with comments describing their history stretching over a hundred years (*Nanyang Siang Pau*, 24 April 1978). Thus, troupes that were able to exhibit such a history were the preferred candidates to achieve heritage status. Identifying troupes that could represent the authenticity of Chinese street opera became an urgent issue. It was clearly stated that Hokkiens troupes would be given a low priority as they were too "modernized", whereas Teochew troupes were favoured as they had the "best" quality (*Straits Times*, 27 March 1978). Interestingly, being modern was seen as being unable to echo traditional antiquity, and thus failed to capture the essence of heritage. Furthermore, during the Hong Lim Park opera series, it was the "ancient costume opera" 古裝戲 that were exclusively staged for the event, with actors performing in classic Ming dynasty garb (*Straits Times*, 27 June 1978).[4] A well-known local Teochew opera practitioner who once participated in the opera festival recalled: "because many of the audience were Europeans, we usually rendered the performances with more dazzling costumes and exciting fight scenes; these are the favourite bits for those foreign tourists".[5] The marks of previous ages generated a sense of exoticism for modern people in the same way as an alien culture does for foreign tourists; gradually, the Chinese street opera that was performed became increasingly enclosed by a foreign country.

In the process of heritage-making, while certain elements were deliberately emphasized, other elements that were crucial when it was a "living" culture were rendered useless and had to be discarded. For example, choosing Hong Lim Park as the only venue for these opera performances was a meaningful decision. It was claimed that this central location with convenient access to transportation made it ideal for attracting both local residents and tourists. However, what went unstated was the fact that organizers took pains to preserve the most important feature of Chinese street opera: that of the "street". Performing in an open-air street environment was the most outstanding feature that came to define the tradition of Chinese street opera. Lowenthal once pointed out that people try to maintain their connection with the past through an attachment to a familiar locale; thus the locale should be shaped and preserved (Lowenthal 1985, p. 42). Hence, the street environment was seen as a cultural heritage that should be preserved to draw older folks who are used to sticking to their old habits. However, it should be pointed out that the Hong Lim Park opera series was more like a process of renovation — a carefully planned refinement of traditional practice — than true preservation. It was impossible to perform street opera in the way they had used to, especially considering the traumatic experience the opera underwent during the "anti-noise campaign". Instead, the concept of "street" was redefined by the Hong Lim Park series such that not only was its traditional religious context stripped off but it was also strictly circumscribed within an ordered, designated and rational public space. Beyond this, it was noticed that at the end of the show there was a photo-taking session where the audience could go backstage to get a feel for the lives of the opera practitioners; they could easily capture the moment with their cameras (*Straits Times*, 14 April 1978). Hence, not only was Chinese street opera enshrined as a heritage, but also the lives of the folk artists were regarded as part of the heritage displayed for popular consumption. The meaning of Chinese street opera was drastically changed as well, from that of a living culture that people regarded as part of who they were to more a display of heritage encapsulated from the past.

To sum up this section, the "mini-revival" refers not only to the fact that more positive attention had been placed on salvaging the tradition of Chinese street opera, but it also denotes organized top-down state efforts at redefining, articulating, appropriating and selecting traditional practices so as to make it a "displayable" cultural heritage of Singapore. Heritage-making was understood as a common process of nation building through which a unique national culture and identity would be solidly grounded in the shared history, memories and tradition (Kong and Yeoh 2003, p. 23). However, rooted in the sub-ethnic dialect culture, Chinese opera found itself uncomfortably framed in the national culture undergirded by the official ideology of multiculturalism and pragmatism. This irreconcilable gap between Chinese opera and state ideology determined the transient nature of Chinese operatic heritagization, and it was doomed to fail. Our study on people's memories in the following section will further reveal the degree of complexity and alternative voices from those who saw their livelihoods and social lives dramatically displaced by the operatic heritage-making efforts.

Displacement by Operatic Heritage-Making: Nostalgia and De-territorialized Travelling

Despite the enthusiastic appraisals of government efforts at preserving the traditional culture of Chinese street opera, many opera practitioners had unsettling experiences which have long been silenced. In 1980, two years after the Hong Lim Park Opera Series, the idea of Chinese street opera as a "dying art" still hung over the professional opera circle. Mr Ng Eng Lay, an eighty-year-old master of an itinerant puppet troupe recalled bitterly of how in the past their performances attracted large crowds during the three biggest Chinese religious festivals, but nowadays he called it a "feat" to draw more than twenty people (*Straits Times*, 26 August 1980). The sense of doom for these traditional cultural expressions could be traced partly to the irreconcilable gap between a dialect-based traditional practice and the dominant ideology of multiculturalism, underwritten by the four racial categories — CMIO (Chinese, Malay, Indian and Others) — and the subsequent elevation of Mandarin as the lingua franca of the Chinese speaking community. Significantly, the use of Mandarin not only wiped out the ethnic and linguistic diversities within the Chinese community but also made dialects and the related cultural expressions irrelevant to and incomprehensible for the younger generations. The latter was particularly detrimental to Chinese street opera, as it basically cut off the ways in which traditional knowledge could have been passed down. Mr Tan Tiong Ghee, who inherited the troupe from his father thirty years ago, confirmed that "the puppet theatre is slowly dying because nobody wants to learn the art". Endorsed by the ideology of multiculturalism, in 1986 the open-air display of Chinese street opera was terminated; it was replaced by a multicultural Traditional Theatre Festival, held in an air-conditioned, indoor environment (Kong and Yeoh 2003, p. 194). Chinese street opera lost all its contextual significance, despite the fact that the government still claimed its firm support for the preservation of tradition and culture. As a result the knowledge of Chinese street opera and many other traditional practices were lost with the passing away of the older generations.

Along with the feelings of pessimism that regarded Chinese street opera as a dying art, public discourse also increasingly saw expressions of nostalgia for the golden days of street opera. From a sociological point of view, this nostalgia was not simply a feeling drawn from the past but was also a product of the present. By "using the past in specially reconstructed ways", for example, by screening out painful episodes of life and elevating happy experiences to prominence, nostalgia helps to alleviate the unsettling experiences people currently suffered (Davis 1979). David Lownthal echoes this by saying that "what is old is necessarily good" (Lowenthal 1985, p. 4). In two essays titled "Chinese Wayangs and Me" 街戏与我, the writers recall how the dazzling opera actors captivated their childhood attention for the first time: "With a strong curiosity, I gazed at their playing of the water sleeves, fell in astonishment with their adept body movement and the breathtaking cadences" (*Nanyang*

Siang Pau, 16 January 1976). "I was too young to understand the lyrics, but I immediately fell in love with the beautiful characters" (*Nanyang Siang Pau*, 5 June 1976). Nostalgia emerges when the writers compare the experiences of the present with those from their memories: "something is lost", "the flavour has changed" (*Nanyang Siang Pau*, 16 January 1976). Through such narratives, Chinese street opera became associated with a lost past from when life was pure and simple.

It should be pointed out that a nostalgic craving for the past is a motivation not so much to relive it but rather to yearn for it, to collect its relics and celebrate its virtues (Lowenthal 1985, p. 7). It is more about past thoughts — the perspectives of childhood — than past things in actuality. Therefore, people's memories about Chinese street opera might not be solely about the performances per se; rather, they are about how people in the past thought about Chinese street opera in relation to their social life: going out with their parents for opera rituals in the temple, grandpa's gentle humming of a opera tune, and sometimes entire neighbourhoods sharing the same enthusiasm towards Chinese street opera. Simply being part of the event was all what mattered, despite the fact that many could not understand the performances. Therefore, the ways in which people thought about Chinese wayangs in childhood were intimately bound with a familiar and comfortable communal life that they grew up with. It was the displacement of a familiar social life that drove the collective nostalgic quest for the old Chinese street opera.

A thing that always accompanies feelings of nostalgia for this period is a sense of anxiety regarding the historical transition, filled as it was with drastic social change brought about by post-war modernity and nation building. For example, people have tended to emphasize this time as a critical period where they struggled hard to make a living and therefore had no leisure time for opera or other cultural entertainment (*Nanyang Siang Pau*, 16 January 1976). These personal memories seem to further confirm the state's stress on economic growth for nation building since the 1960s. Moreover, such anxiety was reinforced by the drastic socio-spatial transformation. As "social practices are spatially patterned and ... these patterns substantially affect these ... social practices" (Chong 2006, p. 295), the act of uprooting Chinese street opera from the rural areas to HDB flats, Hong Lim Park and, finally, indoor theatres tremendously altered the practice of street opera itself. It explains why the feelings of displacement often found expression through the preservation of sites with historical value, such as Wayang Street located not far from Chinatown (*Straits Times*, 3 February 1987).

Evidently, what Chinese street opera meant to ordinary citizens differed greatly from the state's heritage-making projects. It is commonly understood that heritage-making is a top-down process with unequal power relations being played out. More and more sociological studies are being undertaken to reveal the hidden voices of the "subaltern" classes. Terence Chong, for instance, conducted thirty-two semi-structured interviews with opera practitioners in order to penetrate the struggle, bitterness and sense of loss that characterize most of his interviewees' narratives. According to Chong, the language policy that favoured English and Mandarin and the ideology of multiculturalism and pragmatism led to a reduction in cultural capital of Chinese opera and, by extension, Chinese identity. The loss of power drove marginalized opera practitioners to appeal to the discourse of "heritage" and "authenticity", whereby an imagined golden past with roots in Chinese history and civilization was evoked. "It becomes clear that when migrant ethnic identities are not able to struggle successfully for symbolic or cultural capital in the national sphere … it is just as likely that they will transcend the national sphere and tap into the collective memories and histories of the imaginary homeland to arouse ethnic pride in the struggle for recognition and power within the national" (Chong 2006, p. 293).

For Chong, "heritage" was used as a rhetoric and discursive device in the struggle for power. Yet, taking a micro-history approach, we would like to add that in spite of being simply discursive, "heritage" did have actual significations for opera practitioners in the ways they tried to understand and position themselves in the drastically changing society. For these people, Chinese street opera, or to be more precise, the practice of a particular opera, say Teochew opera, was both livelihood and heritage. Different from the heritage rendered as a tool for nation building or a discursive device for power struggle, opera practitioners saw it as the key to form their subjectivity: where they came from, who they were/are and why they held on to it.

The life histories of opera practitioners all attest to the identical origin of their operatic practice: family heritage/inheritance. It was emphasized that Teochew opera practitioners identified Teochew opera as their family heritage passed down from their parents' generation from the "homeland" Chaoshan to Nanyang. Chng Gek Huay 庄玉花 was one of the most outstanding *huadan* 花旦 (actress) in the Xin Rong He Xing opera troupe. She recalls that before moving to Singapore her whole family was engaged in Teochew opera in Siam: her father played Teochew musical instruments; her two elder sisters sang opera songs; the whole family made a living by performing Teochew opera. Naturally, for Chng, leading a life in opera troupes was a natural decision to make, not because acting was the only skill she had but because it was an important thing that her family passed to her.[6] Therefore, opera became an indispensable element for one's self-making. Cheah Gek Song 谢玉松[7] recalled his childhood of growing up in chaotic wartime China. Performing and teaching in the opera troupes, his father was a well-known master of Teochew opera in Jieyang 揭阳 (a town adjacent to Chaozhou and Shantou). Cheah developed his operatic skills by observing his father's performances from an early age. His recollection of Teochew opera was therefore closely tied to the memory of his family in the same way as for Chng Gek Huay. Hence, for these two, Chinese street opera represented a past that defined who they were and the kind of people they hoped to be. They, of course, maintained the practice out of passion and love; but, above all, for them opera represented their family heritage, one which required that they continue it through every means.

Poverty and destitution are common themes to be brought up. Cheah's family was already in such a destitute state that his elder brother had to be sold to a Siam Teochew opera troupe. The family used the money to buy two acres of land, which sustained their livelihood for a long time. Chng Gek Huay also described her family's early situation: "my family was poverty-stricken in Siam, so my father decided to look for a better livelihood in Nanyang (Singapore). On the way to Nanyang, the whole family was engaged with *zouchang* 走唱 (walking and singing), playing Teochew music, singing and performing Teochew opera to earn some travelling fare. That was how we made a living on the road. I would call it a vagrant life" (Chng 1988). These expressions of personal experiences during difficult times refer to what historians call "mass migration". These painful childhood memories kept rising to the fore, reinforcing the beliefs of these Teochew opera practitioners that regardless of all their hardships they had come a long way. The bitter memories of their "vagrant life" are thus essential in defining their sense of self.

What are especially revealing in these oral narratives are the references to a number of connected localities, by which we could chart the life trajectories of these itinerant performers. For example, both Cheah's and Chng's families had connections in Thailand and Malaya; they either had family members performing in Siam whilst the rest of them were dispersed in China and Malaya, or the whole family troupe was formed in Siam and then travelled to Malaya to seek their livelihood. Put simply, an itinerant lifestyle across Nanyang was a significant experience that threaded throughout their life histories; it formed part of their subjectivities as people, always diasporic, transnational and "on the road".

Here, the life history of Chua Hong Kee and his troupe, Kim Eng 金鹰 (the golden eagle), provides a synopsis of what a diasporic itinerant livelihood meant to opera practitioners and professional opera troupes. Firstly, the ways Chua made plans for his troupe reveals how people on the ground understood their livelihoods. The name Kim Eng expressed Chua's ambition to bring the troupe overseas, like an eagle that could fly as far and high as possible. To set up the troupe, he began by purchasing costumes from Hong Kong, inviting opera gods to the troupe by obtaining incense ashes from Thailand, and getting new opera scripts from China. All these gestures implied that, from Chua's perspective, Teochew opera was a de-territorialized culture, rooted in local soils but which should aspire for "glocal" outreach.

Secondly, de-territorialized travelling was essential to the survival of professional opera troupes like Kim Eng. By inducing the flows of people and ideas across geographical boundaries, it ensured a dynamism and vibrancy for the performances. Kim Eng was one of the troupes to be established in post-war Singapore when traditional culture such as Chinese wayangs began to be sidelined for the cause of nation building. It would not be an exaggeration to claim that Chua Hong Kee carved out a niche for Teochew opera against all the odds. Significantly, what undergirded Chua's achievements was his ten years' of experience of itinerant performances in troupes in Penang, Siam and Hong Kong. According to Chua, after having served for seven years in Sin Yong Hua 新荣和 Teochew opera troupe, he decided to leave Singapore to join the newly established Chaoyi 潮艺 (Teochew Art and Opera) troupe in Penang in 1960. It was here that he learnt how to play three musical instruments — Teochew strings, suona horn, and dulcimer — by following a Teochew music master from China (Chua 2007). Consisting of performing artists from Siam, China and Malaya, the Chaoyi opera troupe gathered all kinds of de-territorialized resources which formed a dynamic and diversified performing environment under which Chua Hong Kee was nurtured.

Interestingly, the musical techniques he acquired during his sojourn in Penang put him in such a cutting-edge position that he was not only recruited back by Xin Rong He as a leading musician in 1965, he was also invited by Xin Tian Cai — a renowned Hong Kong Teochew opera troupe — to lead their musical accompaniment from 1973 to 1977 (Chua 2007). In the 1970s, Hong Kong had already replaced Shanghai as the avant-garde centre of art, culture and entertainment. Located at the crossroads between the East and West, Hong Kong cultivated groups of cultural entrepreneurs, such as left-wing filmmakers, local movie stars and transnational entertainment corporates whose innovative strategies greatly enhanced the aesthetic and commercial value of traditional dialect opera. In the recollection of Chua Hong Kee, Hong Kong even became the "holy land" that diasporic opera practitioners always longed for, a place where they believed they could learn the finest performing skills. Chua described his time spent in Hong Kong as an experience of learning everything "new" that could be applied in Singapore (Chua 2007). Chua Hong Kee's accounts of his travels are significant in telling a nuanced story about the drifting life of an opera troupe. But such an experience was definitely not uncommon. It is representative of a large group of opera practitioners whose life on the road could shed much light on the trans-regional transmission of ideas and the movement of people and goods. The flows of people, together with the skills and ideas they brought with them, could be likened to an automobile engine, generating energy to stage good opera performances.

However, with stricter immigration controls and a greater emphasis on nation building in the independent nation states, trans-border travel became increasingly difficult. It was particularly the case for post-war Malaya, which witnessed a painful struggle and separation in 1965, resulting in the current Singapore and Malaysia. This historical episode remained an awkward moment in the memories of many travelling opera troupes, which were forced to forsake their itinerant ways of life. Chua Hong Kee, a Singapore-born Teochew opera practitioner who had led an itinerant performing life since the 1950s, recalled that, upon separation, the overall atmosphere was still flexible. "With a blue passport, we were granted two weeks in Malaysia, performing all the way from the south to the north. Approaching the expiry date, we simply went to perform in Johor (southern tip of Malaysia, a state bordering Singapore), crossed the border to Singapore and then we re-entered Malaysia again so that we were granted another two weeks in Malaysia" (Chua 2007). It was not until two decades after separation that Malaysia began to enforce stricter policies to regulate the movement of peoples. It required troupes from Singapore wishing to travel to Malaysia to perform to apply for a permit in Kuala Lumpur. The person applying for the permit would usually need to travel to and fro at least three times and sometimes had to pay bribes in order to get the permit.

The emergence of independent nation states in the 1960s also inevitably obstructed the free travel of de-territorialized operatic sources. Chua recalled an unforgettable episode in 1987 when, suddenly, the immigration bureau rejected any extension of the visas of his foreign actors. Two Thais and three Malaysians were forced to leave Singapore within twenty-four hours. The rest of the Malaysians were too scared to stay, and they packed up to leave the troupe a few days later (Chua 2007). He had no other alternative than to beg for help from his former employees. It was a disaster for Chua; he described it "as if the whole world went out of light all of sudden". Since then he faced a deteriorating situation in which many scripts went unperformed due to lack of actors. He tried to recruit young local actors but his efforts were futile (Chua 2007). When the engine was cut off, the travelling opera troupes became a "vanishing trade". Chua's troupe stopped entering Malaysia from the 1980s, as any profits that could be made would hardly match the expenditure needed for the entry permit. As Chua put it: "Our people would rather stay in Singapore, it was more comfortable here" (Chua 2007). This reflection also rightly captured a subtle change in people's mindsets. The formerly itinerant opera practitioners had now turned into citizens of the independent nation state.

The antithesis of being de-territorial/diasporic and national lay at the centre of heritage-making (Ang 2011, pp. 82–95). At this point I would propose that it is helpful to take a revisionist approach towards what Lee Tong Soon observed as the fundamental factor that contributed to the rift between the "elevated" amateurs and the "sidelined" opera professionals in post independence Singapore (2009). Lee holds that Chinese street opera as a traditional performing culture was redefined and represented by amateur groups in the framework of the cultural nationalism that emphasized Singapore as a country of "educated, historically informed, culturally vibrant, technologically advanced and artistically well versed" citizens (p. 154). The professional opera troupes and practitioners who represented the true legacy of Chinese street opera lost all their cultural capital in the construction of the new national culture of Singapore and they gradually died out. Lee criticized the ways in which local opera circles attributed the tragic destiny of opera professionals to their low aesthetic values, yet amateurs suddenly became the representatives of Chinese opera as if it was a natural selection.[8] He follows this with bitter sociological criticism that lays the blame on the top-down state policies and the all-powerful elite construction (pp. 138–58). For example, he argues that for the Hong Lim Park Opera Series, the government gave preference to amateur troupes, which gradually became dominant in representing the tradition of Chinese street opera (p. 140).

Here, Lee overlooks the fact that that less professional troupes were represented because "most of them have gone abroad on engagement" (*Straits Times*, 27 March 1978). This statement suggests that the diasporic and de-territorialized tradition of the professional troupes made them so mobile and unstable that they were deemed unsuitable for a national festival. Therefore, while being critical of the state's cultural policies, Lee ignores the underlying incompatibility between two forces: the diasporic and the national. Lee tends to oversimplify the multiple forces that affected the existential being of the performing culture, especially the changes within the performing art itself, which were underwritten by the irreconcilable gap between the "diasporic" and the "national". In essence, Chinese street opera among the diaspora, or Chinese opera as a whole, had evolved historically as a migrant culture — the people, art form and business of which heavily relied on the de-territorialized/diasporic flows of ideas, practices and talent. The post-independence nation building of Singapore imposed great pressures on the de-territorialized operatic exchanges, which was greatly detrimental to the art form itself.

Conclusion

Chinese street opera was a typical representation of a migrant culture, with origins in specific localities of South China and which followed the footsteps of Chinese migrations to Nanyang since the early nineteenth century. Moreover, Chinese street opera and opera troupes had been intimately associated with the network of diasporic temple-theatres and later the development of diasporic trading connections, which were afforded by key mobile and resourceful diasporic merchants. This unique historical ecology characterized by pre-war Nanyang connectedness, mobility and interaction sustained the lifeblood of Chinese street opera as an art form, as a business practice, and its practitioners. However, the post-independence nation building of Singapore revealed not only a contrasting destiny for Chinese street opera but also spoke to the constant struggle between being diasporic/de-territorial and national.

The moves to make street opera into a cultural heritage necessarily altered its basic format. The act of displaying the tradition within a modern regulated space was seen as a necessary step in refining street opera. It was a struggle to recall the past, but at the same time it was a struggle to properly curb the overwhelming influence of the past. The same could be argued for the ways in which the nation state tried to balance the past and the present. For instance, the state abandoned traditional culture for the sake of economic development but then later sought to hark back to its cultural roots in order to construct a national identity.

However, this process was not as smooth or successful as it has usually been described in the public discourse. The recollections of individuals who had been practising Teochew opera all their lives often articulate bitterness, a sense of loss and displacement. For them, opera as heritage has two levels of meaning. First, opera represents their mark of identity through which they can trace their family continuity to Siam, South China, and Penang. The de-territorialized operatic practices entered into their diasporic subjectivities/mentality in defining who they were and where they came from. However, confronting the strictly defined national boundaries in the 1970s and the 1980s, personal memories were often silenced for the larger sake of nation building. It has been the attempt of this chapter to bring back these alternative voices of street opera so that they may testify on the dynamics of nation building from a micro-perspective.

Notes

1. Cheang Hong Lim 章芳琳 (1825–93), a wealthy businessman, invested in opium farms. He was also a well-known philanthropist and the headman of the Hokkien community in Singapore. For details about the life of Cheang Hong Lim, see Song (1967, pp. 168–69).
2. State campaigns included the National Courtesy Campaign, Speak Mandarin Campaign, Keep Singapore Clean Campaign, and the Public Health Campaign. Information gained from the online project, "Remember Singapore" <http://remembersingapore.wordpress.com/2013/01/18/singapore-campaigns-of-the-past/>.
3. "Speech by Dr. Ahmad Mattar, Minister for the Environment at the 'Residents

and HDB Area Office' Day at Queenstown Sports Complex", Stirling Road, 5 Oct 1986". Singapore Government Press Release. National Archives of Singapore, release no. 15/Oct, 07-1/86/10/05.

4. For example, one of them performed a scene from the historical fiction *The Romance of the Three Kingdoms*, featuring heroic figures such as Ling Chong 林冲. "Chinese Opera Show", *Straits Times*, 27 June 1978.

5. Chua Hong Kee 蔡奉岐, Oral History Interview, National Archives of Singapore, accession number 00029279, 11 April 2007.

6. Chng Gek Huay 庄玉花, Oral History Interview, National Archives of Singapore, accession number 000860, 14 January 1988.

7. Cheach Gek Song 谢玉松, Oral History Interview, National Archives of Singapore, accession number 000932, 26 May 1988.

8. The local opera circle, represented by Chua Soo Pong and Joana Wong, had extensive discussions on the decline of professional opera troupes. See, for example, Chua (1995, pp. 91–102) and Wong (1995, pp. 103–8).

References

Ang, Ien "Unsettling the National: Heritage and Diaspora". In *Heritage, Memory & Identity*, edited by Helmut Anheier and Yudhishthir Raj Isar. Thousand Oaks, CA: Sage, 2011.

Chen Jinghe 陈荆和 and Chen Yusong 陈育崧, eds. *Xinjiapo huawen beiming jilu* 新加坡华文碑铭集录 [Chinese epigraphy in Singapore]. Hong Kong: Hong Kong Chinese University Press, 1975.

Chong, Terence. "Chinese Opera in Singapore: Negotiating Globalization, Consumerism and National Culture". *Journal of Southeast Asian Studies* 34, no. 3 (2003): 449–71.

———. "Ethnic Identity and Cultural Capital: An Ethnography of Chinese Opera in Singapore". *Identities: Global Studies in Culture and Power* 13 no. 2 (2006): 283–307.

Chua, Beng Huat. *Communitarian Ideology and Democracy in Singapore*. London: Routledge, 1995.

Chua Soo Pong. "Reaching Out for Cultural Roots: A Singapore Example in Reviving Traditional Theatre". In *Traditional Theatre in Southeast Asia*, edited by Chua Soo Pong. Singapore: UniPress, 1995.

Davis, Fred. *Yearning for Yesterday: A Sociology of Nostalgia*. New York: Free Press, 1979.

Duncan, James, and Nancy Duncan. "Rereading the Landscape". *Environment and Planning D: Society and Space* 6 (1998): 117–26. Quoted in Kong and Yeoh (2003, p. 2).

Frost, Mark Ravinder. "Emporium in Imperio: Nanyang Networks and the Straits

Chinese in Singapore, 1819–1914". *Journal of Southeast Asian Studies* 36, no. 1 (2005): 29–66.

Kong, Lily, and Brenda S.A. Yeoh. *The Politics of Landscapes in Singapore: Constructions of "Nation"*. Syracuse: Syracuse University Press, 2003.

Kuhn, Philip A. *Chinese among Others: Emigration in Modern Times*. Singapore: NUS Press, 2008.

Kwa, Chong Guan, Derek Heng, and Tan Tai Yong. *Singapore: A 700-year History: From Early Emporium to World City*. Singapore: National Archive of Singapore, 2009.

Lee, Tong Soon. *Chinese Street Opera in Singapore*. Urbana: University of Illinois Press, 2009.

Lin Chunjun 林淳钧. *Chaoju wenjianlu* 潮剧闻见录 [Anecdotes about Teochew operas]. Guangzhou: zhongshan daxue chubanshe, 1993.

Lin Xiaosheng 林孝胜. "Qingyunting yu shijiu shiji xinhua shehui" 青云亭与十九世纪新华社会 [Cheng Hoon Temple and the Chinese society in eighteenth century Singapore]. In *Xinhua lishi yu renwu yanjiu* 新华历史与人物研究 [Index to famous historical figures of Singaporean Chinese], by Lin Xiaosheng 林孝胜 and Ke Mulin 柯木林. Singapore: Nanyang xuehui, 1986.

Ling Yuanfu 林源福. *Nanhai mingzhu* 南海明珠 [The pearl of the South Seas]. Singapore: Xinjiapo Fujian huiguan, 2010.

Loh, Kah Seng. "Kampong, Fire, Nation: Towards a Social History of Postwar Singapore". *Journal of Southeast Asian Studies* 40, no. 3 (2009): 613–43.

Lowenthal, David. *The Past is a Foreign Country*. Cambridge: Cambridge University Press, 1985.

Ozouf, Mona. *Festivals and the French Revolution*. Cambridge, MA: Harvard University Press, 1991.

Scott, James C. *Seeing Like a State: How Certain Schemes to Improve the Human Condition Have Failed*. New Haven: Yale University Press, 1998.

Song Ong Siang. *One Hundred Years' History of the Chinese in Singapore*. Singapore: University Malaya Press, 1967.

Vaughan, Jonas Daniel. *The Manners and Customs of the Chinese of the Straits Settlements*. Kuala Lumpur: Oxford University Press, 1971.

Wong, Joana Quee Heng. "Chinese Opera in Singapore: An Overview". In *Traditional Theatre in Southeast Asia*, edited by Chua Soo Pong. Singapore: UniPress, 1995.

Newspapers

Straits Times
"Letters to the Editor". 8 September 1970.
"Litterbugs Fined". 30 May 1972.

"Untidy Wayang Men Fined". 12 September 1972.
"Wayang Men Fined $80". 19 September 1972.
"Ministry Looking for Best Wayang Troupes". 21 February 1978.
"Only the Best Opera for Hong Lim Park Plan Hits Snag". 27 March 1978.
"Goodbye to All These". 26 August 1980.
"Street Opera goes Indoors in New Festival". 23 July 1986.
"More and More Just A Memory". 3 February 1987.

Nanyang Siang Pau 南洋商报
Xin Guang 新光. "Xin huanjing, xin shenghuo" 新环境新生活 [A new environment, a new life]. 4 May 1971.
"Zhuzhaiqu yanxi tingche cheng wenti" 住宅区演戏停车成问题 [Street operas cause problems to the parking spaces of our residential areas]. 15 August 1973.
"Quanli zhichi xiang chaosheng xuanzhan" 全力支持向吵声宣战 [Fully support the anti-noise campaign]. 29 July 1974.
Huang Mushen 黄木申. "Chaozhou yinyue yu xiju" 潮州音乐与戏剧 [Teochew music and dramas]. 24 January 1975.
"Zaijiezaili chu zaosheng yu bailei" 再接再厉除噪声与败类 [Keep on to eradicate noise and dregs of society]. 26 April 1975.
Wu Yan 吴彦. "Jiexi de moluo yu zhengdun wenti" 街戏的没落与整顿问题 [Issues on street operas' declining and reforming]. 3 September 1975.
Dong Er, "Jiexi yu wo" 街戏与我 [Chinese wayangs and me]. 16 January 1976.
"Huang Shuren yiyuan zuori piping wenhuabu buying pianzhongyu guangbo gai guli bendi yishu kejiang benguo fazhan dongtai miaohui xialai" 黄树人议员昨日批评文化部不应偏重于广播该鼓励本地艺术可将本国发展动态描绘下来 [Parliament member Huang Shuren encouraged to record the development of local art]. 20 March 1976.
"Jiexi yu wo" 街戏与我 [Chinese wayangs and me]. 5 June 1976.
"Fanglin xitai niucheshui juchang jiang chengwei difangxi zhuyao changsuo" 芳林戏台牛车水剧场将成为地方戏主要场所 [Hong Lim Park stage will become the main venue for regional operas]. 20 February 1978.
"Wenhuabu difang xiju xilie" 文化部地方戏剧系列 [Regional opera series by the Ministry of Culture]. 24 April 1978.

Oral Interviews, National Archives of Singapore
Chua Hong Kee 蔡奉岐. Oral History Interview, accession number 00029279, 11 April 2007.
Chng Gek Huay 庄玉花. Oral History Interview, accession number 000860, 14 January 1988.
Cheach Gek Song 谢玉松, Oral History Interview, accession number 000932, 26 May 1988.

11

Policy Formation and Civil Society Engagement in Heritage-Making in Taiwan: A Historical Examination

Min-Chin Chiang, Li-Ling Huang, Shu-Mei Huang
and Hsin-Huang Michael Hsiao

In Taiwan the discussion of civil society emerged in the 1980s and peaked in the early 1990s, when the society underwent political democratization. Civil society was considered a public sphere, enjoying relatively autonomy from the control of the state or the market. The birth of civil society in Taiwan came about by the proliferation of non-profit organizations, community organizations, and professional and voluntary groups through continuous social mobilization. Lawmaking was indispensable for the consolidation of civil society. New ordinances, ranging from human rights, environmental regulation to cultural preservation, were brought to the agenda. The emergence of civil society allowed people to leverage themselves from the control of the state and the market. In addition to this, the new Taiwanese identity that took shape in the 1990s reinforced the civil society that was in the making. However, across the turn of the millennium, as the state–society relationship reconfigured, civil society also differentiated. Both the market and the state tried to entrench civil society, which more often than not led to many different voices within civil society. Conflicts among various social groups have become a noticeable feature in the debates and decision-making processes of public affairs.

Against this backdrop we would like to trace the early history of the development of the idea of heritage preservation in Taiwan. The emergence of the heritage preservation movement and related policies is closely intertwined with the changing cultural politics that reflect the contested meanings of national and local identities in Taiwan. Before the lifting of martial law in 1987, civil society had played a significant role in heritage-making. Since 1987, civil society has further pushed the state to change the laws and policies governing heritage preservation.

The first piece of legislation in this area, the Cultural Heritage Preservation Act, was promulgated in Taiwan in 1982, while the country was still under authoritarian rule. The implementation of the Heritage Act and associated cultural policies inevitably reflected the Chinese nationalist historical narrative; however, at the same time, it created negotiable spaces for diverse narratives through the imported notion of "cultural heritage", which could be seen as an indirect challenge to the dominant narrative. The materiality of cultural heritage and its connection to local contexts shed light on the initially "invisible Taiwan" that the dominant Chinese nationalist narrative neglected. Furthermore, variant claims of heritage also opened space for civil society to negotiate different versions of its local development. In the process of legitimating the Heritage Act, civil society played a core role by being involving in the conservation movement and through growing public interest and academic discussions. The Cultural Heritage Preservation Act has undergone several amendments. Each amendment reflects a re-contextualization of the imported notion of cultural heritage, its associated social dynamics, and the changing role of civil society in the heritage-making process.

In this chapter, we have taken a cultural and institutional approach to examine how the rise of civil society and the heritage preservation movement have reconfigured each other. We have analysed state–society relations at different periods in time and the changing nature of cultural identity in Taiwan. The lifting of martial law was identified as a milestone, since it challenged the strong state authority and the professionals in interpreting the historical significance of heritage. Cultural activists and local organizers started to have an impact on heritage listings. We have selected some representative cases at different stages in order to highlight these social changes. They include Lin An Tai Old House, Dihua Street and Wen Men Lou. In parallel to these cases studies we will discuss the introduction and development of the Cultural Heritage Preservation Act to bring out the main agendas, challenges and conflicts that have occurred in heritage preservation in Taiwan.

1950s to 1970s: Distorted Cultural Policies

The tragic incident of 28 February 1947, which saw the massacre of local political and cultural elites by the Kuomintang (KMT; Chinese Nationalist Party) troops, marked the traumatic beginnings of KMT rule in Taiwan after the Japanese colonial period. After the civil war in China, in 1949 the KMT government retreated to Taiwan. In the same year, martial law was enforced in Taiwan. Thousands of political dissidents were arrested during the White Terror, which lasted for four decades. As a result, social engagement and political participation by the Taiwanese population has been strictly limited. Civil society was highly suppressed, and over time almost all local Taiwanese culture had been marginalized.

In 1966, as the decade-long Great Proletarian Cultural Revolution raged in the People's Republic of China (PRC), the KMT regime in Taiwan initiated the Chinese Cultural Renaissance Movement (Zhonghua Wenhua Fuxing Yundong;中華文化復興運動), positioning itself as the representative of authentic Chinese culture. This cultural policy lasted until the 1970s. As a result, in the capital city Taipei, numerous public architectural works built or renovated during this period were designed in the Chinese nationalist fashion (Kuo 2004). For example, the East Gate (Jin-Fu Gate) and South Gate (Li-Cheng Gate) of the Old City of Taipei, that had originally been built in the Fu-kien style of Southern China, were remodelled in the Northern Chinese Palace Style. Meanwhile, the industrial modernization policies successfully created high economic growth and helped to consolidate the legitimacy of the KMT regime. But these rapid developments also proved to be destructive to the physical environment.

During the post-war KMT authoritarian period, the government did not consider the issue of historical preservation except in the light of tourism demands of members of the U.S. army[1] and the Chinese Cultural Renaissance Movement of the 1960s and 1970s. In the 1960s, Taiwan experienced dramatic change — rapid industrialization, urbanization and domestic migration — which evoked nostalgia for the lost traditions and lifestyles, an emerging demand for domestic tourism, and a growing awareness of historical preservation. At the same time, social and economic change was informed by the propaganda of the KMT's Chinese nationalist narrative. In this context, in the 1960s two groups of preservationists sparked awareness for architectural conservation: scholars interest in collecting data on Taiwanese traditional architecture, and artists and architects concerned with traditional buildings and the folk culture of Taiwan. Their efforts brought about the *guji* (古蹟; monument) preservation movement in the 1970s.

In the 1970s a series of political and economic crises occurred. The 1973 oil crisis affected the economy. The sovereignty disputes between Taiwan and Japan over Diao-yu Island were followed by waves of student protests against Japan. The KMT's loss of representation at the United Nations to the PRC was another heavy blow to the government's legitimacy. In this social milieu of uncertainty, the post-war generation began to develop a consciousness of "returning to reality" and "back to the land of Taiwan". Through cultural actions, they sought collectively for a new national narrative, and attempted to construct the collective memory. This was the emergence of the awareness of "cultural localization (本土化)" or "Taiwanization (臺灣化)" (Hsiau 2008).

Some urban elites began to examine and to value the vernacular cultures of Taiwan, while others looked to local society for inspiration of cultural creativity. Writers, painters and dancers dedicated themselves to the cultural movement of reconstructing local identity. In 1971, Reed Dillingham and Lin Hua, then scholars associated with the Architecture Department of Tong-Hai University, completed their book *A Survey of Traditional Architecture of Taiwan*, with the financial support of the Asia Foundation. The book echoed the work of Lin Heng-dao (林衡道) and other renowned Taiwanese historians; it represented a landmark as the first publication to systematically examine Taiwan's architecture from a perspective that was not the government's. Meanwhile, *Echo Magazine* (漢聲雜誌) also began to publish its investigatory reports of folk arts in Taiwan. These social mobilizations explored the value of Taiwanese vernacular culture. Moreover, the vernacular literature movement that burst on to the scene in the late 1970s led to further debate over local identity.

The case of the Lin An Tai Old House (林安泰古厝) most represents the emerging social awareness for preservation of the 1970s. The ancestor of

Lin's family emigrated from Fukien, in the southeast of China, moving to Taiwan in the mid-eighteenth century. In 1822 the Lin An Tai Old House was built according to the traditional folk residency style of Southern China. Reed Dillingham and Lin Hua's survey documented the Lin An Tai Old House well and attracted people's attention to it. However, in 1976 plans were made to tear down the house to make way for a road as part of urban development for the Da-An area. Historians and architectural scholars mobilized renowned figures in the cultural sphere and appealed to the government to reroute the road and to preserve the house. In 1978 the house escaped destruction and was instead relocated to Taipei Shin-sheng Park along the Keelung River. This illustrates a solution of compromise in the face of government plans for economic and urban development.

Early 1980s: Authorized Heritage

The systematic conceptualization and practice of historical preservation was first brought to Taiwan under Japanese rule. The Japanese government enacted the Preservation Act of Historic Sites, Resort and Natural Heritage (史蹟名勝天然紀念物保存法) in 1922, as well as thirty-five other pieces of Japanese domestic legislation.[2] However, except for a number of announcements of listings between 1933 and 1941, the Japanese legislation was never fully implemented in Taiwan. In 1930, the Preservation Act of Antiques (*Guwu Baocunfa*; 古物保存法) was promulgated by the Republic of China (ROC) government (led by the KMT) in China. After the Second World War, Japan ceded Taiwan to the ROC government, and the Chinese Preservation Act of Antiques replaced the Japanese Preservation Act of Historic Sites, Resort and Natural Heritage as the official legislation for historical preservation in Taiwan. However, not until the Cultural Revolution in China did the ROC government begin to consider issues concerning historical preservation. In the late 1960s the Ministry of the Interior initiated the process of revising the Preservation Act of Antiques in order to show the cultural superiority of the ROC over the Communist PRC, and so prioritized heritage that would strengthen the linkage between Taiwan and the authorized tradition inherited from mainland China (Lin 2011). The event of the preservation for the Lin An Tai Old House in the late 1970s also pushed for an institutional change for cultural preservation.

This process of revision ended with the enactment of the Cultural Heritage Preservation Act in 1982. The expression "cultural heritage" was translated as *wenhua zichan* (文化資產; cultural assets). In comparison to the strong personal linkage and sense of rootedness suggested by the Western term "heritage", the translation *wenhua zichan* is more connected to material quality and economic value. On the other hand, the criterion of "antiquity" underlying the legislation of the 1980s embodied the Chinese nationalist narrative of the KMT government. By stressing the significance of the historical connection to Chinese civilization, sites of Taiwanese, Japanese or aboriginal culture were excluded, and the status of the KMT in leading an authentic cultural "China" was legitimated.

The first series of designations after the implementation of the Cultural Heritage Preservation Act included eighteen sites. Composed largely of citadels, temples and city gates, these sites contributed to a national narrative of Taiwan's inseparable cultural and historical connection to China under KMT governance. As Yan (2009) has noted, the sites either related to resistance to foreign invasions by the Han people, or to Taiwanese assistance to Qing repression of rebellion in Taiwan. Other sites, such as those pertaining to indigenous or Japanese remnants, were excluded. The criterion of "age" helped to disqualify Japanese colonial sites from a national preservation list (Taylor 2005). This criterion for what could be regarded as "historic" remained in place until the 1990s.

Late 1980s to 1990s: Heritage and New Identity Formation

A few years after the inauguration of the Cultural Heritage Preservation Act, the political framework of Taiwan witnessed a new social landscape. Political and social movements emerged in the 1980s to challenge the political regime and call for reform. Under the influence of social mobilization, martial law was lifted and an opposition party was formed. Hsiao and Liu (2002) categorized the seventeen types of social movements. They included a middle-class consumer movement, anti-pollution action, an environmental movement, a movement to represent aboriginal people, one for Hakka people, a student movement, and so on. This wide spectrum of movements helped to reclaim power for the people and redefined state–society relations. The community movement led by the urban middle class concerned with the environment and urban liveability, despite its limitations, has challenged the dominant approach of city as a growth-machine shaped by the ruling party, industrial capitalists and real estate developers.

In contrast to the Chinese cultural nationalism of the post-war era, the 1980s and 1990s marked a shift to Taiwanese cultural nationalism. The people's knowledge, as well as the government's policies in regard to literature, language and history, experienced landslide changes. Social mobilization also expressed the people's aspirations for redefining ethnic identity and for collective memories (Hsiau 2012). A new social consensus formed in the 1990s that the Taiwanese population is made up of four ethnic groups: the Holo, the Hakka, Chinese-immigrants after 1949, and the aboriginal population.

Government policies have played an important role in pushing for social changes. In 1988, President Chiang Ching-Kuo, the son of Chiang Kai-shek, passed away. Lee Teng-hui was inaugurated as the new president, becoming the first Taiwan-born president. In 1996 he ran in the first presidential election and gained the majority vote. By the end of his term in 2000 he had played an important role in reshaping Taiwanese cultural nationalism. In 1991 he announced an end to the "Period of Mobilization for the Suppression of Communist Rebellion" (動員戡亂時期) and launched the first amendment to the Constitution. The "Additional Articles of the Constitution of the Republic of China" were incorporated, which allowed the Constitution to meet the requirements of the nation and the political status of Taiwan. In 1993, as the anchor of the new national identity, President Lee initiated a cultural campaign to "Build the Great Taiwan, Shape the New Central Land" (經營大臺灣、 建立新中原). The main agency for this endeavour was the Council for Cultural Affairs (CCA) (Huang 1995). In 1997 the term "multi-culture" was incorporated into the "Additional Articles of the Constitution of the Republic of China".

The 1990s saw the beginning of Taiwan's "era of localism". Local places, as well as the idea of Taiwan as a place, were to gain unprecedented status in both political narrative and social practice. "Place" in Taiwan has been imbued over time with social attachments by a variety of agents, each with their own motives. In 1993 President Lee Teng-hui bound Taiwan to the narrative of "Community of Life" (生命共同體) in order to legitimize the nation-state. Local governments held festivals to turn the spotlight on products or attractions with local distinctiveness, groups participated in recollecting local memories, and architectural and planning professionals worked on the conservation of historical buildings. These acts, as well as place-based social and environmental movements, gradually converged into the state-led Comprehensive Community Development Program (shequ zongti yingzao; 社區總體營造), which was officially inaugurated in 1994.

Chen Chi-Nan, the vice director of the CCA at the time, followed the Machizukuri (まちづくり; community making) approach of Japan, and formulated the Comprehensive Community Development Program with an emphasis on the participation of civil society. From 1994 to 2000, funds of approximately US$400 million were allocated for improving both the physical and the soft environment, such as consolidating cultural activity centres, conducting cultural preservation and developing local society. The policy promoted the previously marginalized local culture of Taiwan into the core of Chinese culture (from the perspective of the ROC). The former elite-oriented cultural policies gradually shifted towards incorporating the meanings and values embraced by the communities and NGOs, which included a focus on ethnic diversity. In 1997 the cultural preservation of Hakka and aboriginal people were listed on the agenda of the second National Cultural Congress by the CCA.

The 1990s: Community Development and Local Museums

Amid the prevailing place-centred phenomena, local museums and heritage sites in Taiwan rapidly increased in number from the 1990s. They serve what we might call "memory tactics" (De Jong and Rowlands 2007) in determining the distinctiveness of a place — that is, strategically rebuilding the sense and identity of a place according to the present needs — and as a medium through which a better future for the island can be built.

Meanwhile, the local governments that arose within the new political landscape played an important role in promoting locality through cultural tourism, utilizing such means as museums, cultural festivals and the production of local artefacts. Within this social and historical context, the idea of developing museums and heritage sites was born and grew rapidly during the 1990s and the following decade. The recollection of local memories was sought by both the government and local residents in order to reconstruct local identities that had become intertwined with the Taiwanese national identity. The representation of the past, as well as the construction of locality, is a dynamic process that is constantly reshaped by diverse actors within a complex social framework. The interpretation of memory was not only restrained by this grand social framework but was also influenced by conflicting conceptions of memory during the actual practice of planning, construction and recollection.

With regard to heritage designation, a coalition was formed by planning scholars, local cultural activists and political representatives to counter the traditional top-down model dominated by the cultural elites and government officers. The interaction between these two approaches created competition/collaboration dynamics and shaped a new state–society relationship. Particularly in the aftermath of the earthquake of 21 September 1999, the preservation actions initiated by local groups greatly increased in scale (Lin 2006, 2011). No longer confined by party politics, many political activists attempted to redefine the public realm through local participation, and they advocated a social vision based on land ethics, community life and local culture (Lee 2014).

From 2000: Amendments to Heritage Policies

The confluence of heritage-making and community-making movements enabled the models of heritage preservation to be more progressive and diversified. However, it also revealed the relative backwardness of the legal framework of the time. As a result, between 1997 and 2005, with collaboration between the government and civil groups, there was a series of five amendments to the Cultural Heritage Preservation Act. Major amendments were made with regard to categorizing, designation, and property compensation.

Replacing Chinese Culture with Multi-culture

Article 1 of the original Cultural Heritage Preservation Act stated that its mission was to promote Chinese culture. In the revision of 2005, this was updated to read as, "to preserve and enhance cultural heritage, enrich the spiritual life of the citizenry, and promote the multi-cultural environment of the Republic of China". This illustrated the clear shift in the cultural view of Taiwan that had taken place over two decades. In addition to amendments to the legal framework, the CCA also attempted to respond to the issue of ethnicity with the introduction of multicultural policies. These efforts included the establishment of Shi-wa-wu Hakka Cultural Preservation Park, identifying potential sites of aboriginal cultural heritage, and the preservation of the military dependents' villages. The influence of the early Comprehensive Community Development Program continued as the CCA proceeded to promote the preservation of regional cultural heritage and to re-use programmes from 2006. This approach stressed the desire to link regional cultural facilities, enhance local economies, and to preserve the historic milieu by community participation. The definition of heritage was further broadened to cover the social landscape of daily life.

Decentralization for Designation and Registration

An important revision was about the right for designation at the government level. Prior to 1985 the entire process of designating a historic monument came under the purview of the central government. Between 1985 and 1997 the municipal governments were given the power of conducting primary investigations and proposing potential lists to the provincial and central government for further examination. With the emerging importance of local politics, a tendency towards decentralization had an influence on heritage policy with the modification of the Cultural Heritage Preservation Act. The amended version of 1997 extended the full right of designation for historic sites to the local governments; local people and communities can nominate sites of potential heritage and request the local government to review them.

In 2002 a new category, "historical building", was added to the act in response to requests from society, particularly influenced by the post-quake reconstruction after the 1999 Chichi earthquake. Figure 11.1 illustrates the initial peak in the number of historic monuments registered in the initial years following the promulgation of the Cultural Heritage Preservation Act of 1982. After 1997 the number of designated historical sites rose rapidly, mostly from designations made by municipal-level governments, and then accelerated much more after 2002.

Expanding Categories of Heritage

The amendment of 2005 expanded the definition of cultural heritage to seven distinct categories as follows:[3]

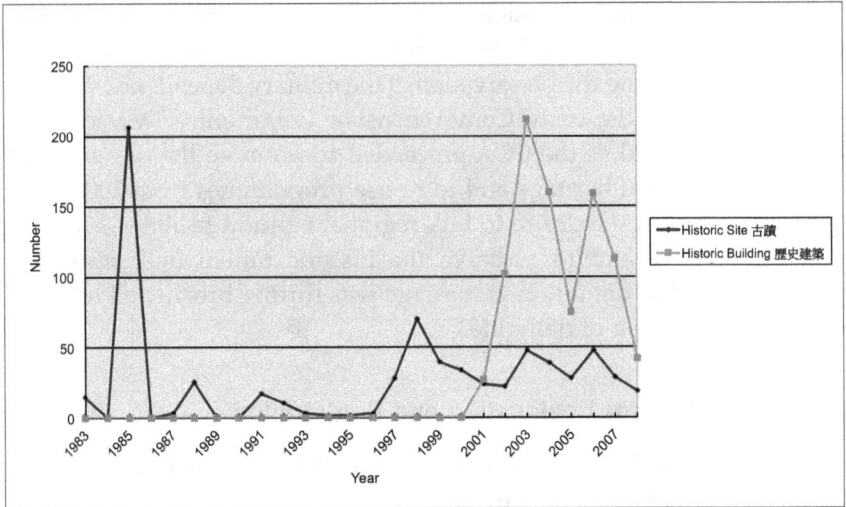

FIGURE 11.1 Annual number of monuments and historical buildings registered, 1982–2008.
Source: Chiang 2012.

(1) Monuments, historical buildings and settlements: the buildings and/or ancillary facilities built for the needs of human life with historic and/or cultural value.

(2) Historical sites: the places which contain the remains or vestiges of past human life with historic and/or cultural value and the spaces upon which such remains and vestiges are erected.

(3) Cultural landscapes: the location or environment which is related to any myths, legends, record of events, historical events, social life or ceremonies.

(4) Traditional arts: traditional crafts and skills descended from different ethnic groups and locales, which includes traditional arts and crafts, and/or performing arts.

(5) Folk customs and related cultural artifacts: customs, beliefs, festivals or any other related cultural artifacts which are related to the tradition of citizen life and has special cultural meaning.

(6) Antiquities: any arts, utensils of life or civility [sic], and books or documents having cultural significance and of value of different eras and from different ethnic groups.

(7) Natural landscapes: natural areas, land formations, plants, or minerals, which are of value in preserving natural environments.

The separation of the category of cultural landscape from that of the natural landscape and the inclusion of the industrial, transportation and water conservancy landscape marked a major development in the conceptualization of heritage. This version of the Cultural Heritage Preservation Act also emphasized preservation skills and the agents of preservation who would consolidate the preservation of intangible heritage.

Protecting Potential Heritage Sites

To address the trend of potential heritage sites being destroyed by rapid urban development, the 2005 version of the act regulated that no construction or development work should damage the integrity of, obscure, or obstruct access to monuments. In urgent cases, prior to a formal review process, the competent authority may declare any building that has the value of a monument as an "Interim Monument", and shall notify the owners, users or managers of such.

Offering Incentives to Private Property Owners to Protect Heritage

In order to ease conflict over heritage preservation of private property, an amendment of 1997 introduced the mechanisms of "Transfer of Floor Area Ratio" to compensate owners for loss. Other amendments introduced at this time offered tax breaks as incentives for owners of private property. The most representative case is provided by the campaign to preserve Dihua Street. Civic groups working with academics challenged the urban renewal plan that was put forward in 1977 which would have widened the street and wiped off the historical shop-houses along it. At the time the preservation campaign was strongly opposed by the property owners. Owing to the long-term campaign and the alternatives proposed to make up for the property owners' losses through transfers of floor area, the urban renewal plan was changed and the houses along the street were designated as a historical preservation district. A total of seventy-seven of the buildings were categorized as Historical Buildings. The preservation movement that initially set out to save Dihua Street has expanded over the last three decades into a broader movement for inner city regeneration. The movement is connected to the establishment of several Urban Regeneration Stations in the district. In these programmes the city government provides spaces — mostly heritage sites or historical buildings — and the private sector, including NGOs, community groups and even small companies, bid for the privilege of managing the proposals. The designation of the Historical Landscape Preservation District around Dihua Street represents a breakthrough for urban design in Taipei through the collaboration between government and civil society. An institution of heritage conservation linked to planning tools was enacted, with a result that satisfied different stakeholders.

Enhancing Access to and Use of Publicly Owned Heritage

To encourage the use of heritage owned by the public sector, the revised articles allowed for fees to be charged to visitors. Such fees, which went to the managing agencies, were intended to cover management and maintenance costs for the monuments. In practice, however, many public heritage sites were put into operation for commercials reasons — the goal

FIGURE 11.2   Preservation of shop-houses in Dihua Street. Photograph © Liling Huang 2017.

of serving the public interest and enhancing cultural values was often left behind.

New Challenges Ahead

As illustrated above, the series of amendments to the Cultural Heritage Preservation Act between 1997 and 2005 reflected the adjustments made by the government in the face of rising demands for cultural preservation from civil society. Despite the accomplishments, the task of preservation became more difficult though after state–society relations underwent another round of transformation. Taiwan's economy has not been able to continue the high rate of growth it used to have. Along with industrial restructuration, an increasing number of production sites have become defunct. Meanwhile, the government has become more financially dependent on the private sector. The Urban Renewal Ordinance was announced in 1998 as a way to stimulate the national economy. In addition, large expanses of public land were sold by the government to the private sector in order to demonstrate effective "re-use" of public properties.

Civic groups, for their part, extended the scope of preservation and diversified the categories of heritage to include community living landscapes, industrial landscapes, and negative heritage. But unlike the earlier competition/collaboration model, the gap between the government and civil society has been increasing. And, obviously, government capacity to address the demands of civil society is becoming weaker.

The increasing gap between the government and civil society is reflected in the most recent revision to the Cultural Heritage Preservation Act, completed in July 2016. During the last two revisions a critical institutional change was the establishment of the Ministry of Culture in May 2012. The aim was for the Cultural Heritage Preservation Act of 2016 to better address the ministry's labour and organizational structure. It was also aimed at enhancing the visibility of cultural affairs in government administration. The officers from the Ministry of Culture claimed that the "mismatch" of categories between UNESCO's Convention Concerning the Protection of the World Cultural and Natural Heritage and Taiwan's Cultural Heritage Preservation Act over the past decade was the main reason for the ineffectiveness of heritage preservation in Taiwan. To connect to the global society, the major attempt of the Ministry of Culture was to introduce categories and international definitions of tangible and intangible heritage, linking this to to its "continuous endeavors of evaluating the potential of listing sites in Taiwan for World Heritage Sites".[4] This concern, however, does not meet with the general concerns and expectations of the grass-roots preservation movement. Some scholars have commented that the division of tangible and intangible heritage was dangerous and could be a regressive step for the preservation movement in Taiwan. Scholars, experts and community activists have also pointed out that many other important issues need to be addressed by the Ministry of Culture. For example, sources of funds for the restoration and management of and research into heritage should be secured. The loose process of review for designation should be improved. And civil society often expects the government to play a more aggressive role in conducting preservation. The challenge, however, is that in comparison with the huge profits to be made from the development of land, the amounts of compensation for heritage preservation or the penalties for the failure to do so are dwarfed.

It is important to note that there are many faces to "civil society"; a fact often ignored in public debates. Different conceptualizations of civil society — such as "the public", "urban citizens", and "the communities" — have been mobilized interchangeably in heritage debates over the past two decades. What are the cultural and political implications of these classifications for considering cultural heritage? This issue is related to the ways in which the notion of "localness" has been implicitly established in the political and sociocultural peripheries, and which has had the power over the practice of inheriting selective properties while disinheriting others in a (post-)colonial city.

One of the most recent cases is the saga to save the old Taipei Railway Depot. Built in 1935, the Taiwan Railway Administration initially considered the depot as nothing more than an old factory that would only attract railway fans. With the depot being successfully designated a site of national heritage in March 2015, it may represent a chance of challenging the narrative of "revitalizing state assets" as the dominant discourse in imagining the future of heritage-making in the country.

It is also important to understand that a successful heritage designation does not necessarily ensure a more inclusive interpretation of the many pasts. In many cases we see communities fluctuating between progressive planning and the conservative politics of historical preservation, and in so doing have approached new possibilities of "insurgent planning" (Miraftab and Wills 2005) in the shadow of the colonial state. "The colonial state" may be understood in two senses; it can refer to the Japanese government that ruled Taiwan from 1895 to 1945; it can also refer to the (neo)colonial state hidden in modernist city planning, which privileges the abstract conceptualization of development as the only public interest.

The case of Wen Men Lou is a critical one for us to examine, representing one of the many issues that remain in the ongoing struggle over designated heritage. Built in the 1920s, the Wen Meng Lou building was the first heritage site designated to showcase Taiwan's historical sex industry and the country's sex workers' movement of the 1990s (Wang and Chang 2014). It was one of the very last legal brothels to operate in the city before licensed sex work was officially abolished in 2001, and it became the centre of an emerging social movement against the policy change and social stigma towards sex work. The Collective of Sex Workers and Supporters (COSWAS) has been one of the key organizations in the campaign and, as a result, made it possible for the building to be recognized as a heritage site in 2006.

The battle, however, was not over. The fact that the building was private property standing on a parcel of land owned by the semi-public Bank of Taiwan made the site vulnerable to speculation and at risk of redevelopment. COSWAS, as a tenant, was excluded ongoing discussions as to the future of the building. A developer has included nearly seventy per cent of public land owned by the Bank of Taiwan — stretching from Gui-shui Street to Ning-hsia Road and including Wen Meng Lou — in an urban regeneration plan. Eyeing profits from the regeneration plan, in March 2011 a realtor bought Wen Meng Lou for NT$3,300,000. Were it not for intervention from the Bureau of Cultural Affairs in response to the campaign by COSWAS, the collective would have been displaced (Wang and Chang 2014). Yet, the campaign by COSWAS has met with increasing opposition from local residents. Some have voiced their disappointment at a site marked by such an infamous history becoming an obstacle to redeveloping the neighbourhood. The deep-seated stigma against sex work has led residents to exclude sex workers and their everyday lives from the representation of heritage. At one point a campaign was even launched to seek the abolition of Wen Meng Lou's designation as a heritage site. The battle has not yet been resolved, and this example clearly demonstrates how heritage-making is a contested process intertwined with politics and socio-economics, a process which, given the diversity of civil society, may never finish.

Concluding Remarks

This chapter has contextualized the development of heritage preservation in post-war Taiwan, with a focus on how civil society has played a critical role in shaping its policy and politics. Despite significant progress since the late 1980s, there will be new challenges to be faced.

As a relatively young, energetic democratic country, the case of Taiwan sheds light on how engagement with civil society in heritage-making continues to contribute to the process of democratization by challenging the definition of the state and *the public* that the state aims to manage, implicitly or explicitly. Examples can be seen most clearly in cases of publicly owned heritage. The ongoing revisions to the Cultural Heritage Preservation Act suggests that no consensus has been reached. It also reflects the increasingly diversified requests for heritage preservation that are being received in the face of a continuously growing civil society. It is worth noting, however, that the rampant land speculation and pro-capitalist policies of recent years have alienated civil society (or at least a segment of it) to a much greater extent than previously, which especially threatens the cultural rights of marginalized people. The current social context is different to that of the 1980s and 1990s when amendments proceeded under a competition/collaboration relationship between the state and society. It appears that a time for new confrontation has arrived. Ironically, it seems increasingly difficult for civil society to engage in revising the institution when they are continuously struggling to save historical buildings from demolition driven by land speculation. The latest major revision to the Cultural Heritage Preservation Act took place over a decade ago; the problems of heritage are reflected in the conflicts occurring between state and society as well as within civil society itself — conflicts which demand more thorough discussion and public debate. We believe that it is, after all, the momentum from civil society in the realm of heritage-making that will allow the cultural to contribute to democracy.

Notes

1. During the Cold War, Taiwan was located along the defensive line of the United States. U.S. forces resided in Taiwan in support of the Korean War of the 1950s. In recent years the increasing tourism demands of U.S. army members has resulted in renovations by the KMT authorities to create sites of rich Chinese cultural significance in order to provide an exotic tourist experience.

2. On 29 December 1922 the office of Taiwan's governor-general promulgated the "Order of Implementing Administrative Laws in Taiwan" (行政諸法臺灣施行令). Thirty-six domestic laws in Japan were officially implemented in Taiwan; the Preservation Act of Historic Sites, Resort and Natural Heritage was among them (Lin 2011).
3. Ministry of Culture, Laws and Regulations Retrieving System <http://law.moc.gov.tw/law/EngLawContent.aspx?Type=E&id=3>.
4. "The Report of Public Hearing on Revision of Cultural Heritage Preservation Act". Legislative Yuan, May 2015. Committee of Educational and Culture, Legislative Yuan, p. 16.

References

Chiang, M. *Memory Contested, Locality Transformed: Representing Japanese Colonial Heritage in Taiwan*. Leiden: Leiden University Press, 2012.

Chiang, Y. "A Research on the Executive System of Designated Procedure of Current Historical Sites in Taipei" (in Chinese). Master's thesis, National Taiwan University of Science and Technology, 2004.

Hsiao, H.H.M., and H.J. Liu. "Collective Action toward a Sustainable City: Citizens' Movement and Environmental Politics in Taiwan". In *Livable Cities? Urban Struggle for Livelihood and Sustainability*, edited by Peter Evens. University of California Press, 2002.

Hsiau, A. *Return to Reality: Political and Cultural Change in 1970s Taiwan and the Postwar Generation* (in Chinese). Taipei: Linking Books, 2008.

———. *Reconstructing Taiwan: The Cultural Politics of Contemporary Nationalism* (in Chinese). Taipei: Linking Books, 2012.

Huang, L. "Transformation of Community in the Face of New Nationalism: Discourse Analysis of 'Living Community' in Taiwan" (in Chinese). Master's thesis, Graduate Institute of Building and Planning, National Taiwan University, 1995.

Huang, S. "Dancing in the Ruins: Locating Space of Insurgent Planning in the Shadow of the Colonial State". In *We Own the City: Enabling Community Practice in Architecture and Planning*, edited by Miazzo and Kee, pp. 218–25. Hong Kong: Hong Kong University Press, 2014.

Kuo, C. "Palace Style of Architectures: Nationalism and Modern Taiwan Architectures 1949–1980" (in Chinese). Project report of National Science Council, Executive Yuan, 2004.

Lee, D. "Community Building and Civil Society". In *Rooted: Theories and Practices of Community Building in Taiwan*, pp. 19–40. Taipei: Tang Shan, 2014.

Lin, H. "Comparison between the Old and New Versions of Heritage Preservation Act" (in Chinese). In *Proceeding of 2006 International Conference on Cultural Heritage Administration*, pp. 121–44. Taipei: CCA, Executive Yuan, 2006.

―――. *History of Cultural Preservation in Taiwan*. Taipei: Yuan Liu, 2011.

Miraftab, F., and S. Wills. "Insurgency and Spaces of Active Citizenship: The Story of Western Cape Anti-eviction Campaign in South Africa". *Journal of Planning Education and Research* 25, no. 2 (2005): 200–217.

Rowlands, M., and Ferdinand de Jong, eds. *Reclaiming Heritage: Alternative Imaginaries of Memory in West Africa*. Walnut Creek, CA: Left Coast, 2007.

Taylor, J.E. "Reading History through the Built Environment in Taiwan". In *Cultural, Ethnic and Political Nationalism in Contemporary Taiwan: Bentuhua*, edited by John Makeham and A-Chin Hsiau, pp. 159–83. New York: Palgrave Macmillan, 2005.

Wang, F.P., and R.C. Chang. "Wen Men Lou: Preservation of Historical Brothel and the Campaign of the Collective of Sex Workers and Supporters (COSWAS)" (in Chinese). *Taiwan Human Rights Journal* 2, no. 4 (2014): 151–68.

Yan, L. *Memory and Landscape* (in Chinese). Taipei: Garden City, 2009.

12

Becoming Taiwanese: Appropriation of Japanese Colonial Sites and Structures in Cultural Heritage-Making — A Case Study on the Wushantou Reservoir and Hatta Yoichi

Yoshihisa Amae

Wushantou Reservoir and the adjacent waterways, known as the Chianan Canal, are located in Southern Taiwan, just beneath the Tropic of Cancer (Figure 12.1). They were constructed in 1930 by the Japanese colonizers who aimed to solve Japan's rice shortage by turning the 150,000 hectares of dry land into a sea of fields that would produce rice twice a year. The project took nearly ten years. The completion of the infrastructure transformed not only the regional landscape but also the colonial economy, as well as the livelihoods of the local farmers. At the time it was completed the reservoir was the largest in Asia and the third-largest in the world (Furukawa 2009, p. 104).

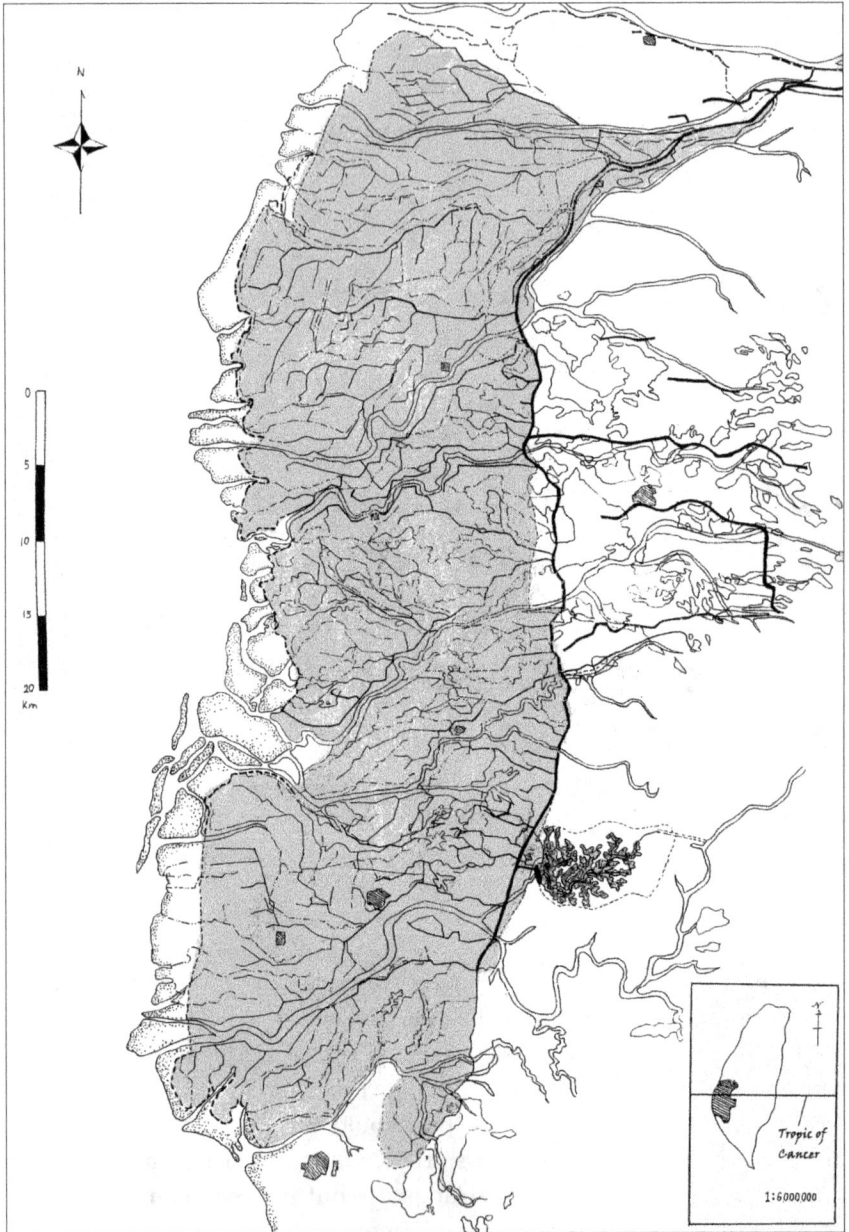

FIGURE 12.1   Aerial view of Wushantou Reservoir and Chianan Canal. Designed by Chihiro Ohara.

Today, some eighty-five years later, this Japanese-built structure is still in use, daily providing tons of water to local farmers. It has also become a site of outstanding cultural heritage in Taiwan — an island that was ruled by Japan for five decades (1895–1945). For instance, in 2001 the Chinese Civil Engineering Association selected Wushantou Reservoir as one of the ten most important historic constructions in Taiwan (Ding 2001). And, in 2009, Taiwan's Ministry of Culture selected it as one of the eighteen "Potential World Heritage Sites".[1] It is also a popular tourist site, attracting more than twenty thousand visitors a year (Taiwan Jianan nongtian shuilihui 2014, p. 66).

Heritage, as the literature suggests, is more concerned with the present than it is with the past (Lowenthal 1997; Harrison 2009). David Lowenthal (1997, p. x), for example, sees heritage as "not an inquiry into the past, but a celebration of it … a profession of faith in a past tailored to present-day purposes". The questions this chapter raise then are as follows: How did Wushantou Reservoir and the Chianan Canal — structures built by the Japanese colonizers — come to earn the status as representative cultural heritage in Taiwan? What does it mean for Taiwan to list these Japanese-era structures as its own cultural heritage? And what present-day purposes do they serve?

As strange as it may sound, heritagization of the Wushantou Reservoir is not an anomaly but a reflection of the social and political reality of present-day Taiwan, in which Japanese imperialism/colonialism is remembered as an era of rapid social transformation and economic development and not so much as an infamous past of shame and terror — something to be rejected and disposed of. In fact, as of December 2016, more than half of Taiwan's 2,180 historic sites and structures are those dating from the Japanese era (Bureau of Cultural Heritage 2017). From the Presidential Office in Taipei to local train stations and administrative buildings, they are ubiquitous on the island, and are cherished by the local communities as important cultural symbols. Unlike in South Korea, "colonial modernity" — a perspective which looks into the intricate relationship between coloniality and modernity in an endeavour to go beyond the Manichean binary of demonizing colonialism and praising modernization — has not gained currency among Taiwanese intellectuals. This is mainly due to the lasting legacy of the post-war Chinese Nationalist Party, or Kuomintang (KMT), government, under which the native Taiwanese had experienced political and economic hardship greater than that under Japanese colonial rule. In particular, the infamous "February 28 Incident" of 1947 — an island-wide protest against the corrupt government which was brutally crushed, claiming more than ten thousand lives — shattered all hope of native Taiwanese embracing the new Chinese regime as their own and created a vast rift between the native Taiwanese and the mainlander Chinese.[2] The distaste for the KMT and nostalgia for Japan — as a reaction as well as in retrospect — were, however, not expressed in public during the martial law period (1949–87). It was not until the island nation had undergone democratic transition in the 1990s that nostalgia for the Japanese past became a social phenomenon and a nationwide movement, whether by preserving Japanese-era buildings or producing literature and films romanticizing the colonial past.[3] Against the backdrop of anti-Japanese sentiments in China and South Korea, Taiwan's "pro-Japanese" phenomenon has attracted scholarly discussion (Kushner 2007; Sakai 2010; Lin 2013). As far as the preservation of Japanese-era structures is concerned, scholars have pointed out the multiple purposes they serve, varying from boosting tourism and producing locality, to building national pride (Lu 2002; Taylor 2005; Chan 2010; Chiang 2010; Amae 2011; Chang and Chiang 2012; Matsuda 2013).

This chapter examines the appropriation of Japanese colonial structures as part of Taiwanese cultural heritage, a social and cultural phenomenon that has been commonly observed on the island since the mid-1990s. As the cases are countless, here I will deal primarily with the Wushantou Reservoir — one of the two major Japanese-era constructions.[4] Subscribing to the perspectives that view heritage as "social process" (Samuel 1994) and "discursive practice" (Hall 2008, p. 221), this chapter will investigate the meanings — cultural, national and post-colonial — that are being produced in heritage-making: an ongoing process of production and consumption. What Paul Du Gay called "a circuit of culture", offers a model to understand how heritage works. Call it "circuit of heritage" (Graham and Ashworth 2000, pp. 2–3); heritage is given meaning through the process of production and consumption by different agents — governmental and societal, as well as collective and individual — that represent different interests. Heritage also constitutes a cultural space of political contestation — more discursive than physical — in which agents compete for meaning. My argument is that the appropriation of Japanese period structures — long neglected after the Second World War — as "national" heritage has contributed to the construction of a "Taiwan" that is imagined as multicultural and hybrid.

Such national imagination deconstructs and debunks "China" (Allio 2009; Chuang 2011). At the same time, it constitutes a post-colonial discourse — "pro-Japanese" that may be, but not necessarily, a "pro-colonial" one (Amae 2011).

Politics of National Heritage-Making

In the past, heritage in Taiwan was imposed entirely from above. The post-war KMT government deemed only sites and structures that symbolized the history of Han Chinese as heritage, and rendered Japanese structures no historic or cultural value, or, worse, something to be eradicated. Heritage, as Rodney Harrison (2009, p. 18) states, is "primarily about establishing a set of social, religious, and political norms that the nation-state requires to control its citizens, through an emphasis on the connection between its contemporary imposition of various state controls and the nation's past". The KMT government implemented a "predatory" approach in selecting and managing national heritage. While many governmental, administrative and commercial buildings from the Japanese era survived destruction despite their origins, structures that more obviously represented Japanese imperialism and its traces in Taiwan, such as war memorials and Shinto shrines, were destroyed, replaced and altered (Johnson 1994; Amae 2011). This coincided with the island-wide "purge" of Japanese culture: Chinese Mandarin replaced Japanese as the official language, and the government banned the use of the Japanese language in public, along with other vernacular languages, including Hokkien used by the majority Hoklo.[5] Collective memories of the Japanese past were systematically blotted out from public discourse, and school history textbooks made no reference to the social transformation and modernization that took place during Japanese rule. In its efforts to mould the island population as "Chinese", the sites and relics selected to have historic significance for Taiwan were those connecting the island's past to mainland China; for instance, relics and structures from the Ming/Zheng (1662–1683) or Qing eras (1683–1895). Sites that commemorate the legacy of the Republic of China or the KMT were also considered to have historic value. For instance, in 1953 thirteen historic sites were chosen by the government that included the Sun Yat-sen Memorial Museum and the *Guangfu* Auditorium of Zhongshan Hall in Taipei — the place where the Japanese authorities signed the surrender document on 25 October 1945 (Lin 2011, p. 71).[6] These cultural policies —

known as "de-Japanization" policies — were driven by the party-state's need to establish political legitimacy in the newly occupied territory, on the one hand, and to compete for Chinese cultural legitimacy against the Chinese Communists in the international arena, on the other. Heritage, thus, was an extension of politics, or politics by other means, through which a Chinese nation was imagined within Taiwan's territorial space by re-tracing historic continuity with the Chinese past — namely the Ming and Qing eras. These assets, however, were not protected by law until the Cultural Heritage Preservation Act was enacted in 1982. It was no surprise that the fifteen first class historic sites (*guji*) selected by the central government in 1983, as well as the 206 sites added in 1985, included no Japanese-era structures (Lin 2011, p. 74).

Production of Taiwan as Locality/Nationality

The situation changed with the island's democratization in the 1990s. Democratization rendered discourses of Taiwanese civic nationalism, which were previously suppressed, to emerge in the public sphere. Since then the nation has been undergoing a process of rewriting national narratives, through changes in school textbooks and names in public spaces and by demythologizing political heroes. Such a movement, needless to say, has affected heritage-making on the island; it has become decentralized and democratized, and as a result diversified and "de-Sinicized". This has taken place at two levels. First, the government made legal changes. In 1997 the Cultural Heritage Preservation Law was revised to change the classifications of national historic sites (abolishing the ranks of first, second and third class) and to authorize local governments to designate historic sites. In 2000 the government introduced a new category, "historic structures (*lishu jianzhu*)", encouraging local governments to register structures for preservation.[7] The revision to the law in 2000 also made it possible for owners of historic buildings to renovate and revitalize their spaces as coffee shops and restaurants (Matsuda 2013, p. 854). Second, in 1994 an Integrated Community-building Project (*shequ zongti yingzao*), spearheaded by Chen Chi-nan, the head of the Council of Cultural Affairs, empowered civic society to participate in the revitalization of community spaces and to develop a new economic model by industrializing local culture. This initiative brought together local scholars, businesses, those working in the fields of culture and history, and local residents to produce a distinct culture and industry utilizing recollected local memories and historic buildings. Successful cases of community revitalization include Qiaotou Sugar Factory Museum and Cultural Park in Kaohsiung and Jinguashi Gold Ecological Park in New Taipei (Chiang 2010).

These changes opened the floodgate for Japanese-era structures to be embraced as heritage, since they were large in number and often served as important catalysts in producing locality. Statistics show that Japanese-era structures and sites have been preserved as heritage in great numbers since the first one (the former Tainan District Court) appeared in 1991. Prior to 1997 there were only seventeen sites from the Japanese period that were designated as historic assets; within two decades this number had mushroomed to 1,142 (Bureau of Cultural Heritage 2017).[8] Jeremy Taylor describes the situation: "suddenly the structures associated with Japanese colonialism were given the highest historical importance ... local government bodies throughout Taiwan have been busy excavating (literally) Shinto shrines ... and other architectural residua of these structures that survived postwar spoliation" (Taylor 2005, pp. 170–71).

Arjun Appadurai's work suggests that the production of locality is at odds with a sense of nation, as local uniqueness defies the "needs for spatial and social standardization" which is a "prerequisite for the disciplined national citizen" (Appadurai 1996, p. 191). Yet, the production of locality, in the particular context of Taiwan, translates into producing a new national political imagining, since the appropriation of Japanese-period structures as national heritage inevitably connects the island's present to the Japanese past, allowing Taiwan to be imagined on an historic trajectory independent of mainland China. In other words, the nationwide movement to produce locality has reconfigured the nation; the inclusion of structures and sites associated with the Japanese period as national heritage has not only transformed the nature of national heritage from being "purely Chinese" to becoming "Taiwanese" in cultural terms, but it has also redefined the idea of the "national" from being a mono-ethnic (i.e., Sino-centric) nation to being a civic and multicultural one.

The Legacy of Hatta Yoichi and the Heritagization of the Wushantou Reservoir

With the exception of the Chiang Kai-shek Memorial Hall in Taipei, no other cultural or industrial heritage site in Taiwan is as closely linked to the legacy of a single individual as Wushantou Reservoir and Chianan Canal. Hatta Yoichi (1886–1942), the Japanese engineer who designed the massive reservoir and oversaw its construction, is a legend in Taiwan, thanks to the power of mass media and popular culture. Hatta today is culturally reproduced and remembered as more than just a competent engineer; he is depicted as a compassionate "miracle maker" who turned the dry land of the Chianan Plains into a massive granary, improving the livelihoods of the local farmers (Amae 2015). To most Taiwanese and Japanese, the legacy of Hatta and the heritagization of Wushantou are virtually two sides of the same coin.

As heritage, Wushantou Reservoir and the Chianan Canal are one of Taiwan's forty-nine "cultural landscapes (*wenhua jingguan* 文化景觀)" (Bureau of Cultural Heritage 2015).[9] The Tainan City government designated them with such a title in 2009. The reasons given for this recognition were that (1) it had contributed to Taiwan's economic development, especially its impact on the agriculture, ecology and society of the Chianan area; (2) it features distinct hydraulic engineering of the 1920s in terms of the method used and its size; (3) the beautiful scenery of the reservoir and the complex waterways running through the vast Chianan Plains are "world-class" (Bureau of Cultural Affairs 2009). Wushantou, I argue, also represents intangible cultural heritage when taking into account the social practices and religious rituals that occur within the given physical space, as well as the discursive practices concerning the material structures and the people involved in the construction.[10]

Wushantou as Industrial Heritage

The Wushantou Reservoir covers an area of thirteen square kilometres and can store up to 150 million tons of water. The construction involved two main components: the building of the embankment and the digging of the tunnel. A unique semi-hydraulic fill technique was used to build the embankment, which is fifty-six metres high and 1,272 metres long. The technique entailed placing multiple layers of different fine-grained material around the core concrete wall and tightened them using jets of water. The method was adopted to give longevity to the structure on the earthquake-prone island. While the method itself was not new, it had never before been used to construct a dam on the scale of Wushantou. Its success thus earned Hatta a place in the history of hydraulic engineering.[11]

The tunnel, which was drilled through the mountain in order to draw in water from the bigger river on the other side, is 3,109 metres long, 5 metres high, and 5 metres wide. The construction — unprecedented in terms of scale — claimed fifty lives as the result of a gas explosion (Furukawa 2009, pp. 148–50).

With its elevation, the reservoir can irrigate 150,000 hectares of land via its many waterways. Including the 6,000-kilometre waterways used to carry waste water from the fields, the total length of the Chianan Canal comes to 16,000 kilometres, which is equivalent to almost half the distance of the earth's circumference (Saito 2009, p. 123). Steel bridges both large and small were built to carry water over the rivers, and numerous gates were installed to control the water. Due to their uniqueness, the Tainan Municipal government designated the three main bridges as historic sites in May 2014. In order to accomplish the construction as quickly as possible, a steam locomotive and other state-of-the-art machinery such as steam shovels and air dump cars were purchased from the United States for the project. Some of these pieces of machinery are displayed at the reservoir. The total budget for the construction was 54.1 million yen, which amounted to roughly half of the colonial government's annual expenditure for 1927 (Saito 2009, p. 55). As a result, rice production in the region saw a seven-fold increase, while sugarcane production increased three-fold (Shimizu 2015, p. 48).[12]

Wushantou as Cultural Landscape

Wushantou Reservoir is also known as "Coral Lake" because the aerial view of the site resembles the shape of a coral (Figure 12.1). The area is a habitat for wild birds and animals, and the fresh air and beautiful scenery attracts tourists, especially in the spring when the cherry trees planted by the roadside blossom. Besides the natural and industrial values, the reservoir is a focal point for the legacy of Hatta Yoichi, represented by his statue and the graveyard dedicated to him and his wife.

Graveyard of Hatta Yoichi and Toyoki

There exist several cultural landmarks in the area. First and foremost are the gravestone of the couple and the bronze statue of Hatta. The grave is located on the small hill overlooking the reservoir. In 1931, celebrating the completion of the construction, a bronze statue of Hatta was made and installed at this location (Figure 12.2). During the Second World World, citing the need for metal, the statue was taken away by the local authorities and was considered missing. In 1942, Hatta was killed in the East China Sea when the ship that was carrying him, along with hundreds of other engineers and army officials, was sunk by a U.S. submarine. The Japanese-style tomb at the site was erected in 1946 following the tragic death of Toyoki, Hatta's wife, who threw herself into the spillway of the reservoir. After the war the missing statue was found by the staff of the Chianan Irrigation Association; in 1981 it was restored to its original site. It is one of only a very few statues of Japanese figures in Taiwan to have survived into the post-war era. The statue, together with the gravestone, constitute a sacred site "where memory crystallizes and secretes itself " (Nora 1989, p. 7). A commemoration service is held at the site every year on 8 May, attracting a huge crowd. It is said that the commemoration service had been held by the local Taiwanese every year since the building of the tomb (Nagoshi and Kusabiraki 1996, p. 176).

FIGURE 12.2 Statue of Hatta Yoichi. Photo © Yoshihisa Amae 2017.

Monument for the Victims

There also stands within the compound beside the reservoir a stone monument for those who died during the construction of the tunnel and embankment. Erected in 1930, it commemorates the lives of 137 men and women who died during the construction. The names of those who died are listed on bronze plates attached to three sides of the square stone foundation. Japanese names of victims are interspersed with Taiwanese ones, suggesting that the names were inscribed according to the time of their deaths, and not divided along racial lines (Nagoshi and Kusabiraki 1996, p. 178). This was an uncommon practice in the Japanese colony, where the native Taiwanese were routinely subjected to segregation and discrimination. The names also include those of the families of construction workers who died due to sickness such as malaria. The fourth plate displays the words of commemoration given by Hatta:

> You have lost your lives in a foreign land due to unexpected accidents and diseases.... it is unbearable pain and sorrow, yet great is your sacrificial martyrdom, which has inspired other workers to complete the construction.... Your names shall be forever remembered, just as the water in the canals never stop running...

Hatta Yoichi Memorial Park

There is an exhibition hall in Wushantou where old photos and documents of the construction, as well as personal items of Hatta, are displayed. The hall was opened in 2000 to provide visitors with information on the massive construction and its designer. Leveraging on Hatta's growing popularity, the government built the Hatta Yoichi Memorial Park in 2011 on the site that was once the community for the workers on the construction. The Ministry of Transportation spent a total of NT$120 million (US$4.2 million) to repair and rebuild four Japanese-style residences — including that of Hatta — that had lain in ruins for many years. In order to reconstruct the houses as authentically as possible, the Taiwanese experts flew to Japan to interview Hatta's daughters concerning the layout of their childhood home and the neighbouring houses. In addition, Japanese experts were brought in to provide technical assistance to the local architects. This act of heritage-making also involved ordinary citizens. In response to an appeal made in a local Japanese newspaper, the people of Kanazawa — Hatta's hometown — donated 169 items of Japanese-style furniture and artefacts with which to decorate the reconstructed houses (*Hokkoku Shinbun*, 15 February 2011).

The opening ceremony of the Memorial Park, held on 8 May 2011, was attended by President Ma Ying-jeou, his cabinet members, and dignitaries from Japan, including former prime minister Mori Yoshiro (Figure 12.3). The main attraction at the park is the residence of the Hatta family, which, along with three other Japanese houses, is open to the public at no charge. The latest addition to the park is the statue of Toyoki, which was installed in September 2013 to commemorate her dedication to her husband and her great love for Taiwan (Figure 12.4). The funds for the statue were raised in Japan and Taiwan. Two hundred and fifty people, including Hatta's daughter-in-law, came from Japan to attend the dedication ceremony (Yoshimura 2013).

Wushantou as Intangible Cultural Heritage

Wushantou Reservoir is a living heritage. After more than eight decades, it still provides water to the local farmers for agriculture, as well as serving

FIGURE 12.3   President Ma Ying-jeou at the ribbon-cutting ceremony of the Hatta residence.
Photo © Yoshihisa Amae 2017.

FIGURE 12.4 Statue of Toyoki and child.

as a recreational space for visitors to walk or cycle along the banks of the reservoir or have a barbecue with family and friends. And, as has already been mentioned, the anniversary of Hatta's death has been commemorated each year on 8 May. The commemoration service had originally been held by the staff of the Chianan Irrigation Association. Later, from the 1980s, they were joined by family members and friends from Japan. It was not until the late 1990s that Hatta Yoichi received wider recognition thanks to publications released about him, in particular by Shiba (1997), Kobayashi (2000), Lee (2003), and Furukawa (2009). As publicity surrounding him increased, attendance at Hatta's annual commemoration service grew. Over the last decade, dignitaries have included the mayor of Tainan City, the commissioner of Chiayi County, a representative of the Japan-Taiwan Exchange Association (a de facto ambassador), and many other local and state legislators. President-elect Ma Ying-jeou attended the ceremony for the first time in 2008 (and again as President of the Republic of China in 2009 and 2011). The commemoration service traditionally runs for about two hours. It begins with the offering of gifts and a Buddhist chant by Taiwanese monks, followed by that of Japanese monks — each pay their respects in their own language and cultural style (Figure 12.5). This is then followed by a ritual performed by family members, and then by central and local government leaders. They offer gifts, flowers and prayers to the dead. After that, distinguished guests take turns in giving eulogies. Finally, all other participants are invited to lay flowers and give prayers at the feet of the statue and the gravestone. Every year, several hundreds of worshippers flock to attend the service.

Drawing from Edward Casey (2000, p. 253) who stated that "commemoration brings together such seemingly disconnected things as past and present, self and other, body and mind … it draws on powers of participation that are at play in every act of remembering", the annual commemoration of Hatta Yoichi is a powerful showcase of how historical ties between Japan and Taiwan — deliberately and systematically severed by the post-war KMT government — are being mended through the commemoration of a colonial engineer. Such an act of remembering is

FIGURE 12.5 A scene from the commemoration service. The two female monks in the front are Taiwanese. The male ones behind them, patiently waiting their turn, are from Japan. Photo © Yoshihisa Amae 2017.

not confined to a single day of the year at an official event organized by the Chianan Irrigation Association — a public sector organization. There exist other commemorative activities arranged by local civic groups, such as music concerts and a bicycle tour, every year during the first week of May. In 2014, local Taiwanese artists held a concert at the Tainan Cultural Center, singing songs dedicated to Hatta as well as songs expressing love for Taiwan. Another event, organized by a local civic group on the first Sunday of May, is run as a kind of pilgrimage whereby participants cycle to the Wushantou Reservoir from different places in Tainan — some of them completing a round trip of nearly seventy kilometres. Nearly three hundred people participated in this event in 2016, including students from local universities and elementary schools, their teachers, environmental activists, and ordinary citizens from the Tainan region. This event, which has been organized for over a decade, aims to cultivate ecological awareness as well as love for the homeland. The group meets up at noon on the hill where Hatta's statue is located and together hold a ceremony. They lay flowers at the feet of the statue, sing songs, read the declaration of "Love Our Land and Protect Our Water", then take their lunch (Liu 2016). Besides these public events in May, visitors, as individuals or in groups, in a public or private capacity, from near or far, come to pay their respects to the late Japanese engineer, offering prayers and gifts throughout the year. Expressed in a Chinese proverb, *yinshui siyuan* (thinking of the source whenever one drinks the water), it is said that local residents and farmers remember Hatta every time they use the water from the reservoir. In sum, the commemoration of Hatta — a colonial figure — has become a routine practice in post-colonial Taiwan, where the colonial has been appropriated as cultural in the quest for a national selfhood and in the embodiment of democratic citizenship. All of this makes Wushantou a unique example of cultural heritage on the island.

Heritage of Wushantou as Discursive Practice

The heritagization and popularization of Wushantou were made possible thanks to powerful narratives about Hatta Yoichi that appeared in the form of books, comics, film, TV dramas, song, musicals, and a traditional Taiwanese puppet show. The highest profile production among them is *Pattenrai!! Minami no Shima no Mizu Monogatari* (Hatta Has Come!! Tales of Water from a Southern Island), an animated film directed by Ishiguro

Noboru for Mushi Productions, a major Japanese animation studio. The film was released in 2008 in Japan and a year later in Taiwan with Chinese subtitles. It depicts the human drama and friendship between a Japanese boy and a Taiwanese boy, revolving around Hatta and the construction of Wushantou in the 1920s. These productions have transfigured the Japanese engineer into a saint-like person who preaches racial equality between Japanese and Taiwanese (including the Taiwanese aboriginals) and who dedicates his life, together with his wife, for Taiwan (Amae 2015). For instance, repeated several times in *Pattenrai*, Hatta utters the mantra, "(As an engineer) there is no Japanese or Taiwanese". Similarly, in the Taiwanese TV drama series *Shuise Jianan*, Hatta and his wife Toyoki are portrayed as "good Japanese" who side with the Taiwanese farmers vis-à-vis exploitative Japanese capitalists and brutal policemen. Hatta, in this production, has three subordinates: Abe (a Japanese), A-shan (a Hoklo, Han Chinese), and Aiueo (a Siraya, Taiwanese aborigine). Hatta mediates their differences and conflicts and brings harmony among them.

Consuming Hatta Yoichi/Wushantou

Through the "circuit of culture", the "ongoing process of production and consumption" (Du Gay 1997) of Hatta, Wushantou has, since the late 1990s, become a representative cultural heritage for Taiwan. In practice, however, the distinction between production and consumption is not always as clear as is suggested in the literature. Like the yin-yang symbol where there is a small part of yang in yin and vice versa, production can be a form of consumption while consumers produce meanings through consumption. Harrington and Bielby (2001, p. 4) point out that consumers are not passive participants; they, as individuals or a group, are agents that fix, alter or reject particular meanings presented by the producers. Whether intentionally or not, producers/consumers often commit the sin of emphasizing certain elements while downplaying others.

The Nihongo Sedai and Pro-Taiwan Independence Groups

One of the primary consumers of Hatta is the so called *Nihongo Sedai* 日本語世代, or "Japanese-speaking generation". They are Taiwanese old-timers who were born in Taiwan during Japanese colonial rule and received a Japanese education. They have a good command of the Japanese language as well as a fair understanding of Japanese culture and ethics. These people suffered the most when the Chinese Nationalists took control of the island after the Second World War, as they were seen by the new rulers as Japanese collaborators, if not traitors to the Chinese nation (*hanjian*). Representative figures of this generation are elites such as former president Lee Teng-hui and the entrepreneur and founder of Chimei Enterprise, Hsu Wen-long (1928–). Since the early 1990s they have become willing agents of the Hatta legacy, contributing to the heritagization of Wushantou and the Chianan Canal. For instance, Lee calls Hatta the "paragon of Japanese spirit", embodying virtues such as loyalty and sincerity and setting an example for others through his own deeds (Lee 2003, pp. 308–9). Hsu Wen-long, an amateur artist, has made busts of Hatta, as well as of other representative Japanese figures in commemoration of their contributions to Taiwan. These busts have been erected at sites of memory of the subjects they depict, such as their places of birth in Japan or their workplaces in Taiwan. Busts of Hatta can be found at the Exhibition Hall in Wushantou and in a museum in Kanazawa.

Hatta/Wushantou is often discursively consumed by these figures to strengthen Taiwanese national identity (Tainaka 2007; Amae 2015). Praise for Japanese colonizers such as Hatta and Gotō Shinpei, civil chief administrator of the Office of the Governor-General of Taiwan (1898–1906), is a vote of non-confidence against the KMT government, if not open defiance of the KMT's legitimacy to rule Taiwan. To this extent, Hatta is used as the antithesis or counterweight of what "China (ROC and PRC alike)" mis/represents. Thus, it was no coincidence that Lee Teng-hui visited Wushantou Reservoir in 2012 and exalted Hatta for his contribution to Taiwan at the time when President Ma Ying-jeou was being criticized by the public for "selling out Taiwan" in striking trade deals with China (Lin 2012). There even exists a popular narrative of comparing the Chianan Canal to the Great Wall of China: "the total length of the water supply canal is 16,000km. This amounts to a length six times longer than the Great Wall" (Kobayashi 2000, p. 140; Furukawa 2009, p. 111).[13] This narrative, most likely originally intended to simply emphasize the size of the canal, has been utilized by pro-Taiwan figures like Lee Teng-hui to distance Taiwan from China. Together with narratives such as "Japan made Taiwan modern" and "Without Japanese rule, Taiwan would be no different from Hainan Island" (Tsai 2000, p. 54), they constitute a "pro-Japanese/anti-Chinese" discourse in Taiwan. It is no accident therefore that a group of Taiwanese academics and activists have, since 2009, organized a petition to register the Wushantou Reservoir as a World Heritage site.[14] Pro-Taiwan civic groups such as the Taiwanese Presbyterian Church — the oldest and largest Protestant denomination on the island — and the Taiwanese Association of University Professors are major supporters of the movement.[15]

KMT and Ma Ying-jeou

The election in 2000 of Chen Shui-bian, the pro-Taiwan president of the Democratic Progressive Party (DPP), further allowed the legacy of Hatta to proliferate and consolidate. Many of the cultural productions that feature the Japanese engineer were produced after 2000. President Chen issued a posthumous presidential award to Hatta in 2007 in recognition of "his important contribution for Taiwan's agriculture". Yet, Chen, in contrast to his successor, the KMT's Ma Ying-jeou, barely leveraged on Hatta's popularity for political gain. For instance, Chen, during his presidency (2000–2008), never attended Hatta's commemoration service. This may be due to the fact that the pro-Taiwan party already enjoyed wide support in Southern Taiwan, especially in Tainan, Chen's hometown.[16]

Such was not the case for the KMT, which traditionally lacks political support in Southern Taiwan. Ma Ying-jeou consumed Hatta to the fullest, overriding his party's traditional stance of neglecting the Japanese colonial legacy. In 2008, Ma praised Hatta and his construction projects during his election campaign stop in Tainan. While it is unlikely that such a move alone granted him victory, it marked the first time Ma championed a Japanese-era construction project (Guo 2011). After his victory, the president-elect attended Hatta's commemoration service at Wushantou on 8 May 2008, becoming the first head of state to do so. The president attended the service again in 2009.[17] He also attended the screening of the film *Pattenrai* in Tainan in November 2009 (Li 2009).[18] In May 2011, President Ma and several members of his cabinet attended the opening ceremony of the Hatta Yoichi Memorial Park, a historic event that attracted a large crowd, including more than two hundred visitors from Japan (Lai 2011). In his prepared speech, Ma hailed Hatta and referred to his character as sincere, honest, hardworking, enterprising and tolerant, which, he added, "coincides with the core values of the people of Taiwan" (Office of the President 2011). The president did not neglect to take credit for building the park by telling the audience that he was the one who came up with the idea three years previously when he first visited the Wushantou Reservoir (Office of the President 2011). It was obvious that by showing respect to Hatta, Ma was attempting to diffuse the party's pro-China image and gain a foothold in the southern constituencies that have traditionally supported the DPP.

Becoming a Taiwanese Deity

While the contributions of popular political and business leaders have been undeniable, Hatta has become a legacy — even a legend — due to the actions of ordinary citizens, who, through various events and activities, both private and public, have venerated him. And there is no better way to perpetuate an individual's fame than to deify him or her. To many Taiwanese, the late Japanese engineer is more than a cultural icon and historical hero; he is a god. This is ever possible in a culture that boasts more than a hundred gods, including human beings who made great achievements (Dong 2008).

In addition to the aforementioned annual commemoration service, Hatta is featured in a 350-year-old Daoist temple in the neighbourhood, which worships *shennong dadi*, the god of farmers. While no records suggest any ties between the temple and the Japanese engineer, in 2009 it built an exhibition hall dedicated to him. The main exhibit is a wooden sculpture of Hatta and his wife, along with Chen Yonghua — one of Zheng Chenggong/Koxinga's military generals who was a pioneer in the area in the late seventeenth century.[19] The temple inaugurated the exhibition at an opening ceremony held in May 2009, which was attended by descendants of Hatta, the mayor of Tainan, and important political figures from either side of the political divide. The temple also organizes an annual *"raojing"* (deity procession) to thank Hatta and bless the neighbourhood. This event sees the participation of a dozen other temples in the neighbourhood (Lin 2011).

There also exists a group in central Taiwan called "February 28 (Incident) Taiwan gods (*ererba Taiwan shen* 二二八台灣神)", which recognises Hatta as one of the forty-nine deities of Taiwan. Hatta has been chosen as a "Taiwanese deity" due to the contribution he made to the island with his construction project (Chen 2014, p. 186). While the practice seems innocent enough, one could argue that the true intention behind the move is purely political. Revering Hatta, a Japanese colonial engineer, as a deity, represents a subtle yet powerful stance of defiance of the post-war KMT regime. This point makes more sense when seen in the larger context: thirty-seven of the deities are Taiwanese elites who were murdered during the February

28 Incident; the other eleven are those who dedicated their lives to the island's human rights and democracy (Chen 2014).

Heritage Tourism and International Grass-roots Diplomacy

Hatta's legacy and the heritagization of Wushantou have led to Tainan County[20] and Kanazawa Prefecture building a special relationship — the two local governments and their city councils signed a friendship agreement in December 2006 (Tainan County Government Information Division 2006) and political and business leaders of the two cities signed a de facto sisterhood city agreement in 2011 (Taiwan The Heart of Asia 2011).[21] The Wushantou Reservoir is a popular destination for students from Kanazawa. In 2009, students from Hanazono Elementary School — Hatta's alma mater — visited Chianan Elementary School, the school that was built for the children of the staff and workers at Wushantou. In 2010 a local educational fund in Kanazawa invited nine students from Chianan to visit their school in Kanazawa to participate in an international exchange programme (*Toyama Shinbun*, 21 August 2010). In both regions, the story of Hatta is taught in schools through the supplementary textbook for elementary school students (Tainan County Government 2010). Teachers and students of Hanazono wrote a song for Hatta, which is sung by students of both schools during visits. In 2012 the Tainan city government organized a "Kanazawa Week" (7–13 May), during which Kanazawa traditional arts, crafts and food were showcased. In response, Kanazawa city held a "Tainan Week" in Kanazawa in September of the same year.

In addition, Hatta is featured in a "City of Love" event organized by the Tainan City Government on "Chinese Valentine's Day". Hatta Memorial Park was featured on one of the eight memorial postcards the city issued to promote its Lovers' Festival (*Qingrenjie*) in 2011 (Tainan City Government 2011). The postcard depicts a young couple sitting on the doorstep of Hatta's residence. The city government seems to have capitalized on the popular perception that views the relationship between Hatta and his wife, who followed her husband into the afterlife, "romantic".

Conclusion: Heritage as Rite of Passage

This chapter has examined how and why Japanese colonial structures that were previously regarded by the KMT government as reminders of

FIGURE 12.6 Toyoki's death depicted in a Taiwanese comic book. The first paragraph, in Chinese, reads: "I have no way to leave you and this island which you've loved so deeply.... Thus, at this point, allow me to dive into your arms...". Source: Xu and Liu 2002, p. 55.

a notorious colonial past — structures to be either destroyed or altered, and not worth protecting — have been appropriated into Taiwanese cultural heritage since the late 1990s. By focusing on the case of Wushantou Reservoir, I have examined how colonial heritage became national and international through the "circuit of culture", a process of production and consumption of the Japanese engineer. Such a transformation was made possible by collaboration between the state and civil society, which together engaged in the production of locality in pursuit of status in the global market as a "cultural great power" (Lu 2002, p. 166) and national selfhood. Moreover, the legacy of Hatta consumed by different agents in popular culture, everyday life, and identity politics has contributed to the heritage-making of Wushantou. In the process, Hatta, a Japanese colonial engineer, became a signifier for "love for Taiwan". His narratives suggest that he loved the Taiwanese, as he treated his workers — both Japanese and Taiwanese — equally. Even his untimely death in the Second World War and his burial in Taiwan, later joined by his wife, have been interpreted as demonstrating his deep love for Taiwan. This troubling representation of Hatta has been sanctified through the public commemoration of and deification of this colonial figure. In other words, Wushantou became cultural heritage through everyday social and discursive practices involving ordinary Taiwanese people.

Various meanings have been produced in the process of heritage/legacy making, for example, Hatta as a preacher of racial equality, a paragon of the Japanese spirit, a lover of Taiwan, and even a deity. But, most importantly, the legacy of Hatta Yoichi and the heritagization of Wushantou, together with the island-wide movement of appropriating Japanese structures as "national heritage", have transformed the meaning of Taiwan and what this island nation represents in the present day: Taiwan no longer represents the sole legitimate China, as it once claimed to be. Nor does it represent China, in full or in part. It has been transformed into a multicultural and hybrid community, in which China is merely one of its traits — not denied but dethroned. This argument makes more sense when one pans back from the single case of Wushantou and looks at the bigger picture of heritagization: The potential World Heritage sites in Taiwan include the Jinmen and Matsu cultural zone, which is a site of memory of the fiercely fought Chinese civil war, and the Beinan Cultural Park, an important archaeological site with particular significance for Taiwanese Austronesians. Taiwan has been reimagined and transformed as the decentralization and democratization of heritage politics has enabled civic groups and ordinary citizens to participate in the making of heritage. Viewing heritage-making as what anthropologists call "rites of passages" (Harrison 2008), one can argue that, through the reconfiguration of its national heritage, in particular the appropriation of Japanese colonial sites and structures, Taiwan has moved into a new stage: that of a new and independent nation — liminal it still may be, but certainly not marginal.

Notes

1. Taiwan (officially known as the Republic of China) has no World Heritage sites, as the island nation is not a member of UNESCO. Wushantou was voted the most popular among the eighteen sites in 2010 through online voting.
2. While the exact number of victims is hard to determine, it is believed that between 18,000 and 28,000 were killed in the name of "sedition". This included many elites, such as politicians, lawyers and educators, who had attempted

to mitigate the crisis. It is believed that the government used this occasion to eradicate all the native Taiwanese social and political elites that it considered could threaten its political legitimacy. George Kerr, a consulate of the U.S. Embassy at the time of the tragedy, referred to is as the "March Massacre", as most of the killings took place in early March with the arrival of supplementary troops from mainland China (Kerr 1966, pp. 254–310).

3. Taiwan is considered to be one of the most "pro-Japan" nations in the world. For example, according to government data, 2.8 million people visited Japan from Taiwan in 2014 (Japan National Tourism Organization 2015). That is one out of every twelve in a nation of twenty-three million people! It is the highest number of visitors from a single country. Moreover, Taiwanese also donated the largest amount of money during the relief effort for the victims of the 3/11 Great Eastern Japan Earthquake in 2011.

4. The other one is the building of the hydraulic power plant at Sun Moon Lake.

5. Hoklo people migrated to the island from Fujian Province in the mid-seventeenth century. Accounting for seventy-three per cent of the total population, they speak a variant of Hokkien that has incorporated Japanese and Plains Aboriginal vocabularies.

6. What is ironic is that both sites have Japanese origins. The Sun Yat-sen Museum was a formerly luxurious Japanese hotel called Umeyashiki, where Sun resided during his visit to Taipei in 1913. Zhongshan Hall was the former Taipei City Hall built by the Japanese in 1936.

7. Besides historic structures being credited with less historic importance, the biggest difference between the two is to do with the nature of protection. While the protection of historic sites is mandatory, for historic structures it is only "recommended", and no penalty is imposed on violators (Lin 2011, p. 133).

8. As of December 2016, the Japanese-era structures include 397 historic sites and 745 historic structures.

9. Other categories of cultural heritage are historic sites and buildings, archaeological sites, communities, relics, traditional arts, and folk culture.

10. According to the UNESCO Convention for the Safeguarding of Intangible Cultural Heritage (2003), intangible cultural heritage is defined as "the practices, representations, expressions, knowledge, skills — as well as the instruments, objects, artifacts and cultural spaces associated therewith — that communities, groups and, in some cases, individuals recognize as part of their cultural heritage. This intangible cultural heritage, transmitted from generation to generation, is constantly recreated by communities and groups in response to their environment, their interaction with nature and their history, and provides them with a sense of identity and continuity, thus promoting respect for cultural diversity and human creativity…" (article 2, paragraph 1).

11. The American Society of Civil Engineers named it the "Hatta Dam" (Furukawa 2009, p. 172).

12. The colonial authorities adopted and enforced a plan to divide the area into three parts and to rotate farmers to plant rice, sugar cane and millet on an annual basis on the argument that there was not enough water for all the farmers to plant rice. However, the real motive beyond the three years' rotation was most likely to secure sufficient quantities of sugar cane. Economist Yanaihara Tadao criticized this "planned economy" and predicted that the Chianan irrigation project would further accelerate the monopoly of the capital by sugar companies in Taiwan, which formed a cartel (Yanaihara [1929] 1988, pp. 280–83).

13. A different book written by a Japanese author, for example, refers to the length of the water supply canal as "half way around the globe" (Saito 2009, p. 123). However, such descriptions of the canal are not as popular as its reference to the Great Wall of China. Interestingly enough, the earlier edition of Furukawa's book (1989) makes no reference to the Great Wall. The comparison was first made by Shiba Ryōtarō in his travel essays published as a book in 1997.

14. Since Taiwan is not a member of the United Nations, the group seeks to accomplish the goal of membership with the help of Japan (Yang 2009). As of 26 January 2014, 78,370 signatures had been collected (Hatta Wang 2014).

15. For example, the Presbyterian Church runs an informative website about the Wushantou Reservoir and the TAUP has organized a public viewing of *Pattenrai*. For more information, see <http://www.pct.org.tw/wusanto/>.

16. Tsai Ing-wen, DPP candidate in the 2008 presidential election, visited Wushantou Reservoir on 16 March 2011. She laid flowers by Hatta's statue as a mark of respect for his work (*Light Up Taiwan*, 16 March 2011).

17. The 2010 ceremony was attended by the vice-secretary of the Presidential Office (Liu 2010).

18. The screening in Taipei was attended by former president Lee Teng-hui and former premier and DPP heavyweight Frank Hsieh. Ma's decision to attend the screening in Tainan was seen as an appeal to southern voters.

19. All the Chens in the village — which are many — are believed to be descendants of this great general. Shi Zhi-hui, a treasured national artist, carved these figures. It is reported that it was the first time Shi had carved a figure other than deities (Cao 2009).

20. Tainan County ceased to exist in December 2010 when it was merged with Tainan City to become a special municipality known as "Greater Tainan".

21. The City of Kanazawa, which has a sister city agreement with Suzhou, was afraid that an official agreement with Taiwan would cause the Chinese city to scrap the agreement.

References

Allio, Fiorella. "Capturing Intangible Culture and Ephemeral Manifestations: The Perpetuation of Taiwanese Traditions in Temple Processions". In *Objects, Heritage and Cultural Identity*, edited by Frank Muyard, Liang-Kai Chou, and Serge Dreyer. Nantou, Taiwan: Taiwan Historica, 2009.

Amae, Yoshihisa. "Pro-colonial or Postcolonial? Appropriation of Japanese Colonial Heritage in Present-day Taiwan". *Journal of Current Chinese Affairs* 40, no. 1 (2011): 19–62.

———. "A Japanese Engineer Who Became a Taiwanese Deity: Postcolonial Representations of Hatta Yoichi". *East Asian Journal of Popular Culture* 1, no. 1 (2015): 33–51.

Appadurai, Arjun. *Modernity at Large*. Minneapolis: University of Minneapolis Press, 1996.

Cao, Ting-ting 曹婷婷. "Gan'en Chen Yonghua, Batian Yuyi dezhe Shi Zhihui fengdaoqian lizuo" [Thanking Chen Yonghua and Hatta Yoichi's good work, Shi Zhihui seals his final piece]. *China Times*, 13 April 2009 <http://tw.myblog.yahoo.com/jw!kHeWvYqAFQ.aVJYbL.PC5g--/article?mid=9059> (accessed 7 November 2013).

Casey, Edward. *Remembering: A Phenomenological Study*, 2nd ed. Bloomington: Indiana University Press, 2000.

Chan, Selina Ching. "Imagining and Consuming Cultures: Nostalgia and Domestic Tourism Development in Taiwan". *Canadian Journal of Development Studies* 31, nos. 3–4 (2010): 367–80.

Chang, Lung-chih, and Min-chin Kay Chiang. "From Colonial Site to Cultural Heritage". *The Newsletter* 59 (Spring 2012): 28–29.

Chen, Meng-juan 陳孟娟. *Taiwan shen xinyang: Da'ai de xiuxing* [Faith of Taiwan gods: Practicing great love]. Taipei: Feibianshe, 2014.

Chiang, Min-chin. "The Hallway of Memory: A Case Study on the Diversified Interpretation of Cultural Heritage in Taiwan". In *Becoming Taiwan: From Colonialism to Democracy*, edited by Ann Heylen and Scott Sommers. Wiesbaden: Harrassowitz, 2010.

Chuang, Chia-yin. "Divorcing China: The Swing from the Patrilineal Genealogy of China to the Matrilineal Genealogy of Taiwan in Taiwan's National Imagination". *Journal of Current Chinese Affairs* 40, no. 1 (2011): 159–85.

Ding, Rong-sheng 丁榮生. "Quanguo 10 da tumu shiji chulu" [10 largest historic sites revealed]. *China Times*, 30 November 2001.

Dong, Fang-yuan 董芳苑. *Taiwanren de shenming* [Taiwanese deities]. Taipei: Qianwei, 2008.

Du Gay, Paul, ed. *Production of Culture/Cultures of Production*. London: Sage, 1997.

Fu, Chao-Ching 傅朝卿. *Tushuo Taiwan Jianzhu Wenhua Zichan: Rizhi shiqi bian 1895–1945*. Tainan: Taiwan Jianzhu Wenhua, 2009.

Furukawa, Katsumi 古川勝三. *Taiwan wo aishita nihonjin: doboku gishi Hatta Yoichi no shōgai* [A Japanese who loved Taiwan: The life of Hatta Yoichi, a civic engineer], rev. ed. Matsuyama, Ehime: Sōfūsha, 2009.

Graham, Brian, Greg Ashworth, and John Tunbridge. *A Geography of Heritage: Power, Culture and Economy*. London: Arnold, 2000.

Guo, Yu-fu 郭譽孚. "Jia'nan dazunyu Batian Yuyi wenti yanjiu zhi jiben ziliao: zhanhou bianzao de guocheng" [Basic information on the studies of Jia'nan irrigation and Hatta Yoichi: The process of post-war changes]. *Zhenzhengde Taiwanshi Yanjiu* [Studies on Taiwan's true history], 26 June 2011 <http://city.udn.com/50077/4659005> (accessed 5 May 2015).

Hall, Stuart. "Whose Heritage? Un-settling 'The Heritage,' Re-imagining the Post-nation". In *The Heritage Reader*, edited by Graham Fairclough, Rodney Harrison, John H. Jameson Jnr, and John Schofield, pp. 219–28. Abingdon: Routledge, 2008.

Hamamura, Isamu 浜村勇. "Nihon tōchi jidai no Taiwan de damu kensetsu" [Constructing a dam in Taiwan during the Japanese era]. *Yomiuri Shinbun*, 19 April 2013, Tsukuhō region edition, p. 13S.

Harrington, Lee, and Denise Bielby, eds. *Popular Culture: Production and Consumption*. Malden, MA: Blackwell, 2001.

Harrison, Rodney. "The Politics of the Past: Conflict in the Use of Heritage in the Modern World". In *The Heritage Reader*, edited by Graham Fairclough, Rodney Harrison, John H. Jameson Jnr, and John Schofield, pp. 177–90. Abingdon: Routledge, 2008.

———. *Understanding the Politics of Heritage*. Hampshire: Palgrave Macmillan, 2009.

Hokkoku Shinbun. "Raigetsu, fukugenn shukushahe zenyi no kagu, Taiwan ni muke [Goodwill furniture to Taiwan's renovated houses next month]. 15 February 2011 <http://www.47news.jp/localnews/hotnews/2011/02/post-20110215093452.html> (accessed 5 May 2015).

Johnson, Marshall. "Making Time: Historic Preservation and the Space of Nationality". *positions: east asia cultures critique* 2, no. 2 (1994): 177–249.

Kerr, George, H. *Formosa Betrayed*. London: Eyre & Spottiswoode, 1966.

Kobayashi, Yoshinori 小林よしのり. *Taiwan ron* [On Taiwan]. Tokyo: Shōgakukan, 2000.

Kushner, Barak. "Nationality and Nostalgia: The Manipulation of Memory in Japan, Taiwan, and China since 1990". *International History Review* 29, no. 4 (2007): 793–820.

Lai, Yourong 賴友容. "Batian Yuyi yuanqu qiyong Sen Xilang shuaituan zhuisi" [Hatta Yoichi Park opens, Mori Shirō leads the group to commemorate]. *Epoch*

Times, 9 May 2011 <http://tw.epochtimes.com/11/5/9/165085.htm> (accessed 7 November 2013).

Lee, Teng-hui 李登輝. *'Bushidō' kaiden: Nōburesu oburiijyu towa* [Understanding 'Bushido': The meaning of noblesse oblige]. Tokyo: Shōgakukan, 2003.

Li, Shuhua 李淑華. "Batian donghua dengtai Ma Yingjiu chuxi Tainan shouying" [Hatta animation arrives in Taiwan, Ma Ying-jeou attends Tainan viewing]. *Epoch Times*, 31 October 2009 <http://www.epochtimes.com/b5/9/10/31/n2707401p.htm> (accessed 7 November 2013).

Light Up Taiwan. "Jianzheng Batian Yuyi yuanjian Cai Yingwen: 'nanfang jingshen' " [Witnessing Hatta Yoichi, Tsai Ing-wen foresees: 'southern spirit']. 16 March 2011 <http://www.iing.tw/2011/03/blog-post_16.html> (accessed 5 May 2015).

Lin, Hui-cheng 林會承. *Taiwan Wenhua Zichan Baocun Shigang* [Guidebook on cultural heritage preservation in Taiwan]. Taipei: Yanliu, 2011.

Lin, Mengting 林孟婷. "Gan'en Batian Yuyi Guantian Cishenggong raojing qifu" [In appreciation of Hatta Yoichi, Guantian Cisheng Temple dedicates prayer journey]. *Liberty Times*, 14 March 2011 <http://www.libertytimes.com.tw/2011/new/mar/14/today-south14.htm> (accessed 7 November 2013).

Lin, Xiuhui 林修卉. "Zhuisi Batian Yuyi Li Deng-hui shudu gengye" [Commemorating Hatta Yoichi, Lee Teng-hui chokes several times]. *NOWnews*, 17 May 2012 < http://www.nownews.com/n/2012/05/17/72059> (accessed 3 February 2017).

Lin, Yi-chun 林怡君. "Shuxiede duanlie: Riben jiyi zai taiwan de zhuanhuan" [Rupture in writing: Japanese colonial memory in Taiwan discourse]. *Monumenta Taiwanica*, 7 April 2013, pp. 89–120.

Liu, Wan-jun 劉婉君. "Zhuisi Batian Yuyi xian baiju shuo ganxie" [Remembering Hatta Yoichi, showing thanks by offering white chrysanthemums]. *Liberty Times*, 9 May 2010 <http://www.libertytimes.com.tw/2010/new/may/9/today-south11.htm> (accessed 5 May 2015).

———. "Xiang Batian Yuyi zhijing jin sanbai ren Jianan dazun tiema suyuan" [Showing respect to Hatta Yoichi, nearly 300 ride their bikes up Chianan Canal to its source]. *Liberty Times*, 1 May 2016 <http://news.ltn.com.tw/news/life/breakingnews/1682149> (accessed 8 February 2017).

Lowenthal, David. *The Heritage Crusade and the Spoils of History*. Cambridge: Cambridge University Press, 1997.

Lu, Hsin-yi. *The Politics of Locality: Making a Nation of Communities in Taiwan*. New York: Routledge, 2002.

Matsuda, Hiroko 松田ヒロ子. "Taiwan ni okeru nihon tōchika no ikō no hozon to saisei: taihokushi aotagai no nihonshiki mokuzō kaoku wo chūshin ni" [Preservation and revitalization of Japanese-era structures in Taiwan: A study on Japanese-style residences in Qingtian street, Taipei City]. In *Teikokugo no hito no idō: postcolonialism and globalization no kōsakuten* [Post-imperial movement of people: Interaction of post-colonialism and globalization], edited by Araragi Shinzō. Tokyo: Bensei, 2013.

Nagoshi, Futaaranosuke 名越二荒之助 and Shōzō Kusabiraki 草開省三, eds. *Taiwan to Nihon Kōryū hiwa* [Untold stories on cultural interactions between Taiwan and Japan]. Tokyo: Tentensha, 1996.

Nora, Pierre. "Between Memory and History: Les Lieux de Memorie". Special issue, *Representations* 26 (1989): 7–24.

Office of the President, Republic of China (Taiwan). "Gan'en Jianan dazunzhi fu, Batian Yuyi jinian yuanqu jiyong" [Appreciating the father of Jianan Irrigation, Hatta Yoichi Memorial Park opens]. 10 May 2011 <http://www.president.gov. tw/Default.aspx?tabid=1103&itemid=24202&rmid=2780> (accessed 5 May 2015).

Saito, Michinori 斉藤充功. *Nittai no kakehashi: Hyakunen damu wo tsukutta otoko* [A bridge between Japan and Taiwan: The man who built the Centennial Dam]. Tokyo: Jiji, 2009.

Sakai, Toru 酒井亨. *Shinnichi Taiwan no gensō: genchi de mititisita shinno nihonkan* [The illusion of "pro-Japanese" Taiwan: A local perspective on real views on Japan]. Tokyo: Fusosha, 2010.

Samuel, Raphael. *Theatres of Memory*, vol. 1, *Past and Present in Contemporary Culture*. London: Verso, 1994.

Shiba, Ryotaro 司馬遼太郎. *Taiwan Kikō* [Taiwan journey]. Tokyo: Asahi Shimbun, 1997.

Shimizu, Misato 清水美里. *Teikoku no "kaihatsu" to shokuminchi Taiwan: Taiwan no kanantaishū to jitsugetsutan hatsudensho* [Imperial development and colonial Taiwan: Chianan irrigation and Sun Moon Lake Electric Power Plant in Taiwan]. Tokyo: Yūshisha, 2015.

Tainaka, Chizuru 胎中千鶴. *Shokuminchi wo katarutoiukoto: Hatta Yoichi no 'monogatari' wo yomitoku* [Narrating colonial Taiwan: Reading the narratives of Hatta Yoichi]. Tokyo: Fūkyōsha, 2007.

Tainan City Government. "Hello! Love City". 2011 <http://love.tncity.tw/love_other110.htm> (accessed 7 November 2013).

Tainan County Government. *Renshi Nanying (Xinpian): Tainanxian Guoxiao liunianji bentu jiaocai* [Getting to know Tainan (new edition): Native teaching materials for sixth graders in Tainan County]. 2010 <http://nbooks.tnc.edu.tw/98/9806/index.htm> (accessed 5 May 2015).

Tainan County Government Information Division. "Fuhui furi fangwentuan, yuanman dacheng dimeng renwu" [Tainan Council's Japan visitation group accomplishes its mission to conclude agreement]. 1 September 2006 <http://ifo.tainan.gov.tw/Publish_Detail.aspx?sID=570&sMon=1&sYear=2007&sClass=1> (accessed 5 May 2015).

Taiwan Jianan Nongtian Shuilihui 台灣嘉南農田水利會. *Jishi Wuyu: Batian Yuyi Jinian Yuanqu binfen shilu* [A story of an engineer: Reports from Hatta Yoichi Memorial Park]. Tainan: Taiwan Jianan Nongtian Shuilihui, 2014.

Taiwan Shūhō 台湾週報. "Hōtai shita Kanazawa Gakuin Higashi Kōtō Gakko no shugaku ryokōsei ikkō ga Hatta Yoichi shi no dōzō ni kenka" [Kanazawa Academy East high school students offer flowers to the statue of Hatta Yoichi]. 19 November 2009 <http://www.taiwanembassy.org/ct.asp?xItem=117662&ctNode=3591&mp=202> (accessed 7 November 2013).

Taiwan The Heart of Asia. "Kanazawashi to Tainanshi ga yūkō kōryū kyōtei teiketsu" [Kanazawa City and Tainan City conclude friendship exchange agreement]. 2011 <http://timefortaiwan.tw/JP/cms/newsAction.do?method=viewContentDetail&iscancel=true&contentId=4500&subMenuId=3501&siteId=103> (accessed 27 May 2013).

Taylor, Jeremy. "Reading History through the Built Environment in Taiwan". In *Cultural, Ethnic, and Political Nationalism in Contemporary Taiwan: Bentuhua*, edited by John Makeham and A-chin Hsiau, pp. 159–83. New York: Palgrave MacMillan, 2005.

Toyama Shinbun. "'Hatta gishi jiman' Nittai de kisou Japan Tent tokubetsu puroguramu" [Japanese and Taiwanese compete for 'Hatta Pride', a Japan tent special programme]. 21 August 2010 <http://www.hokkoku.co.jp/subpage/H20100821101.htm> (accessed 7 November 2013).

Tsai, Kun-tsan 蔡焜燦. *Taiwanjin to Nihon seishin* [Taiwanese and Japanese spirit]. Tokyo: Nihon Kyōbunsha, 2000.

Xu, Yu 徐昱 and Liu Xiao-qian 劉曉蒨. "Lianlian Wushantou" [Loving Wushantou]. *Shaonian Taiwan*, November 2002, pp. 52–55.

Yanaihara, Tadao 矢内原忠雄. *Teikoku shugi ka no* Taiwan [Taiwan under Imperialism]. Tokyo: Iwanami [1929] 1988.

Yang, Si-rui 楊思瑞. "Taixuejie faqi zhengqu Wushantou shuiri xitong denglu shijie yichan" [Taiwanese academics initiate a drive to register Wushantou irrigation system as World Heritage site]. *Epoch Times*, 8 May 2009 <http://www.epochtimes.com/b5/9/5/8/n2520235.htm> (accessed 5 May 2015).

———. "Mianhuai Batian Yuyi jinian yuanqu kaiyuan" [Cherishing the memory of Hatta Yoichi, the Memorial Park Opens]. *Yam News*, 8 May 2011 <http://n.yam.com/cna/garden/201105/20110508650132.html> (accessed 5 May 2015).

Yoshimura, Tsuyoshi 吉村剛史. "Suiri jigyō no nihonjin gishi wo sasaeta tsuma wo kenshō Taiwan ni dōzō" [A wife who supported a Japanese engineer of irrigation project honoured by getting a statue built in Taiwan]. *Sankei News*, 1 September 2013 <http://sankei.jp.msn.com/world/news/130901/chn13090119480001-n1.htm> (accessed 7 November 2013).

Websites
Bureau of Cultural Heritage, Ministry of Culture 文化部文化資產局
Hatta Wang 八田網
Japan National Tourism Organization 日本政府観光局

13

Defining Culture in the Heritage Preservation of Taiwanese Veterans' Villages: The Case of Zuoying

Li Danzhou

Introduction: The Origin of Taiwanese Veterans' Villages

After the Chinese civil war spread in February 1947, the troops of the Chinese Nationalist Party (KMT) suffered successive military reversals in the Liaoshen, Pingjin and Huaihai campaigns of 1948. Consequently, the KMT military strategy was to retreat.[1] At a military conference in Dinghai in 1949, from among the three possible strategies — "shift to Xikang", "retreat to Hainan Island" or "retreat to Taiwan" — Chiang Kai-shek elected for the Taiwan option.[2] The retreat to Taiwan in 1949 saw the transportation of governmental agencies and large quantities of antiques to Taiwan. According to statistics, 1.2 million troops and civilians were moved between 1945 and 1953 (Lin 2011, p. 250).

To relocate millions of KMT soldiers and their dependents, Taiwanese veterans' villages (pinyin: *juancun*) gradually emerged on the landscape of Taiwan. According to Guo Guanlin, it is not correct to see the Taiwanese veterans' villages as "villages built up for the soldiers and dependents", because the villages were constructed with the exclusive political motive "to stabilize the morale of the KMT troops" (Guo 2005, p. 1). Early in 1932, military settlements similar to the Taiwanese veterans' villages emerged in Jiangxi Province and Shanxi Province of mainland China. These settlements were built to accommodate KMT troops and to support the fight against the Communist forces. Prior to 1949 the military settlements in Taiwan were mostly quarters and barracks left by the Japanese colonial power. For instance, Whampoa New Village in Fengshan District of Kaohsiung City is typically regarded as the earliest dormitory for Japanese land forces. Gu Chaoguang proposed that due to dissatisfaction with the KMT's internal conflict between the Whampoa warlords and the Baoding warlords, Sun Liren arrived at Fengshan for troop training in October 1947. He established the fourth military training class and arranged the accommodation for soldiers and their dependents in Whampoa New Village. As the civil war in mainland China worsened during the retreat, temporary buildings, rebuilt warehouses, old factories, and even illegal houses were gradually subsumed within the category of Taiwanese veterans' villages.

It should be noted that *The Regulations on Taiwanese Veterans' Villages of the KMT Army*, endorsed by the Department of National Defense on 11 January 1954, marked the debut of the official administration of Taiwanese veterans' villages. Veterans' villages were thus "built up by the public funds, belonged to governmental properties, and were distributed and administrated by subordinated army services". Accordingly, a tightly linked network of military apparatus began to take shape, from individual households to the Department of National Defense. After retreating to Taiwan, both the KMT military authorities and the Chinese Women's Anti-Communism and Anti-Soviet Union Association (*Fulianhui*; dominated by Song Meiling, Chiang Kai-shek's wife) constructed houses for more than five thousand households. The administrative catalogue listed a total of 871 veterans' villages (of these, no specific location could be identified for fifteen of them) (Chen 2009, p. 64).

Grounded in an ethnographic framework and a case study of some disappearing naval veterans' villages in southern Taiwan, this chapter considers the cultural heritage preservation of Taiwanese veterans' villages as a discursive field. In investigating various aspects of "culture" in terms of cultural policy, cultural management, community participation, cultural industry and cultural memory, the heritage-making of Taiwan can indeed be seen to be a cultural-led product. Specifically, I find it to be "a signifying system"[3] through which this sort of urban heritage is socially constructed as a political rhetoric of collective memory, an administrative subject for urban governance, a more "nativism" issue regarding social transformation, as well as a future commodity for the tourist gaze. However, a series of lawsuits initiated by some residents to protest the ultra vires actions of the Department of National Defense and to resist the progressive privatization of land should not be readily neglected, because these local struggles strive for the right of inhabitation that concerns social justice via the politics of everyday life.

The Emergence of "Village Culture"

When I arrived at the naval veterans' village in Zuoying, all the residents I met used the term "village culture" (juancun wenhua). What interested me most was how a military settlement could transform into a type of culture. What did "village culture" mean? It was necessary to examine Taiwanese veterans' villages from a historical perspective.

After the full-scale retreat of the KMT military to the Zhoushan Islands and Hainan Island in May 1950, Chiang Kai-shek delivered a speech over the radio entitled "To All Our Countrymen". This speech demanded political mobilization from the bottom up and a struggle for the final victory of anti-communism. As the outcome of particular historical circumstances, the construction work on houses and the administration of residents was no more than stopgap measures that served the purpose of "striking back to the mainland of China". However, with the death of Chiang Kai-shek in 1975 and radical changes in the political complexion of the ROC (Republic of China) government, the slogan "strike back to the mainland" vanished, and residents who lived in veterans' villages were forced to take root in Taiwanese society.

An official regulation issued by the War Ministry of the Department of National Defense on 31 January 1988, *Some Notes on the Reconstruction Work in the Ramshackle Veterans' Village*, reported on the deplorable conditions of some veterans' villages (p. 1). As an amendment to the previous regulation, *Regulations on the Reconstruction Work in Ramshackle Veterans' Village* made efforts to articulate the reconstruction policy with the revitalization of land in 1997 (Department of National Defense 1999, p. 1). An article issued on 26 April 2000 stated that reconstruction work for Taiwanese veterans' villages was within the scope of urban planning to "promote the recycling of land use and improve the living environment" (Department of National Defense 2000, p. 6111). Therefore, the reconstruction work of the veterans' villages was conducted not only with the motive of renovating the rundown buildings and facilities, but it also anticipated the progressive process of land privatization under the pretext of urban renewal. This was the changing context of Taiwanese veterans' villages that saw their rapid disappearance and the controversy over their preservation verses demolition. The following questions were raised: What should be preserved? What had already been preserved? What had disappeared with deliberate acts of destruction? All these questions are related to the important topic of "village culture".

The Culturalization of the Naval Veterans' Village in Zuoying: A Perspective on Cultural Policy

Both the making of cultural policy and its subsequent implementation help to legitimate the culturalization of Taiwanese veterans' villages. The term "village culture" did not appear in the initial version of *Regulations on the Reconstruction Work in Ramshackle Veterans' Village*, issued on 5 February 1996. However, according to the amended versions issued on 12 December 2007 and 30 December 2011, the term "cultural preservation on Taiwanese Veterans' Village" appeared in article 4 for the first time and was juxtaposed with the act of reconstruction when dealing with the disputes over the ramshackle veterans' villages (Department of National Defense 2011).

Although the responsible agency was defined as "the Department of National Defense" in article 2, the official Ministry of Culture became involved in the implementation of cultural preservation, assisting the Department of National Defense in examining and verifying the qualified veterans' villages. *Measures on the Selection and Approval of Cultural Preservation on the Ramshackle Veterans' Villages*, issued in 2013, clarified the responsibility and function of the Ministry of Culture in the process of cultural preservation. In addition to selecting one or two sites with empty land and old houses remaining to apply for the qualification of cultural preservation, each village's representatives were required to be located in five administrative regions covering the entire Taiwan Island. It was compulsory for the application report to include all information related to geographical location, cultural values, methods of preservation and relevant management. Once the responsible department nominated a veterans' village for further preservation, the local government was obligated to conduct urban planning and then to assign another piece of land to return to the military authority. The organizational structure of the nine-person advisory committee on cultural preservation consisted of two representatives from the Department of National Defense, one representative from the Construction and Planning Agency and the Ministry of the Interior, one representative from the Ministry of Culture, and five representatives from folk society, academia, and the professional world. In general, "culture" referred to the involvement of official departments that were responsible for culture.

On the basis of article 54 in the official cultural law of the *Taiwan Cultural Heritage Preservation Act (wenzifa)*, a stretch of naval veterans' villages in Zuoying were registered as a "cultural landscape"[4] by the Kaohsiung City Government on 9 April 2010. The cultural preservation covered a wide range of naval settlements in Zuoying, including Mingde New Village, Jianye New Village, Hequn New Village and relevant facilities such as Sun Yat-sen Hall. In addition to the legal foundation of the *Taiwan Cultural Heritage Preservation Act*, based on *Measures on the Selection and Approval of Cultural Preservation of the Ramshackle Veterans' Villages*, the Kaohsiung City Government also appealed to the Department of National Defense to nominate Mingde New Village as an industrial park representative of "village culture" in southern Taiwan. As Table 13.1 shows, Mingde New Village and Jianye New Village represent one of the thirteen potential cultural parks in Taiwan.

Culturalization of the Naval Veterans' Village in Zuoying: Power Relations among the Bureaucracy, Academics and NGOs

The implementation of cultural policy was further reified in a power structure among the bureaucracy, academics and folk society. According to the timetable of cultural preservation in the veterans' village of Kaohsiung City, it is obvious that cultural preservation was closely linked to municipal administration. As the convener, the vice mayor founded an organization called the *Consultative Panel of Cultural Preservation of the Veterans' Village in Kaohsiung City*. Five divisions addressed different aspects of cultural preservation. For instance, the Public Works Department was responsible for forestation and beautification; the Urban Development Bureau took

TABLE 13.1

Proposed Cultural Preservation of the Ramshackle Veterans' Villages in Taiwan: A Summary Sheet of Chosen Sites

	Region	Responsible Unit	Name	Military Service
1	Northern	Taipei City Government	Zhongxin New Village (abstention)	Land forces
2	Northern	New Taipei City Government	Sanchong 1st Village	Air forces
3	Northern	Taoyuan County Government	Mazu New Village	Land forces
4	Northern	Hsinchu City Government	Zhongzhen New Village	Air forces
5	Northern	Hsinchu County Government	Hukou Armored Village	Land forces
6	Central	Taichung City Government	Xinyi New Village	Air forces
7	Central	Changhua County Government	Zhongxing New Village	Land forces
8	Central	Yunlin County Government	Jianguo 2nd Village (abstention)	Air forces
9	Southern	Tainan City Government	Zhikai New Village	Air forces
10	Southern	Kaohsiung City Government	Mingde New Village, Jianye New Village	Naval forces
11	Southern	Kaohsiung City Government	Haiguang 4th Village, Juguang 3rd Village, Cihui New Village	Naval forces Land forces
12	Southern	Pingtung County Government	Shengli New Village, Chongren New Village (in Chenggong District)	Land forces Air forces
13	Offshore Island	Penghu County Government	Duxing 10th Village	Land forces

Source: Meng Xiude, Some Ideas on the Cultural Preservation and Revitalization of Zuoying Naval Veterans' Villages.

charge of urban planning for the development of a cultural park for the veterans' village; the Bureau of Cultural Affairs focused on the preservation plan and cultural management; the Tourism Bureau advocated cultural tourism in the veterans' village; and the Economic Development Bureau was responsible for promoting creative industries. Notably, as a branch of the Department of Military Service, the original community service centre was transformed into the "Project Management Center for Cultural & Creative Cluster in Veterans' Village of Zuoying" to perform the duty of industrial park management. The administrative structure explained how "village culture" had been involved in urban governance led by the local government; that is, the local government developed cultural tourism and creative industries in the name of "village culture" (Kaohsiung City Government 2010*b*).

Sponsored by the local Bureau of Cultural Affairs or the Bureau of Cultural Heritage affiliated with the Ministry of Culture, scholars conducted archival studies or on-site fieldwork at the proposed veterans' village and prepared relevant research reports for governmental planning. As the earliest research proposal on the cultural preservation of Zuoying Veterans' Village, *The Research Report on Kaohsiung Museum of Military Dependents Village* concentrated on the feasibility of establishing a cultural museum with the theme of military dependents' villages. It mainly investigated the historical archives (geographical environment, historical development, cultural background and life experiences), site evaluation and selection (location, management and tourism), and curatorship (exhibition design and outdoor display). *The Cultural Association of Old Town in Kaohsiung* and its working team completed a research report in December 2006. In addition to reviewing the political background and historical development of Taiwanese veterans' villages, this report included some case studies of naval veterans' villages in Zuoying, including architecture, facilities, historic sites, oral history, archives, and the cultural and natural landscape.

Authorized by the Bureau of Cultural Affairs, the Department of Creative Design and Architecture at the National University of Kaohsiung submitted two research proposals on the data analysis of spatial resources and a maintenance scheme for the cultural landscape in 2010 and 2011. By contrast, *The Report on the Basic Data of Space and Feasibility of Revitalization in Zuoying Veterans' Village* emphasized the basic spatial data for the strategic evaluation of cultural preservation, which included fundamental information on space (geographical location, land and architectural analysis and transportation) and cultural features (historical development, characteristics of architecture and cultural values). *The Proposal on the Maintenance Scheme of Cultural Landscape in Zuoying Naval Veterans' Village* explored how a series of executive measures would be able to function during the process of cultural preservation, especially after the official registration as a "cultural landscape". For example, preservation methods for planting and greening and protection of the representative architecture, public facilities and historical plaza were comprehensively discussed and analysed in this report. With regard to both revitalization and maintenance, these two reports highlighted the functional role of cultural preservation as an indispensable part of urban planning and regional regeneration.

In contrast to the spatial analysis, a separate research report investigated the life history of female residents living in the veterans' villages. This report was conducted by the Department of Creative Design and Architecture at the National University of Kaohsiung in 2010. This project selected fifteen women from the remaining seven veterans' villages of Zuoying District and documented their oral histories by means of literary texts and audiovisual technology. With attention to gender politics and the cultural identification of Taiwanese ethnicity, *Report on Life History of Women in Veterans' Villages in Kaohsiung City* helped to socially construct a new ethnicity called the "after-war new immigrant" (Kaohsiung City Government 2010c, p. 4).

Non-governmental organizations have been engaged in the cultural preservation of naval veterans' villages since October 2003; the re-construction work had already begun in Zuoying at that time. As a spontaneously formed and early folk society organization, The Folk Association for Promoting Village Culture in Mingde and Jianye New Village consisted of residents who disagreed with the reconstruction policy advocated by the military authority. Mr Qiu Shanliang, a veteran major general who had retired from the KMT ground forces, was forced to flee his hometown in Shandong Province when he was fourteen years old and settled in Taiwan with his brother-in-law. As the director-general of this anti-reconstruction association, he stated that the association's basic appeal was to "make everyone be able to live here". Taking a stance against the planned demolition, his team made efforts towards mediation with the administrative authorities. One part of the association's strategy saw it engaging in a lawsuit with the Department of National Defense to safeguard the rights and interests of residents. On another front, through effective communication with the local government, the team appealed for cultural preservation to retain the original architecture and facilities of Mingde, Jianye and Hequn New Villages. By August 2007, some anti-reconstruction residents in Mingde and Jianye New Villages had unified with anti-reconstruction forces in the other nine veterans' villages. They gained court approval and registration to establish an aggregate corporation called the Cultural Development Association of Veterans' Village in Kaohsiung City. Their guiding principle was to "retain and develop village culture and strive for the justified rights of residents". Their central tasks include:

> (1) retain the disappearing village culture that had been devastated by the reconstruction work; (2) retrieve the distinctive culture in every single veteran's village. For those that have been reconstructed, we suggest preservation by means of oral history or cultural relics; for those that have not been reconstructed, we suggest negotiating with the responsible departments for further preservation; (3) actively promote preservation activities, including traditional culture, lifestyle, ecological environment, humanistic education, architectural landscape, and military history. Promote the establishment of a cultural museum; (4) develop software for cultural promotion and preservation. Cooperate with electronic media or print media to pass village culture to the offspring; (5) coordinate with the cultural policy making of the government, and mediate with relevant departments; (6) actively strive for the legal rights of residents.[5]

As the former director-general, Wang Rulin stated that the primary goal of this association was to oppose reconstruction. However, he gradually noticed the significance of "culture" as a tactic for struggle. According to Rulin, anti-reconstruction did not contradict cultural preservation. Although the lawsuit with the Department of National Defense and the tactical manoeuvring for the right of habitation remained controversial issues, attention had already been paid to cultural preservation and spatial revitalization in the naval veterans' villages. When preparing to construct a cultural museum of military dependents' villages, the association had participated in a bidding procedure. After the establishment of the cultural museum the association had been engaged in military-themed curatorship since 2008. In addition to the concern about the cultural museum, the association cooperated with other commercial companies and organizations to promote the "village culture". For instance, the association applied the budget from some large state-owned enterprises to host cultural activities related to the veterans' village, such as a bicycle competition to cross multiple veterans' villages in Zuoying. The association also cooperated with the Youth Development Administration under the Ministry of Education to encourage youth to walk across Taiwan to understand the local culture. Student workers were welcome to visit veterans' villages, eat the village food and watch open-air cinema. In Kaohsiung City, a dragon boat competition was organized on Love River to promote "village culture" among civilians.

With regard to further development, Wang Rulin proposed the idea of a "village culture cluster" covering the areas of Mingde, Jianye and Hequn New Villages. After extensive renovation, the shabby houses in southern Jianye New Village could be revitalized as youth hostels and areas for dining and shopping. The original No. 1 Mingde Hotel could be reused as a military history museum to introduce the public to the historical development of Taiwan's military. The association even planned to negotiate with the Teresa Teng Foundation to establish a Teresa Teng memorial hall inside the veterans' village.

When envisioning the concept of cultural preservation and spatial revitalization for the near future, it is necessary to mention a newly founded organization, The Community Development Association of Mingde and Jianye New Village. As a civil society group newly registered by the Social Affairs Bureau of Kaohsiung City Government in May 2012, the purpose of this non-governmental organization is to "develop village culture, tourism, hostels, food, and souvenirs" and "improve the hospitality with tourists".[6] The director-general, Meng Xiude, planned cultural festivals for a national day of the Republic of China on 10 October. The most recent activity organized by the association aimed to invite those born in the village to return to Zuoying. By inviting military officers, celebrities and high achievers who were born in the veterans' villages, this ambitious cultural activity guided cultural preservation towards the creative industries and cultural tourism, "attracting the mainlander tourists to understand the multi-culture in Taiwan".[7]

The Contradictory "Culture"?

It is necessary to consider the reinvention of veterans' villages by examining the changing discourse of "historical preservation" during the past few decades in Taiwan. Yen suggested that from the Second World War to the 1970s, there was no systematic idea of "historical preservation" in Taiwan. However, in the 1970s, in addition to the rediscovery of the historical, cultural and social values of traditional Taiwanese architecture by some architectural specialists and the major turning point of the rejection of Taiwan's membership of the United Nations in the late 1970s, the formerly authoritarian state run by Chiang Kai-shek's nationalists was under pressure of regime legitimation. As the first official administration responsible for cultural affairs, the Council for Cultural Affairs in Taiwan was founded in 1981. Another authoritative law, the Taiwan Cultural Heritage Preservation Act, was launched in 1982 to define the criteria and specific classifications of cultural capital. Both the administrative department and cultural policy helped to legitimate the tentative "localization" by means of culture preservation. Although the concern about "culture" had moved from a China-oriented concern to a Taiwan-oriented one, the outlook of cultural history and the appraisal of cultural relics remained in line with the Chinese cultural orientation in comparison with Western culture at that time. Thus, the so-called "localization" in the name of historical preservation was considered a general framework of Taiwanese culture to consolidate the legitimation of the Chinese Nationalist Party (Yen 2006, pp 93–97).

However, in Taiwan in the late 1980s, radical socio-political changes occurred, including the reversal in 1986 of the prohibition against forming political parties, the rescinding of the emergency law (martial measures) in 1987, the end to the prohibition of newspapers in 1988, and the boom in the economy led by export trade. Consequently, in comparison with the top-down discourse of historical preservation, two types of bottom-up ideas appeared in the 1990s: the discourse of settlement preservation (*juluobaocunlunshu*) and the community construction movement (*shequzongtiyingzao*). Xia Zhujiu, a scholar at the Institute of Building and Planning of National Taiwan University, held the idea that civic participation and the collective memory of community residents should be considered in historical preservation. This viewpoint was in line with the urban movement and called for the subjective agency of grass-roots forces inside a community to oppose the property hegemony and ideological apparatus. Another conceptual framework, the community construction movement, was discussed from 1993 to 1997 by Chen Qinan, the vice chairman of the Council for Cultural Affairs in Taiwan. If the early historical preservation in the 1980s aimed to construct an essentialized "local" by the policies of the KMT authorities, the discourse of the community construction movement acted in the opposite direction, claiming that "village construction, street construction, town construction, countryside construction" (Chen 1996, p. 113) would play an important role in constructing a democratic Taiwan. Indeed, Chen's argument coincided with the political tendency by which Taiwan attempted to reposition its national subjectivity in the 1990s. As a result, the Council for Cultural Affairs in Taiwan has made additional implementations in every city and county of Taiwan since 1994 to reinvent the folklore, rituals and cultural relics of local communities.

In this case, the dynamics of "village culture" among the bureaucracy, academics, non-governmental organizations and residents demonstrated an emerging sense of "place". The social construction of the naval veterans' village reflected a persistent entanglement of the discourse of settlement preservation and the community construction movement. If the purpose of community construction was to cultivate a new identification of Taiwan, a number of participants during the process of cultural preservation in the naval veterans' village spontaneously regarded "village culture" as an indispensable part of Taiwan's multi-culture to reinforce the assertion that "Taiwan is a democratic country".[8] I observed a rich diversity of community participation rather than the sense of a presupposed political stance. The anti-reconstruction residents continued to strive for their legal rights to habitation against the military authority, and some university lecturers attempted to bring the student movement into the cultural preservation of the naval veterans' village.[9] As Huang Xiuli's research has shown, in addition to governmental guidance, local organizations and cultural associations became involved in the cultural preservation of the veterans' village, but it has remained difficult to obtain cooperation or funding from private enterprise (Huang 2010, pp. 237–39).

In the case of the naval veterans' village in Zuoying, due to disagreements on all sides about defining "village culture",[10] "culture" has remained an ambiguous signifier. As in the vivid example presented below, a public hearing entitled, "How could a live veteran's village become possible? The prospect of cultural preservation cluster in Mingde new village of Kaohsiung city", provided a centralized reflection to explain how different interest groups responded to the strategy and approach of cultural preservation in Mingde New Village of Zuoying District. Despite different opinions,[11] the ultimate goal was to reach an agreement to carry out the idea of "live revitalization" and vigorously promote cultural and creative industries.

The Culturalization of the Naval Veterans' Village in Zuoying: Industrial Transformation towards Cultural Industry as the Ultimate Goal

Different interest groups were able to reach an agreement about the concept of industrialized culture due to the developmental tendency of the cultural and creative industries claimed by the Council for Cultural Affairs in Taiwan since 2009. With the slogan "antiquity as capital, life as product" (Ministry of Culture n.d.), the comprehensive capitalization of culture greatly influenced the cultural preservation of the naval veteran's village.

As an overall plan, this area of "cultural landscape" that was registered by the Kaohsiung City Government fitted the municipal schemes for transportation, urban planning and the tourism industry. Moreover, the inevitable prospects for Zuoying Veterans' Village conformed to the central government's overall development strategy for southern Taiwan and the industrial transformation of the cultural and creative industries.

According to the *Overall Development Outline for Kaohsiung as an Economic and Trade City* published in June 2010, due to the rising unemployment rate, difficulties with tourism infrastructure and, in particular, the decline of traditional manufacturing industries, it was necessary to upgrade the industrial structure (Kaohsiung City Government 2010*a*). As a new blueprint for Taiwan's economy released by Ma Ying-jeou during the presidential election of 2008, the i-Taiwan 12 Projects (also known as "The Twelve Major Taiwan Construction Projects")[12] aimed to redevelop the Kaohsiung Free Trade Zone and Eco-port. The "promotion of the industrial rebirth in the Kaohsiung area" (Ministry of Economic Affairs n.d.) constituted an indispensable part of this NT$38.8 billion investment plan. The Development Scheme of Spatial Structure, announced in 2010, defined Kaohsiung as the core city in southern Taiwan and the international metropolis in terms of a marine city and cultural innovation. Because of the offshoring manufacturing industry, it was suggested that creative industries, cultural tourism and IT industries should be taken into consideration (National Development Council 2010).

Situated in northern Kaohsiung, Zuoying was adjacent to the new downtown area of Aozidi, which was north of the Nanzi Export Processing

Zone and south of the cultural park of Neiweipi (Kaohsiung City Government 2009). In regard to transportation, both the high-speed rail station and the MTR station were located in Zuoying. The main stadium of the 2009 World Games and the scenic spot of Lianchitan were also in the heartland of Zuoying. Thus, Zuoyiing was positioned as a region of "technology, culture and sports". Given the competitive advantage of an industrial park in terms of transportation, sports and tourism, the local government designed four themed regions in Zuoying to promote relevant industries such as "scenery tourism resources, high-speed industry, leisure and sports, multi-cultural life style" (Kaohsiung City Government n.d.). The block of naval veterans' villages was designated as an assemblage of scenic tourism and multicultural lifestyle. On the one hand, the local government intended to improve the overall environment to coordinate with the surrounding transportation, landscape and land development. On the other, the multicultural lifestyle foregrounded its potential future as a cultural park with a military theme, which was led by the Bureau of Cultural Affairs as part of urban planning in Kaohsiung City (Kaohsiung City Government 2009).

Meanwhile, the cultural preservation of the naval veterans' village was under the guidance of a series of governance policies released by the Council for Cultural Affairs in Taiwan, such as the "Life Aesthetics Movement Schemes" (2012), "the 2nd New Homeland Community Construction Movement" (2013), "the 2nd Local Cultural Museum Schemes" (2013), "Schemes on the Inheritance and Promotion of Traditional Art" (2013), and "Schemes on the Cultural Park of Henan Opera in Taiwan" (2012) (Kaohsiung City Government 2010).

The promotional material from The Community Development Association of Mingde and Jianye New Village may have addressed the core of the problem:

> Kaohsiung used to be an important city in terms of heavy industry, petrochemical industry, electronics industry. However, given that mainland China had become the workshop of the world in the past 20 years through social reform and open policy, the advantage of the manufacturing industry in Taiwan disappeared. The emptiness of industrial structures was the most serious problem in Kaohsiung City. For the future, determining how Kaohsiung could relocate its urban development and stop the tendency toward decline became the important mission for the municipal government and the central government. With the increasing number of

mainlander tourists and commercial dealings, cultural tourism should be considered as a lasting opportunity. According to a survey of mainlander tourists, the favorite place in Taiwan was the 'military academy of land forces'. Because the military academy of land forces, air forces and naval forces were all situated in Kaohsiung City, the relevant museums of military history were also located inside the academies. As the only Taiwanese city with coverage of three military services, it was a great asset for developing cultural tourism.[13]

The Disappearing Landscape That Should Not Be Forgotten: Zhang and Her Graffiti Wall in Chongshi New Village

When I visited Chongshi New Village in 2013, I found that the buildings of this veterans' village were rapidly disappearing. Walls and shacks had collapsed in a heap of ruins and an excavator was devastating the village.

Chongshi New Village was situated adjacent to the naval camp. It was north of Jieshou Road and east of Zhongzheng Road, with the old city wall in the south. The reconstruction work in Chongshi New Village dates from a notice from the War Ministry affiliated with the Department of National Defense on 25 November 2003. With the legal basis of the *Detailed Rules and Regulations on Reconstruction Works of Ramshackle Veterans' Villages*, the military authority initially hosted an explanatory session for ten veterans' villages in Kaohsiung City. Then, all households living in veterans' villages were required to complete consent forms for the reconstruction work within three months of the notice. After authentication by a court of law, application forms, certificates of recognition, copies of residential certificates, and copies of social class certificate were scheduled to be submitted to the administrative military services.[14] Thus, the first phase of the legal explanation session was arranged on 4 December 2003, which was the beginning of the reconstruction work in Chongshi New Village.[15]

To implement the reconstruction policy, detailed regulations were designed for the disbursement of pecuniary compensation. For the households that preferred to exchange private housing for "a type of collective mansion built by the military authority" (*guozhai*), the administrative agency would allocate houses with different covered areas to the veteran soldiers according to military rank. For instance, generals received 112 square meters, colonels received 99 square meters, lieutenants and sergeants received 92.4 square meters, illegal housing estates on public property received 85.8 square meters, and orphans and widows received 39.6 square meters.[16] Furthermore, if the original residents preferred to receive monetary compensation, allowances in terms of purchase, moving expenses, rental fees, and mortgages could be offered by the military administration. Even if the residents applied to purchase other private housing in the real estate market, they would be compensated. In general, the regulations and the consecutive terms and conditions on reconstruction all pointed to the acceleration of the demolition of veterans' villages; that is, the progressive transformation towards well-regulated collective mansions aimed to release the land for the next round of urban regeneration.

However, when the official policy was enacted, inevitably, there were difficulties with the actual conditions in the veterans' villages. First, according to the prospectus for reconstruction that had been distributed to the households in each veteran's village,

> …once there were three-fourths of residents who agreed with reconstruction and had been verified by the law court or notary, this veterans' village was required to attend to the procedure of reconstruction on the basis of the reconstruction plan and relevant regulation. For those who disagreed with reconstruction, the Department of National Defense was obliged to withdraw the residential certificate as well as the corresponding rights, take back the residential houses and transfer to the local court for compulsory execution. Nevertheless, if the number of residents who agreed with reconstruction did not reach three-fourths, this veterans' village was unable to move ahead with the procedure of reconstruction. (Department of National Defense 1999, p. 8)

Indeed, in situations where people disagreed with reconstruction but the total number of residents in the village who agreed with reconstruction exceeded three quarters, these people felt that they were deprived of their right to habitation by this compulsory policy. Second, for veterans' villages that would not experience reconstruction after the ballot, land must be included in the governmental plan for urban redevelopment.[17] Given that the ownership of land and buildings belonged to the state, however, how long could the village remain the same? Would the residents eventually be banished from state-owned assets? How might the developing scheme of urban renovation influence private inhabitation? The vista of the future remained uncertain.

Because the number of original residents who agreed with the reconstruction work was greater than three quarters, Chongshi New Village underwent systematic demolition and relocation. Zhang Wanming was one of the few residents to resist the planned reconstruction. Her isolated two-story house, with a wall covered in graffiti,[18] thus became surrounded by a heap of rubble. She invested in an electronic surveillance system and an anti-theft security mesh, and kept dogs that would bark at strangers. She said, in her desperation, "I fed six dogs and installed the electronic security guard. I heard from somebody that the trees had been stolen, but the Chief of Village just ignored it. This community was getting out of control."

Zhang was born on Penghu Island. As a native Taiwanese who married a man of Fujian descent in 1986, she had lived in Chongshi New Village for more than twenty years. Her father-in-law was a junior officer who came to Taiwan after the retrocession of the Japanese in 1946. Later, her mother-in-law and aunts arrived and lived in a small house inherited from the Japanese. According to Zhang's account, they believed that they would return to the mainland soon, and they never expected to remain in Taiwan for such a long time. During the long stay in Taiwan, Zhang and her husband had renovated the shabby primary room four times since 1965, adding a kitchen, a dining hall and a toilet. In her words, "A room in the east, a room in the west, a room on the left, a room on the right. Sometimes an umbrella was needed for walking from the bedroom to the kitchen." After giving birth to two children, Zhang applied for permission from the military authority and rebuilt a few rooms in 1989, which cost approximately NT$5 million. At the same time the covered area had increased from 26.4 to 165 square metres, of which the self-built space occupied approximately 66 square metres.

Several households, including that of Zhang in Chongshi New Village, submitted an appeal with the Taiwan High Court Kaohsiung Branch Court to protest against the Department of National Defense. Their main argument was that their houses should be treated as private property — thus challenging the legitimacy of the reconstruction policy. In fact, prior to 1979 the occupants of the military dormitories could not make any changes, due to the intense political atmosphere of "striking back to the mainland". However, before the death of Chiang Ching-kuo in 1988, the concepts of "anti-communism and resume the state" became distant and elusive and the households in veterans' villages received permission to rebuild their houses. As *The Guidance Notes on the Allocation of Military Dormitories* and *Main Points on the Reconstruction Work in Ramshackle Veterans' Village* issued by the War Ministry of the Department of National Defense in 1988 noted, after the on-site reconstruction, the properties became privately owned.[19] Consequently, the householders reaffirmed their right to occupy and use the land, and the ultra vires of the Department of National Defense was challenged by tireless and assiduous residents such as Zhang. This strong woman dug deeper into the ultimate goal of the so-called "reconstruction policy", from which the major investors would benefit due to the progressive privatization of state-owned property. However, the two-story building in Chongshi New Village had been part of her memories of the past few decades. Her resistance represented a struggle for an intimate dwelling rather than a desert of concrete.

Unfortunately, similar to the fate of Chongshi, the last several veterans' villages in Zuoying were eventually demolished in 2013. The fractured memories of these disappearing villages have become similar to broken tiles and ruined walls — difficult to scrape together.

FIGURE 13.1 Eastern Zizhu New Village in September 2013.

Conclusion: An "Invisible" Taiwan in the Name of "Culture"

When investigating the cultural politics of heritage-making between preservation and demolition in the naval veteran's village of Zuoying as a carrier of the manifestations of memory, the ambiguous signification of "culture"[20] should be taken into account.

If we consider the preservation of cultural heritage in naval veterans' villages as a discursive field, it is clear that Taiwanese history has been represented as a continually twisting path in contemporary culture, the so-called "post-historical". Along with the decline of leader worship and the bygone slogan of "strike back to the mainland", especially after the death of Chiang Ching-kuo in 1988, most houses were approved for rebuilding. Thus, state-owned land became privately owned. The process of taking root in Taiwanese veterans' villages initiated a wide discussion on "village culture", with each side keeping to its own argument. First, the administrative agencies transformed from the Department of National Defense into multiple departments responsible for culture. Second, the power structure circulating among bureaucratic agencies, academics and folk society pointed to the reinvention of a sense of "place", which was conceived as an indispensable part of the socially constructed "local" and was tightly linked to urban planning for the sake of regional redevelopment and industrial transformation towards cultural and creative industries. Finally, as a sole activist, Zhang's resistance to the reconstruction policy dominated by the Department of National Defense conveyed a sense of emotional attachment and deep-rooted feeling to her homeland. Could this be regarded as a type of alternative memory of Taiwanese veterans' villages?

As a cultural landscape registered by the Taiwan Cultural Heritage Preservation Act, Mingde and Jianye New Villages in Zuoying were planning to welcome tourists, especially from mainland China. When I visited the Kaohsiung Museum of Military Dependents Village in January 2013 for the first time, Ms Lin Fangqi, the person in charge, shared a story with me. At this popular destination in Kaohsiung City for tour groups from the mainland, one such visitor discovered a family photo among the items on display — it depicted him and his sister, then as a little boy and girl. When his uncle came to Taiwan during the migration of 1949, this family photo was kept until it was given to the Kaohsiung

Museum of Military Dependents Village. Cross-strait stories remain one of the inevitable branches of Taiwanese post-historical trajectories. As an outsider, my journey of "looking" from the other side of the Taiwanese Strait indicated that an "invisible" Taiwanese society began to emerge in the name of "culture"; this finding requires further exploration.

Notes

1. In a biography of Chiang Kai-shek, Dong Xianguang (1980) mentioned that "he had decided to choose Taiwan to escape from the threat of the Chinese Communist Party. Once the mainland of China had an emergency, Taiwan Province could serve as the last base for holding the governmental ground and for the subsequent rebound" (p. 510).
2. *Collections of Jiang Jingguo*, vol. 15, p. 439.
3. The resources of "new cultural geography" theory were greatly influenced by the rising discipline of "cultural studies" that emerged in the United Kingdom in the 1960s. The textualizing of society not only triggered interdisciplinary studies between the humanities and the social sciences but, more importantly, this research paradigm also suggested that cultural geographers investigate how social groups of different ethnicities, genders and classes gave meaning to the urban-scape by employing different representational practices.
4. In article 3 of the *Taiwan Cultural Heritage Preservation Act*, a "cultural landscape" was defined as a "space and its related environment associated with mythology, legend, deed, historical event, community life or ritual". Quoted from <http://www.moc.gov.tw/law.do?method=find&id=30>_(accessed 25 March 2014).
5. *A Brief Introduction on Cultural Development Association of Veterans' Village in Kaohsiung City*.
6. *Regulations on "the Community Development Association of Mingde and Jianye New Village"*.
7. *The Proposal on the Homecoming Activity for Villagers in Zuoying*.
8. In-depth interview with a staff member of Kaohsiung Museum of Military Dependents Village, 24 August 2013.
9. As a professor in National Kaohsiung University, Shur-Tzy Hou believed that the involvement of the student movement was not enough because "students dare not to protest the government like the Wenlin Yuan dispute in Taipei, Kaohsiung was more conservative".
10. The definition of "village culture" still reflected a provisional nature and the ethnic divide. For example, an anonymous resident informed me that quite a few Taiwanese maintained that the residents living in Veterans' Villages were *Waishengren* (mainlanders in Taiwan) with vested interests.

11. Representatives from all sides maintained that steps to preserve "village culture" should be implemented as quickly as possible. However, each group had a different focus: Residents were concerned with asserting their rights and in preserving their assets for the long-term. The concerns of scholars lay with further development and industrial transformation, such as whether veterans' villages could be developed into ecological museums through the symbiosis of the original residents and tourists. The elected representatives advocated that both the blue political coalition and the green political coalition should seek a balance between the rights of residents and the cultural industry. And the representatives of agencies such as the Department of National Defense, the Bureau of Cultural Affairs, and the Urban Development Bureau promised to promote cultural preservation in the veterans' villages (Kaohsiung City Council 2013).

12. The "i-Taiwan 12 Projects" plan was put forward by Ma Ying-jeou during the 2008 presidential election. The projects made efforts to promote twelve public constructions to relieve the structural pressure that had resulted from the transformation of the dominant manufacturing industry. Covering four areas — transportation, industrial development, urban and rural development, and environmental protection — the ultimate goal of the "i-Taiwan 12 Projects" was to rebuild Taiwan's competitiveness and reinforce the economy through the investment of an estimated NT$3.99 trillion. The Executive Yuan of the ROC approved the projects on 2 December 2009 (National Development Council 2009.

13. *My Home is Park, Park is My Home* (publicity material of "the folk association for promoting village culture in Mingde and Jianye new village", 2013).

14. *Notice on the 1st Phase of Explanation Session on the Reconstruction Work in Ten Veterans' Villages of Kaohsiung City.* 25 November 2003.

15. *The Schedule for the 1st Phase of Legal Explanation Session on the Reconstruction Work in Zizhi new Village of Kaohsiung City.*

16. *The Manual for the 1st Phase of Explanation Session on the Reconstruction Work in Zizhi new Village of Kaohsiung City.* 4 and 5 December 2003.

17. Self-governing association of Ziqiang new village, *Notice on the Article 11 and Article 12 of the Regulations on the Reconstruction Work in Ramshackle Veterans' Village.* July 2009.

18. The graffiti on the wall included a series of artworks created by Zhang Wanming's daughter, Zhuo Yun. The environment, architecture, figures, and antiquity were sublimated into art to retrieve the last memories of the veterans' village. All of the artistic creations were collected in her master's thesis.

19. See Department of National Defence, May 1988, p. 10 and January 1988*b*, pp. 2–3.

20. "Culture" has always played an important role in the field of human

geography. In the 1920s a representative of the Berkeley school, Carl O. Sauer, referred to "cultural determinism" by criticizing the idea of environmental determinism and emphasizing the influence of culture in a natural landscape. Later geographers distinguished nature from culture, regarding culture as a spontaneous entity with its own rules and disciplines. Since the 1960s there has been increasing criticism of the conceptual framework of "culture as an entity". For instance, in seeking to examine changing social relations, James Duncan saw "culture" as a field filled with conflicts. The "cultural turn" in human geography was a deviation from the traditional Berkley school of the 1980s. The major difference hinged on the understanding of "culture". In comparison with the emphasis on the ontological status of culture based on the influences of history and the environment and the aim of studying reified and materialized cultural artefacts, the "new cultural geography" was intended to understand "culture" as the representational system of all sorts of social relationships, emphasizing the study of the operational mechanisms of culture in order to understand the systems of social production and reproduction (Mitchell 1995) and to determine the reasons, processes and power relations (Duncan and Duncan 1996).

References

Chen, Chaoxing, et al. *Juan Cun De Qian Shi Jin Sheng: Fen Xi Yu Wen Hua Bao Cun Zheng Ce* [The past and present of Taiwanese veterans' village: Analysis of the policy of cultural heritage preservation]. Taizhong: Xing Zheng Yuan Wen Hua Jian She Wei Yuan Hui Wen Hua Zi Chan Zong Guan Li Chu Chou Bei Chu, 2009.

Chen, Qinan. "She Qu Ying Zao Yu Wen Hua Jian She" [Community construction and cultural development]. *Li Lun Yu Zheng Ce* [Journal of theory and policy] 113 (1996).

Denevan, William M., and Mathewson Kent. *Carl Sauer on Culture and Landscape: Readings and Commentaries*. Baton Rouge: Louisiana State University Press, 2009.

Department of National Defense. *Some Notes on the Reconstruction Work in the Ramshackle Veterans' Village*. War Ministry, Department of National Defense, 31 January 1988a.

———. *Main Points on the Reconstruction Work in Ramshackle Veterans' Village*. January 1988b.

———. *Guidance Notes on the Allocation of Military Dormitories*. May 1988.

———. *Laws and Regulations on the Reconstruction Work in Ramshackle Veterans' Village*. Department of National Defense, August 1999.

———. "Regulations on Urban Renewal". In *The Collection of Laws and Regulations on the Reconstruction Work in the Ramshackle Veterans' Village.* Department of National Defense, September 2000.

———. *Regulations on the Reconstruction Work in Ramshackle Veterans' Village,* amended version. Department of National Defense, 13 December 2011. Cited in <http://www.6law.idv.tw/6law/law/国军老旧眷村改建条例.htm#a4> (accessed 25 March 2014).

Dong, Xianguang. *Jiang Zong Tong Zhuan* [The biography of Chiang Kai-shek]. Taipei: Zhong Guo Wen Hua Xue Yuan, 1980.

Duncan, James, and Nancy Duncan. "Reconceptualizing the Idea of Culture in Geography: A Reply to Don Mitchell". *Transactions of the Institute of British Geographers,* n.s., 21, no. 3 (1996): 576–79.

Guo, Guanlin. *Cong Zhu Li Ba Dao Gao Lou Da Sha De Gu Shi: Guo Jun Juan Cun Fa Zhan Shi* [From bamboo fence to the large mansions]. Taipei: Guo Fang Bu Shi Zheng Bian Yi Shi, 2005.

Huang, Xiuli. "Tai Wan Juan Cun Wen Hua Bao Cun Yu Zai Li Yong Fang Shi Fa Zhan Zhi Li Cheng" [The development of cultural preservation and revitalization in Taiwanese veterans' villages]. Master's dissertation, National Kaohsiung University, 2010.

Kaohsiung City Council. "Meeting Minutes on the Public Hearing Called 'How Could a Live Veteran's Village Become Possible? The Prospect of Cultural Preservation Cluster in Mingde New Village of Kaohsiung City' ". 9 December 2013 <http://www.kcc.gov.tw/Upload/NewsActivity/74afa8ce-9bfb-64b9-1ed9-598bb4153960_公听会纪录.pdf?KeyID3=162> (accessed 2 April 2014).

Kaohsiung City Government. "The 3rd Detailed Outline on Changing the Urban Planning of Kaohsiung City (Zuoying District) 變更高雄市都市計畫（左營地區）細部計畫（第三次通盤檢討）案計畫書". December 2009. <http://plan.kcg.gov.tw/KaoPlan_book/AB549/AB549.htm#_Toc265141598> (accessed 5 April 2014).

———. *Overall Development Outline for Kaohsiung City as an Economic and Trade City.* 23 June 2010*a*. Urban Development Bureau, Kaohsiung City Government <http://urban-web.kcg.gov.tw/ksnew/web_page/KDA040100.jsp?PK01=20100830115830&PK02=1&SK01=1&SearchValue=> (accessed 5 April 2014).

———. *The Prospectus on the Cultural Preservation of Naval Veterans' Villages in Zuoying of Kaohsiung City: A Case on the Cultural & Creative Cluster in Zuoying Veterans' Village.* Kaohsiung: Bureau of Cultural Affairs, Kaohsiung City Government, 2010*b* <http://w4.khcc.gov.tw/mdv/pdf/04-04-04.pdf> (accessed 28 March 2014).

———. *Report on Life History of Women in Veterans' Villages in Kaohsiung City.* Department of Creative Design and Architecture in National University of Kaohsiung. Kaohsiung: Bureau of Cultural Affairs, Kaohsiung City Government, 2010*c*.

———. *Report on the Basic Data of Space and Feasibility of Revitalization in Zuoying Veterans' Village.* Department of Creative Design and Architecture in National University of Kaohsiung. Kahsiung: Bureau of Cultural Affairs, Kaohsiung City Government, 2010*d*.

———. "The Functional Positioning of Zuoying and its Developmental Strategy". n.d. <http://urban-web.kcg.gov.tw/data/bu03/board/20091228134752-1.pdf> (accessed 27 March 2014).

Lin, Tongfa. *1949 Da Che* Tui [A big retreat in 1949]. Beijing: Jiu Zhou, 2011.

Ministry of Culture. "Mid-term Schemes of the Council for Cultural Affairs in Taiwan (2009–2012)". n.d. <http://www.moc.gov.tw/ccaImages/adminstration/0/98-101m-target.doc> (accessed 6 April 2014).

Ministry of Economic Affairs. "Investment Opportunities in the I-Taiwan 12 Projects". n.d. <http://hirecruit.nat.gov.tw/TopMenuEng.do?method=aspects&ssid=05_04> (accessed 14 November 2014).

Mitchell, Don. "There's No Such Thing as Culture: Towards a Reconceptualization of the Idea of Culture in Geography". *Transactions of the Institute of British Geographers*, n.s., 20, no. 1 (1995): 102–16.

National Development Council. "I-Taiwan 12 Projects". December 2009 <http://www.ndc.gov.tw/m1.aspx?sNo=0012702&ex=1&ic=0000015> (accessed 5 April 2014).

———. "The Development Scheme of Spatial Structure". February 2010. <http://www.ndc.gov.tw/m1.aspx?sNo=0011780&ex=1&ic=0000015> (accessed 5 April 2014).

Williams, Raymond. *Culture*. London: Fontana, 1981.

Yen, Liang-yi. "Guo Zu Ren Tong De Shi Kong Xiang Xiang: Tai Wan Li Shi Bao Cun Gai Nian Zhi Xing Cheng Yu Zhuan Hua" [Time-space imagination of national identity: The formation and transformation of the conceptions of historic preservation in Taiwan]. *Gui Hua Xue Bao* [Journal of planning] 33 (2006): 91–106.

Zhuo, Yun. "Chong Shi Xin Cun, Lai Zi Juan Cun De Nu Hai: Zhuo Yun Chuang Zuo Zi Shu" [Remapping Chongshi new village: A girl from a veterans' village and Zhuoyun's autography]. Master's dissertation, National Kaohsiung Normal University, 2011.

14

Tobacco Crop Memories in Taiwan: The Heritage of a Deadly Agriculture

Han-Hsiu Chen and Gareth Hoskins

Agricultural landscapes have long been an important vehicle for post-productivist rural economies seeking to repackage themselves as places for tourism. Preservation activities, heritage operations, and commemorative routines are now intensifying their focus on the agricultural past to emphasize their distinctiveness and to shore up fragile local identities by conserving, celebrating and attending to past methods of cultivation, techniques of animal husbandry and other historic forms of land use. These places of agricultural history are labelled "cultural landscapes" by UNESCO's World Heritage sites programme, and include vineyards in Italy (Puleo 2013), rice terraces in the Philippine Cordilleras (Guimbatan and Baguilat 2006), as well as the pastoral landscapes associated with the English picturesque (Matlass 2005). Seemingly without controversy, the historic cultivation of tobacco is counted equally as agricultural heritage and often interpreted in ways similar to crops that are far more benign. Generic interpretive formulae for agricultural heritage such as "the taming of nature through dedicated hard work", "working in harmony with nature", "technological advancement" and "idiosyncratic local practices and architectures" are all familiar examples.

Tobacco heritage's unproblematized repetition of the "human harmony with nature" theme avoids the overwhelmingly destructive effects of this plant's cultivation. According to the World Health Organisation's figures, a hundred million deaths were caused by tobacco in the twentieth century and, they warn, if current trends continue there will be up to one billion deaths in the twenty-first century. It is not insignificant that eighty per cent of these deaths will occur in the developing world.[1] So what are we to do with the historical spaces of tobacco cultivation and manufacture? What kinds of messages do we want to use these spaces to convey?

Most kinds of agricultural heritage is overt and highly visible precisely because it helps to enhance the value of the farmed commodities associated with it, as traditional, natural, pure and wholesome, for example. Tobacco is unusual in that stories of origins and links to the soil, so familiar in artisan products like wine, pasta, cheese or bread, are silenced by state regulations on advertising. This leaves site-specific tobacco heritage in a unique and intriguing position, affiliated to Jeffersonian ideals of the essential goodness of a cultivated landscape and the yeoman farmer as a means to divert attention away from tobacco's well known deleterious aspects. Serious interpretive engagement with smoking-related deaths, suffering and disease is the most obvious omission from tobacco heritage operations, but other negative aspects of the crop's cultivation linked to, for example, pesticide poisoning, deforestation (Geist 1999), child labour (Thompson 2013), associations with slavery (Kulikoff 1986), and the direct link between tobacco cultivation and colonial power, are often lacking.

This chapter examines whether, and if so how, geographically diverse and temporally shifting public attitudes towards tobacco smoking shape the presentation and display of these agricultural heritage sites. We explore how the contemporary awareness of tobacco's capacity to kill (an almost comprehensive public knowledge of its addictive and harmful effects, a growing knowledge of the industry's reliance on pesticides, and child labour) are reconciled with tobacco heritage's potential to generate revenue through attractive preservation-led economic revitalization. At best, tobacco heritage provides a unique opportunity to reflect on and generate discussion around corporate agriculture, colonial economies, labour exploitation, and the nefarious profit-driven requirement of dead labour (Mitchell 2000). At worse, these sites — presented as natural, normal, traditional and harmonious examples of human–land relations imbued with nostalgic appeals to local culture and tradition — give tacit approval for tobacco's continued human consumption.

We ask how do exhibitions, tours and interpretation strategies deal with this history in a sensitive way? This chapter works through the case studies in Taiwan where contemporary attitudes to tobacco smoking differ and demonstrates how those contemporary attitudes shape the way the local tobacco history is encountered. This provides a foundation for thinking in more detail about how Taiwan's tobacco agriculture was transformed into local and national heritage.

The chapter proceeds through four sections. The first explores the physical and conceptual space of agricultural heritage in general and critiques the invariably positive values of "harmony" that are so often used to code nature–culture relations in this context. It shows how tobacco heritage draws unproblematically on those very same comforting tropes of admirable domestication which so commonly apply to other crops, including wine, fruit and pasture. The second section moves to provide the historical context of tobacco agriculture in Taiwan. The third section focuses on the cases of Taiwan's tobacco heritage to illustrate the ways towns attempt to convert their fading tobacco industry and the buildings associated with the leaf's manufacture into a heritage resource for tourism purposes. It considers the political implications of tobacco's second-life as heritage, drawing on interviews with residents, tobacco farmers, heritage institute staff and council representatives. The final section provides a conclusion that critiques notions of universal heritage value and harmonious relations with the land and calls for a more serious engagement with the negative outcomes of tobacco cultivation as well as collaborative effort amongst international heritage bodies to balance positive representations with informed critique.

Addicted to Harmony

When Kirshemblatt, in her book *Destination Culture: Tourism, Museums and Heritage*, wrote about "the reciprocity of disappearance and exhibition" (1998, p. 56), she captured in a wonderfully distinct and memorable phrase how our presumed loss of something, a place or a way of life, for example, leads to an explicit attempt to capture and put it on display. This is as true in spaces of industrial decline (Stanton 2006) as it is in more contemporary spaces of consumption — as the huge public interest in the anticipated ruin of American suburban shopping malls testifies (Lawless 2014). But it is in the agricultural landscape where this sensibility is at its most acute (Lowenthal and Olwig 2013). It is a message that runs through historian Pierre Nora's seven-volume account of the birth of a modern memory culture in France, *Lieux de Memoire* (1996), and one that Leo Marx pays homage to in his account of the modification of pastoral ideals by technology in the United States (1964).

Indeed, a nostalgic longing for pre-industrial times is said by Crang (1999) to have driven the outdoor conservation movement in Dalarna Sweden with an Open Air Museum, and the United States' nineteenth century romantic pursuit of pristine wilderness as a response to rapid industrialization and urbanization (Cronon 1996). Just as wilderness as a concept helped maintain our quixotic belief in the existence a non-human wild, where nature was externalized and conceived of as something "out there" and "unproduced" (Smith 2008), so agricultural landscapes are selected and picked to be heritage precisely to demonstrate the comforting belief in our ability to domesticate nature's otherness. Indeed, cultivated landscapes are often regarded as being "nature enhanced", enabled to reach their full potential by farming and technology. Our affection for these kinds of "humanized" landscapes carries with it an aggressive impulse that geographer Yi Fu Tuan (1984) identifies so well in places such as the English country garden that imposes a "proud and ostentatious restraint" — an aesthetic of containment, control and subordination.

The official designated category of "cultural landscape" has been part of UNESCO's Wold Heritage protocol since 1992. It contains within its portfolio sites where a natural and cultural "balance" and "harmony" result in impressive visual scenes, scenes that illustrate long-running "traditional" customs and "intimate" often "spiritual" relations that reflect both "creative genius" and "sustain biological diversity".[2] The story embodied in each of these places show off humanity at its apparent best.

The agricultural landscape has always served a dual material and symbolic purpose — to produce material sustenance for consumption and to locate cultural identities, collective values and beliefs. Famously, geographer Stephen Daniels referred to this as the "duplicity of landscape" (1989). More recently, scholars have explored these dual functions in far more depth with specific reference to official heritage practice and management. Crang and Tolia-Kelly's (2010) examination of the affective politics of race in the English Lake District National Park is an astute example of the normative power of apparently blind cultural frameworks that universalize whiteness as a default category. And Morris's (2011) organizational history of the environment as a realm of concern for UNESCO clearly outlines our successive efforts to define nature and fix it in place, which "arise[s] for a variety of reasons — from conservation and protection, to development and exploitation, to enjoyment and appreciation" (p. 124). The relationship between nature and culture, human and the environment is not a simple story, especially when it gets incorporated into its production as heritage.

Tobacco, despite its huge influence in global history, is omitted from UNESCO's flagship "Globally Important Agricultural Heritage Systems" programme (Koohafkan and Altieri 2001), but historic locations of tobacco cultivation and manufacture are increasingly recognized as formal parts of the agricultural heritage landscape throughout the world, from the southern United States such as North Carolina, Virginia, Maryland and Florida, through to Cuba, Sweden, the Netherlands, China, Japan and Taiwan. In each instance the negative aspects are more often than not silenced by more positive frameworks, and the passage of time is used to mute the controversy. The Tobacco Heritage Trail of South West Virginia, for example, welcomes visitors to its website with the description, "reflect the area's long agrarian history and the region's principal industry for centuries".[3] The experience on offer here is a generic sense of the quaint long-inhabited rural, and much less about the conditions of slavery that produced it and the deaths its consumption promoted.

Comparing with other agricultural heritage, the most obvious difference between celebrating the history of tobacco and other crops (for example, vineyards or fruits) is that people are not able to try smoking or purchase cigarettes at tobacco heritage sites, but visitors are usually able to taste different wines at vineyards, or even purchase different kinds of final products or grapes there. On the contrary, visitors never have the opportunity to taste local cultivated tobacco; even smoking is not allowed at tobacco heritage sites, like in the museum. This all points to the controversy of celebrating such a deadly crop in society. Tobacco is so controversial because its chemical content makes it deadly to humans, a fact that has significantly stigmatized tobacco heritage. In Kavala, one of the busiest harbours in the north of Greece, and involved in the tobacco trade since the mid-nineteenth century, "smoking as a politically incorrect activity" (Deffner et al. 2009) is conceived of as one of the threats the tobacco museum meets when it attempts to extend its market (Rentetzi 2009). And a representative of the Ohio Tobacco Museum wrote a newspaper article to clarify that their aim in continuing to run the museum is to preserve the cultural and social stories of the local tobacco industry, not to promote tobacco consumption (*New Democrat*, 15 April 2013). These examples all show that the negative image of tobacco significantly affects the ways people conserve tobacco-related history and that preservation of tobacco heritage is challenging work.

Tobacco Industry in Taiwan

Tobacco cultivation has a long history in Taiwan. Indigenous people in Taiwan had established customs of smoking and chewing tobacco and growing indigenous tobacco leaves. Tobacco also has a significant cultural meaning in indigenous society. Tobacco was introduced to the Han Chinese in Taiwan in the fifteenth century. Initially, tobacco cultivation was conducted on small farms scattered widely across Taiwan. The period in which tobacco cultivation developed rapidly and came to be called a "tobacco industry" was during the Japanese colonial period, from 1895 to 1945. The Office of the Governor-General recognized tobacco to be a good source of revenue for the treasury, so from 1905 the tobacco crop became a monopoly of the Japanese colonial government.

A variety of species had initially been grown in Taiwan; however, the Brightleaf variety was the most successful, so the other species were abandoned. Brightleaf tobacco is a type of *Nicotiana tabacum*. It is also known as "Virginia tobacco". In Taiwan, people call it yellow-type or American-type tobacco. It was first cultivated in eastern Taiwan by Japanese colonists in the Japanese immigrant villages. The extension of cultivation of Brightleaf tobacco shaped the landscape in a particular way; many tall tobacco buildings, used for curing tobacco leaves, were built in the fields. Since Brightleaf tobacco cultivation was introduced by the Japanese, the tobacco buildings were built in a Japanese style. Most tobacco buildings in Taiwan are described as being in Osaka-style, because the design is reminiscent of Osaka Castle in Japan. The buildings feature a small tower at the top that serves as a ventilator. This special style of architecture is quite different from the tobacco barns of other tobacco-cultivating countries, and they were the most important equipment in tobacco production. They were also the symbols of both the tobacco landscape and the Japanese village during the Japanese period.

After the Second World War the policy of a government monopoly over tobacco cultivation was continued under the Kuomintang (KMT), which meant that the tobacco leaves were consistently purchased for a guaranteed price by the monopoly bureau. The KMT authorities tried to extend this industry in an attempt to increase government revenues, just as the Japanese had done over the preceding fifty years. Moreover, in an attempt to increase domestic demand for cigarettes, Vice President Cheng Chen, in a public speech in 1963, said that "Non-smokers are good people but smokers are good citizens" — neglecting to mention tobacco's deadly nature. The tobacco industry began to decline in the 1980s because of the trade surplus with the United States and the United States' proposition to open the tobacco and liquor market to them in an attempt to decrease their trade deficit (Lee 2006). Additionally, because of its isolated diplomatic relations and a tendency for trade liberalization, the Taiwanese government actively sought to join the World Trade Organisation, becoming a member in 2002. In the same year, the monopoly bureau was reformed as a private company called the Taiwan Tobacco and Liquor Cooperation. The market became severely contested for two reasons. Firstly, the market had been opened up to international competitors. And secondly, health awareness had increased, leading to a fall in domestic demand and a shrinking of Taiwan's tobacco industry. Maintaining the market for domestic cigarettes became a huge challenge.

As a valuable cash crop, tobacco generated large revenues for the state, manufacturers and growers. But as a dangerous crop it was criticized by the entire world. The current situation sees the tobacco landscape as having a new role as heritage, and this dramatic story continues. Landscape production never ends. Landscape is not a final result; it is a continuing process (Daniels 1989; Schein 1997). The creation of Taiwan's tobacco landscape as heritage is a complex process that has been influenced by various ways of understanding tobacco. It is currently being developed for different purposes.

Tobacco Heritage in Taiwan

The Case of Fonglin, Eastern Taiwan

Fonglin Township is located in the middle of Hualien County, eastern Taiwan, and was among the first three Japanese immigrant villages in the country. Tobacco was introduced to the immigrant villages as a new cash crop for the Japanese colonists because the environment was unsuitable to make a living from other crops. Tobacco was unexpectedly successful and brought the colonists a new life; tobacco was a kind of saviour for the Japanese. After the Japanese left, the people of Fonglin took over the Japanese properties and continued the tobacco cultivation. Tobacco was a significant local cash crop until it faced a steady decline from the 1980s. Tobacco cultivation in eastern Taiwan saw a reduction from more than a thousand hectares in 1968 to a hundred and fifty hectares in 1995. The changing circumstances saw tobacco farmers facing the challenge of having to relinquish the cultivation that had been the main source of income for their families for more than forty years. Fonglin's tobacco industry finally ended in 2010. The stories, however, never end; they are just told in a different way. The landscape has become a heritage site, and tobacco legacies have been recognized from different perspectives: The Hakka Cultural Museum now hosts a small exhibition about the history of local tobacco cultivation. Four abandoned tobacco buildings have been conserved through public funding to commemorate the history. And tobacco production in Fonglin is commemorated for its connection to Japanese colonial history, conceived of as a unique selling point for Fonglin's past.

The conservation of old tobacco buildings is a significant way to protect the legacy of Fonglin's tobacco agriculture. Visitors walking around Fonglin can find many tobacco buildings dotting the landscape. Many of them are abandoned or have been destroyed. One has been conserved by the owner and operates as a bed and breakfast. Another has been preserved as a private residence. The other four have been conserved by the use of public funds from the Construction and Planning Agency of the Ministry of the Interior (CPAMI) and the Council for Hakka Affairs in Taiwan (HAC).

Following the completion of the conservation work sponsored by CPAMI and HAC, one of the four conserved tobacco buildings became famous due to its Western appearance — the building has a Tudor-style architecture and features an outdoor seat in the style of the Spanish architect Gaudi (Figure 14.1). This unusual approach to reconstruction led to some criticism. Responding to such criticism, a Fonglin Township official who was part of the examining committee for the reconstruction project asked why tobacco buildings must look like a "traditional tobacco building?"[4]

The conservation led to a great deal of debate, since Western-style architecture was alien to the local cultural context. For example, one township official said,

FIGURE 14.1   Tudor-style conserved tobacco building. Photo provided by a local resident in Fonglin.

Generally speaking, the tobacco building conservation work should be done according to its original style. As you can see, the Western style one, the second building in the first village, at that corner, I have no idea how they do such a thing.... the Western style is really weird, it is inharmonious.[5]

A local tobacco farmer echoed this opinion:

Many people said I should demolish the small ventilator tower at the top of the tobacco building. I told them that if I demolish that part, I will not preserve my tobacco building anymore. Keeping the original form of the tobacco building so that subsequent generations will know what the tobacco buildings looked like in the past. The Western-style conserved one, it is not a tobacco building. Its shape is not the correct original form.[6]

The conservation work on the Tudor-style tobacco building is an attempt to present the image of a beautiful Western estate. This kind of picturesque depiction of agriculture as traditional and beautiful is consistent with international heritage practice: agriculture-related heritage sites that are recognized as official heritage highlight the harmonious relationship between nature and culture. In this context, we argue that this kind of heritage practice too often underlines the positive narratives of agricultural landscape as heritage. While we believe that it is important to commemorate great beauty or the coexistence between culture and nature in the world, we do not see tobacco to be a symbol of this harmony, entwined as it is with stories of struggle and controversy between people, tobacco and the environment. Tobacco is harmful to human health; its cultivation causes deforestation; the pesticides used in tobacco cultivation are also harmful to the tobacco labourers, and the residues of such leach into the soil, further damaging the environment. These uneasy narratives are often erased in the celebration of harmonious scenery, just as the presentation of the beautiful Western-style farmland and Tudor-style conserved tobacco building in Fonglin masks the destructive social effects of tobacco agriculture. This argument echoes the Marxist stance of geographer Don Mitchell (2000) and Ashworth and Tunbridge's argument on dissonant heritage (2007), that the representation of agricultural history and the stories underlying the harmonious scene are not consistent.

Nowadays, this Western picturesque conserved tobacco building is still popular with tourists, and its image is often used to promote local tourism. For example, it has been featured on the cover of Fonglin's tourist brochure (Figure 14.2).

Fonglin's Unique Selling Point in the Tobacco Memories

The definition of heritage is transformed from valuable personal belongings inherited from the previous generation (Hardy 1988; Lowenthal 1996; Tunbridge et al., 1996), to an idea of public treasure. Recently, geographers have provided a more abstract description of heritage, saying that "it is a view from the present, either backward to a past or forward to a future" (Graham et al., 2000, p. 2), while archaeologists see it as a "way of interacting with the world" (Sørensen et al., 2009, p. 12). These statements imply that heritage is not always fixed or simple, since it is constantly changing over time. Such an idea could well be seen in Fonglin's tobacco heritage. Fonglin's interpretation of the history of the local tobacco industry continuously changes so as to help local economic and historical

FIGURE 14.2 Fonglin's tourist brochure.

regeneration, which goes beyond the controversies of celebrating a dangerous crop and colonial history.

What makes Fonglin's historical representation of tobacco more complicated is its colonial history and it marginalization within contemporary commemoration of tobacco. Fonglin is not the only place to commemorate its tobacco history; local tobacco heritage is also recognized in Meinong District in southern Taiwan. Meinong District is the largest and most well-known tobacco settlement in Taiwan; when people think of a tobacco settlement in Taiwan, Meinong District is the first place that comes to mind. In this context, Fonglin's tobacco heritage is marginalized in comparison to the commemorative efforts in Meinong in southern Taiwan. For this reason Fonglin Township adopted a strategy to distinguish itself from Meinong by highlighting its historical connection to the Japanese colonial period. According to the township mayor,

> Fonglin is not famous, but we cultivate tobacco too.... Therefore, if our marketing was strong enough, people would understand that our tobacco culture equals that of Meinong. We will work hard so that, in the future, if people talk about tobacco buildings, both Fonglin and Meinong will come to their mind. Based on our promotion over the past eight years, people are gradually coming to know Fonglin and coming to visit our tobacco buildings and Hakka Cultural Museum.... We have also regenerated the Japanese culture, and the Japanese shrine will attract some people. The Japanese would come to Fonglin rather than Meinong, because they lived here in the past, so they would come to see where their ancestors lived. Our promotion is different from theirs [Meinong]. They draw on tobacco buildings, while our focus is the inheritance of immigrant culture to the tobacco history, and this distinguishes us from each other.[7]

In this context, the tobacco-related historical regeneration plan in Fonglin focuses on preserving the Japanese colonial legacy by such steps as reconstructing a Japanese shrine and preserving a Japanese police office in order to preserve aspects of the Japanese immigrant village that was located in Fonglin a hundred year ago. This demonstrates how people in Fonglin have reinterpreted their local history in order to distinguish its tobacco heritage from those of other localities in Taiwan, in order to overcome the township's marginalization in the broader context of Taiwan's tobacco heritage. However, this unique selling point of Fonglin's tobacco heritage tourism masks the controversy of celebrating colonization in a post-colonial society.

The Case of Liudui Hakka Cultural Park, South Taiwan

Brightleaf tobacco was first cultivated in the south of Taiwan in 1935 when the Japanese authorities set up three immigrant villages, all three of which were involved in tobacco cultivation. After the Second World War it was found that the environmental conditions in southern Taiwan were suitable for tobacco growing; therefore, in order to have high quality tobacco leaves, the monopoly bureau extended the cultivation area in the south. Soon, the northern Pingtung Plain was the biggest area of tobacco cultivation in Taiwan. During that period, twenty-one townships in the south of Taiwan were engaged in tobacco cultivation, including Meinong, Gaoshi, Gangshan, Qishan, Wandan and Jiuru. Following the decline of the industry, tobacco cultivation gradually disappeared from the northwest and east of Taiwan, but the tobacco farmers in the south fought to continue cultivation, and some tobacco farms can still be found in southern Taiwan. However, the Taiwan Tobacco & Liquor Corporation said recently that 2017 would be the final year that tobacco leaves could be purchased from farmers, which means that tobacco agriculture will end soon.

Liudui Hakka Cultural Park, opened in 2011, is a place to commemorate, represent and preserve Hakka folk culture. The park features several different sections that display various stories about Hakka culture and social life. The history of the tobacco industry is permanently displayed there because it was a significant industry in the area of Kaohsiung and Pingtun. The exhibition portrays the labour involved in growing and curing the crop, and displays objects such as a model of a grocery store, a shelf of cigarettes, tools and licences.

The tobacco display area in the park combines a tobacco building (Figure 14.3) donated by a local tobacco farmer, which was taken down and relocated to the park, and open-air farmland that is "coupled harmoniously with garden landscaping and surrounding scenery. The tobacco house (building) fully presents a true image of Hakka industry" (Liudui Hakka Cultural Park 2011). The farmland area was established to assist in integrating Hakka culture and industry, to preserve and develop traditional farming technology and produce, and to aid in the transformation of the traditional industries in Liudui (Liudui Hakka Cultural Park 2011). In this context, the designers have attempted to represent a "harmonious" and "integrated scene" of the tobacco industry rather than just focus on a building or an object, and this "integrated scene" portrays the relationship

FIGURE 14.3 The tobacco building display hall and open-air farmland on the right-hand side. Photo taken by the author in 2011.

between tobacco, the building and the landscape as harmonious, and it is regarded as a "true image" of the local tobacco industry. This kind of picturesque depiction of agriculture as traditional and beautiful is consistent with international heritage practice, as mentioned above. However, it could be disputed whether this is a complete and true image of the local landscape. Does it represent the full story of the tobacco landscape?

According to the assistant researcher of the cultural park, Mr Liu, who was also the designer of the tobacco and farmland display area, the reason for setting it up was because tobacco cultivation was a very important industry in the Liudui area, and this part of the landscape is designed and operated based on the concept of an open-air museum. Thus, it couples a tobacco building and farmland area to represent an agricultural village. Tobacco and rice are grown here, and the cultural park also arranges some immersion programmes for visitors to experience the farming life.[8]

At the end of 2016, Liudui Hakka Cultural Park held a series of activities to commemorate tobacco agriculture in order to mark the end of local tobacco cultivation in 2017. In November 2016 a group of local elementary school students were invited to the park to sow tobacco seeds under the supervision of an experienced tobacco farmer. When the tobacco plants were about to flower, the tobacco farmer was invited to return to the park to demonstrate "topping" and "suckering"[9] on 5 January 2017. Then, on 16 February 2017, the farmland was opened to the public to experience harvesting tobacco leaves. Several experienced tobacco farmers were on site to demonstrate how to harvest, pack and prepare the leaves to be cured. The final activity was planned for 26 February. People are welcome to visit the tobacco farmer to learn about the curing process, as well as the packing and purchasing process when the curing is completed. During these activities, not only are the details of tobacco cultivation demonstrated, but the memories of the tobacco farmer are also shared. For example, visitors can learn just how labour intensive tobacco cultivation is. Those who grew up in families involved in the tobacco industry often become directly engaged in this hard work, whether male or female, adult or child. As a tobacco farmer Mrs Lin recounted,

> I don't know why you were so stupid (laughing). I disagreed with him [Mr Lin] when he said he wanted to build a tobacco building. I told him that our three generations would suffer from the very hard work involved in tobacco cultivation. If we did tobacco work, our sons needed to work at that, too, and if my son got married, his wife needed to work at it as well, and the grandson would cry all day, because no one had time to take care of him.[10]

The farmers further noted how the curing process also entailed very hard work:

> The curing work was so hard. You could not sleep the whole night. The curing process took a week at least. The leaves were cured in the tobacco building, and someone had to be there to monitor the process day and night. If you fell asleep when monitoring the curing temperature during the night, the fire was extinguished and became ashes, the temperature reduced and cold air flowed into the curing space, so that the bottom of the leaves became black. You could not sleep, but you still needed to work in the daytime. It was so tiring.[11]

As we have argued in this chapter, the historical celebration of agriculture has overwhelmingly been focused on the great meaningfulness of the heritage sites, of how they have contributed to improving human life or have created harmony and great beauty, not on how hard the workers have had to labour in order to shape the landscape. The activities that Liudui Hakka Cultural Park have recently implemented offer a valuable complement that bring to light the stories of hardship of the workers, and which makes the commemoration of the tobacco history in Taiwan more comprehensive. However, the controversy of commemorating a dangerous crop in contemporary society is never encountered. The historic cultivation of tobacco is counted equally as agricultural heritage and often interpreted in ways similar to crops that are far more benign.

Conclusion

Tobacco is a high-profit crop. It returns a huge amount of money to cigarette manufacturers. Since the chemical content of nicotine in tobacco makes people addicted to it, smoking becomes increasingly popular. However, when people started to notice that the chemical composition of tobacco is deadly to humans, anti-smoking campaigns led to a reduction of tobacco consumption and cultivation. In the case of Taiwan, when the industry was thriving there were more than seventy tobacco cultivation areas in the country. At the time of writing, however, only a small amount of production was taking place in the south of Taiwan — this was scheduled to end completely in 2017. Several tobacco settlements in Taiwan and historic locations of tobacco cultivation and manufacturing throughout the world have attempted to commemorate their once thriving tobacco agriculture. This means that tobacco cultivation is transformed from productive tobacco agriculture to post-productive agricultural heritage.

Agricultural landscapes have only fairly recently come within the purview of international heritage practice, bringing along with it the concept of the commingling of nature and culture and a celebration of the harmonious relationship between humans and the environment. In this chapter we have argued that the harmonious picture of agricultural heritage is problematic, since there is a dark side to it. If UNESCO World Heritage is often conceived as guidelines to be followed in heritage practice, the celebration of great beauty or harmony of the agricultural landscape should be understood in a more comprehensive way, by exploring the deeper stories masked by the peaceful scenes. This argument is well reflecting in the case of tobacco agricultural heritage, such as Fonglin's conserved Tudor-style tobacco building with its picturesque landscape, and the tobacco display area in Liudui Hakka Cultural Park. These two cases demonstrate that the harmonious scene between culture and nature is an important characteristic in the practice of heritage tourism. Furthermore, Tobacco heritage's unproblematized repetition of the theme of "human harmony with nature" fails to address the overwhelmingly destructive effects of this plant's cultivation. Serious interpretive engagement with smoking-related disease is obviously omitted from tobacco heritage, and other negative aspects of tobacco agriculture — such as environmental issues, child labour, or the direct connection between tobacco cultivation and colonial politics — are often lacking, too. In the case of Fonglin in Taiwan, in order to distinguish itself from the biggest tobacco settlement and to develop its cultural tourism, a new historical interpretation of the local tobacco history was created by highlighting the township's connection to its Japanese colonial history, reshaping the negative image of colonization as a cultural and historical characteristic of Fonglin's tobacco cultivation.

This chapter has examined case studies in Taiwan where contemporary attitudes to tobacco smoking differ and has demonstrated how those contemporary attitudes have shaped the way local tobacco history is encountered. The interpretation of tobacco history in Taiwan explores the historical and cultural significances of tobacco, rather than just its economic contribution to society. Nevertheless, it could be argued that this kind of commemoration only interprets partial stories of the industry's history, erasing the more uncomfortable narratives that are embedded in its heritage. Tobacco is not a benign crop; its cultivation entails various negative aspects. As we have explored in this chapter, the commemoration of tobacco agriculture is inherently complex due to contemporary motives for economic regeneration, historical reinterpretation, heritage tourism, and social responsibility.

Notes

1. <http://www.who.int/tobacco/mpower/tobacco_facts/en/> (accessed 16 February 2017).
2. <http://whc.unesco.org/en/culturallandscape> (accessed 16 February 2017).
3. <http://tobaccoheritagetrail.org> (accessed 17 February 2017).
4. Interview with Mr Liu, Fonglin Township official, 2010.
5. Interview with Mr Wang, Fonglin Township official, 3 March 2011.

6. Interview with Mr Huang, local tobacco farmer, 25 May 2011.
7. Interview with Mayor Peng of Fonglin Township, 29 March 2011.
8. Interview with Mr Liu, assistant researcher at Liudui Hakka Cultural Park, 12 May 2011.
9. This involves the farmers plucking the flowering heads and buds to save the plant's nutrition in order for the leaves to grow bigger and thicker, and hence with more flavour.
10. Interview with Mrs Lin, tobacco farmer, 2 March 2011.
11. Interview with Mr Huang, tobacco farmer, 25 May 2011.

References

Ashworth, G.J., B.J Graham, and J.E. Tunbridge. *Pluralising Pasts: Heritage, Identity and Place in Multicultural Societies*. London: Pluto, 2007.

Crang, M. "Nation, Region and Homeland: History and Tradition in Dalarna, Sweden". *Cultural Geographies* 6, no. 4 (1999): 447–70.

Crang, M., and D.P. Tolia-Kelly. "Nation, Race and Affect: Senses and Sensibilities at National Heritage Sites". *Environment and Planning A* 42, no. 10 (2010): 2315.

Cronon, W. "The Trouble with Wilderness: Or, Getting back to the Wrong Nature". *Environmental History* 1, no. 1 (1996): 7–28.

Daniels, S. "Marxism, Culture, and the Duplicity of Landscape". *New Models in Geography* 2 (1989): 196–220.

Deffner, A., T. Metaxas, K. Syrakoulis, and T. Papatheohari. "Museums, Marketing and Tourism Development: The Case of the Tobacco Museum of Kavala". *Tourismos* 4, no. 4 (2009): 57–76.

Geist, H.J. "Global Assessment of Deforestation Related to Tobacco Farming. *Tobacco Control* 8, no. 1 (1999): 18–28.

Graham, B.J., G.J. Ashworth, and J.E. Tunbridge. *A Geography of Heritage: Power, Culture, and Economy*. London: Arnold, 2000.

Guimbatan, R., and T. Baguilat. "Misunderstanding the Notion of Conservation in the Philippine Rice Terraces — Cultural Landscapes". *International Social Science Journal* 58 (2006): 59–67.

Hardy, D. "Historical Geography and Heritage Studies". *Area* 20 (1988): 333–38.

Kirshenblatt-Gimblett, B. *Destination Culture: Tourism, Museums, and Heritage*. University of California Press, 1998.

Koohafkan, P., and M.A. Altieri. *Globally Important Agricultural Heritage Systems (GIAHS): A Legacy for the Future*. Rome: FAO, 2011.

Kulikoff, A. *Tobacco and Slaves: The Development of Southern Cultures in the Chesapeake, 1680–1800*. University of North Carolina Press, 1986.

Lawless, S. *Black Friday: The Collapse of the American Shopping Mall*. Artivist, 2014.

Lee M.-C. *The Influence of Globalization upon Change of the Tobacco and Alcohol Tax Law in Taiwan*. Master's dissertation, National Chung Kung University, 2006.

Liudui Hakka Cultural Park. "Liudui Hakka Cultural Park". Preparatory Office of Taiwan Hakka Cultural Centre, CFHA. Liudui Hakka Cultural Park, 2011.

Lowenthal, D. *The Heritage Crusade and the Spoils of History*. London: Viking, 1998.

Lowenthal, D., and K. Olwig, eds. *The Nature of Cultural Heritage, and the Culture of Natural Heritage*. New York: Routledge, 2013.

Marx, L. *The Machine in the Garden: Technology and the Pastoral Ideal in America*. Oxford University Press, 1964.

Matless, D. *Landscape and Englishness*. London: Reaktion Books, 2005.

Mitchell, D. "Dead Labor: The Geography of Workplace Violence in America and Beyond". *Environment and Planning A* 32, no. 5 (2000): 761–64.

———. *Cultural Geography: A Critical Introduction*. Malden, MA: Blackwell, 2000.

Morris, B. "Not Just a Place: Cultural Heritage and the Environment. In *The Cultures and Globalization Series 4: Heritage, Memory & Identity*, edited by H. Anheier and Y. Isar, pp. 124–37. London: Sage, 2011.

Nora, P., and L.D. Kritzman, eds. *Realms of Memory: Conflicts and Divisions*, vol. 1. Columbia University Press, 1996.

Puleo, T.J. "Parasitizing Landscape for UNESCO World Heritage". *Geoforum* 45 (2013): 337–45.

Rentetzi, M. "The Tobacco Museum of the City of Kavala". *Technology and Culture* 50, no. 3 (2009): 649–57.

Schein, R.H. "The Place of Landscape: A Conceptual Framework for Interpreting an American Scene". *Annals of the Association of American Geographers* 87 (1997): 660–80.

Smith, N. *Uneven Development: Nature, Capital, and the Production of Space*. Athens: University of Georgia Press, 2008.

Sørensen, M.L.S., and J. Carman. *Heritage Studies: Methods and Approaches*. London: Routledge, 2009.

Stanton, C. *The Lowell Experiment: Public History in a Postindustrial City*. University of Massachusetts Press, 2006.

Thompson, G. "Leaves of Poison". *The Nation*, 14 November 2013.

Tuan, Y.F. *Dominance & Affection*. London: Yale University Press, 1984.

Tunbridge, J.E., and G.J. Ashworth. *Dissonant Heritage: The Management of the Past as a Resource in Conflict*. Chicester: Wiley, 1996.

Index